Dragan Bošnački
Stefan Edelkamp (Eds.)

Model Checking Software

14th International SPIN Workshop
Berlin, Germany, July 1-3, 2007
Proceedings

Springer

Volume Editors

Dragan Bošnački
Department of Biomedical Engineering
WH 3.101 Eindhoven University of Technology
513 5600 MB Eindhoven, The Netherlands
E-mail: dbosnack@yahoo.com

Stefan Edelkamp
Computer Science Department
University of Dortmund
Otto Hahn Straße 14
44227 Dortmund, Germany
E-mail: stefan.edelkamp@cs.uni-dortmund.de

Library of Congress Control Number: 2007929430

CR Subject Classification (1998): F.3, D.2.4, D.3.1, D.2

LNCS Sublibrary: SL 1 – Theoretical Computer Science and General Issues

ISSN 0302-9743
ISBN-10 3-540-73369-8 Springer Berlin Heidelberg New York
ISBN-13 978-3-540-73369-0 Springer Berlin Heidelberg New York

Springer is a part of Springer Science+Business Media

springer.com

Typesetting: Camera-ready by author, data conversion by Scientific Publishing Services, Chennai, India
Printed on acid-free paper SPIN: 12084210 06/3180 5 4 3 2 1 0

Preface

The SPIN workshops focus on techniques for the validation and analysis of software systems based on explicit representations of state spaces, or combination of the latter with other representations. One of the main goals of the workshops is to encourage the interaction of researchers and practitioners in this area and the exchange of ideas with scientists working in related areas in software engineering.

The evolution and success of the SPIN workshops reflects the maturing of model checking into a dominant technology for the formal verification of software systems. The first SPIN workshop was held in Montreal in 1995. In its first instances the workshop was intended as a forum for presenting extensions and applications of the model checker SPIN, to which the workshop owes its the name. As from the year 2000, the scope of the event clearly broadened to more general topics on software verification. To promote the interaction with other areas, since 1996, SPIN workshops have been organized as more or less closely affiliated events with bigger conferences. Since 1999, the proceedings of the SPIN workshops have appeared in Springer Verlag's *Lecture Notes in Computer Science* series.

This volume contains the proceedings of the 14th SPIN workshop, held in Berlin, Germany, on July 1–3, 2007, collocated with CAV 2007, the 19th Computer-Aided Verification Conference. The topics of interest that were listed in the call for papers for SPIN 2007 were: algorithms for state space-based verification; innovative implementation techniques; manual or automatic modeling of systems for state space tools; manual or automatic derivation of properties that are to be checked of the systems; techniques for alleviating state explosion; techniques for dealing with infinite state spaces and infinite families of systems; techniques for dealing with timed or probabilistic systems; derivation of code, test cases, or other useful material from state spaces; innovative or otherwise particularly significant case studies; theoretical results on the limits and possibilities of state space methods; unpublished, insightful surveys or historical accounts on topics of relevance to SPIN workshops; directed model checking and accelerated error detection; as well as short tool presentations.

The submitted papers covered a vast majority of these topics. We received 39 submissions of which 31 were full technical papers and 8 short tool papers. Of those the Program Committee finally selected 14 technical and 4 tool papers to be presented during the workshop and included in the proceedings. papers was withdrawn afterwords, which reduced the final The competition was particularly strong this year. As a result, regrettably, a substantial number of good papers had to be rejected.

Each paper was rigorously reviewed by at least three reviewers. One paper for which both PC co-chairs had a possible conflict of interests was handled by a sub-committee chaired by Willem Visser. For most of the submissions the decision on acceptance was reached by consensus. In a couple of cases, where this was not possible, the opinion of the majority prevailed.

In addition to the selected papers we had an invited talk that was given by Dennis Dams, an invited tutorial held by Luboš Brim, and a seeded discussion on the *end of reduction techniques in software model checking.*

Apart from the high quality, this year's presentations were characterized also by the broad spectrum of topics in software model checking that they featured. These ranged from emerging techniques, e.g., directed model checking, model checking with multi-core systems via more established ones, e.g., abstraction and partial-order reduction, to interesting case studies and tool demonstrations.

We would like to thank the PC committee members as well as their sub-reviewers for their reviews and for their help in composing a strong program for SPIN 2007. Also, we are indebted to all members of the Steering Committee for their advice and tremendous help with the organizational questions. Springer allowed us to use the OCS on-line conference service free of charge for which we are very grateful. The system was maintained by Martin Karusseit and Holger Willebrandt whose prompt reactions to all technical problems were invaluable. Also we would like to thank our universities in Eindhoven and Dortmund, respectively, for their support. Last but not least, we would like to thank the CAV organizers for giving us the opportunity to hold SPIN together with CAV, as well as for their organizational help.

May 2007

Dragan Bošnački
Stefan Edelkamp

Organization

Program Committee

Dragan Bošnački (Eindhoven, Netherlands) (co-chair)
Matthew Dwyer (U. Nebraska, USA)
Stefan Edelkamp (Dortmund, Germany) (co-chair)
Jaco Geldenhuys (Stellenbosch, South Africa)
Patrice Godefroid (Microsoft, USA)
Susanne Graf (Verimag, France)
Alex Groce (NASA/JPL, USA)
Jörg Hoffmann (DERI, Austria)
Gerard Holzmann (NASA/JPL, USA)
Radu Iosif (Verimag, France)
Marta Kwiatkowska (Birmingham, UK)
Stefan Leue (Konstanz, Germany)
Alberto Lluch Lafuente (Pisa, Italy)
Pedro Merino (Malaga, Spain)
Kedar Namjoshi (Bell Labs, USA)
Corina Păsăreanu (NASA Ames, USA)
Doron Peled (Warwick, UK and Bar Ilan, Israel)
Paul Pettersson (Mälardalen, Sweden)
Theo Ruys (Twente, Netherlands)
Antti Valmari (Tampere, Finland)
Willem Visser (SEVEN Networks, USA)
Pierre Wolper (Liege, Belgium)

Steering Committee

Patrice Godefroid (Microsoft, USA)
Susanne Graf (Verimag, France)
Stefan Leue (Konstanz, Germany)
Antti Valmari (Tempere, Finland)
Moshe Vardi (Rice U., USA)
Pierre Wolper (Liege, Belgium)

Advisory Board

Gerard Holzmann (NASA/JPL, USA)
Amir Pnueli (Weizmann Inst., Israel)

Additional Referees

Husain Aljazzar
Markus Bauhan
Marius Bozga
Vincenzo Ciancia
Bob Coecke
Dennis Dams
Alexandre David
Dejan Nickovic
Ann-Marie Ericsson
Blaise Genest
John Håkansson
Henri Hansen
Corné Inggs
Shahid Jabbar
Mark Kattenbelt
Timo Kellomäki
Masud Khokhar
Birgitta Lindström
Johannes Leitner
Jesús Martínez
Laurent Mounier
Adam Rogalewicz
Cristina Seceleanu
Sarah Thompson
Xu Wang
Wei Wei

Table of Contents

Invited Contributions

Directed Model Checking

Partial Order Reduction

Program Analysis

Exploration Advances

Modeling and Cases

Tools

StackSnuffer: Curing Orion's Unsoundness*

Dennis Dams

Bell Laboratories, Murray Hill, NJ 07974, USA

Software analysis and verification require abstraction of the program under consideration. As a result, many reported errors may in fact be false alarms. The Orion static analyzer reduces the ratio of false alarms by performing a state space exploration at two levels of precision. At the first level, a conservative analysis is performed. This detects all errors of a certain kind, but with a potentially high number of superfluous warnings. At the second level, each potential-error trace that is produced at the first level, is subjected to a feasibility analysis using symbolic reasoning - typically by invoking third-party decision procedures. If a trace cannot be shown to be infeasible, it is reported. Orion's precision can be tuned by varying the resources spent in the second level.

This approach results in an excellent signal-to-noise ratio. Orion has uncovered many errors in well-tested open source code, with only little human processing required to separate the wheat from the chaff. However, the interaction between the two levels causes Orion to miss certain errors, and when used to prove absence of bugs, it therefore needs to be run with the second level switched off.

In this talk, we present an adaptation of the depth-first search algorithm, called StackSnuffer, aimed at finding all errors without sacrificing Orion's signal-to-noise ratio. We formalize correctness and discuss the condition under which StackSnuffer is correct. This condition turns out to be equivalent to reducibility of the analyzed program's flow graph.

Experiments with StackSnuffer confirm that previously missed errors are now found. Furthermore, another small adaptation to the algorithm results in an intriguing new approach to deal with loops.

* This work is supported in part by NSF grant CCR-0341658.

D. Bošnački and S. Edelkamp (Eds.): SPIN 2007, LNCS 4595, p. 1, 2007.

Tutorial: Parallel Model Checking*
(Extended Abstract)

Luboš Brim and Jiří Barnat

Faculty of Informatics, Masaryk University, Brno, Czech Republic

With the increase in the complexity of computer systems, it becomes even more important to develop formal methods for ensuring their quality. Various techniques for automated and semi-automated analysis and verification have been proposed. In particular, model-checking has become a very practical technique due to its push-button character. The basic principle behind model-checking is to build a model of the system under consideration together with a formal description of the verified property in a suitable temporal logic. The model-checking algorithm is a decision procedure which in addition to the yes/no answer returns a trace of a faulty behaviour in case the checked property is not satisfied by the model. One of the additional advantages of this approach is that verification can be performed against partial specifications, by considering only a subset of all specification requirements. This allows for increased efficiency by checking correctness with respect to only the most relevant requirements that should be fulfilled.

Conventional model checking techniques have high memory requirements and are very computationally intensive; they are thus unsuitable for handling real-world systems that exhibit complex behaviours which cannot be captured by simple models having a small or regular state space. Various authors have proposed ways of solving this problem by either using powerful shared-memory multiprocessors (e.g. multi-core machines) or by distributing the memory requirements over several machines (e.g. on a cluster of workstations).

The work on parallel verification is quite extensive, growing in recent years. There are attempts to consider both the symbolic as well as the enumerative techniques, theorem-provers as well as sat-solvers, etc. In this tutorial we focus on basic elements of enumerative parallel model-checking of temporal properties formulated in linear time temporal logic (LTL).

Model checking traditionally terms the task of verifying an implementation with respect to its specification. However, model checking could and probably should also be considered as a flexible analysis tool—as long as the object to analyse is representable as a finite-state system and the analysis can be formulated in a suitable temporal logic. In consequence, model checkers are at the heart of many modelling and analysis tools and will be in the future. We will briefly introduce some technical aspects related to the design of a parallel model-checker.

* This work has been partially supported by the Grant Agency of Czech Republic grant No. 201/06/1338.

D. Bošnački and S. Edelkamp (Eds.): SPIN 2007, LNCS 4595, pp. 2–3, 2007.

Parallel verification is a new emerging field. Extending the techniques as known from the sequential world adds significant complications. Efficient parallel solution of many problems often requires invention of original, novel approaches radically different from those used to solve the same problems sequentially. Several methods for parallel model-checking did succeed in making its way into industrial tools. Performance results on either parallel machines or on a cluster of workstations show significant improvements with respect to sequential techniques, both in extension of the size of the problem and in computational times, along with adequate scalability with the number of processors.

References

1. Barnat, J., Brim, L., Černá, I.: Cluster-Based LTL Model Checking of Large Systems. In: FMCO, November 2005. LNCS, vol. 4111, pp. 259–279. Springer, Heidelberg (2005)
2. Barnat, J., Brim, L., Černá, I., Moravec, P., Ročkai, P., Šimeček, P.: DiVinE – A Tool for Distributed Verification (Tool Paper). In: Ball, T., Jones, R.B. (eds.) CAV. LNCS, vol. 4144, pp. 278–281. Springer, Heidelberg (2006)
3. Behrmann, G., Hune, T.S., Vaandrager, F.W.: Distributed Timed Model Checking – How the Search Order Matters. In: Emerson, E.A., Sistla, A.P. (eds.) CAV. LNCS, vol. 1855, pp. 216–231. Springer, Heidelberg (2000)
4. Bollig, B., Leucker, M., Weber, M.: Parallel Model Checking for the Alternation Free μ-Calculus. In: Margaria, T., Yi, W. (eds.) TACAS. LNCS, vol. 2031, p. 543. Springer, Heidelberg (2001)
5. Garavel, H., Mateescu, R., Smarandache, I.: Parallel State Space Construction for Model-Checking. In: Dwyer, M.B. (ed.) Model Checking Software. LNCS, vol. 2057, pp. 216–234. Springer, Heidelberg (2001)
6. Grumberg, O., Heyman, T., Schuster, A.: Distributed Model Checking for μ-calculus. In: Berry, G., Comon, H., Finkel, A. (eds.) CAV. LNCS, vol. 2102, pp. 350–362. Springer, Heidelberg (2001)
7. Haverkort, B.R., Bell, A., Bohnenkamp, H.C.: On the Efficient Sequential and Distributed Generation of Very Large Markov Chains From Stochastic Petri Nets. In: Proc. 8th Int. Workshop on Petri Net and Performance Models, pp. 12–21. IEEE Computer Society Press, Los Alamitos (1999)
8. Holzmann, G., Bosnacki, D.: The Design of a multi-core extension of the Spin Model Checker. In: Presented at FMCAD'06 (journal version submitted, January 2007) (2006)
9. Inggs, C., Barringer, H.: CTL* Model Checking on a Shared Memory Architecture. Formal Methods in System Design 29(2), 135–155 (2006)
10. Jabbar, S., Edelkamp, S.: Parallel External Directed Model Checking with Linear I/O. In: Emerson, E.A., Namjoshi, K.S. (eds.) VMCAI 2006. LNCS, vol. 3855, pp. 237–251. Springer, Heidelberg (2005)
11. Lerda, F., Sisto, R.: Distributed-memory model checking with SPIN. In: Dams, D.R., Gerth, R., Leue, S., Massink, M. (eds.) Theoretical and Practical Aspects of SPIN Model Checking. LNCS, vol. 1680, Springer, Heidelberg (1999)
12. Stern, U., Dill, D.L.: Parallelizing the Murφ Verifier. In: Grumberg, O. (ed.) CAV 1997. LNCS, vol. 1254, pp. 256–267. Springer, Heidelberg (1997)

Local Abstraction-Refinement for the mu-Calculus*

Harald Fecher[1] and Sharon Shoham[2]

[1] Christian-Albrechts-University Kiel, Germany
hf@informatik.uni-kiel.de
[2] The Technion, Haifa, Israel
sharonsh@cs.technion.ac.il

Abstract. Counterexample-guided abstraction refinement (CEGAR) is a key technique for the verification of computer programs. Grumberg et al. developed a CEGAR-based algorithm for the modal μ-calculus. There, every abstract state is split in a refinement step. In this paper, the work of Grumberg et al. is generalized by presenting a new CEGAR-based algorithm for the μ-calculus. It is based on a more expressive abstract model and applies refinement only locally (at a single abstract state), i.e., the *lazy abstraction* technique for safety properties is adapted to the μ-calculus. Furthermore, it separates refinement determination from the (3-valued based) model checking. Three different heuristics for refinement determination are presented and illustrated.

1 Introduction

One of the most successful techniques to checking correctness of large or even infinite programs is predicate abstraction [8] with *counterexample-guided abstraction refinement* (CEGAR) [3]. This approach consists of three phases: abstraction, model checking, and refinement. A typical tool based on that technique is SLAM [2], where an efficient approximation of the post-transitions of a concrete system is calculated by using cartesian approximation, and where a spurious counterexample found during the model checking phase is used for determining the refinement. Another prominent tool based on CEGAR is BLAST [14], where, contrary to SLAM, refinement is applied locally (called *lazy abstraction*), i.e., only the relevant abstract states of a trace being a spurious counterexample are refined. Both tools mentioned are only capable of verifying safety properties.

Grumberg et al. [9,10] present CEGAR-based algorithms for the verification of the μ-calculus [19], which is a powerful formalism for expressing branching time[1] and reachability properties by using fixpoint constructions. These approaches have as underlying abstract models *Kripke modal transition systems* [15], which have may and must transitions (over, resp., under approximation of the concrete transitions), as in *modal transition systems* [20]. Two transition relations are essential in order to preserve branching time properties. They also allow to preserve both *validity* and *invalidity* from the abstract model to the concrete model, at the cost of introducing a third truth value

* This work is in part financially supported by the DFG project *Refism* (FE 942/1-1).

[1] Branching time is relevant whenever nondeterminism occurs from external factors (e.g., user input), from random behavior, or from the modeling of faulty systems or channels.

D. Bošnački and S. Edelkamp (Eds.): SPIN 2007, LNCS 4595, pp. 4–23, 2007.

unknown, which means that the truth value in the concrete model is unknown. This leads to a *3-valued semantics*. In this setting, refinement is no longer needed when the result is *invalid*, as in traditional CEGAR approaches. Instead, refinement is needed when the result is *unknown*. As such, the role of a counterexample as guiding the refinement is taken by some cause of the indefinite result.

In [9], a 3-valued satisfaction game is defined, where the Verifier tries to obtain validity, and the Falsifier tries to obtain invalidity. In order to win, a player must not use may transitions. The third truth value is captured by the possibility that none of the players wins. Furthermore, their model checking algorithm, which is a generalization of the parity game algorithm of Zielonka [28], determines an abstract state z and a predicate p such that the splitting of z with respect to p leads to less spurious behavior. This approach is generalized in [10] by making the approach independent from the Zielonka algorithm, i.e., allowing more efficient algorithms [18]. There, the model checking is performed via a reduction of the 3-valued satisfaction game into two games: one for validity and one for invalidity. The predicate determining the splitting is derived from the trace obtained after playing the *non-losing* strategies of the players in these games against each other. In both approaches, every configuration (abstract states combined with subproperties) where the (in)validity is not yet shown is split, i.e., only a weak form of *lazy abstraction* is made.

Contribution. A new CEGAR-based model checking algorithm for the μ-calculus is presented. This algorithm improves the approaches of [9,10] in the following way:

- A more expressive underlying abstract model is used, namely *generalized Kripke modal transition systems* [26], where must hypertransitions, as in *disjunctive modal transition systems* [21], are used, i.e., a must transition points to a set of states rather than to a singleton. Consequently, a smoother refinement determination can be obtained [26] and more properties can in principle be shown [6].
- A stronger notion of *lazy abstraction* is used: only a single abstract state is split. Even better, some but not all configurations having the same underlying abstract state are split. Thus the state space remains smaller and verification is sped up.
- The algorithm provides a separation of the refinement determination from the model checking. This is done by providing a structure that encodes all possible causes for the indefinite result. On this structure, heuristics for determining the local refinement step can be defined. In particular, three different heuristics are presented and illustrated. The most promising one can only be defined in a local refinement setting.

Further related work. A CEGAR-approach to branching time properties is given in [24], where, contrary to our approach, only the transition relation is under, resp., over approximated (the state space remains equal). In [12], the techniques used in SLAM are generalized to branching time properties, where the underlying abstract model is equivalent to Kripke modal transition systems. In [23] models are abstracted by *alternating transitions systems* with *focus predicates*. These resemble game-graphs with must hypertransitions. Refinement is not discussed in this paper. A CEGAR-approach for the more general alternating μ-calculus is given in [1], which is a generalization of [5]. In [1] the underlying abstract model has must as well as may hypertransitions. Refinement is made globally (not locally) and the refinement determination depends on the

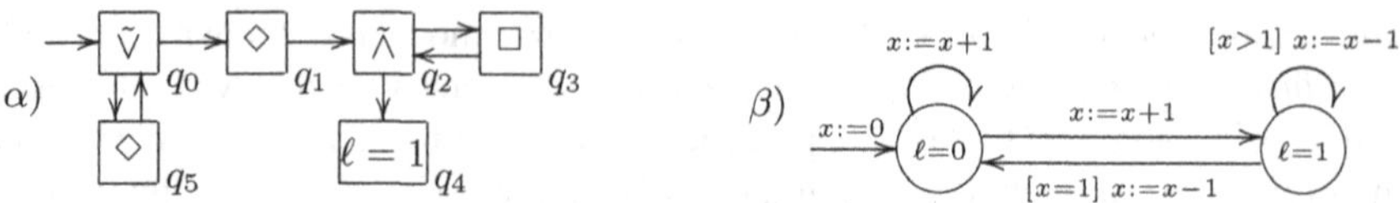

Fig. 1. A μ-calculus formula (α) in terms of automata (see Section 3.3), and a system (β). α): The property at the initial state q_0 holds if (i) there is a transition such that $\ell = 1$ holds on every possible path or (ii) there is a transition such that q_0 holds again (consequently, if there is an infinite path then q_0 holds). β): The range of ℓ is $\{0, 1\}$ and of x is $\mathbb{N}$, both initialized with 0. The actions of the transitions can be executed, including the modification of ℓ, whenever the guard, depicted in rectangular brackets, is valid. When the guard is $true$, it is simply omitted.

model checking algorithm, i.e., no separation is used. Must and may hypertransitions are also used in [7], where finite-state abstractions can be computed (for any μ-calculus formula) by a generalization of predicate abstraction. No CEGAR-based algorithm is presented there. In [25] a different kind of may hypertransitions is used in order to improve precision for non-partitioning abstraction functions. Our approach does not need these may hypertransitions for precision, since our abstraction function locally corresponds to partitions. [25] also suggests a CEGAR-based algorithm, however they consider only the alternation-free fragment of the μ-calculus. Moreover, their refinement follows [9], resulting in a weak form of lazy abstraction. In [11] the techniques of testing and verification interact with each other, improving the refinement heuristic. Similar improvements can be obtained by using 3-valued abstract models, which we do.

Outline. The new CEGAR-based algorithm is illustrated by an example in Section 2, made precise in Section 4, and is improved in Section 6. Section 3 presents the underlying concrete/abstract models, game structures, and the μ-calculus in terms of alternating tree automata. The heuristics for refinement determination are developed in Section 5 and Section 7 concludes the paper. An appendix contains pseudo codes of less important procedures. Proofs are omitted due to space constraints.

2 Example

Our model checking algorithm is illustrated by checking the μ-calculus formula, presented via a tree automaton description in Figure 1 (α), at the system depicted in Figure 1 (β). Note that both the formula and the system are used for illustration purposes and do not claim practical relevance.

The model checking is based on a configuration structure, where each configuration consists of a subproperty and a (possibly abstract) state of the system. The outgoing transitions of a configuration define 'subgoals' for determining the value (valid, invalid or unknown) of the subproperty in the (abstract) state of the system. Subproperties are given by the automaton states, which are labeled either by a predicate (e.g. $\ell = 1$) or by $\tilde{\wedge}, \tilde{\vee}, \Diamond, \Box$. Intuitively, $\tilde{\wedge}$ and $\tilde{\vee}$ stand for the logical connectives $\wedge$ and $\vee$ resp. Similarly, $\Diamond$ stands for "exists a successor", while $\Box$ stands for "all successors".

The first configuration structure is obtained by combining all subproperties (automaton states) with the single abstract-state $true$, which abstracts any concrete system-state.

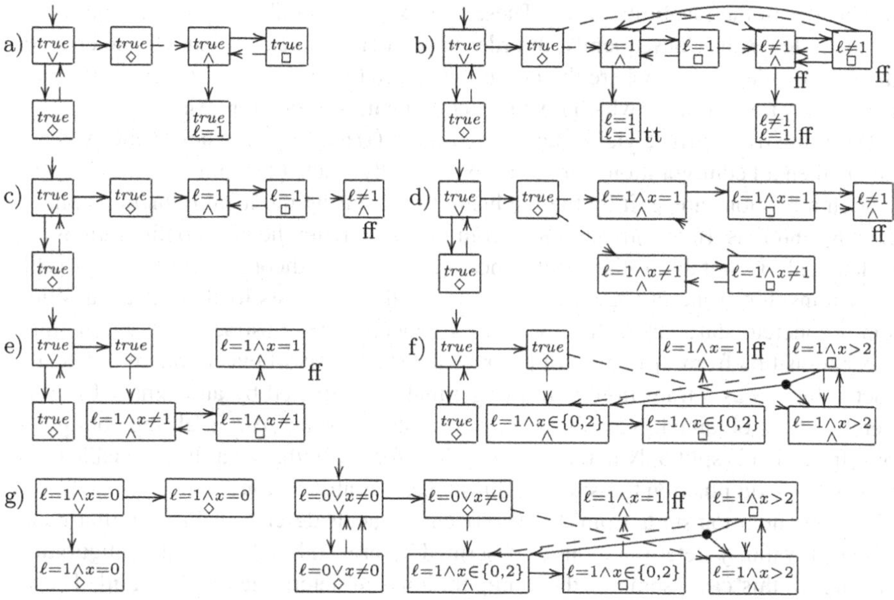

Fig. 2. Example of a property check via local refinement. May transitions are depicted as dashed arrows and must, as well as junction, transitions as solid arrows.

In addition, the transition relation of the system is overapproximated by a may transition from *true* to itself. No must transition (underapproximation) is used in the initial abstraction. The obtained configuration structure is presented in Figure 2 (a). For readability, the figure uses the labels of the automaton-states, rather than their names. May and must transitions leave $\Diamond$- or $\Box$-configurations and the other transitions, which imitate the automaton transitions, are called *junction transitions*.

In general, the algorithm iterates four phases: (in)validity determination, simplification of the configuration structure, refinement determination by some heuristic, and local refinement. The validity of the configurations is determined via a parity game algorithm, where the Verifier moves in $\tilde{\vee}$- and $\Diamond$-configurations, and the Falsifier moves in $\tilde{\wedge}$- and $\Box$-configurations. In the validity game the Verifier can only use must and junction transitions, whereas the Falsifier can additionally use may transitions. The valid configurations become labeled with tt. Thereafter, the same is done via an invalidity check where the Falsifier can only use must and junction transitions, whereas the Verifier can additionally use may transitions. The invalid configurations become labeled with ff. No validity or invalidity can be determined in (a). As a result no simplification is possible in this case. The unknown values in (a) result from four possible causes. One is the configuration $(true, \ell = 1)$, where the validity of the predicate $\ell = 1$ in the state $true$ is unknown, thus neither the Verifier nor the Falsifier can win. The others are the three may transitions in the configuration structure, which result from the may transition from the $true$ state to itself. For example, the fact that the may transition from $(true, \Diamond)$ to $(true, \vee)$ is not a must transition prevents the Verifier from winning the validity game, and on the other hand, its existence interferes with the winning of the Falsifier in the invalidity game. These causes represent all the possible causes for an indefinite result. Consequently, in order to refine the system, a heuristic determines either (i) a configuration where the property is a predicate and the validity is unknown or (ii) a may transition for which no corresponding must transition exists.

Assuming the heuristic yields the configuration $(true, \ell = 1)$, whose validity is unknown, then all configurations forwardly/backwardly reachable from $(true, \ell = 1)$ via junction transitions are split by the predicate $\ell = 1$ during the local refinement phase. The may and must (hyper)transitions incoming and leaving the new configurations are recalculated via suitable satisfiability checks solved by a theorem prover. As in [26], a may transition from an abstract state z_1 to another z_2 exists iff there is a transition from a concrete state abstracted by z_1 to a concrete state abstracted by z_2. A must (hyper)transition from z_1 to a set of abstract states $\widetilde{Z}$ exists iff every concrete state abstracted by z_1 has a transition with a target that is abstracted by an element from $\widetilde{Z}$. Thereby, (b) is obtained. Note that we do not split the state *true* in all the configurations. Instead, it is split only in the configurations forwardly/backwardly reachable from $(true, \ell = 1)$ via junction transitions. This makes our abstraction *lazy*.

The next iteration starts from (b). The tt and ff labels describe the result after making the (in)validity-determinations as described before. Unlike the initial configuration structure, in this case, some of the configurations are determined as (in)valid. Thereafter, configurations and transitions having no further influence on the (in)validity-determinations, are removed in the simplification phase, yielding (c). For example, the junction transition from $(\ell = 1, \wedge)$ to $(\ell = 1, \ell = 1)$ along with the target configuration, which is labeled tt, are removed, since knowing that one conjunct has value tt, makes the value of $\wedge$ depend on the value of the other conjunct. The algorithm continues with the simplified structure. Assuming the heuristic determines the may transition pointing to $(\ell \neq 1, \wedge)$, then the source (and all configurations connected to it via junction transitions) are split by the weakest precondition to reach $\ell \neq 1$ in the concrete system, which is $\ell = 0 \vee x = 1$. Thus we obtain (d). Proceeding with (in)validity-determinations and simplifications, we obtain (e). Assuming the heuristic yields the may transition into $(\ell = 1 \wedge x \neq 1, \wedge)$, then the source (and all configurations connected to it via junction transitions) are split by the weakest precondition to reach $\ell = 1 \wedge x \neq 1$ in the concrete system, which is $(\ell = 0 \wedge x \neq 0) \vee (\ell = 1 \wedge x > 2)$. Thus we obtain (f), where a must hypertransition arises. No further validity or invalidity can be determined in (f), thus no simplification takes place. Assuming the heuristic yields the may transition into $(true, \vee)$, then the source (and all configurations connected to it via junction transitions) are split by the weakest precondition to reach *true*, which is $\ell = 0 \vee x \neq 0$. Thus we obtain (g), where the initial configuration is also recalculated. Now the initial configuration becomes valid and thus the property is verified.

3 Preliminaries

Throughout, $\mathbb{P}(B)$ denotes the power set of a set B. Functional composition is denoted by $\circ$. Given a relation $\rho \subseteq B \times D$ with subsets $X \subseteq B$ and $Y \subseteq D$ we write $X.\rho$ for $\{d \in D \mid \exists b \in X\colon (b, d) \in \rho\}$ and $\rho.Y$ for $\{b \in B \mid \exists d \in Y\colon (b, d) \in \rho\}$.

The projection to the i-th coordinate is denoted by π_i. Let $\mathrm{map}(f, \Phi)$ be the sequence obtained from the sequence Φ by applying function f to all elements of Φ pointwise.

3.1 System

Without loss of generality, we will not consider action labels on models in this paper. A *rooted transition system* $T = (S, s^{\mathrm{i}}, \rightarrow, \mathcal{L})$ consists of a (possibly infinite) set S of states, an initial state $s^{\mathrm{i}} \in S$, a transition relation $\rightarrow \subseteq S \times S$, and a *predicate language* $\mathcal{L}$, which is a set of predicates that are interpreted over the states in S (i.e., each predicate $p \in \mathcal{L}$ denotes a set $[\![p]\!] \subseteq S$ of states), such that the following three conditions are satisfied. (i) There exists $p^{\mathrm{i}} \in \mathcal{L}$ with $[\![p^{\mathrm{i}}]\!] = \{s^{\mathrm{i}}\}$. (ii) The boolean closure of $\mathcal{L}$, denoted by $\overline{\mathcal{L}}$, is a decidable theory (i.e., satisfiability is decidable). (iii) $\overline{\mathcal{L}}$ is effectively closed under exact predecessor operations; that is, for every formula ψ in $\overline{\mathcal{L}}$ we can compute the boolean combination $\mathrm{pre}(\psi)$ of predicates from $\mathcal{L}$ such that $[\![\mathrm{pre}(\psi)]\!] = \rightarrow .[\![\psi]\!]$. In the following we assume a fixed rooted transition system $T = (S, s^{\mathrm{i}}, \rightarrow, \mathcal{L})$.

3.2 Strong-Weak-Parity-Game

Here, three valued parity games having under/over approximated transitions are presented. These games will be used to encode the satisfaction of a property in a system. They generalize the three-valued parity games of [10] by adding a validity function.

Definition 1. *A* strong-weak-parity-game $G = (C, C_1, C_2, c^{\mathrm{i}}, R^-, R^+, \theta, \omega)$ *has*

- *a set of game states C divided (not necessarily completely) by two players; $C_1 \subseteq C$ for Player 1 and $C_2 \subseteq C \setminus C_1$ for Player 2,*
- *an initial game state $c^{\mathrm{i}} \in C$,*
- *a set of strong and a set of weak game transitions $R^-, R^+ \subseteq C \times C$,*
- *a parity function $\theta : C \rightarrow \mathbb{N}$ with finite image, and*
- *a validity function $\omega : C \rightarrow \{\mathrm{tt}, \mathrm{ff}, \bot\}$, into the values true, false, and unknown.*

The source (target) of a transition t in G is denoted by $\mathrm{sor}(t)$, resp. $\mathrm{tar}(t)$.

Definition 2

- *Finite validity plays for strong-weak-parity-game G have the rules and winning conditions as stated in Table 1. An infinite play Φ is a* win *for Player 1 iff* $\sup(\mathrm{map}(\theta, \Phi))$ *is even; otherwise it is won by Player 2.*
- *Finite invalidity plays for G have the rules and winning conditions as stated in Table 2. An infinite play Φ is a* win *for Player 2 iff* $\sup(\mathrm{map}(\theta, \Phi))$ *is odd; otherwise it is won by Player 1.*
- *G* is valid *(*is invalid*) in $c \in C$ iff Player 1 (resp. Player 2) has a strategy for the corresponding validity (resp. invalidity) game such that Player 1 (resp. Player 2) wins all validity (resp. invalidity) plays started at c with her strategy. G* is valid *(*is invalid*) iff G is valid (resp. is invalid) in c^{i}.*

Remark 1. The validity, as well as the invalidity, game obviously corresponds to a parity game. Therefore, decidability of validity, resp. invalidity, is in UP $\cap$ coUP [17].

Table 1. Moves of validity game at game state c, specified through a case analysis. If a Player is unable to move at his turn, the other Player wins. Validity plays are sequences of game-states generated thus

$\omega(c) \neq \bot \vee c \notin C_1 \cup C_2$: Player 1 wins iff $\omega(c) = \text{tt}$
$c \in C_1 \wedge \omega(c) = \bot$: Player 1 picks as next configuration $c' \in \{c\}.R^-$;
$c \in C_2 \wedge \omega(c) = \bot$: Player 2 picks as next configuration $c' \in \{c\}.(R^- \cup R^+)$;

Table 2. Moves of invalidity game at game state c, specified through a case analysis. If a Player is unable to move at his turn, the other Player wins. Invalidity plays are sequences of game-states generated thus

$\omega(c) \neq \bot \vee c \notin C_1 \cup C_2$: Player 2 wins iff $\omega(c) = \text{ff}$
$c \in C_1 \wedge \omega(c) = \bot$: Player 1 picks as next configuration $c' \in \{c\}.(R^- \cup R^+)$;
$c \in C_2 \wedge \omega(c) = \bot$: Player 2 picks as next configuration $c' \in \{c\}.R^-$;

Proposition 1. *Validation over strong-weak-parity-game is 3-valued, i.e., a strong-weak-parity-game is either valid, invalid, or neither of them.*

Definition 3. *A strong-weak-parity-game G is* simplified *if (i) it is valid or invalid in $c \in C$ iff $\omega(c) \neq \bot$ and (ii) there are no transitions (a) leaving (in)valid game-states, (b) leaving game-states from C_1 and point to invalid ones, or (c) leaving game-states from C_2 and point to valid ones, i.e., $\forall t \in R^+ \cup R^- : \omega(\text{sor}(t)) = \bot \wedge (\text{sor}(t) \in C_1 \Rightarrow \omega(\text{tar}(t)) \neq \text{ff}) \wedge (\text{sor}(t) \in C_2 \Rightarrow \omega(\text{tar}(t)) \neq \text{tt})$.*

Intuitively, G is simplified if the validity function encodes correctly all the (in)valid game-states, and in addition, only transitions that "explain" an unknown value exist.

Theorem 1. *For any strong-weak-parity-game G there is an equivalent simplified one G' in the sense that $C = C'$ and for all $c \in C$ we have: G is valid (is invalid) in c iff G' is valid (resp. is invalid) in c. Moreover, the algorithm from Table 3 calculates a corresponding G'.*

3.3 Property Language

We will present the modal μ-calculus [19] in its equivalent form of automata [27].

Definition 4 (Tree automata). *An* alternating tree automaton $A = (Q, q^{\text{i}}, \delta, \Theta)$ *has*

- *a finite, nonempty set of states $(q \in)Q$ with the initial element $q^{\text{i}} \in Q$*
- *a transition relation δ mapping automaton states to one of the following forms, where q, q_1, q_2 are automaton states and $p \in \mathcal{L}$: $p \mid q \mid q_1 \tilde{\wedge} q_2 \mid q_1 \tilde{\vee} q_2 \mid \Diamond q \mid \Box q$*
- *an acceptance condition $\Theta \colon Q \to \mathbb{N}$ with finite image.*

An alternating tree automaton is depicted in Figure 1 (α), where all automaton-states have acceptance value 0. The labels of the automaton states and their outgoing transitions encode the transition relation δ. In the following, we assume a fixed alternating tree automaton $A = (Q, q^{\text{i}}, \delta, \Theta)$. Set Q_{qua} consists of those automaton-states of the form $\Diamond$ or $\Box$, i.e., $Q_{\text{qua}} = \{q \in Q \mid \exists q' : \delta(q) \in \{\Diamond q', \Box q'\}\}$. The successor state of

Table 3. Algorithm for the determination of equivalent, simplified strong-weak-parity-games, where $G = (C, C_1, C_2, c^{\mathrm{i}}, R^-, R^+, \theta, \omega)$

Algorithm Simplify (G : a strong-weak-parity-game)

1: Use a parity-game algorithm to determine the valid game-states and adapt ω accordingly.

2: Use a parity-game algorithm to determine the invalid game-states and adapt ω accordingly.

3: Remove in G all weak/strong transitions that (i) leave (in)valid game-state, (ii) leave elements from C_1 and point to invalid game states, or (iii) leave elements from C_2 and point to valid game states.

$q \in Q_{\mathrm{qua}}$ is denoted by $\mathrm{succ}(q)$, i.e., $\mathrm{succ}(q) = q'$ if $\delta(q) \in \{\Diamond q', \Box q'\}$. Furthermore, $Q_1 = \{q \in Q \mid \delta(q) \in \bigcup_{q_1, q_2 \in Q}\{q_1, q_1 \tilde{\vee} q_2, \Diamond q_1\}\}$ denotes the automaton-states under control of Player 1 and $Q_2 = \{q \in Q \mid \delta(q) \in \bigcup_{q_1, q_2 \in Q}\{q_1 \tilde{\wedge} q_2, \Box q_1\}\}$ those under control of Player 2. Satisfaction of a rooted transition system with respect to an alternating tree automata is obtained via transformation into a strong-weak-parity-game:

Definition 5. *The* property-game *for T and A, denoted $P_{T,A}$, is the strong-weak-parity-game $(S \times Q, S \times Q_1, S \times Q_2, (s^{\mathrm{i}}, q^{\mathrm{i}}), R^-, \{\}, \Theta \circ \pi_2, \omega)$, where*

$$\begin{aligned} R^- = {} & \{((s,q),(s,q')) \mid \exists q'' : \delta(q) \in \{q', q' \tilde{\wedge} q'', q'' \tilde{\wedge} q', q' \tilde{\vee} q'', q'' \tilde{\vee} q'\}\} \cup \\ & \{((s,q),(s',q')) \mid \delta(q) \in \{\Diamond q', \Box q'\} \wedge (s,s') \in \rightarrow\} \end{aligned}$$

$$\omega(s,q) = \begin{cases} \mathrm{tt} & \text{if } \delta(q) \in \mathcal{L} \wedge s \in [\![\delta(q)]\!] \\ \mathrm{ff} & \text{if } \delta(q) \in \mathcal{L} \wedge s \notin [\![\delta(q)]\!] \\ \bot & \text{otherwise.} \end{cases}$$

Furthermore, we write $T \models q$, whenever $P_{T,A}$ is valid, and otherwise, we write $T \not\models q$ (which is equivalent to $P_{T,A}$ is invalid).

All the transitions in $P_{T,A}$ are strong. The transitions that leave game-states whose automaton component q is in Q_{qua} correspond to the transitions in the underlying system. In all other cases, the transitions reflect the automaton transitions, and the system component remains unchanged. The parity conditions also reflect the acceptance conditions of the automaton. ω evaluates game-states whose automaton component q is such that $\delta(q) \in \mathcal{L}$. In this case, the evaluation is determined by the value of the predicate $\delta(q)$ in s. The (in)validity of such game-states provides the basis of the (in)validity evaluation of the game. Note that our definition of $T \models q$ coincides with the standard definition of satisfaction, and $T \not\models q$ coincides with the satisfaction of the dual formula, i.e., corresponds to negation.

Next, special strong-weak-parity-games derived for alternating tree automata satisfaction on abstracted systems, in terms of generalized Kripke modal transition systems [26], are introduced. These are called *abstract property-games*. Unlike previous works, we do not define the abstract system separately. Instead, its description is intertwined with the property in the game structure. This is most convenient to enable a *lazy abstraction* where the same part of the system can be abstracted differently in different contexts. The abstract property-games are obtained by combining the abstract-states

$z \in Z$ with the property-states and encoding hypertransitions via additional game-states (hyper-points) where subsets of abstract-states $\widetilde{Z} \in \mathbb{P}(Z)$ are combined with Q_{qua}. The hyper-points are used to model hypertransitions. The classification of game-states to players is based on the property-states as before, except that in hyper-points the responsibility of the players switches. Furthermore, an abstract state z has a formula describing the concrete states that are abstracted by z. In particular, the same concrete state can be abstracted by multiple abstract states. However, it will only be abstracted by a single abstract state in each context (property-state). Formally:

Definition 6. *An* abstract property-game *P is a tuple (Z, ϱ, G), where Z is a set of abstract states, $\varrho : Z \to \overline{\mathcal{L}}$ is an abstraction function, and G is a strong-weak-parity-game such that*

- $C \subseteq (Z \times Q) \cup (\mathbb{P}(Z) \times Q_{\text{qua}})$,
- $C_i = C \cap ((Z \times Q_{\text{i}}) \cup (\mathbb{P}(Z) \times (Q_{\text{qua}} \setminus Q_{\text{i}})))$ *for* $i \in \{1, 2\}$,
- *an element $(\widetilde{Z}, q) \in \mathbb{P}(Z) \times Q_{\text{qua}}$ encodes an* hyper-point *connecting $(z, q) \in Z \times Q_{\text{qua}}$ to (a subset of) the elements of $\widetilde{Z}$ combined with the next automaton state,* $\text{succ}(q)$, *i.e.,* $\forall(\widetilde{Z}, q) \in C \cap (\mathbb{P}(Z) \times Q_{\text{qua}}) : R^{-}.\{(\widetilde{Z}, q)\} \subseteq \{(z, q) \mid z \in Z\}$ *and* $\{(\widetilde{Z}, q)\}.R^{-} \subseteq \{(z', \text{succ}(q)) \mid z' \in \widetilde{Z}\}$.

P is simplified *if G is.*

To simplify the presentation of the paper, we refrain from formalizing the additional constraints of an abstract property-game. Instead, we describe them informally. Similarly to the property-game, the abstract property-game maintains the structure of the property automaton. In particular, whenever the automaton component is not in Q_{qua}, the outgoing game transitions are strong-transitions that reflect the automaton transitions, thus the system component does not change. When the automaton component is in Q_{qua}, the outgoing transitions reflect the transitions of the underlying system, except that they can now either overapproximate the system transitions, via weak-transitions, or underapproximate the system transitions, via strong-transitions that point to hyper-points. In analogy to generalized Kripke modal transition system, the weak transitions of an abstract property-game are also called *may transitions*, since they are used to represent may transitions of the underlying abstract model. The strong transitions of an abstract property-game that point to hyper-points are called *must transitions* (they represent must hypertransitions of the underlying model) and the other strong transitions are called *junction transitions*.

Recall that the may and must transitions leave game-states whose automaton state q is in Q_{qua}. In principle, *if some* concrete state abstracted by z has a transition to *some* concrete state abstracted by z', i.e. $\varrho(z) \wedge \text{pre}(\varrho(z'))$ is satisfiable, then there exists a may transition from (z, q) to $(z', \text{succ}(q))$. This is called the *may condition*. A must transition from (z, q) to the hyper-point $(\widetilde{Z}, q)$ exists *only if* the *must condition* holds, namely *every* concrete state abstracted by z has a transition whose target state is abstracted by *some* state in $\widetilde{Z}$, i.e. the implication $\varrho(z) \Rightarrow \text{pre}(\bigvee_{z' \in \widetilde{Z}} \varrho(z')))$ holds. The hyper-point $(\widetilde{Z}, q)$ is connected via junction transitions to the game-states in $\{(z', \text{succ}(q)) \mid z' \in \widetilde{Z}\}$. However, simplification can damage these rules. Including additional may transitions that do not fulfill the may condition, or not including some of the must transitions although they do fulfill the must condition, is sound. However, a smaller set of may transitions, resp. a bigger set of must transitions makes the over, resp. under, approximation tighter and hence more precise. Similarly, the smaller the set $\widetilde{Z}$ in a hyper-point is, the more precise the must transition is.

The validity function ω is used as in the concrete property-game, except that now the evaluation of the predicate $p = \delta(q) \in \mathcal{L}$ in an abstract state z depends on the value of the predicate in *all* the concrete states abstracted by z. Namely, $\omega(z,q) = \text{tt}$, resp. ff, if $\varrho(z) \Rightarrow p$, resp. $\varrho(z) \Rightarrow \neg p$, holds. Otherwise, $\omega(z,q) = \bot$. The parity function is defined as in the concrete property-game (since it only depends on the automaton).

The initial abstraction for T, which contains only a single abstract state z abstracting everything (i.e., $\varrho(z) = true$), corresponds to the following abstract property-game:

Definition 7. *The initial abstract property-game $P^I_{T,A}$ for T and A is* $(\{z\},\{(z, true)\}, (\{z\} \times Q, \{z\} \times Q_1, \{z\} \times Q_2, (z, q^{\mathrm{i}}), R^-, R^+, \Theta \circ \pi_2, \omega))$, *where z is an arbitrary element and*

$$
\begin{aligned}
R^- &= \{((z,q),(z,q')) \mid \exists q'' : \delta(q) \in \{q', q'\tilde{\wedge}q'', q''\tilde{\wedge}q', q'\tilde{\vee}q'', q''\tilde{\vee}q'\}\} \\
R^+ &= \{((z,q),(z,q')) \mid \delta(q) \in \{\Diamond q', \Box q'\}\} \\
\omega(z,q) &= \bot \qquad \textit{for } q \in Q\,.
\end{aligned}
$$

Note that the initial abstract property-game does not depend on T. This reflects the fact that we start with a fully abstracted system. In particular, no must transitions exist, and the may transitions correspond to a may transition from z to z in the underlying abstract system. The validity function interprets all the predicates as $\bot$ in z.

Examples of abstract property-games for the system from Figure 1 (β) and the tree automaton from Figure 1 (α) appear in Figure 2. In particular, Figure 2 (a) presents the initial abstract property-game. In the figure, a game-state $(z,q) \in Z \times Q$ is labeled by $\varrho(z)$, which is the predicate describing the concrete states abstracted by z, and by the label of the automaton-state q, which reflects $\delta(q)$. To simplify the figure, hyper-points are omitted. Namely, instead of including a must transition from (z,q) to the hyper-point $(\widetilde{Z},q)$ and junction transitions from the hyper-point to $\{(z', \mathrm{succ}(q)) \mid z' \in \widetilde{Z}\}$, Figure 2 directly connects (z,q) to $\{(z', \mathrm{succ}(q)) \mid z' \in \widetilde{Z}\}$ using a must transition, or, if necessary, a hypertransition.

4 CEGAR Locally Applied on Configurations

In the verification algorithm, a simplified abstract property-game is calculated, starting from the initial abstract property-game. If the validity of the initial game-state remains unknown, a *refinement heuristic* is applied on the simplified abstract property-game.

Definition 8. *A* refinement heuristic *is a function mapping an abstract property-game to a game-state c in $Z \times Q$ combined with an element p from $\overline{\mathcal{L}}$.*

Suppose the refinement heuristic Heuristic yields (c, p). Then c as well as the game states $\tilde{c}$ forwardly/backwardly reachable from c via junction transitions are split by p

Table 4. A model checking algorithm for μ-calculus properties, where refinement is made locally on configurations, i.e., on abstract-states combined with properties. Here, the components of P and G are denoted as in Definition 6, resp. 1. Procedure Simplify is given in Table 3, Refine in Table 5, Add is explained in Section 4, and Heuristic is discussed in Section 5.

Algorithm PropertyCheck (A : pointed automata, T : rooted transition system)
Local variables P : an abstract property-game, initialized with $P^I_{T,A}$

Simplify (G)
while ($\omega(c^{\mathrm{i}}) = \bot$) do
  Redirect every transition t pointing to a hyper-point $(\widetilde{Z}, q) \in \mathbb{P}(Z) \times Q_{\mathrm{qua}}$ such that it points to $(\pi_1(\{(\widetilde{Z}, q)\}.R^-), q)$, where this hyper point (together with their maximal allowed outgoing transitions) is added to C (for example by using procedure Add).
  % This step updates $\widetilde{Z}$ in case that some of the outgoing junction transitions of the hyper-point were removed during simplification. Note that the newly added game-states cannot be (in)valid.
  Remove from G every game-state $c \in C$ that is unreachable (from the initial game-state c^{i}), unless $c = (z, q) \in Z \times Q$ and there exists some reachable game-state $c' = (z', q')$ such that $\omega(c') = \bot$ and in addition, either $\delta(q') = \Diamond q \wedge \omega(c) = \mathrm{tt}$, or $\delta(q') = \Box q \wedge \omega(c) = \mathrm{ff}$. % Game-states that have no influence on (in)validity are removed. States fullfilling the last constraint are not removed, since they are needed for the computation of precise must hypertransitions in Refine.
  Refine (P, Heuristic (P)) % Heuristic(P) yields a game-state combined with an element from $\overline{\mathcal{L}}$
  Simplify (G)
return $\omega(c^{\mathrm{i}})$

in the abstract property-game. The transitions incoming/leaving such a new game-state $\tilde{c}'$ split from $\tilde{c}$ are calculated by taking the transitions incoming/leaving $\tilde{c}$ into account. This procedure of simplification and local refinement is repeated until the property for the initial game-state is verified or falsified. The verification algorithm PropertyCheck is presented in Table 4 and its used Refine-procedure, which calculates the local refinement, is presented in Table 5. Note that the initial abstraction in PropertyCheck can be imprecise (if every concrete state has an outgoing transition or if none of them has one), but this imprecision will be eliminated after refinement steps.

In the following, the Refine-procedure is described in more detail. Its used procedures are informally described below, with the pseudo codes of OutgoingMayCalculation and OutgoingMustCalculation given in Appendix A. Let (c, p), where $c = (z, q)$, be the game-state and predicate returned by Heuristic. In Line 1, the new abstract-states z_1 and z_2 are determined, as the result of splitting z based on p. Here the abstract states and ϱ are encoded as in cartesian predicate abstraction, i.e., an abstract-state is a function from a set of predicates into a three valued domain, indicating whether the corresponding predicate is used, its negation is used, or is not considered. Consequently, if suitable refinement heuristics (e.g., those presented in Section 5) are used, the resulting substates z_1 and z_2 can effectively be calculated.

Q' is used to collect the states that have to be split, i.e., are connected via junction transitions to c. It is sufficient to collect in Q' only automaton-states, since it is an invariant that the first component of game-states connected to c via junction transitions is always z. Set Q' is initialized to q, representing c. Every state $\tilde{q}$ in Q', representing

Table 5. An algorithm for local refinement calculation, where the components of P are denoted as in Definition 6, resp. 1. The occurring procedures are explained in Section 4.

Algorithm Refine (P: an abstract property-game, $((z,q),p)$: $(Z \times Q) \times \overline{\mathcal{L}}$)
Local variables Q': $\mathbb{P}(Q)$ initialized with $\{q\}$

1: Determine $z_1, z_2 \in Z$ (and possibly add those elements to Z and adapt ϱ) such that $[\![\varrho(z_1)]\!] = [\![\varrho(z) \wedge p]\!]$ and $[\![\varrho(z_2)]\!] = [\![\varrho(z) \wedge \neg p]\!]$
2: while $Q' \neq \{\}$ do
3: remove an element $\tilde{q}$ from Q'
4: Add $(P, (z_1, \tilde{q}))$; Add $(P, (z_2, \tilde{q}))$ % Adding of the game-states obtained from splitting.
5: if $c^{\mathrm{i}} = (z, \tilde{q})$ then (if Satisfiable $(p^{\mathrm{i}} \wedge \varrho[z_1])$ then $c^{\mathrm{i}} := (z_1, \tilde{q})$ else $c^{\mathrm{i}} := (z_2, \tilde{q})$) % Relocation of the initial game-state.
6: if $\tilde{q} \notin Q_{\mathrm{qua}}$ then
7: while $\{(z,\tilde{q})\}.R^- \neq \{\}$ do % Calculation of the outgoing junction transitions
8: remove an element $(z', \tilde{q}')$ from $\{(z,\tilde{q})\}.R^-$ % By an invariant $z' = z$
9: $Q' := Q' \cup \{\tilde{q}'\} \setminus \{\tilde{q}\}$; $R^- := R^- \cup \{((z_1,\tilde{q}),(z_1,\tilde{q}')),((z_2,\tilde{q}),(z_2,\tilde{q}'))\}$
10: else % $\tilde{q} \in Q_{\mathrm{qua}}$
11: OutgoingMayCalculation $(P, z, z_1, z_2, \tilde{q})$
12: OutgoingMustCalculation $(P, z, z_1, z_2, \tilde{q})$
13: while $(R^-.\{(z,\tilde{q})\}) \cap (Z \times Q) \neq \{\}$ do % Calculation of the incoming junction transitions
14: remove an element $(z', \tilde{q}')$ from $(R^-.\{(z,\tilde{q})\}) \cap (Z \times Q)$ % By an invariant $z' = z$
15: $Q' := Q' \cup \{\tilde{q}'\} \setminus \{\tilde{q}\}$; $R^- := R^- \cup \{((z_1,\tilde{q}'),(z_1,\tilde{q})),((z_2,\tilde{q}'),(z_2,\tilde{q}))\}$
16: IncomingMayCalculation $(P, z, z_1, z_2, \tilde{q})$
17: IncomingMustCalculation $(P, z, z_1, z_2, \tilde{q})$
18: $C := C \setminus \{(z,\tilde{q})\}$; $C_1 := C_1 \setminus \{(z,\tilde{q})\}$; $C_2 := C_2 \setminus \{(z,\tilde{q})\}$

the game-state $\tilde{c} = (z, \tilde{q})$, is split by splitting z to z_1 and z_2. The resulting game-states are added to the abstract property-game, using Add (Line 4). If necessary, the initial game-state is recalculated via a satisfiability check that checks which of the substates of z abstracts s^{i}, characterized by p^{i} (Line 5).

After the substates of $\tilde{c}$ are added as game-states, the transitions incoming/leaving $\tilde{c}$ are recalculated, as ingoing/outgoing transitions of the new game states. Consider first the outgoing transitions (Lines 6-12). In case when $\tilde{q} \notin Q_{\mathrm{qua}}$, the junction transitions leaving the game-state $\tilde{c}$ being split are removed and correspondingly added to the two new game-states. Q' is extended with the target states (Line 9). In case when $\tilde{q} \in Q_{\mathrm{qua}}$ the may as well as the must transitions leaving the new states are calculated by OutgoingMayCalculation and OutgoingMustCalculation resp. In this case the target game-states are not split (i.e., they are not added to Q'). This captures the laziness of the abstraction. In general, this step removes may-transitions that become redundant after refinement, as they do not represent any concrete transition. It also adds must transitions that did not exist before. It therefore makes the over and under approximations tighter.

More specifically, OutgoingMayCalculation checks if the may transition leaving $\tilde{c} = (z, \tilde{q})$ into $\tilde{c}' = (\tilde{z}', \mathrm{succ}(\tilde{q}))$ also exists for the new states $(z_i, \tilde{q})$. This is done by using a theorem prover to check if z_i and $\tilde{z}'$ fulfill the may condition.

In OutgoingMustCalculation, hypertransitions leaving $(z, \tilde{q})$ are taken for the new states without calculation. This is because when the must condition holds for z and some $\widetilde{Z}$, it is guaranteed to also hold for any substate of z, representing a subset of concrete states. In addition, a must transition from the new game-state $(z_i, \tilde{q})$ into the hyper point $(\widetilde{Z}, \tilde{q})$ is 'added' if z_i and $\mathcal{U}_G(\tilde{q}) \cup \widetilde{Z}$ fulfill the must condition, where $\mathcal{U}_G(\tilde{q})$ denotes the game-states that (depending on the type of $\tilde{q}$) are valid, resp. invalid, at the succeeding state of $\tilde{q}$ (i.e., at $\mathrm{succ}(\tilde{q})$). Formally, for $\tilde{q} \in Q_{\mathrm{qua}}$,

$$\mathcal{U}_G(\tilde{q}) = \begin{cases} \{z \mid \omega(z, \tilde{q}') = \mathrm{tt}\} & \text{if } \delta(\tilde{q}) = \Diamond \tilde{q}' \\ \{z \mid \omega(z, \tilde{q}') = \mathrm{ff}\} & \text{if } \delta(\tilde{q}) = \Box \tilde{q}' . \end{cases}$$

The consideration of $\mathcal{U}_G(\tilde{q})$ when checking the must condition, although it is not part of the hyper-point, is sound and is made for maintaining precision. It can be viewed as a shortcut for first including $\mathcal{U}_G(\tilde{q})$ in the hyper-point, and then removing it during simplification. Checking the must condition involves checking implication. Implication $a \Rightarrow b$ is checked by checking unsatisfiability of $a \wedge \neg b$. In order to reduce the number of theorem prover calls, only those $\widetilde{Z}$ are considered that are subsets of the targets of the may transitions leaving the corresponding new game-state. Furthermore, $\widetilde{Z}$ is automatically not considered if a superset is already determined to not fulfill the must condition. Similarly, once $\widetilde{Z}$ is determined to be a hypertransition, none of its supersets is checked. This is justified by the fact that including only *minimal* sets $\widetilde{Z}$ as hyper-points does not damage precision [26].

Consider now the incoming transitions (Lines 13-17). The incoming junction transitions of $\tilde{c}$ originating in game-states that are not hyper-points are calculated similarly to the outgoing junction transitions, where also Q' is extended (Line 15). The incoming may transitions are calculated, analogously to the outgoing may transitions, in IncomingMayCalculation, where may transitions can possibly be removed, making the overapproximation tighter.

The calculation of the incoming must transitions is made in IncomingMustCalculation. Here a difference arises compared to the outgoing must transitions. Since must transitions always lead to hyper-points, no must transition points directly to the split game-state $\tilde{c} = (z, \tilde{q})$, but a must transition can indirectly point to $\tilde{c}$ via a hyper-point $(\widetilde{Z}', \tilde{q}')$. We consider such must transitions as incoming must transitions. The hyper-point $\widetilde{Z}'$ that contains the abstract-state z being split is possibly refined (and made tighter) by keeping only one of the substates z_1 or z_2 in it. The existence of such a tighter hypertransition is checked (and resp. added) by checking if the must condition is fulfilled when replacing z by z_1 or z_2. In case that none of these two refined hypertransitions exists, the one where z is replaced by both new states in $\widetilde{Z}'$ is added without a necessary calculation. Note that if a refined hypertransition is discovered, then the latter hypertransition is redundant (as it is less precise), and is hence not included. Compared to the calculation of the outgoing must transitions, where transitions could possibly be added, in this case we simply make the existing ingoing must transitions more precise.

Note that after the calculation of the outgoing may and must transitions, the game-state $\tilde{c}$ being split (which will be removed in the end) is still allowed as target, i.e., it is possible that a new game-state can point to $\tilde{c}$. But after the recalculation of incoming may and must transitions, these cases, where $\tilde{c}$ is the target are handled. Thus, when Refine terminates it is ensured that no transition incoming/leaving $\tilde{c}$ can exist. In particular, self-loops are adequately refined by our approach.

New game-states are added with the Add-procedure, which is also responsible for updating the validity function ω. Procedure Add $(G, (\eta, \tilde{q}))$ adds to G the game-state $(\eta, \tilde{q}) \in (Z \times Q) \cup (\mathbb{P}(Z) \times Q_{\text{qua}})$, if it is not already present, such that it yields an abstract property-game. In particular, if $(\eta, \tilde{q}) \in \mathbb{P}(Z) \times Q_{\text{qua}}$, then all possible transitions leaving the new hyper-point to $\{(z, \text{succ}(\tilde{q})) \mid z \in \eta\}$ are also added. Furthermore, if the automaton component $\tilde{q}$ of an added game-state $(\eta, \tilde{q}) \in Z \times Q$ is such that $\delta(\tilde{q})$ is a predicate in $\mathcal{L}$, then the function ω is determined at it by calculating if $\varrho(\eta) \Rightarrow \delta(\tilde{q})$ or $\varrho(\eta) \Rightarrow \neg\delta(\tilde{q})$ holds. Again, implication is checked via the equivalent unsatisfiability check.

Example 1. Consider the abstract property-game depicted in Figure 2 (e), where a refinement heuristic determined that the game-state $c = (\ell = 1 \wedge x \neq 1, \Box)$ needs to split according to the predicate $(\ell = 0 \wedge x \neq 0) \vee (\ell = 1 \wedge x > 2)$. Figure 2 (f) depicts the result of the local refinement. Initially, c is split into $(\ell = 1 \wedge x \in \{0, 2\}, \Box)$ and $(\ell = 1 \wedge x > 2, \Box)$. The outgoing transitions of the substates are recalculated: c has only two outgoing may transitions, pointing to $(\ell = 1 \wedge x = 1, \wedge)$ and $(\ell = 1 \wedge x \neq 1, \wedge)$. The first remains as an outgoing may transitions of $(\ell = 1 \wedge x \in \{0, 2\}, \Box)$, while the second remains as an outgoing may transition of $(\ell = 1 \wedge x > 2, \Box)$. The latter transition is also added as an outgoing must transition of $(\ell = 1 \wedge x > 2, \Box)$, as it now fulfills the must condition (more precisely, a hyper-point $(\{\ell = 1 \wedge x \neq 1\}, \Box)$ is added, with an incoming must transition from $(\ell = 1 \wedge x > 2, \Box)$, and outgoing junction transition to $(\ell = 1 \wedge x \neq 1, \wedge)$). Next, the incoming transitions of c are considered. As a result, the source state, $\tilde{c} = (\ell = 1 \wedge x \neq 1, \wedge)$, of the incoming junction transition of c is also split into $(\ell = 1 \wedge x \in \{0, 2\}, \wedge)$ and $(\ell = 1 \wedge x > 2, \wedge)$. The junction transitions are adapted accordingly, and the rest of the transitions of the substates of $\tilde{c}$ are calculated: the incoming may transitions of $\tilde{c}$ become incoming transitions of both its substates. In addition, the incoming must transition of $\tilde{c}$ from $(\ell = 1 \wedge x > 2, \Box)$, that was added during the refinement, becomes a must hypertransition (more precisely, the hyper-point which previously consisted of a singleton set $\{\ell = 1 \wedge x \neq 1\}$, now consists of the two abstract states to which $\ell = 1 \wedge x \neq 1$ was split, however, the hyper-point is omitted from the figure, and a must hypertransition is used instead).

So far some limitations exist in our model checking algorithm, restricting the practical relevance of the algorithm in its current version. Those points, as well as corresponding optimizations of the algorithm, are discussed in Section 6.

Theorem 2 (Soundness). *Suppose satisfiability checks are sound and complete and* Heuristic *is a refinement heuristic. If* PropertyCheck(A, T) *returns* tt *(*ff*) then* $T \models q$ *(resp.* $T \not\models q$*) holds.*

Theorem 3 (Relative completeness). *Suppose satisfiability checks are sound and complete and* $\mathcal{L}$ *can describe every subset of* S*. If the acceptance function of* A *always maps to zero (i.e.,* A *corresponds to a least fixpoint free* μ*-calculus formula) and* $T \models q$*, then there exists a (not necessarily computable) refinement heuristic* Heuristic *such that* PropertyCheck(A, T) *returns* tt.

Note that the usage of hypertransitions is necessary for Theorem 3, since allowing only singleton targets yields a model that is not complete for safety-properties with respect to predicate abstractions, see, e.g., [6]. Theorem 3 does not hold if we restrict to computable refinement heuristics, since otherwise the halting problem would be decidable. Furthermore, Theorem 3 does not hold for automata with arbitrary acceptance function, since the underlying class of abstract models is not expressive enough. Fairness constraints, as in [4,7], are needed.

5 Heuristics

The CEGAR-based algorithm described in Section 4 uses a refinement heuristic to determine a game-state c that should be split, and a predicate p, according to which c is split, along with the game-states reachable from it via junction transitions. In this section we define the special class of pre-based heuristics and thereafter present and discuss suitable ones.

Definition 9. *Suppose P is an abstract property-game. Then a state $(z, q) \in C$ is* predicate-unknown *if $\delta(q) \in \mathcal{L}$ and $\omega(z, q) = \perp$. A* real may transition *is a $t \in R^+$ that has no corresponding must transition, more precisely, every must transition $t' \in R^-$ that leaves the same source ($\mathrm{sor}(t) = \mathrm{sor}(t')$) has a target $\mathrm{tar}(t')$ whose first component $\widetilde{Z}$ is different from the singleton set consisting of the first component z of the target of t (i.e., $\pi_1(\mathrm{tar}(t')) \neq \{\pi_1(\mathrm{tar}(t))\}$).*

A refinement heuristic Heuristic *is* pre-based *if the return value is derived from a predicate-unknown state or from a real may transition, whenever one of them exists. More precisely, if* $\mathsf{Heuristic}(P) = (c, p)$ *then (i) $c = (z, q)$ is a predicate-unknown state in C and $p = \delta(q)$ or (ii) $c = \mathrm{sor}(t)$ for some real may transition $t \in R^+$ and $p = \mathrm{pre}(\varrho(\pi_1(\mathrm{tar}(t))))$ or (iii) neither a predicate-unknown state nor a real may transition exists.*

Proposition 2. *A simplified abstract property-game, where the initial game-state is neither valid nor invalid, i.e. $\omega(c^{\mathrm{i}}) = \perp$, has a predicate-unknown state or a real may transition.*

Intuitively, predicate-unknown states and real may transitions are good candidates for refinement since they can be viewed as a cause for uncertainty. In particular, the refinement heuristics used in the example of Section 2 are all pre-based. Pre-based refinement heuristics are sufficient for finite state systems:

Theorem 4 (Termination). *Suppose T has a finite bisimulation quotient (with respect to the elements of $\mathcal{L}$ that occur in A), satisfiability checks are sound and complete, and* Heuristic *is a pre-based refinement heuristic. Then* $\mathsf{PropertyCheck}(A, T)$ *terminates, i.e., returns* tt *or* ff.

5.1 Bottom Up Strategy

Determine (i) a predicate-unknown state (z, q) or (ii) a real may transition t that points to an (in)valid game-state, i.e., $\omega(\mathrm{tar}(t)) \neq \perp$. Return $((z, q), \delta(q))$, resp. $(\mathrm{sor}(t),$

$\text{pre}(\varrho(\pi_1(\text{tar}(t)))))$. Note that such states, resp. real may transitions, do not always exist in simplified abstract property-games. In such a case an arbitrary real may transition t is chosen. An advantage of the bottom up strategy is that (if case (i) or (ii) are applicable) at least one of the new game-states is (in)valid after the refinement. A disadvantage of the bottom up strategy is that it can become an unnecessary source of nontermination:

Example 2. Consider the example from Section 2. Then the bottom up strategy will 'run to' Figure 2 (e) and then determine the may transition pointing to the invalid state. Since $\text{pre}(\varrho(\ell = 1 \wedge x = 1)) = (\ell = 1 \wedge x = 2) \vee (\ell = 0 \wedge x = 0)$, the result of refinement will be splitting the source state $\ell = 1 \wedge x \neq 1$ to $\ell = 1 \wedge x = 2$ and $\ell = 1 \wedge x \neq 1 \wedge x \neq 2$. After simplification, an abstract property-game equivalent to (e), which is already equivalent to (c), will be generated (with the abstract state $\ell = 1 \wedge x \neq 1$ replaced by $\ell = 1 \wedge x \neq 1 \wedge x \neq 2$, and the abstract state $\ell = 1 \wedge x = 1$ replaced by $\ell = 1 \wedge x = 2$). This will continue forever, replacing $\ell = 1 \wedge x \neq 1$ by $\ell = 1 \wedge x \neq 1 \wedge \ldots \wedge x \neq i$, and $\ell = 1 \wedge x = 1$ by $\ell = 1 \wedge x = i$.

5.2 Breadth First Strategy

Determine a state (z, q) that (i) is a predicate-unknown state or a source of a real may transition t and (ii) has a minimal distance to the initial game-state. Return $((z, q), \delta(q))$, resp. $(\text{sor}(t), \text{pre}(\varrho(\pi_1(\text{tar}(t)))))$. Note that it is possible that after the refinement step, the distance of the next witness state (z, q) will decrease, since a must transition 'pointing' to $\{(z', q')\}$ can become a hypertransition, pointing to $\{(z'_1, q'), (z'_2, q')\}$, resulting in a real may transition pointing, e.g., to (z'_1, q'), whereas the original may transition pointing to (z', q') was not a real one.

Example 3. Consider the example from Section 2. Then the breadth first strategy will split one of the $(\mathit{true}, \Diamond)$ states in Figure 2 (a) along the weakest precondition of true, as it is made in (f). Thus the property will be shown after a single refinement step.

The success of the breadth first strategy in this example is due to the shallow depth of the loop $q_0 \to q_5 \to q_0$, which ensures that this strategy manages to recognize the infinite must path and thus it finds the property to be valid. But if, e.g., the property of Figure 1 is transformed into the (equivalent) property where the loop $q_0 \to q_5 \to q_0$ is replaced by a 'deeper' loop $q_0 \to q_5 \to q_6 \to \ldots \to q_n \to q_0$ in which $q_6, \ldots, q_n$ are also $\Diamond$-states, then the depth of the loop makes the breadth first strategy run into the same live-lock described in Example 2 after the first few refinement steps, before it finds the infinite must path. Thus, it fails to terminate.

5.3 Youngest First Strategy

Determine a state (z, q) that (i) is a predicate-unknown state or a target of real may transition t and (ii) is minimal with respect to the number of splits used to obtain z. Return $((z, q), \delta(q))$, resp. $(\text{sor}(t), \text{pre}(\varrho(\pi_1(\text{tar}(t)))))$. Point (ii) can easily be determined if the abstract states are encoded via the afore mentioned cartesian predicate approach, since only the positions where the cartesian function does not map to 'unused' have to be counted. Note that this kind of heuristics cannot be defined, if a global refinement approach is used, where every state is split by the new predicate.

Example 4. In Figure 2 (a) the youngest first strategy will split either the source state of one of the three real may transitions along the weakest precondition of $true$ or the state $(true, \ell = 1)$. If the split state in the first refinement step is one of the two $(true, \Diamond)$ states, then in particular the initial state is split and the property will be shown. If one of the other two states is split, then both of them are split, and so is the target of the real may transition leaving the upper $(true, \Diamond)$ state (as these states are connected via junction transitions). This ensures that the lower $(true, \Diamond)$ state, whose outgoing real may transition leads to a yet unsplit state, will be split along the weakest precondition of $true$ in the second refinement step. Thus, at latest in the second refinement step the initial state will be split along the weakest precondition of $true$, and the property will be shown. The youngest first strategy also succeeds for the modified property described in Example 3.

In order to maintain the advantage of the bottom up strategy, real may transitions to (in)valid states can be restrictively favored by, e.g., doubling the 'age' of the states that are unknown. Sometimes pre-based refinement heuristics are not sufficient:

Example 5. Consider the property $\rightarrow \Diamond$ checked on system $\xrightarrow{x:=0}$ $[x{=}0]$ $[x{>}1]\ x{:=}x{-}1$,

where $x \in \mathbb{N}$. Then any pre-based refinement heuristics will produce after n refinements the (simplified) abstract property-game $\rightarrow$ $x{=}0 \vee x{>}n$ $\Diamond$, i.e., the property cannot be verified. On the other hand if first the initial state is separated, then $\rightarrow$ $x{=}0$ $\Diamond$ $x{\geq}1$ $\Diamond$ is obtained. Thus the property can be shown.

6 Optimizations of the Algorithm

For the sake of completeness, we present some possible optimizations of the algorithm.

Too many Simplify calls. The Simplify procedure is called after every local refinement. Thus an expensive algorithm is calculated, while expecting only small improvements, since only a local refinement was made. To remedy this, more refinement iterations can be made before Simplify is called again. Further optimization is obtained, if the validity function is also adapted during the refinement calculation, e.g., by backwards search when a state is determined to become (in)valid, and Simplify is only called for more exact determination of least fixpoint properties.

No reuse of theorem prover calls. Typically the same satisfiability checks are calculated multiple times, since they (mainly) depend on the abstract state and not on the property of the configuration. Therefore, those calls can be reused by caching, or by using an additional generalized Kripke modal transition system, where the abstract states and their may and must (hyper)transitions are stored, resp. negatively stored, whenever a corresponding satisfiability check is made. Here, a tradeoff between time and space arises. Furthermore, the heuristics can be tuned to prefer those game-states for which no (or less) new satisfiability checks have to be made to determine the refinement.

Unnecessary many theorem prover calls. In case of refinement, a forward search of game-states reachable via junction transitions always takes place. However, it is possible that the current refined game-state will immediately become (in)valid (e.g., due to the first optimization) and thus the (in)validity of its reachable game-states will be irrelevant. Therefore, such a forward search should only take place if the validity of the current game-state cannot be determined immediately.

Complex $\mathtt{pre}(\psi)$-calculations. The algorithm starts with the most general abstraction consisting of only one abstract state, thus coarse abstractions arise. Such abstractions have the disadvantage that the calculation of $\mathrm{pre}(\psi)$ is in general expensive. Therefore, it is beneficial to start with a less coarse initial abstraction, which can be determined by pre-examination of the underlying systems (e.g., by partitioning the code-lines). The techniques of interpolations [13,22] might also help to avoid the high cost of $\mathrm{pre}(\psi)$-calculations.

Too complex formulas for the theorem prover. Due to satisfiability checks of complex formulas, the calculation time of the theorem prover can outweigh the calculation time of the parity game algorithm. A remedy is to drop precision and use further approximations. A refinement step can, in addition to the extension of the abstract state space, perform a more precise calculation of the used approximations. We suggest the following approximations:

- Approximate the predicates of the different states by using two formulas: one for an over and the other for an under approximation of the precise formula. In each calculation those approximation formulas that guarantee soundness are used.
- Approximate the must transitions, i.e., only calculate a subset of possible must transitions. For example, first calculate those having a single target and as a refinement step calculate those having two elements as target, etc. Alternatively, only calculate the hypertransitions on demand inside the parity game algorithm, as in [25].
- Approximate the system, e.g., instead of using T, use an approximated system for which $\mathrm{pre}(\psi)$ can be more efficiently calculated.
- Approximate the theorem prover queries by clustering predicates [16]. In this approach, one theorem prover call is split into many having less complex formulas and their results are combined afterwards, where precision is lost.

How exactly these approximation techniques can be applied is a topic of future work.

7 Conclusion

We presented a new CEGAR-based algorithm for the μ-calculus, where refinement is local and the refinement determination is separated from the model checking algorithm. Three different refinement heuristics are developed, where the most promising one heavily depends on the local refinement approach. It is even possible that our algorithm will yield improvements for safety properties, since by using a 3-valued abstract model better refinement heuristics can be obtained. Exact examinations will take place after the implementation of our algorithm, which is future work. The investigation of other refinement heuristics is also the subject of future work.

References

1. Ball, T., Kupferman, O.: An abstraction-refinement framework for multi-agent systems. In: LICS, IEEE Computer Society Press, Los Alamitos (2006)
2. Ball, T., Podelski, A., Rajamani, S.K.: Boolean and cartesian abstraction for model checking C programs. In: Margaria, T., Yi, W. (eds.) TACAS. LNCS, vol. 2031, pp. 268–283. Springer, Heidelberg (2001)
3. Clarke, E.M., Grumberg, O., Jha, S., Lu, Y., Veith, H.: Counterexample-guided abstraction refinement for symbolic model checking. J. ACM 50(5), 752–794 (2003)
4. Dams, D., Namjoshi, K.S.: The existence of finite abstractions for branching time model checking. In: LICS, pp. 335–344. IEEE Computer Society Press, Los Alamitos (2004)
5. de Alfaro, L., Godefroid, P., Jagadeesan, R.: Three-valued abstractions of games: Uncertainty, but with precision. In: LICS, pp. 170–179 (2004)
6. Fecher, H., Huth, M.: Complete abstraction through extensions of disjunctive modal transition systems. Technical Report 0604, Christian-Albrechts-Universität zu Kiel (2006)
7. Fecher, H., Huth, M.: Ranked predicate abstraction for branching time: Complete, incremental, and precise. In: Graf, S., Zhang, W. (eds.) ATVA 2006. LNCS, vol. 4218, pp. 322–336. Springer, Heidelberg (2006)
8. Graf, S., Saidi, H.: Construction of abstract state graphs with PVS. In: CAV (1997)
9. Grumberg, O., Lange, M., Leucker, M., Shoham, S.: Don't know in the μ-calculus. In: Cousot, R. (ed.) VMCAI 2005. LNCS, vol. 3385, pp. 233–249. Springer, Heidelberg (2005)
10. Grumberg, O., Lange, M., Leucker, M., Shoham, S.: When not losing is better than winning: Abstraction and refinement for the full μ-calculus. Information and Compuatation (2007) doi: 10.1016/j.ic.2006.10.009
11. Gulavani, B., Henzinger, T.A., Kannan, Y., Nori, A., Rajamani, S.K.: Synergy: A new algorithm for property checking. In: FSE, ACM Press, New York (2006)
12. Gurfinkel, A., Chechik, M.: Why waste a perfectly good abstraction? In: Hermanns, H., Palsberg, J. (eds.) TACAS 2006. LNCS, vol. 3920, Springer, Heidelberg (2006)
13. Henzinger, T.A., Jhala, R., Majumdar, R., McMillan, K.L.: Abstractions from proofs. In: POPL, pp. 232–244. ACM Press, New York (2004)
14. Henzinger, T.A., Jhala, R., Majumdar, R., Sutre, G.: Lazy abstraction. In: POPL (2002)
15. Huth, M., Jagadeesan, R., Schmidt, D.A.: Modal transition systems: A foundation for three-valued program analysis. In: Sands, D. (ed.) Programming Languages and Systems. LNCS, vol. 2028, pp. 155–169. Springer, Heidelberg (2001)
16. Jain, H., Kroening, D., Sharygina, N., Clarke, E.M.: Word level predicate abstraction and refinement for verifying RTL verilog. In: DAC, pp. 445–450. ACM Press, New York (2005)
17. Jurdzinski, M.: Deciding the winner in parity games is in UP $\cap$ co-UP. Inf. Process. Lett. 68(3), 119–124 (1998)
18. Klauck, H.: Algorithms for parity games. In: Grädel, E., Thomas, W., Wilke, T. (eds.) Automata, Logics, and Infinite Games. LNCS, vol. 2500, pp. 107–129. Springer, Heidelberg (2002)
19. Kozen, D.: Results on the propositional μ-calculus. Theor. Comput. Sci. 27, 333–354 (1983)
20. Larsen, K.G., Thomsen, B.: A modal process logic. In: LICS, pp. 203–210 (1988)
21. Larsen, K.G., Xinxin, L.: Equation solving using modal transition systems. In: LICS, pp. 108–117. IEEE Computer Society Press, Los Alamitos (1990)
22. McMillan, K.L.: Lazy abstraction with interpolants. In: Ball, T., Jones, R.B. (eds.) CAV 2006. LNCS, vol. 4144, pp. 123–136. Springer, Heidelberg (2006)
23. Namjoshi, K.S.: Abstraction for branching time properties. In: Hunt Jr., W.A., Somenzi, F. (eds.) CAV 2003. LNCS, vol. 2725, pp. 288–300. Springer, Heidelberg (2003)

24. Pardo, A., Hachtel, G.D.: Incremental CTL model checking using BDD subsetting. In: DAC, pp. 457–462 (1998)
25. Shoham, S., Grumberg, O.: 3-valued abstraction: More precision at less cost. In: LICS'06
26. Shoham, S., Grumberg, O.: Monotonic abstraction-refinement for CTL. In: Jensen, K., Podelski, A. (eds.) Tools and Algorithms for the Construction and Analysis of Systems. LNCS, vol. 2988, Springer, Heidelberg (2004)
27. Wilke, T.: Alternating tree automata, parity games, and modal μ-calculus. Bull. Soc. Math. Belg. 8(2), 359–391 (2001)
28. Zielonka, W.: Infinite games on finitely coloured graphs with applications to automata on infinite trees. Theor. Comput. Sci. 200(1-2), 135–183 (1998)

A Pseudo Code of Additional Procedures

Table 6. Procedures for the calculation of the outgoing may, resp. must, transitions

Algorithm OutgoingMayCalculation $(P,\ z,\ z_1,\ z_2,\ \tilde{q})$ % calculation of the weak transitions leaving $(z_1, \tilde{q})$ or $(z_2, \tilde{q})$

While $\{(z,\tilde{q})\}.R^+ \neq \{\}$ do
  remove an element $(\tilde{z}', \tilde{q}')$ from $\{(z,\tilde{q})\}.R^+$
  if Satisfiable $(\varrho(z_1) \wedge \text{pre}(\varrho(\tilde{z}')))$ then $R^+ := R^+ \cup \{((z_1,\tilde{q}),(\tilde{z}',\tilde{q}'))\}$
  if Satisfiable $(\varrho(z_2) \wedge \text{pre}(\varrho(\tilde{z}')))$ then $R^+ := R^+ \cup \{((z_2,\tilde{q}),(\tilde{z}',\tilde{q}'))\}$
od

Algorithm OutgoingMustCalculation $(P,\ z,\ z_1,\ z_2,\ \tilde{q})$ % calculation of the must transitions leaving $(z_1, \tilde{q})$ or $(z_2, \tilde{q})$

Local variables $M_1, M_2, N_1, N_2 : \mathbb{P}(Z)$ % M_i stores the yet determined relevant must transition for $(z_i, \tilde{q})$; N_i stores the not yet considered, relevant must transition for $(z_i, \tilde{q})$

$M_1 = \{\widetilde{Z} \cap \pi_1(\{(z_1,\tilde{q})\}.R^+) \mid \widetilde{Z} \in \pi_1(\{(z,\tilde{q})\}.R^-)\}$
$M_2 = \{\widetilde{Z} \cap \pi_1(\{(z_2,\tilde{q})\}.R^+) \mid \widetilde{Z} \in \pi_1(\{(z,\tilde{q})\}.R^-)\}$
remove all elements from $\{(z,\tilde{q})\}.R^-$
$N_1 := \pi_1(\mathbb{P}(\{(z_1,\tilde{q})\}.R^+)) \setminus \{\widetilde{Z}_1 \mid \exists \widetilde{Z} \in M_1 : \widetilde{Z} \subseteq \widetilde{Z}_1\}$
$N_2 := \pi_1(\mathbb{P}(\{(z_2,\tilde{q})\}.R^+)) \setminus \{\widetilde{Z}_2 \mid \exists \widetilde{Z} \in M_2 : \widetilde{Z} \subseteq \widetilde{Z}_2\}$
for i=1 to 2 do
  While $N_i \neq \{\}$ do
    take (not remove) an element $\widetilde{Z}$ from N_i
    % Check if a must transition exists (iff $\varrho(z_i) \Rightarrow \text{pre}(\bigvee_{\tilde{z} \in \mathcal{U}_G(\tilde{q}) \cup \widetilde{Z}} \varrho(\tilde{z}))$) by using a satisfiability check
    if $\neg$ (Satisfiable $(\varrho(z_i) \wedge \neg(\text{pre}(\bigvee_{\tilde{z} \in \mathcal{U}_G(\tilde{q}) \cup \widetilde{Z}} \varrho(\tilde{z})))))$ then
      $M_i := M_i \cup \{\widetilde{Z}\} \setminus \{\widetilde{Z}_i \mid \widetilde{Z} \subset \widetilde{Z}_i\}$; $N_i := N_i \setminus \{\widetilde{Z}_i \mid \widetilde{Z} \subseteq \widetilde{Z}_i\}$
    else $N_i := N_i \setminus \{\widetilde{Z}_i \mid \widetilde{Z}_i \subseteq \widetilde{Z}\}$
  od
  For $\widetilde{Z} \in M_i$ do % Add the calculated hyper-transitions
    Add $(P, (\widetilde{Z}, \tilde{q}))$; $R^- := R^- \cup \{((z_i,\tilde{q}),(\widetilde{Z},\tilde{q}))\}$
  next
next

Minimal Counterexample Generation for SPIN

Paul Gastin[1] and Pierre Moro[2]

[1] LSV, ENS Cachan & CNRS
61, Av. du Prés. Wilson, F-94235 Cachan Cedex, France,
Paul.Gastin@lsv.ens-cachan.fr
[2] LIAFA, Univ. Paris 7
2 place Jussieu, F-75251 Paris Cedex 05, France
moro@liafa.jussieu.fr

Abstract. We propose an algorithm to compute a counterexample of minimal size to some property in a finite state program, using the same space constraints than SPIN. This algorithm uses nested breadth-first searches guided by a priority queue. It works in time $\mathcal{O}(n^2 \log n)$ and is linear in memory.

1 Introduction

Model checking is used to prove correctness of properties of hardware and software systems. When the program is incorrect, locating errors is important to provide hints on how to correct either the system or the property to be checked. Model checkers usually exhibit counterexamples, that is, faulty execution traces of the system [CV03]. The simpler the counterexample is, the easier it will be to locate, understand and fix the error. A counterexample may mean that the abstraction of the system (formalized as the model) is too coarse; several techniques allow to refine it, guided by the counterexample found by the model-checker. The refinement stage can be done manually or automatically, but since even the automatic computation of refinements can be very expensive, it is very important to compute *small* counterexamples (ideally of minimal size) in case the property is not satisfied.

It is well-known that verifying whether a finite state system $\mathcal{M}$ satisfies an LTL property φ is equivalent to testing whether a Büchi automaton $\mathcal{A} = \mathcal{A}_{\mathcal{M}} \cap \mathcal{A}_{\neg\varphi}$ has no accepting run, where $\mathcal{A}_{\mathcal{M}}$ is a Kripke structure describing the system and $\mathcal{A}_{\neg\varphi}$ is a Büchi automaton describing executions that violate φ. It is easy, in theory, to determine whether a Büchi automaton has at least one accepting run. Since there is only a finite number of accepting states, this problem is indeed equivalent to finding a reachable accepting state and a loop around it. A counterexample to φ in $\mathcal{M}$ can then be given as a path $\rho = \rho_1\rho_2$ in the Büchi automaton, where ρ_1 is a simple (loop-free) path from the initial state to an accepting state, and ρ_2 is a simple loop around this accepting state (see Figure 1). Our goal is to find short counterexamples. The first trivial remark is that we can reduce the length of a counterexample if we do not insist on the fact

D. Bošnački and S. Edelkamp (Eds.): SPIN 2007, LNCS 4595, pp. 24–38, 2007.

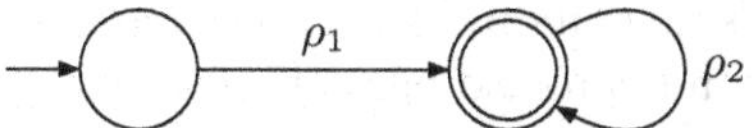

Fig. 1. An accepting path in a Büchi automaton

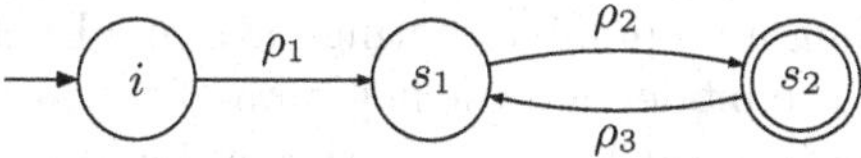

Fig. 2. An accepting path in a Büchi automaton

that the loop starts from an accepting state. Hence, we consider counterexamples of the form $\rho = \rho_1\rho_2\rho_3$ where $\rho_1\rho_2$ is a path from the initial state to an accepting state, and $\rho_2\rho_3$ is a simple loop (see Figure 2).

A minimal counterexample can then be defined as a path of this form, such that the length of ρ is minimal.

A minimal counterexample can of course be computed in polynomial time using minimal paths algorithms based on breadth first searches (BFS). Since the model of the system frequently comes from several components working concurrently, the resulting Büchi automaton to be checked for emptiness may be huge. Therefore, memory is a *critical resource* and, for instance, we cannot afford to store the minimal distances between all pairs of states. Actually, even linear space may be a problem if the constant is too high. In tools like SPIN, only one integer and a few bits per state are stored for the computation of a "small" counterexample (it is well-known that SPIN does not compute a *minimal* counterexample). The aim of this paper is to give a polynomial time algorithm for computing a minimal counterexample using no more memory than SPIN does, i.e., one integer and a few flags per state.

There exists several algorithms [CVWY92, HPY96, GMZ04, SE05] to check a Büchi automaton for emptiness and to construct a counterexample when the language is nonempty. All these algorithms use nested depth first search (DFS) and therefore they cannot be easily adapted to compute a minimal counterexample. It is also possible to use Tarjan like algorithms to find a counterexample, see e.g. [Cou99, VG04].

In [GMZ04], an algorithm computing a minimal counterexample is presented. As far as the memory is concerned, this algorithm is as efficient as SPIN. However, it is still based on DFSs and its time complexity is exponential.

In [HK06], the authors propose an algorithm based on interleaved BFSs. They use three integers and some bits per state, which is more than SPIN does. Moreover, they need to explore the edges badkwards which would be difficult in practice with SPIN.

Our contribution is the following:

– We propose a polynomial time algorithm to compute a counterexample of minimal size. This algorithm only uses forward edges and does not use more memory than SPIN does when trying to reduce the size of counterexamples,

i.e., one integer and some bits per state. It is based on a BFS which is driven by a priority queue and can also be seen as several BFSs interleaved.
- We improve this algorithm with several optimizations.

Note that, we do not address the problem of finding the smallest counterexample, given an LTL property and a finite system. We only focus in this paper on the problem of finding a minimal accepting path in a Büchi automaton representing the product of the model and the negation of the property to be checked.

In the case of symbolic model checking, the problem is slightly different. In particular, in [SB05], the authors show that classical techniques for checking LTL properties (without past) give the smallest counterexample.

The paper is organized as follows. We first recall some notations and the development context in the Section 2. Then we present in Section 3 an algorithm that computes a minimal counterexample, and prove its correctness. We also present an algorithm to recover the trace of a counterexample when only the states s_1 and s_2 are known (see Figure 2). This is needed when using bit-state hashing techniques. In Section 4, we propose several optimizations in order to obtain a more efficient algorithm. We conclude in Section 5.

2 Context and Notations

Let $\mathcal{A} = (S, E, i, F)$ be a Büchi automaton where S is a finite set of states, $E \subseteq S \times S$ is the transition relation, $i \in S$ is the initial state and $F \subseteq S$ is the set of accepting states. Usually transitions are labeled with actions but since these labels are irrelevant for the emptiness problem, they are ignored in this paper. In pictures, the initial state is marked with an ingoing edge and accepting states are doubly circled.

Recall that a path in an automaton is a sequence of states $s_1 s_2 \cdots s_k$ such that for all $i = 1, \ldots, k-1$ there is a transition from s_i to s_{i+1}. We denote by $d(r, s)$ the *distance* between r and s, that is the length of a minimal path from r to s. Note that $d(r, s) = 0$ if $r = s$ and $d(r, s) = \infty$ if s is not reachable from r. A loop is a path $s_1 s_2 \cdots s_k$ with $k > 1$ and $s_k = s_1$. A path $s_1 s_2 \cdots s_k$ is *simple* if $s_i \neq s_j$ for all $i \neq j$. A loop $s_1 s_2 \cdots s_k$ is a *cycle* if $s_1 s_2 \cdots s_{k-1}$ is a simple path. A loop (resp. a cycle) is *accepting* if it contains an accepting state. Finally, an *accepting path* is of the form $\gamma = i \cdots s_k \cdots s_{k+\ell}$ where $i \cdots s_{k+\ell-1}$ is a simple path and $s_k \cdots s_{k+\ell}$ is an accepting cycle. We call $i \cdots s_k$ the *head* of γ. Note that an accepting path starts in the initial state. We also call *counterexample* an accepting path.

2.1 Space Constraints

When checking for emptiness a Büchi automaton that arises from a model and the negation of an LTL formula, we often run out of memory. Hence, it is crucial to use as little memory as possible. This is why SPIN only uses one integer and a few bits per state when reducing the size of a counterexample. Our aim is to use no more memory than SPIN does. Since we want to compute shortest paths we will use BFS and store some distances. The memory constraint implies that only one distance per state can be stored at any given time of the algorithm.

3 An Algorithm to Find the Smallest Counterexample

We will describe an algorithm to compute a minimal counterexample. We do not include any optimization in this section. Section 4 will describe the improvements yielding an efficient algorithm that can be implemented.

The main algorithm is presented in Section 3.5. It uses several algorithms that are presented first.

Actually, instead of computing directly a counterexample $\rho_1\rho_2\rho_3$ as described in Figure 2, we will only compute the key-states s_1 and s_2 so that ρ_2 is a path from s_1 to s_2. The next section shows how the counterexample can be reconstructed from s_1 and s_2.

3.1 Reconstructing the Counterexample

Let $\rho_1\rho_2\rho_3$ be a minimal counterexample (see Figure 2). Assume that only the states s_1 and s_2 that are at the beginning and the end of ρ_2 are known. The problem is to reconstruct the counterexample.

If states are stored in an hash table as usual, one can recover the trace of the counterexample using a BFS algorithm [CSRL01] that stores, when a state is visited for the first time, a pointer to its father. It then suffices to apply this BFS from the initial state i to s_1 to generate ρ_1, then to apply it from s_1 to s_2 to generate ρ_2 and finally to apply it once more from s_2 to s_1 to generate ρ_3.

But if one wants to use bit-state hashing techniques [WL93, Hol98], one cannot generate the trace using the backward pointer technique. Since all informations about a state are not stored in the hash table, once a state is removed from the queue, the only remaining informations for this state are the one stored in the hash table, i.e., some flags and depth informations. A pointer to this memory location does not give complete information about the state.

We propose a simple algorithm to reconstruct the counterexample, when pointer to fathers cannot be used, e.g., when bit-state hashing techniques are used. Since we know states i, s_1 and s_2 we only need to compute a shortest path between a pair (r, r') of states. We first use a BFS to store $d(r, s)$ for each state visited until r' is reached. Then we use a DFS starting from r, that visits a successor s' of a state s iff its distance to r is $d(r, s) + 1$. This condition enforces the DFS to visit states in the order implied by their minimal distance from r. Once r' is reached, the shortest path is stored in the DFS stack. The description is given in Algorithm 1.

Note that, once the distances are computed by a BFS, a backward search in the graph starting from s and following edges for which the distance decreases until r (hence distance 0) is reached, allows to construct efficiently the shortest path from r to s. Unfortunately, backward searches cannot be used in practice

Algorithm 1. An algorithm to generate a shortest path from r to r'

```
void BFS_trace (State r, State r')
Queue F;
F.enqueue(r,0); r.bfs_flag = true;
while F ≠ ∅ do
    (s,n) = F.dequeue();
    for all s' ∈ E(s) do
        if ¬ s'.bfs_flag then
            F.enqueue(s', n+1); s.bfs_flag = true;
            s.depth = n+1;
        end if
        if s' == r' then
            goto 15;
        end if
    end for
end while
DFS_trace(r,r');

void DFS_trace (State s, State r')
cp.push(s,s.depth);; s.dfs_flag = true;
if s == r' then
    exit all recursive calls of DFS_trace
end if
for all s' ∈ E(s) do
    if ¬ s'.dfs_flag and s'.depth == s.depth+1 then
        DFS_trace(s',r');
    end if
end for
cp.pop();
```

with SPIN since it would be hard to compute the set of predecessors of a state. Indeed, the number of potential predecessors may be use, e.g., if the state is reached by an assignment to some integer variable.

3.2 Distances from the Initial State

The first step is to compute with a BFS the distances between the initial state and each state. They correspond to the possible length of the path ρ_1 of the counterexample (see Figure 2). Moreover, we also store in a queue called `Accept`, all the accepting states that are reachable from the initial state. All this is quite standard and presented in Algorithm 2 for the sake of completeness.

3.3 Another Breadth First Search

Once Algorithm 2 has completed, we have stored in `Accept`, all reachable accepting states. We will now find the smallest counterexample going through one

Algorithm 2. A BFS to store distances from the initial state

```
Queue BFS_distance(State i)
 1: Queue F, Accept;
 2: F.enqueue(i,0);
 3: i.depth = 0; i.bfs_flag = true;
 4: while (F ≠ ∅) do
 5:    (s,n) = F.dequeue();
 6:    if (s ∈ F) then
 7:       Accept.enqueue(s);
 8:    end if
 9:    for all s' ∈ E(s) do
10:       if ¬ s'.bfs_flag then
11:          s'.depth = n+1;
12:          F.enqueue(s',n+1);
13:          s'.bfs_flag = true;
14:       end if
15:    end for
16: end while
17: return Accept;
```

of these states, and we will repeat this operation for each accepting state. Note that, since we used a queue to store accepting states, we will start with the accepting state which is the closest to the initial state.

We denote by `r` the current accepting state we are working on. Algorithm 3 will fill a *priority queue* (see [CSRL01][1]) with the set of states reachable from `r`. The priority that will be associated with a state s will be $d(i,s) + d(r,s)$, i.e., $|\rho_1| + |\rho_3|$ in the sense of the Figure 2. We already know $d(i,s)$ from Algorithm 2. This information is stored as the s`.depth`. To fill the priority queue, we perform another BFS starting from `r` that visits all states reachable from `r`. We use a global variable `maxdepth` that contains the size of the smallest counterexample found so far (∞ if no counterexamples were found yet).

Once Algorithm 3 has been performed, we have in the priority queue `PQ` the states reachable from r ordered according to $d(i,s) + d(r,s)$. We will use this information to find the smallest counterexample passing through `r`.

Lemma 1

1. *For all* $(s,n) \in$ `PQ`*, we have* $n = d(i,s) + d(r,s) <$ `maxdepth`*.*
2. *For all state* s*, if* $d(i,s) + d(r,s) <$ `maxdepth` *then* $(s, d(i,s) + d(r,s)) \in$ `PQ`*.*

Proof. (1) For each state, we have s`.depth` $= d(i,s)$. The property is clear when $s = r$. Now, when s' is inserted in `PQ` at line `12`, we have $n+1 = d(r,s')$ by classical properties of the BFS. Since this is guarded by the test in line `11`, the result follows.

[1] There are different implementations for a priority queue (binary heap, binomial heap, Fibonacci heap). They all give the same (theoretical) complexity for our purpose.

Algorithm 3. A BFS to construct the priority queue

```
Priority Queue BFS_PQ(State r)
 1: Queue F; Priority Queue PQ;
 2: F.enqueue(r,0); r.bfs_flag = true;
 3: if r.depth < maxdepth then
 4:    PQ.enqueue(r, r.depth);
 5: end if
 6: while F ≠ ∅ do
 7:    (s,n) = F.dequeue();
 8:    for all s' ∈ E(s) do
 9:       if ¬ s'.bfs_flag then
10:          F.enqueue(s', n+1)); s'.bfs_flag = true;
11:          if s'.depth + n + 1 < maxdepth then
12:             PQ.enqueue(s', s'.depth + n + 1);
13:          end if
14:       end if
15:    end for
16: end while
17: return PQ;
```

(2) If $s = r$ then line 4 is executed and we get the result. Let now s' be such that $d(i, s') + d(r, s') <$ `maxdepth`. Since $d(r, s') <$ `maxdepth` we deduce that $d(r, s') < \infty$ and s' is reachable from r. Hence s' will be considered and lines `11-13` will be executed with s'. Since s'`.depth` $= d(i, s')$ and $n + 1 = d(r, s')$ we deduce from the hypothesis that $(s', d(i, s') + d(r, s'))$ is inserted in `PQ`. □

3.4 BFS Guided by a Priority Queue

Algorithm 4 finds the smallest counterexample whose loop goes through a specified repeated state `r`. Again, our search is limited by `maxdepth` but we omit this optimization from our intuitive description. After Algorithm 3 we have in the priority queue `PQ` all pairs (s, n) with $n = d(i, s) + d(r, s)$ (Lemma 1). The aim is to find a state s such that $d(i, s) + d(r, s) + d^+(s, r)$ is minimal (here $d^+(s, r)$ denotes the length of a shortest *nonempty* path from s to r). Note that the corresponding counterexample can then be reconstructed using Algorithm 1.

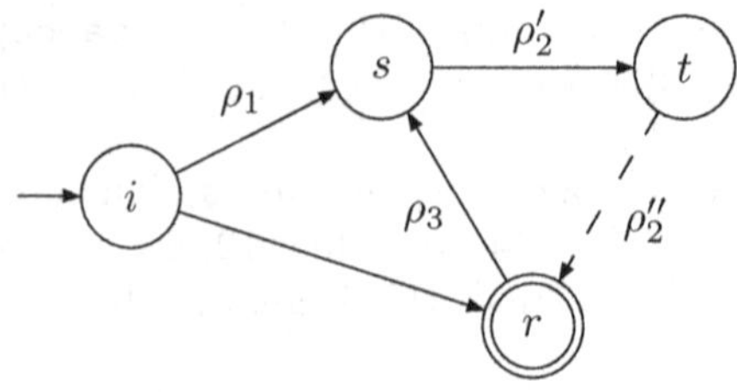

Fig. 3.

Algorithm 4. Algorithm for finding the smallest counterexample

```
(State,State,int) Prio_min(State r, Priority Queue PQ)
Queue G;
n = PQ.PrioMin();
while (PQ ≠ ∅ or G ≠ ∅) and (n + 1 < maxdepth) do
   /* Put in G pairs (s,s) such that s is in PQ with priority n,
   without being marked.*/
   while (PQ.min() == n) do
      (s,m) = PQ.extract_min();
      if ¬ s.marked then
         G.enqueue(s,s);
         s.marked = true;
      end if
   end while
   G.enqueue(#);
   while G.head() ≠ # do
      (s,t) = G.dequeue();
      for all t' ∈ E(t) do
         if t' == r then
            return (s,n+1);
         else if ¬ t'.marked then
            G.enqueue(s,t');
            t'.marked = true;
         end if
      end for
   end while
   G.dequeue(); /* symbol # */
   n++;
end while
return (r,∞);
```

The idea is to use simultaneous (interleaved) BFSs. We begin with a BFS starting from some state s with $d(i,s)+d(r,s)$ minimal. Assume we have reached a state t (see Figure 3). If $d(i,s)+d(r,s)+d(s,t)$ is smaller than the minimal priority in PQ then we continue the BFS from state t. If, on the other hand, there is some state s' with $d(i,s')+d(r,s') < d(i,s)+d(r,s)+d(s,t)$ then we start a new BFS from state s' instead. We use a single queue G for all the interleaved BFSs. In this queue, we store pairs (s,t) since, when we eventually reach r, we need to know from which state s we started with.

The algorithm proceeds in rounds (separated by # in the queue G). In the initialization phase, we put in G all pairs (s,s) with $n = d(i,s)+d(r,s)$ minimal. Then we consider all successors t' of states t such that (s,t) is in G for some s. The "rank" of these states t' is $n+1$ and we add (s,t') to G for the next round if t' has not yet been reached. We also add for the next round the pairs (s,s) such that $(s,n+1)$ is in PQ. When we reach state r we have found our smallest counterexample whose loop goes through r.

Lemma 2. *Invariant for Algorithm 4: there is exactly one # in* `G` *between lines* `13-23` *and there is no # in* `G` *outside lines* `12-24`.

Proof. At the beginning of the algorithm, `G` is empty. We insert a # in the queue at line `12` and no # is inserted or deleted between lines `13-23`. Hence, the # inserted at line `12` is popped at line `24`. The result follows. □

The invariants for the loops of Algorithm 4 are given by the following table

Invariants for loop 3 : (1, 2, 3, 4)
Invariants for loop 5 : (1, 2, 3, 4)
Invariants for loop 13 : (2, 3, 5, 6, 7)

where

$$\forall s \quad d(i,s) + d(r,s) + d^{+}(s,r) > n \tag{1}$$

$$\forall t \quad t \text{ is marked} \vee (t,n) \in \texttt{PQ} \vee \forall s, d(i,s) + d(r,s) + d(s,t) > n \tag{2}$$

$$\forall s,t \quad (s,t) \in G \Longrightarrow t \text{ is marked} \tag{3}$$

$$\forall s,t \quad (s,t) \in G \Longrightarrow d(i,s) + d(r,s) + d(s,t) = n \tag{4}$$

$$\forall s,t \quad (s,t) \in G \text{ before } \# \Longrightarrow d(i,s) + d(r,s) + d(s,t) = n \tag{5}$$

$$\forall s,t \quad (s,t) \in G \text{ after } \# \Longrightarrow d(i,s) + d(r,s) + d(s,t) = n + 1 \tag{6}$$

$$\texttt{PQ.PrioMin}() > n \tag{7}$$

Loop 3. We first show that (1, 2, 3, 4) hold initially for loop 3, i.e., after line 2:

(1) Since $\texttt{PQ.PrioMin}() = n$, we deduce from Lemma 1 that $d(i,s) + d(r,s) \geq n$ for all s. The result follows since $d^{+}(s,r) > 0$.
(2) Assume that $d(i,s)+d(r,s)+d(s,t) \leq n$ for some s. Since $\texttt{PQ.PrioMin}() = n$, we deduce using Lemma 1 that $d(i,s) + d(r,s) = n$ and $d(s,t) = 0$. Using Lemma 1 again we obtain $(t,n) = (s,n) \in \texttt{PQ}$.
(3, 4) Holds trivially since `G` is empty.

Loop 5. Assuming that (1, 2, 3, 4) are invariants for loop 3, we obtain immediately that (1, 2, 3, 4) hold initially for loop 5. We show that they are preserved by the execution of lines (6-10):

(1) Clear since n is unchanged.
(2) If t is marked or $(t,n) \in \texttt{PQ}$ before line 6 then the same holds after line 10. Moreover n is unchanged in this loop hence the third part of (2) is also invariant.
(3) Clear since whenever a pair (s,s) is inserted in `G` at line 8 then s is marked at line 9 .
(4) When a pair (s,s) is inserted in `G` at line 8 then we have $d(i,s) + d(r,s) = n$ by Lemma 1.

Loop 13. First, note that (2) and (7) hold after line 11 and are invariants by lines (12-24): `PQ` and n remain unchanged in the body of loop 13 and once a state is marked, it remains so forever.

Also, (3) holds after line 11 and when a pair (s, t') is inserted in G at line 19 then t' is marked at the next line. Hence, (3) is preserved by the execution of lines (14-22).

Now, since (4) holds after line 11 then (5, 6) hold after line 12 (by Lemma 2 there are no # in G except from lines (13-23) where there is exactly one # in G). Equation (5) is clearly preserved by lines (14-22) since new pairs are inserted in G after #.

It remains to show that (6) is preserved by lines (14-22). Consider the pair (s, t') inserted in G at line 19. By (5) we have $d(i, s) + d(r, s) + d(s, t) = n$. Since $t' \in E(t)$, we get $d(t, t') \leq 1$ and we deduce that $d(i, s) + d(r, s) + d(s, t') \leq n+1$. Now, t' was not marked (line 18) and $(t', n) \notin$ PQ by (7). We deduce from (2) that $d(i, s) + d(r, s) + d(s, t') > n$. Therefore, $d(i, s) + d(r, s) + d(s, t') = n + 1$ and (6) still holds after the insertion of (s, t') in G.

Loop 3 continued. Finally, we have to show that (1, 2, 3, 4) still hold after line 25. We know that after line 23, the first element in G is # and that (2, 3, 6) hold. We deduce immediately that (3, 4) hold after line 25.

We consider (1), so assume that $d(i, s) + d(r, s) + d^+(s, r) = n + 1$ for some s. Let t be such that $r \in E(t)$ and $d^+(s, r) = d(s, t) + 1$. Then, we deduce that $d(i, s) + d(r, s) + d(s, t) = n$. Now, after line 11 we have $(t, n) \notin$ PQ by (7). We deduce from (2) that t is marked. Let s' be such that $(s', t) \in G$. Since $r \in E(t)$ we deduce that line 17 will be executed before the end of loop 13. Therefore, if line 24 is reached, this means that $d(i, s) + d(r, s) + d^+(s, r) > n + 1$ for all s. We deduce that (1) still holds after line 25 (if reached).

It remains to show that (2) still holds after line 25. This is a direct consequence of the following:

Claim. Assume that after line 23 there are s, t' such that t' is not marked and $d(i, s) + d(r, s) + d(s, t') \leq n + 1$. Then, $(t', n + 1) \in$ PQ.

Let s, t' satisfy the hypotheses of the claim. By (7) we know that $(t', n) \notin$ PQ hence, by (2), we get $d(i, s) + d(r, s) + d(s, t') > n$. Therefore, $d(i, s) + d(r, s) + d(s, t') = n + 1$. We prove that $t' = s$ by contradiction. So assume that $t' \neq s$. Then $d(s, t') > 0$ and there exists t such that $d(s, t') = d(s, t) + 1$ and $t' \in E(t)$. We obtain $d(i, s) + d(r, s) + d(s, t) = n$. We deduce that t was already marked before line 12 by (7, 2). Therefore, there exists s' such that (s', t) has been inserted in G before line 12 (maybe in some previous execution of the body of loop 3). Therefore, after line 23, all successors of t have already been considered and must be marked. This is a contradiction with $t' \in E(t)$ and t' is not marked. Therefore, $t' = s$ and we have $d(i, s) + d(r, s) = n + 1$. Since $n + 1 <$ maxdepth (test line 3), using Lemma 1 we obtain $(t', n+1) = (s, n+1) \in$ PQ, which proves the claim.

Lemma 3. *Either* $d(i, s) + d(r, s) + d^+(s, r) \geq$ maxdepth *for all state* s *and Algorithm 4 exits at line 27, or Algorithm 4 exits at line 17 with a pair* $(s, n+1)$ *such that* $d(i, s) + d(r, s) + d^+(s, r) = n + 1 <$ maxdepth *and for all state* s' *we have* $d(i, s') + d(r, s') + d^+(s', r) > n$.

Proof. Follows easily from the invariants, in particular (1) and (5). □

Algorithm 5. The complete algorithm

```
Stack Minimal_Counterexample (State i)
Queue Accept = BFS_distance(i);
maxdepth = ∞;
while Accept ≠ ∅ do
   State r = Accept.dequeue();
   Priority Queue PQ = BFS_PQ(r);
   (s,n) = Prio_min(r, PQ)
   if n < maxdepth then
      s1 = s; s2 = r;
      maxdepth = n;
   end if
end while
if maxdepth < ∞ then
   Stack cp;
   BFS_trace(i,s1); BFS_trace(s1,s2); BFS_trace(s2,s1);
   return cp;
end if
return ∅;
```

3.5 Synthesis

We give now the complete algorithm which computes the smallest counterexample. This algorithm works in time $\mathcal{O}(|E| \cdot |F| \cdot \log(|S|))$, the factor $\log(|S|)$ is due to the operations on the priority queue. The algorithm works in linear space. More precisely, for each state we store an integer (depth field) and a few bits (`bfs_flag` or `marked`). In fact, these flags should be erased after each call to an algorithm, this is omitted for simplicity. The size of each queue is at most linear in the number of states.

4 Improvements

The first improvement is to use, before calling Algorithm 5, a nested-DFS algorithm such as [CVWY92, HPY96, SE05, GMZ04], or a Tarjan-like algorithm [Cou99, VG04][2]. This allows to perform a linear time search to detect whether there exists some counterexample, and in this case it can also initialize `maxdepth` to the size of the counterexample found in order to speed-up Algorithm 5.

We can further improve the computation time by applying the following optimizations.

Improving the initial value of `maxdepth`

For Algorithm 2, suppose that a counterexample has already been found and stored in a path called `cp`. Then, if an algorithm like a nested-DFS was used,

[2] In fact, a nested-DFS algorithm can also prevent revisiting some states, see the end of Algorithm 6.

Algorithm 6. A BFS to store distances from the initial state

```
Queue BFS_distance(State i)
 1: Queue F, Accept;
 2: F.enqueue(i,0);
 3: i.depth = 0; i.bfs_flag = true;
 4: maxdepth = size(cp); n = 0; saved = 0
 5: while (F ≠ ∅) ∧ (n < maxdepth) do
 6:   (s,n) = F.dequeue();
 7:   if (s ∈ F) then
 8:     Accept.enqueue(s);
 9:   end if
10:   for all s' ∈ E(s) do
11:     if s'.color != black and ¬ s'.bfs_flag then
12:       s'.depth = n+1;
13:       F.enqueue(s',n+1);
14:       s'.bfs_flag = true;
15:     end if
16:   end for
17:   if s.color == blue and s.is_in_cp and depth(s,cp) - n > saved then
18:     saved = depth(s,cp) - n;
19:     maxdepth = size(cp) - saved;
20:   end if
21: end while
22: return Accept;
```

one knows if a state is on the head of the counterexample (it will be `blue` (see [SE05, GMZ04] for more information on the `blue` flag[3]) and in the current stack). Algorithm 2 computes the minimal distances between the initial state and all the states. So for each state that belongs to the head of the counterexample `cp`, one can compare its distance from the initial state in the path `cp`, and its minimal distance. Then, if the latter is smaller, one can already update the maxdepth field at this point. These modifications are described in Algorithm 6, lines 4, 11 and 17-20.

Looking for counterexample in Algorithm 3

If a successor of a state is also the current accepting state, then we have found a counterexample (and it has the form of Figure 1). Since we know its length we can update `maxdepth` (see lines 19-21 in Algorithm 7).

Limiting the state space in Algorithm 3

We can also add a condition in the body of the loop saying that we are looking for counterexamples for which the loop size is at most `maxdepth` (see lines 9-11 in Algorithm 7).

---

3 The blue color is described in these papers, but it is common to all the nested-DFS approaches.

Algorithm 7. A BFS to construct the priority queue

```
Priority Queue BFS_PQ(State r)
 1: Queue F; Priority Queue PQ;
 2: F.enqueue(r,0); r.bfs_flag = true;
 3: if r.depth < maxdepth then
 4:    PQ.enqueue(r, r.depth);
 5: end if
 6: loop = false;
 7: while F ≠ ∅ do
 8:    (s,n) = F.dequeue();
 9:    if n + 1 ≥ maxdepth then
10:       break;
11:    end if
12:    for all s' ∈ E(s) do
13:       if ¬ s'.bfs_flag then
14:          F.enqueue(s', n+1)); s'.bfs_flag = true;
15:          if (s'.depth + n + 1 < maxdepth) and (s'.depth < s.depth) then
16:             PQ.enqueue(s', s'.depth + n + 1);
17:          end if
18:          loop = loop ∨ (s' == r);
19:          if (s' == r) and (s'.depth + n + 1 < maxdepth) then
20:             maxdepth = s'.depth + n + 1;
21:          end if
22:       end if
23:    end for
24: end while
25: if loop then
26:    return PQ;
27: else
28:    return ∅
29: end if
```

Call to Algorithm 4 iff a smaller counterexample may exist

There is also in Algorithm 7, a local boolean named `loop`, which records if there exists an accepting path into the limited state space (limited by maxdepth). If this boolean `loop` is false at the end of the execution, then there are no useful loop passing through `r` and there is no need to continue the computation for this state (see lines 6, 18 and 25-29 in Algorithm 7).

Including only useful states in `PQ`

Recall that we are looking for a state s for which $d(i,s) + d(r,s) + d^+(s,r)$ is minimal. Algorithm 3 inserts in `PQ` pairs $(s, d(i,s) + d(r,s))$ which are then used by Algorithm 4 to find some state which minimizes the quantity above.

At line 10 of Algorithm 3, we have $d(r,s) = n$, $d(r,s') = n+1$ and $s' \in E(s)$. Then, $d^+(s,r) \leq 1 + d(s',r)$. We deduce that if $d(i,s) \leq d(i,s')$ then $d(i,s)+d(r,s)+d^+(s,r) \leq d(i,s')+d(r,s')+d^+(s',r)$. Therefore, if s' minimizes this quantity, so does s and there is no need to insert s' in the priority queue PQ. This is prevented by the additional constraint on line 15 of Algorithm 7.

Note that this only saves some memory in the priority queue PQ. Indeed, with the notation above, we have $d(i,s) + d(r,s) < d(i,s') + d(r,s')$ (still assuming that $d(i,s) \leq d(i,s')$). Hence, even if we insert $(s', d(i,s') + d(r,s'))$ in PQ, when this pair is extracted from PQ at line 6 of Algorithm 4, the state s' is already marked and therefore, (s', s') is not inserted in G.

5 Conclusion

We have proposed an algorithm to compute the smallest counterexample of a property represented by a Büchi automaton. We have presented a set of improvements that can immediately be used to get a more efficient algorithm.

Our algorithm has nice properties. First, it can find all smallest counterexamples for all accepting states, if the variable **maxdepth** is always set to ∞.

Second, the ordering of the transitions has no impact on the computation time. For nested-DFS approaches, the result can strongly depends on the order of the transitions.

Third, our algorithm can also be used for bounded explicit model checking, setting the maxdepth variable to some value. The algorithm properties ensure that it will found the smallest counterexample passing through the state space bounded by the maxdepth value. This is not the case for classical nested-DFS algorithms which fail to answer properly for some graph configurations (depending on the ordering for the visit).

References

[Cou99] Couvreur, J.M.: On-the-fly verification of linear temporal logic. In: FM 1999. LNCS, vol. 1708, pp. 253–271. Springer, Berlin Heidelberg New York (1999)

[CSRL01] Cormen, T.H., Stein, C., Rivest, R.L., Leiserson, C.E.: Introduction to Algorithms. McGraw-Hill Higher Education (2001)

[CV03] Clarke, E.M., Veith, H.: Counterexamples revisited: Principles, algorithms, applications. In: Verification: Theory and Practice. LNCS, vol. 2772, pp. 208–224. Springer, Heidelberg (2003)

[CVWY92] Vardi, M.Y., Wolper, P., Yannakakis, M.: Memory-efficient algorithms for the verification of temporal properties. Formal Methods in System Design 1(2/3), 275–288 (1992)

[GMZ04] Gastin, P., Moro, P., Zeitoun, M.: Minimization of counterexample in SPIN. In: Proc. of SPIN'04. LNCS, vol. 2989, pp. 92–108. Springer, Berlin Heidelberg New York (2004)

[HK06] Hansen, H., Kervinen, A.: Minimal counterexamples in O(n log n) memory and O(n^2) time. In: Proc. of ACDC'06, pp. 133–142. IEEE Computer Society Press, Los Alamitos, CA, USA (2006)

[Hol98] Holzmann, G.: An analysis of bitstate hashing. Formal Methods in System Design, 13(3), pp. 287–305, extended and revised version of Proc. PSTV95, pp. 301–314 (1998)

[HPY96] Holzmann, G., Peled, D., Yannakakis, M.: On nested depth first search. In: Proc. of SPIN'96. American Mathematical Society (1996)

[SB05] Schuppan, V., Biere, A.: Shortest counterexamples for symbolic model checking of LTL with past. In: Halbwachs, N., Zuck, L.D. (eds.) TACAS 2005. LNCS, vol. 3440, pp. 493–509. Springer, Heidelberg (2005)

[SE05] Schwoon, S., Esparza, J.: A note on on-the-fly verification algorithms. In: Halbwachs, N., Zuck, L.D. (eds.) TACAS 2005. LNCS, vol. 3440, pp. 174–190. Springer, Heidelberg (2005)

[VG04] Valmari, A., Geldenhuys, J.: Tarjan's algorithm makes on-the-fly LTL verification more efficient. In: Jensen, K., Podelski, A. (eds.) TACAS 2004. LNCS, vol. 2988, pp. 205–219. Springer, Heidelberg (2004)

[WL93] Wolper, P., Leroy, D.: Reliable hashing without collosion detection. In: Courcoubetis, C. (ed.) CAV 1993. LNCS, vol. 697, pp. 59–70. Springer, Heidelberg (1993)

Generating Counter-Examples Through Randomized Guided Search

Neha Rungta and Eric G. Mercer

Department of Computer Science
Brigham Young University
Provo, UT 84602, USA

Abstract. Computational resources are increasing rapidly with the explosion of multi-core processors readily available from major vendors. Model checking needs to harness these resources to help make it more effective in practical verification. Directed model checking uses heuristics in a guided search to rank states in order of interest. Randomizing guided search makes it possible to harness computation nodes by running independent searches in parallel in a effort to discover counter-examples to correctness. Initial attempts at adding randomization to guided search have achieved very limited success. In this work, we present a new low-cost randomized guided search technique that shuffles states in the priority queue with equivalent heuristic ties. We show in an empirical study that randomized guided search, overall, decreases the number of states generated before error discovery when compared to a guided search using the same heuristic. To further evaluate the performance gains of randomized guided search using a particular heuristic, we compare it with randomized depth-first search. Randomized depth-first search shuffles transitions and generally improves error discovery over the default transition order implemented by the model checker. In the context of evaluating randomized guided search, a randomized depth-first search provides a lower bound for establishing performance gains in directed model checking. In the empirical study, we show that with the correct heuristic, randomized guided search outperforms randomized depth-first search both in effectively finding counter-examples and generating shorter counter-examples.

1 Introduction

The current trend in micro-processor design is to group multiple processors into a single silicon die and package. For example, dual-core processors are quickly becoming mainstream, and quad-core packages are readily available from most vendors. CEO Paul Otellini, at a recent Intel development forum, displayed an 80 core prototype chip capable of terabyte per second data exchange and pledged production runs in the next five years [25]. The trend is clearly to put more processors on a single die rather than to increase clock speed and computation in a single processor. This is leading to an explosion in computational resources.

D. Bošnački and S. Edelkamp (Eds.): SPIN 2007, LNCS 4595, pp. 39–57, 2007.

The question for the model checking community given the growth in multi-core processors, as well as parallel and distributed systems, is how can we harness this computation power? At the heart of explicit state model checking is an exhaustive proof to show the absence of a specific behavior. The proof literally enumerates, in a largely brute-force manner, the entire behavior space of the system being verified [4]. The complexity of the systems, however, limits practical application of model checking in both time and space. Aggregating the available computation resources to solve the model checking problem can help to improve the situation.

Parallel and distributed model checking has shown some limited promise in utilizing large amounts of computation resources [35, 21, 1, 20, 3, 19]. The focus of the community is to find ways to harness several computation nodes to cooperatively construct the exhaustive proof. These approaches generally look appealing in low node counts but are less efficient as more computation nodes are added [22]. Seminal work goes so far as to prove that depth-first search itself is inherently sequential and does not lend itself to parallel computation [29]. This may explain the lack of scaling in current approaches and possibly suggest that we need a fundamentally different algorithm for model checking that is less sequential and more amenable to parallelization.

As a counterpoint, it is possible to parallelize model checking by moving away from an exhaustive proof and instead focus on counter-example generation. In other words, run several independent experiments with some degree of randomization on individual computation nodes to find a counter-example to the proof. This is in contrast to several computation nodes cooperatively constructing an exhaustive proof. The shift in focus from exhaustive proof to counter-example generation began in the directed model checking community, and it opens new avenues for distributed model checking.

Early researchers of parallel and distributed model checking explored the concept of random walk for counter-example generation with modest success [17,34,24]. Random walk has inherently low memory requirements, and the work distributes these random walk based searches over many computation nodes in hopes of discovering a counter-example. The effectiveness of random walk in terms of coverage is critically dependent on the structure of the model [28,2,18]. Empirical studies show that random walk is not very useful for error discovery in the models where it achieves poor coverage. This creates a need for effective randomized searches which better harness the computation resources.

Recent work studying default search order in model checker performance contributes a key insight to randomization of a regular depth-first search [7]. Controlling for default search order in depth-first search by randomly choosing transitions to explore (randomized DFS) dramatically improves counter-example generation [6]. Independent randomized DFS searches easily distribute to any number of computation nodes, however, like any search method, randomized DFS breaks down in certain models [32]. The issue in randomized DFS is that it blindly moves through the behavior space even when there is information readily available about the structure of the model and the property being invalidated that can improve the search.

Directed model checking uses heuristics to rank interest in states and guide the search of the behavior space to efficiently generate counter-examples [37,9, 10,16,27,33,8,31]. The heuristics generally consider either the model structure or the property being validated to rank the states. A guided search then orders the states in a priority queue based on the path cost and heuristic ranking where states estimated to lead more quickly to a counter-example are explored before other states. Guided search is effective in counter-example generation and often succeeds where depth-first search fails. More importantly, the length of the counter-examples generated by guided search algorithms are often shorter than those generated by depth-first search. This simplifies the developer's task of understanding the counter-example.

Guided search also benefits from randomization, and like depth-first search, once randomized, it can be run independently in parallel (randomized GDS[1]). Preliminary work in randomized GDS chooses randomly from the first n-best entries of the priority queue when selecting the next state to explore [23]. The effectiveness of the randomization is not clear from the empirical study. In some instances, the randomization helps; while in other instances, the randomization hurts. The control, n, in [23] only ranges over a limited set of values between two and five, and the algorithm also does not distinguish between states in the priority queue with different heuristic values. In Java PathFinder v4.0 (JPF), it is also possible to execute a randomized GDS by randomizing the transition order in generating successors before adding them to the priority queue. This randomization, however, has very limited impact on the actual default search order in the guided search. Clearly, there are several open questions in randomized GDS left to be explored.

This paper presents a new randomized GDS algorithm that completely shuffles states in the priority queue with equal heuristic rankings. We show that full randomization of the guided search improves the effectiveness of the search over default search order in an empirical study. The empirical study uses characterized benchmarks from [7,32] and published heuristics for the JPF, [36], and Estes, [26], model checkers. This paper also presents a second empirical study on the new randomized GDS algorithm in context of randomized DFS using the previously mentioned models and heuristics. The second study highlights the role of the heuristic in performance. When the heuristic is correctly matched to the models and properties, the new randomized GDS algorithm outperforms randomized DFS in both the effectiveness of the search in finding counter-examples and the length of the counter-examples. When the heuristic is not correctly matched to the models or properties, randomized DFS is more effective in error discovery which demonstrates a need to develop better heuristics for those classes of models and properties.

---

[1] We use randomized GDS to refer generally to any algorithm that adds randomization into guided search, and we will clearly indicate how the search is randomized in the context in which it appears.

The algorithm and empirical studies in this paper underscore a need to develop methods that match heuristics to models and the properties being disproved. This work and other work such as [23] and [6] also revisit a new way to view randomization, model checking, and search techniques. It motivates a need to study and understand how to best use randomization in model checking and parallelization for counter-example generation. Research in this area is especially timely given the rapid increase in computational resources, and more importantly, the ever increasing need for practical model checking in system design.

2 Background

It is important to control for default search order when evaluating model checking algorithms because implementation details in the model checker itself affect performance to a larger degree than previously supposed [7]. For example, in a simple depth-first search, the state at the top of a search stack may have several enabled transitions that move the current state to the next state of computation. The choices arise from non-determinism in the model, where the non-determinism is usually a result of scheduling decisions or input locations. The principle observation in [7] is that controlling for the default order in which a model checker selects transitions during depth-first search dramatically affects the outcome of counter-example generation. The work in [7] proposes a randomized DFS that controls for default transition order by shuffling transitions enabled at each state. Follow-on work in [6] shows that randomized DFS is effective in counter-example generation across their benchmark set[2]. In the words of [7], "*[T]hese findings tell a strong cautionary tale*", because default search order significantly affects performance of the techniques being evaluated in comparison studies. This is especially critical for directed model checking which relies on comparison studies to establish performance gains.

Directed model checking uses a guided search rather than depth-first or breadth-first search to find counter-examples for the property being verified. The fundamental assumption is that an error does exist in the model, and the goal is to find the error before exhausting computation resources. The work in this paper focuses on a greedy best-first search; although, the ideas are equally applicable to other best-first search techniques that make no guarantee on the optimality of the counter-example. In other words, the results of an A^* search are not significantly affected by our approach. A greedy best-first search is illustrated in Fig. 1. The top state in Fig. 1 is the initial state. At each iteration of the search, a state is removed from a priority queue, its successors are generated, ranked by a heuristic function, and inserted into the priority queue. For example, the initial state in Fig. 1 has three successors which are ranked 12, 9, and 2. These states are inserted into the priority queue. The next iteration of the search

[2] There are other default orders in model checkers that are yet to be controlled as evidenced in [32], where different versions of JPF yield different results in randomized DFS.

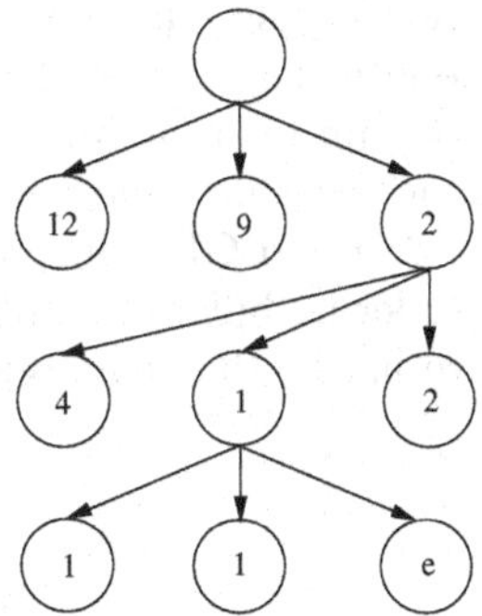

Fig. 1. An illustration of greedy best-first search that chooses the state nearest to the goal state to expand in the search based on a heuristic function

removes the state with rank 2 from the priority queue and repeats the process. The heuristic function estimates the nearness of a state to an actual goal state. The goal state in our example is marked with the 'e' character. The goal state in directed model checking is an error state from which we build a counter-example to the specified property. A good heuristic for a greedy best-first search often converges quickly to an error state, and the length of the counter-example is near minimal.

Directed model checking critically relies on empirical studies to show performance gains over depth-first search, and like depth-first search, must control for default search order. For example, consider a priority search queue that contains over 100,000 states and a heuristic function that assigns an integer value between one and six to each state. Invariably, there are many thousand states with equivalent heuristic values. The order in which they are explored is largely controlled by the order in which they are generated by the model checker and ordered in the priority queue. During a guided search, some function compares the heuristic value of a newly generated state to the heuristic values of existing states in the queue before inserting the new state in the queue based on its ranking. Most often, this function uses a pre-determined ordering to sort states that have the same heuristic value. For example, when comparing a newly generated state, s_1, with a heuristic value, x, to an existing state in the priority queue, s_2, with a heuristic value, x, the state ordering function always inserts state s_1 after s_2 in the priority queue. The order in which states s_1 and s_2 are explored can potentially affect the total number of states generated before error discovery—a fact disregarded by the ordering function. The lesson from [7] is that these default choices in the model checker need to be controlled. This gives rise to randomized GDS which in the context of this paper refers to a greedy best-first search with some randomization to control for default order.

There are several ways to implement randomized GDS, and each controls for default order in the priority queue to a certain extent. For example, [23] randomly chooses between the n-best entries in the priority queue, and JPF v4.0 allows the transition order to be shuffled during state generation. The former method shows some potential while the later method is not effective in randomization. This paper presents a new algorithm for randomized GDS that controls for all heuristic ties in the priority queue. We show that with the correct heuristic function, our new algorithm for randomized GDS outperforms not only the greedy best-first search using default ordering but randomized DFS as well. This is especially true in models that are hard—that is, models where randomized DFS is not successful.

3 Randomized GDS

Current techniques for randomization of guided search are not effective in exploiting the full potential of the randomization. For example, as mentioned previously, the approach presented in [23] limits the randomization to the n-best entries in the priority queue, where n is specified by the user. As another example, JPF allows for randomization in its searches. To understand its approach, we need to first look at its priority queue implementation; specifically, the `DefaultComparator` class. The class uses state identifiers and hash values to resolve heuristic ties between states in the priority queue. The state identifiers and hash values map to the same states in every single run of a guided search and deterministically resolve the heuristic ties. Turning on the `randomize_choices` option in JPF successfully modifies the order in which successors, for a particular state, are added to the priority queue because the successors are now assigned different state identifiers every time we execute a guided search trial. This randomized GDS approach causes only a small amount of variance in the number of states generated before error discovery when compared to the guided search since the randomization is limited to the successors of a given state. Our studies show that the limited amount of randomization is not effective in significantly changing the default search order.

To fully exploit the potential of randomization in directed model checking we define a randomized GDS algorithm that randomly shuffles states with equivalent heuristic ranking in the priority queue. The pseudo-code for this algorithm is presented in Fig. 2. The algorithm is *embarrassingly parallel* [15]. Several trials of the new randomized GDS algorithm can be launched in parallel on different computation nodes since each randomized GDS trial is completely independent of the other trials. There is no communication overhead between the trials which allows the algorithm to scale up to an arbitrary number of computation nodes.

In the randomized GDS algorithm, we associate a random value with each state generated during model checking in addition to its heuristic value. The tuple $\langle s_i, h_i, r_i \rangle$ in Fig. 2 is an element stored in the priority queue where s_i is the state, h_i is the heuristic ranking of s_i, and r_i is the random value associated with s_i. The randomized GDS algorithm employs a new comparator function, compare_vals, that is also shown in Fig. 2 and uses the random values as a secondary key to sort states with the same heuristic rankings. The approach enables us to effectively randomize the order of states with same heuristic values

```
  /* N is the set of computation nodes */
procedure randomized_guided_search_init(N)
  for each i ∈ N do
    execute(randomized_guided_search(), i)
  wait_for_all_nodes_to_terminate_execution()
  gather_results(1...N)
  return

  /* Add initial element ⟨s0, h0, r0⟩ to PriorityQueue PQ */
  /* Add s0 to the Visited set */
procedure randomized_guided_search()
  while PQ ≠ ∅ do
    ⟨si, hi, ri⟩ := PQ.dequeue()
    for each s' ∈ successors(si) do
      if error(s') then
        return Error Statistics
      if s' ∉ Visited then
        Visited := Visited ∪ {s'}
        PQ.enqueue(⟨s', heuristic(s'), rand_val()⟩)
  return No Errors Found

  /* PriorityQueue PQ uses compare_vals to order states */
procedure compare_vals(⟨s1, h1, r1⟩, ⟨s2, h2, r2⟩)
  if h1 > h2 then
    return true
  else if h1 < h2 then
    return false
  else
    if r1 > r2 then
      return true
    else
      return false
```

Fig. 2. Pseudo-code for randomized GDS that shuffles states with the same heuristic values using a secondary key from a random number generator

across different states and search levels. The new randomized GDS algorithm has a low cost of randomization because maintaining the random value is the only additional cost it incurs when compared to a regular guided search.

We present two empirical studies that compare randomized GDS to default order guided search. The first study is in JPF v4.0 uses Java benchmarks and the second study is in Estes uses C benchmarks. JPF contains a suite of structural heuristics, [16], that exploit thread properties in Java programs and also has a heuristic for finding feasible abstract counter-examples [27,16]. The Java models used in this study are small to medium sized programs that contain concurrency errors. These models have been collected from different sources: original papers presenting the heuristics [16], concurrency literature [12], research describing Java specific errors [14], and the IBM benchmark suite [13]. Additionally, these models are characterized to a certain degree having been used recently in two extensive benchmarking studies [7, 32].

Our empirical study is conducted on a super-computing cluster with 618 nodes. We conduct a single experiment of executing 100 trials of our randomized GDS algorithm in parallel for each subject in the study. The choice of 100 trials is arbitrary, but we believe its size is sufficient to indicate general trends in performance. The randomized GDS trials and the guided search are allocated 7GB RAM, and the execution time is bounded at 1 hour. The 1 hour is again arbitrary but together with 100 trials constitutes an upper bound of 100 hours of computation for each model—a significant amount of resources.

Table 1 is a comparison between the default order guided search and our new randomized GDS algorithm in JPF. We present results for four different heuristics in JPF: choose-free heuristic, most-blocked heuristic, interleaving heuristic, and the prefer-thread heuristic. Based on the description of the heuristics in [16] and our knowledge of the models, we pick heuristics that are most likely to work well for a given model. We present, in Table 1, the number of states generated for a default order guided search (`GDS`). The values in Table 1 with the form, x^*, indicate that the search generated x number of states before running out of either time or memory. For the new randomized GDS algorithm (`Randomized-GDS`), in Table 1, we present the following statistics: path error density (`PED`), minimum (`Minimum`) and maximum (`Maximum`) number of states generated in a single error discovering randomized GDS trial among all the trials, mean (`Mean`) number of states generated in all the error discovering randomized GDS trials, and the 95% confidence interval (`95% CI`) for the mean number of states. The path error density is the ratio of the number of error discovering randomized GDS trials to the total number of trials executed.

The results in Table 1 show that the new randomized GDS algorithm, overall, improves the error discovery for a given heuristic over default search order. In the `AccountSubtype(2,2)` model, the default order guided search does not find an error even after exploring over 2.22 million states. In contrast, all 100 trials of the new randomized GDS algorithm find an error and explore only 193, 313 states—on average—before error discovery. Furthermore, the maximum number of states generated—642,193—by a single randomized GDS run of the new algorithm is also dramatically lower than the number of states generated by the default order guided search. Similar behavior is observed in all the `ProducerConsumer` models, and some `TwoStage`, `Piper`, and `Wronglock` models. In certain models, the mean number of states generated by the new randomized GDS algorithm is more than the states generated by the default order guided search, as seen in the `Deos(abstracted)` and `Reorder(1,5)` models; however, even in these models, the minimum number of states generated by the new randomized GDS algorithm is less than the number of states generated by the default order guided search.

Table 2 presents the results of running our new randomized GDS algorithm on different distance heuristic functions implemented in the Estes model checker [26]. We evaluate three specific distance heuristic functions in Table 2: FSM [11], EFSM [30], and e-FCA [31]. The only change in the setup for evaluating

Table 1. Comparing the performance of default order guided search (GDS) and randomized guided search (Randomized-GDS) using the heuristics in JPF and published benchmarks

Model	GDS	Randomized-GDS				
		PED	Minimum	Mean	Maximum	95% CI
ChooseFree Heuristic						
Deos(abstracted)	16	1.00	11	40	423	14
RwNoExcpChk(2,100,1)	372,826	1.00	769	6,419	20,865	739
MostBlocked Heuristic						
Clean(1,1,12)	188	1.00	33	377	993	59
Piper(2,2,2)	16,437	1.00	240	1,338	3,909	171
Piper(2,4,4)	2,478,360*	0.87	138,916	1,229,530	2,274,249	116,015
Interleaving Heuristic						
Raxextended(4,3)	1,225,743*	1.00	404	20,774	670,813	14,480
PreferThreads Heuristic						
Accountsubtype(2,2)	2,225,914*	1.00	30,726	193,313	642,193	94
Producerconsumer(1,10,4)	1,783,620*	0.93	2,774	145,466	742,693	36,519
Producerconsumer(1,12,4)	1,781,899*	0.90	13,830	238,092	960,610	52,981
Producerconsumer(1,16,4)	1,781,530*	0.49	7,280	257,131	889,248	67,850
Producerconsumer(1,8,4)	1,835,216*	1.00	1,148	156,428	925,537	38,689
Producerconsumer(2,2,4)	2,591,457*	1.00	10,902	109,394	313,929	13,602
Producerconsumer(2,4,4)	2,016,936*	1.00	2,592	213,491	1,122,008	45,523
Producerconsumer(2,8,4)	1,721,824*	0.68	21,055	434,401	1,098,461	77,976
Reorder(1,1)	144	1.00	40	98	163	6
Reorder(1,5)	545	1.00	36	14,864	64,447	4,312
Reorder(10,1)	1,727,521	0.00	-	-	-	-
Reorder(5,1)	15,207	1.00	393	10,850	30,790	1,473
Reorder(8,1)	274,125	0.80	10,789	714,454	2,624,613	120,013
Reorder(9,1)	691,264	0.32	324,035	861,445	1,412,937	110,618
Twostage(1,1)	218	1.00	53	134	246	9
Twostage(2,5)	24,187	0.96	218	361,571	1,681,177	97,480
Twostage(5,2)	322,593	0.96	5,419	417,841	2,170,752	95,440
Twostage(6,1)	716,413	0.94	31,346	486,830	1,626,718	76,994
Twostage(7,1)	2,354,460*	0.36	81,218	867,382	1,411,624	120,191
Twostage(8,1)	2,119,657*	0.05	178,476	755,151	1,259,085	514,492
Wronglock(1,1)	156	1.00	37	67	122	4
Wronglock(1,10)	7,391	1.00	94	98,616	1,805,704	58,614
Wronglock(1,20)	7,391	0.78	97	562	2328	99
Wronglock(10,1)	2,330,993*	1.00	795	4,848	26,070	834
Wronglock(20,1)	2,056,532*	1.00	3,176	32,484	163,642	6,282

heuristics in Estes from the study in JPF is that the randomized GDS trials and guided search using default search order are allocated 2 GB of RAM. The performance of the FSM distance heuristic function improves with the new randomized GDS algorithm as seen in Table 2. In the `Barbershop(11)` model, the default order guided search does not find an error in over 1.2 million states

Table 2. Comparing the performance of default order guided search (GDS) and randomized guided search (Randomized-GDS) using the Estes model checker

Model	GDS	Randomized-GDS				
		PED	Minimum	Mean	Maximum	95% CI
FSM Heuristic						
Barbershop(5)	132,376	1.00	13,917	59,496	154,473	5,948
Barbershop(9)	492,166	0.59	61,732	785,698	2,003,928	118,996
Barbershop(11)	1, 292, 835*	0.15	381,808	813,644	1,247,461	157,172
e-fca Heuristic						
Barbershop(5)	814	1.00	921	1,012	1,308	13
Barbershop(9)	1,070	1.00	1,543	1,692	1,918	18
Barbershop(11)	1,196	1.00	1,939	2,243	2,671	27
Barbershop(20)	1,767	1.00	5,099	6,319	8,439	131
Barbershop(25)	2,086	1.00	7,654	9,873	12,657	233
EFSM Heuristic						
Barbershop(5)	21,706	1.00	4,950	19,849	67,875	1,853
Barbershop(9)	17,537	0.65	94,357	816,848	1,999,595	129,344
Barbershop(11)	30,256	0.06	293,893	701,278	1,181,985	412,829

while the new randomized GDS algorithm explores only 813, 644 states—on average—in 15 error discovering trials.

It is interesting to note that for some models, the default order guided search outperforms the new randomized GDS algorithm using the EFSM and e-FCA distance heuristics. For example, in the `Barbershop(20)` model, 1767 states are generated with guided search while the minimum number of states generated by the randomized GDS algorithm is 5099. The examples where default order guided search outperforms the new randomized GDS algorithm support the hypothesis presented in [7] that certain reported performance gains of directed model checking techniques can potentially be an artifact of the default order implemented by the model checker rather than the technique itself.

This empirical study shows—on average—that the new randomized GDS algorithm is a better search technique than a default order guided search with no randomization. As a side note, we omit the results on the n-best algorithm in [23] and JPF's random choice generator because they are not competitive with the new randomized GDS algorithm. For the remainder of this paper, we use randomized GDS to refer to our new randomized GDS algorithm. The next section shows in another empirical study that with the correct heuristic, randomized GDS performs well in the models where randomized DFS is unable to find an error. We refer to these models as *hard* [32].

4 Evaluation

Randomized DFS serves as a good standard for comparison when we evaluate the performance gains of randomized GDS [32]. Randomized GDS and randomized

DFS both effectively control for the default search of the model checker implementation which makes them well-suited for comparison. Also, when evaluating the performance of a new heuristic, it is sometimes hard to find another heuristic that is designed to work on the same class of programs or properties. Randomized DFS serves as an ideal comparison technique to evaluate the performance of such heuristics. It also provides a tighter lower bound on performance than say a metric based on stateless random walk, [32], and is a significant bar to overcome when showing performance gains in stateful techniques such as randomized GDS.

We design an empirical study to compare the performance of existing heuristics, using randomized GDS, to randomized DFS implemented by JPF. Like the previous study, we run 100 trials of randomized GDS for each model and an equal number of randomized DFS trials. We bound the execution time at 1 hour for each trial. In our initial experiments, the size of the frontier, states in the priority queue, increases rapidly in randomized GDS trials which causes the searches to run out of memory in JPF before reaching the specified time bound. To overcome this issue, we bound the size of the queue in JPF at 100,000 states. This allows randomized GDS trials to successfully run for an hour in JPF without exhausting the available memory. Bounding the size of the queue turns the complete search into a partial search; however, guided search aims to find a counter-example efficiently rather than to do an exhaustive proof. An earlier study, [16], and our experiments show that bounding the size of the queue does not affect, in general, the number of randomized GDS trials that discover an error. The system configuration used to conduct this empirical study is the same as described in the previous section.

We record and normalize values of five different metrics in the randomized GDS and randomized DFS trials to study the performance gains of randomized GDS over randomized DFS. We measure the path error density, number of states generated, time taken before error discovery, length of the counter-example, and total memory utilized for each of the search trials. Recall that the path error density is the ratio of the error discovering trials over the total number of trials executed. We measure the minimum, mean, and maximum values for all metrics, except path error density, generated during the error discovering trials since the randomization generates different results in each trial. The minimum, mean, and maximum values generated by the search trials are normalized between 0.00 and 1.00 for each metric. Here is an explanation of the normalization process for states generated: the smallest number of states generated among the trials of both search techniques, for a given model, is mapped to the value of 1.00; similarly, the largest number of states generated among the trials is mapped to the value of 0.00. All other values for states generated, in the given model, are normalized between these two values. The values are normalized to the maximum or minimum values since these represent the extremes in the observed performance across several trials. The normalization process is conducted separately for each metric in a model. Intuitively, values close to 1.00 indicate good performance for a given metric while values close to 0.00 indicate the opposite. The normalization technique helps us in better understanding and visualizing

Table 3. Comparing the average values generated in error discovering trials of randomized guided search (RGDS), using the Prefer-Thread heuristic, and randomized DFS (DFS)

	PED		States		Time		Trace		Memory	
	DFS	RGDS	DFS	RGDS	DFS	RGDS	DFS	RGDS	DFS	RGDS
Accountsubtype(1,1)	1.00	1.00	0.98	0.58	0.58	0.68	0.37	0.45	0.62	0.60
Accountsubtype(2,2)	1.00	1.00	1.00	0.59	0.99	0.60	0.42	0.36	0.99	0.37
Wronglock(10,1)	1.00	1.00	1.00	0.79	0.89	0.70	0.34	0.65	0.98	0.78
Wronglock(1,1)	1.00	1.00	0.89	0.52	0.55	0.94	0.70	0.49	0.58	0.56
Wronglock(1,10)	1.00	0.97	0.47	0.98	0.45	0.98	0.57	0.53	0.90	0.93
Twostage(1,1)	1.00	1.00	0.83	0.48	0.66	0.83	0.39	0.54	0.40	0.67
Twostage(2,5)	1.00	0.96	0.52	0.91	0.54	0.94	0.44	0.59	0.39	0.78
Twostage(6,1)	1.00	0.98	0.60	0.87	0.62	0.92	0.31	0.64	0.87	0.63
Reorder(5,1)	1.00	1.00	0.34	0.72	0.34	0.83	0.45	0.75	0.44	0.79
Reorder(8,1)	1.00	0.89	0.36	0.84	0.40	0.92	0.41	0.72	0.89	0.61
ProdCons(1,16,4)	0.67	0.87	1.00	0.88	0.99	0.85	0.55	0.72	1.00	0.67
Twostage(7,1)	0.41	0.73	0.42	0.76	0.42	0.89	0.17	0.58	0.97	0.53
Wronglock(1,20)	0.28	0.81	1.00	0.99	1.00	0.99	0.50	0.62	1.00	0.99
Reorder(9,1)	0.06	0.57	0.31	0.75	0.16	0.87	0.10	0.74	0.99	0.48
Twostage(8,1)	0.04	0.57	0.70	0.70	0.40	0.74	0.01	0.50	0.99	0.43
Reorder(10,1)	0.00	0.34	0.00	0.63	0.00	0.70	0.00	0.51	0.00	0.38

the performance of the heuristic in different models because it puts all metrics on the same scale and graph across both search techniques.

The prefer-thread heuristic, using randomized GDS, performs well in the models shown in Table 3. Please note that this table omits the data for the minimum and maximum values across our several metrics. Table 3 only presents the average values that have been normalized. The values given in Table 3 are as follows: path error density (`PED`), number of states (`States`), time taken (`Time`), length of counter-example (`Trace`), and memory utilized (`Memory`) measured in error discovering trials of randomized GDS and randomized DFS. In a large number of models, the path error density is the same, 1.00, for both randomized DFS and randomized GDS. In models where randomized DFS has a path error density of 1.00, finding an error is not difficult, and the results on these models do not convey much information on the effectiveness of the heuristic.

To overcome some of the weakness in the benchmarks, our study uses hard models generated in [32] to evaluate the true effectiveness of the heuristic, which are the last six entries in Table 3. For example, in the `Wronglock(1,20)` model, the measured path error density of randomized DFS is 0.28 while the path error density of the randomized GDS is dramatically higher at 0.81. The average values for states, time, and memory are close to 1.00 for both search techniques in the `Wronglock(1,20)` model; however, the average length of the counter-example for randomized GDS is smaller than the average length of the counter-example recorded from the randomized DFS trials. In understanding the length of a counter-example, values closer to 1.00 depict a shorter counter-example while values close to 0.00 indicate a longer counter-example. There are other models like `Reorder(9,1)`, `Twostage(8,1)`, and `Reorder(10,1)` where randomized GDS improves over randomized DFS.

The high path error density of randomized GDS in models where randomized DFS struggles to find an error makes a compelling argument for the use of the heuristic in the given models. The results in Table 3 show that randomized GDS, using the prefer-thread heuristic, successfully overcomes the lower bound on the performance set by randomized DFS in the given models.

In Fig. 3 we visualize the comparative performance of randomized DFS and randomized GDS using the prefer-thread heuristic for the models shown in Table 3. The minimum, mean, and maximum values for all the different metrics and models are aggregated in Fig. 3(a). The different edges along the graph show which search technique generates the best and worst boundary values. The points in the graph along the axis where $x = 0$ show all the worst values that are contributed by randomized DFS for the measured metrics while the points along the axis where $y = 0$ show all the worst values generated by randomized GDS. Similarly, points along $x = 1$ represent the best values contributed by randomized DFS while points along $y = 1$ represent the best values contributed by randomized GDS. The points above the dashed diagonal line in Fig. 3(a) show the values of the metrics where randomized GDS improves over randomized DFS. In general, there is a high density of points above the diagonal that show for the given set of models, it is more effective to use randomized GDS, with the prefer-thread heuristic, over randomized DFS. There is also a high density of points in the upper right corner of the graph. These points represent the values where both randomized GDS and randomized DFS perform well and do not help us in evaluating the true effectiveness of the search and heuristic over randomized DFS. We now look at each of the metrics separately to understand the areas in which randomized GDS scores over randomized DFS.

There are three metrics where randomized GDS clearly outperforms randomized DFS in the benchmark suite using the prefer-thread heuristic. These three metrics are the path error density, length of the counter-example, and time taken before error discovery as shown in Fig. 3(b), (c), and (d) respectively. The points in the upper right corner of the graph in Fig. 3(b) show that in all trials, both search techniques are equally successful in finding the error; however, points that are above the dashed diagonal line show that a larger number of randomized GDS trials find an error in models where only a small number of randomized DFS trials find an error. The high path error density of randomized GDS is a very compelling measure that depicts the improvement of randomized GDS over randomized DFS. Randomized GDS also performs extremely well in generating shorter counter-examples. The high density of points above the diagonal in Fig. 3(c) indicates that randomized GDS has dramatically shorter counter-examples compared to randomized DFS across all the models in test. Similarly, the distribution of points in Fig. 3(d) indicates that randomized GDS takes less time to find an error when compared to randomized DFS.

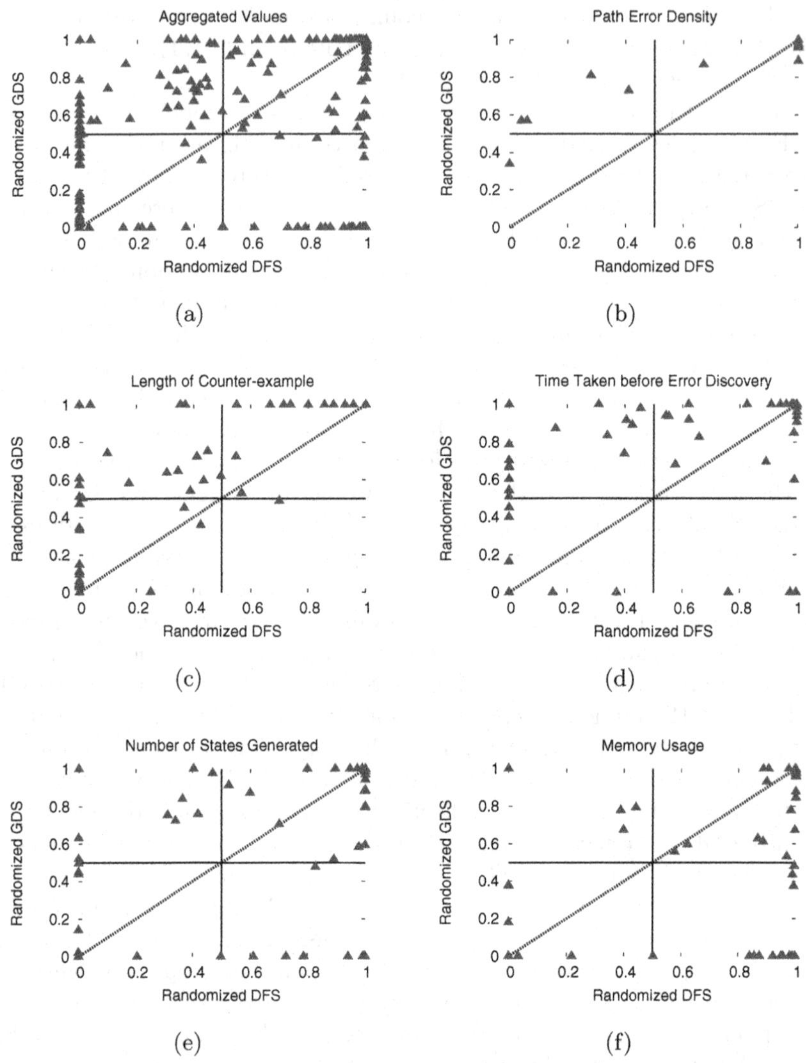

Fig. 3. Visualizing the normalized minimum, mean, and maximum values of different metrics comparing randomized GDS, using the Prefer-Threads heuristic, to randomized DFS. (a) An aggregation of all values for the different metrics. (b) Values comparing path error density. (c) Values comparing length of counter-example. (d) Values comparing time taken before error discovery. (e) Values comparing number of states generated. (f) Values comparing memory usage.

In Fig. 3(e), it is hard to discern which search technique performs better in generating fewer number of states before error discovery; however, the randomized DFS clearly outperforms randomized GDS in the amount of memory utilized as shown in Fig. 3(f). Randomized GDS maintains the frontier of states

Table 4. Comparison of results using the Most-Blocked Heuristic with a randomized guided search (RGDS) to results from randomized DFS (DFS)

	PED		States		Time		Trace		Memory	
	DFS	RGDS	DFS	RGDS	DFS	RGDS	DFS	RGDS	DFS	RGDS
Clean(1,1,12)	1.00	1.00	0.09	0.59	0.52	0.87	0.34	0.25	0.42	0.65
Piper(2,4,4)	1.00	1.00	0.96	0.65	0.96	0.63	0.60	0.85	0.94	0.25
Piper(2,8,4)	0.96	0.00	0.92	0.00	0.92	0.00	0.52	0.00	0.47	0.00
Clean(10,10,1)	0.96	0.00	0.95	0.00	0.96	0.00	0.37	0.00	0.85	0.00
Piper(2,16,8)	0.00	0.00	0.00	0.00	0.00	0.00	0.00	0.00	0.00	0.00

Table 5. Comparison of results using the Interleaving Heuristic with a randomized guided search (RGDS) to results from randomized DFS (DFS)

	PED		States		Time		Trace		Memory	
	DFS	RGDS	DFS	RGDS	DFS	RGDS	DFS	RGDS	DFS	RGDS
Airline(6,1)	1.00	1.00	0.75	0.99	0.74	0.99	0.22	0.62	0.53	0.90
Airline(6,2)	1.00	1.00	0.96	1.00	0.95	1.00	0.25	0.60	0.89	0.97
Raxextended(4,3)	1.00	1.00	0.96	0.99	0.96	1.00	0.67	0.99	0.87	0.96
Airline(20,4)	0.03	0.00	0.55	0.00	0.59	0.00	0.47	0.00	0.39	0.00
Airline(20,3)	0.01	0.00	1.00	0.00	1.00	0.00	1.00	0.00	1.00	0.00
Airline(20,2)	0.01	0.00	1.00	0.00	1.00	0.00	1.00	0.00	1.00	0.00

that need to be explored. The increasing frontier size, however, has a dramatic impact on the memory usage. The unbounded priority queue in JPF causes a serious explosion in memory usage while executing the randomized GDS. In fact, as mentioned earlier, we restrict the size of the priority queue to only 100,000 states so that 7 GB of RAM is not exhausted before reaching the specified time bound. Overall, across the different metrics, randomized GDS using the prefer-thread heuristic improves performance over randomized DFS by effectively finding counter-examples and generating shorter counter-examples.

We present results for the most-blocked, interleaving, and choose-free heuristics in Table 4, Table 5, and Table 6 respectively. These heuristics do not perform well on the class of models for which they are designed, and the comparison with randomized DFS makes these heuristics even less appealing in our benchmarks. For example, the randomized DFS path error density for `Piper(2,8,4)` model is 0.96 while the path error density of randomized GDS using the most-blocked heuristic as seen in Table 4 is 0.00. Similar behavior is seen for the model `Clean(10,10,1)`. The choose-free, most-blocked, and interleaving heuristics do not overcome the randomized DFS lower bound and are not effective in generating counter-examples for models in the tables. The sub-par performance of these heuristics argues a greater need to identify models where they are effective.

The results in this section indicate that given the correct heuristic for a set of models, randomized GDS is effective in finding errors where randomized DFS

Table 6. Comparison of results using the Choose-Free Heuristic with a randomized guided search (GDS) to results from randomized DFS (DFS)

	PED		States		Time		Trace		Memory	
	DFS	RGDS	DFS	RGDS	DFS	RGDS	DFS	RGDS	DFS	RGDS
Deos(true)	1.00	1.00	0.72	0.97	0.56	0.96	0.36	0.95	0.60	0.92
Replicated(5,2)	0.97	0.00	0.81	0.00	0.87	0.00	0.57	0.00	0.88	0.00
RWNoExpChk	0.77	1.00	0.97	0.72	0.72	0.55	0.75	0.99	0.94	0.69

struggles. It is also important to note that better error discovery, shorter counter-examples, and reduced error discovery time in randomized GDS comes at the cost of increased memory usage due to the large search frontier.

5 Conclusions and Future Work

This paper presents a new randomized GDS algorithm that completely shuffles states in the priority queue with equal heuristic rankings. The algorithm is easily implemented, efficient, and has low overhead in terms of memory and time. We show that full randomization of the guided search improves the effectiveness of the search over the regular guided search. To evaluate the performance of randomized GDS using a particular heuristic, we compare it with randomized DFS because randomized DFS creates a lower bound for establishing performance gains in directed model checking. Also, when the heuristic is correctly matched to the models and properties, the new randomized GDS algorithm outperforms randomized DFS in both the effectiveness of the search in finding counter-examples and the length of the counter-examples. The approach is timely given the recent explosion in computation resources and is easily distributed to several computation nodes to improve the likelihood of error discovery.

There is a need to explore other avenues for combining randomization and directed model checking. For example, can we use randomization to balance exploring new parts of the behavior space and use heuristics to exploit the information available about the model? Also, as we develop heuristics appropriate for use in a randomized GDS algorithm, there is a need to understand the intended problem domain for the heuristic. In other words, we need to characterize heuristics in terms of the models for which they are expected to be effective. Without this characterization, it is not obvious which heuristic best fits a given property and model. There also a need to define language and metrics to characterize heuristics for their intended problem domains. An interesting avenue of research is to use something similar to the *"Patterns"* categorization for specifications [5].

Acknowledgments

We thank Matt Dwyer and Suzette Person at the University of Nebraska for sharing with us the models presented in [7] and the discussions of their work on the quality of models. We also thank Shmuel Ur for providing us access to the models developed at the IBM Research Center in Haifa. We finally thank Ira and Mary Lou Fulton for their generous donations to the BYU Supercomputing laboratory which made it possible for us to run the extensive analysis presented in this paper.

References

1. Barnat, J., Brim, L., St, J.: Distributed LTL model checking in SPIN. In: Dwyer, M.B. (ed.) Model Checking Software. LNCS, vol. 2057, pp. 200–216. Springer, Heidelberg (2001)
2. Barnat, J., Brim, L., Černá, I., Moravec, P., Ročkai, P., Šimeček, P.: DiVinE – A Tool for Distributed Verification (Tool Paper). In: Ball, T., Jones, R.B. (eds.) CAV 2006. LNCS, vol. 4144, pp. 278–281. Springer, Heidelberg (2006)
3. Brim, L., Cerna, I., Moravec, P., Simsa, J.: How to order vertices for distributed LTL model-checking based on accepting predcessors. Electronic Notes in Theoretical Computer Science 135(2), 3–18 (2006)
4. Clarke, E.M., Emerson, E.A., Sistla, A.P.: Automatic verification of finite-state concurrent systems using temporal logic specifications. ACM TOPLAS 8(2) (1986)
5. Dwyer, M.B., Avrunin, G.S., Corbett, J.C.: Property specification patterns for finite-state verification. In: Ardis, M. (ed.) FMSP-98. Proceedings of the 2nd Workshop on Formal Methods in Software Practice (FMSP-98), pp. 7–15. ACM Press, New York (1998)
6. Dwyer, M.B., Elbaum, S., Person, S., Purandare, R.: Parallel randomized state-space search. In: Proceedings of the 29th International conference of Software Engineering 2007 (To Appear)
7. Dwyer, M.B., Person, S., Elbaum, S.: Controlling factors in evaluating path-sensitive error detection techniques. In: SIGSOFT '06/FSE-14. Proceedings of the 14th ACM SIGSOFT international symposium on Foundations of software engineering, pp. 92–104. ACM Press, New York (2006)
8. Edelkamp, S., Jabar, S.: Large-scale directed model checking LTL. In: Valmari, A. (ed.) Model Checking Software. LNCS, vol. 3925, pp. 1–18. Springer, Heidelberg (2006)
9. Edelkamp, S., Lafuente, A.L., Leue, S.: Directed explicit model checking with HSF-SPIN. In: Proceedings of the 7th International SPIN Workshop. LNCS, vol. 2057, Springer, Heidelberg (2001)
10. Edelkamp, S., Lafuente, A.L., Leue, S.: Trail-directed model checking. In: Stoller, S.D., Visser, W. (eds.) Electronic Notes in Theoretical Computer Science, vol. 55, Elsevier Science Publishers, Amsterdam (2001)
11. Edelkamp, S., Mehler, T.: Byte code distance heuristics and trail direction for model checking Java programs. In: Workshop on Model Checking and Artificial Intelligence (MoChArt), pp. 69–76 (2003)
12. Eytani, Y., Havelund, K., Stoller, S.D., Ur, S.: Towards a framework and a benchmark for testing tools for multi-threaded programs: Research articles. Concurrency and Computation: Practice & Experience 19(3), 267–279 (2007)
13. Eytani, Y., Ur, S.: Compiling a benchmark of documented multi-threaded bugs. In: Proceedings of the Workshop on Parallel and Distributed Systems: Testing and Debugging, p. 266. IEEE Computer Society Press, Los Alamitos (2004)

14. Farchi, E., Nir, Y., Ur, S.: Concurrent bug patterns and how to test them. In: IPDPS '03. Proceedings of the 17th International Symposium on Parallel and Distributed Processing, p. 286. IEEE Computer Society Press, Los Alamitos (2003)
15. Foster, I.: Designing and Building Parallel Programs: Concepts and Tools for Parallel Software Engineering. Wesley Longman Publishing, Boston, MA, USA (1995)
16. Groce, A., Visser, W.: Model checking Java programs using structural heuristics. International Symposium on Software Testing and Analysis , 12–21 (July 2002)
17. Haslum, P.: Model checking by random walk. In: Proceedings of ECSEL Workshop (1999)
18. Holzmann, G.J.: The model checker SPIN. IEEE Transactions on Software Engineering 23(5), 279–295 (1997)
19. Holzmann, G.J.: The design of a distributed model checking algorithm SPIN. FMCAD 2006 Invited Presentation (November 2006)
20. Inggs, C.P., Barringer, H.: CTL* model checking on a shared-memory architecture. Formal Methods in System Design 29(2), 135–155 (2006)
21. Jabbar, S., Edelkamp, S.: Parallel external directed model checker with linear I/O. In: Emerson, E.A., Namjoshi, K.S. (eds.) VMCAI 2006. LNCS, vol. 3855, pp. 237–251. Springer, Heidelberg (2005)
22. Jones, M., Mercer, E., Bao, T., Kumar, R., Lamborn, P.: Benchmarking explicit state parallel model checkers. In: 2nd International Workshop on Parallel and Distributed Methods in Verification (2003)
23. Jones, M.D., Mercer, E.: Explicit state model checking with Hopper. In: Graf, S., Mounier, L. (eds.) Model Checking Software. LNCS, vol. 2989, pp. 146–150. Springer, Heidelberg (2004)
24. Jones, M.D., Sorber, J.: Parallel search for LTL violations. Software Tools for Technology Transfer 7(1), 31–42 (2005)
25. Krazit, T.: Intel pedges 80 cores in five years. CNET News.com (September 2006)
26. Mercer, E.G., Jones, M.: Model checking machine code with the GNU debugger. In: Godefroid, P. (ed.) Model Checking Software. LNCS, vol. 3639, pp. 251–265. Springer, Heidelberg (2005)
27. Pasareanu, C., Dwyer, M., Visser, W.: Finding feasible abstract counter-examples. Springer International Journal on Software Tools for Technology Transfer (STTT) 5(1), 34–48 (2003)
28. Pelanek, R., Hanzl, T., Cerna, I., Brim, L.: Enhancing random walk state space exploration. In: FMICS '05. Proceedings of the 10th International Workshop on Formal methods for industrial critical systems, pp. 98–105. ACM Press, New York (2005)
29. Reif, J.H.: Depth-first search is inherently sequential. Information Processing Letters 20(5), 229–234 (1985)
30. Rungta, N., Mercer, E.G.: A context-sensitive structural heuristic for guided search model checking. In: 20th IEEE/ACM International Conference on Automated Software Engineering, pp. 410–413, Long Beach, California, USA (November 2005)
31. Rungta, N., Mercer, E.G.: An improved distance heuristic function for directed software model checking. In: Formal Methods in Computer Aided Design (FMCAD), pp. 60–67, San Jose, CA, USA (November 2006)
32. Rungta, N., Mercer, E.G.: Hardness for explicit state software model checking benchmarks. In: Technical Report SMC-BYU-0107, Brigham Young University, Department of Computer Science (2007)
33. Seppi, K., Jones, M., Lamborn, P.: Guided model checking with a bayesian meta-heuristic. Fundamenta Informaticae 70(1-2), 111–126 (2006)

34. Sivaraj, H., Gopalakrishnan, G.: Random walk based heuristic algorithms for distributed memory model checking. In: Proceedings of Workshop on Parallel and Distributed Model Checking (2003)
35. Stern, U., Dill, D.L.: Parallelizing the Murϕ verifier. In: Grumberg, O. (ed.) CAV 1997. LNCS, vol. 1254, pp. 256–267. Springer, Heidelberg (1997)
36. Visser, W., Havelund, K., Brat, G., Park, S.: Java PathFinder: Second generation of a Java model checker. In: Gopalakrishnan, G. (ed.) Proceedings of the Workshop on Advances in Verification (WAVE'00) (July 2000)
37. Yang, C.H., Dill, D.L.: Validation with guided search of the state space. In: 35th Design Automation Conference (DAC98), pp. 599–604 (1998)

Distributed Dynamic Partial Order Reduction Based Verification of Threaded Software*

Yu Yang, Xiaofang Chen, Ganesh Gopalakrishnan, and Robert M. Kirby

School of Computing, University of Utah
Salt Lake City, UT 84112, U.S.A.
{yuyang, xiachen, ganesh, kirby}@cs.utah.edu

Abstract. Runtime (dynamic) model checking is a promising verification methodology for real-world threaded software because of its many features, the prominent ones being: (i) it avoids the need to extract a model and instead runs the actual code, and (ii) the precision of information available at run-time allows techniques such as dynamic partial order reduction (DPOR) [1] to dramatically cut down the number of interleavings examined. Unfortunately, DPOR does not have many implementations for real thread libraries such as POSIX Pthreads, and suffers from high computational overheads due to a stateless search that requires re-executions. In our previous work [2], we designed a runtime model checker, `inspect`, that overcomes the first of these drawbacks. `Inspect` has been shown capable of detecting data races, deadlocks and other incorrect API usages in real-world PThreads C programs. In this paper, we describe a distributed version of `inspect`, which implements an extended DPOR algorithm. Our two key contributions are: (i) a practical algorithm for distributed dynamic partial order reduction; (ii) the innovations that helped distributed `inspect` attain nearly linear (with respect to the number of CPUs) speedup on realistic examples.

1 Introduction

Runtime (dynamic) model checking (e.g., as in [3]) is a promising verification methodology for real-world threaded software because of its many features. It avoids the (implicit or explicit) overhead of modeling programs that is usually required by other model checkers [4,5,6,7]. The precision of information available at run-time allows techniques such as dynamic partial order reduction (DPOR) [1] to dramatically cut down the number of interleavings examined. In our previous work [2], we designed a runtime model checker, `inspect`, that (to the best of our knowledge) is the first implementation of DPOR that handles the widely used POSIX Pthreads library. `Inspect` explores *relevant* interleavings (generated by DPOR) of a multithreaded C program with a specific testing scenario. In this setting, `Inspect` has detected data races, deadlocks, and other incorrect API

* Supported in part by NSF award CNS00509379, Microsoft HPC Institute Program, and SRC Contract 2005-TJ-1318.

D. Bošnački and S. Edelkamp (Eds.): SPIN 2007, LNCS 4595, pp. 58–75, 2007.

usages in real-world PThreads C programs. However, we observed that run-time is a major limiting factor of `inspect`. `Inspect` explores the state space by executing the program concretely and observing its visible operations. As it is not easy to capture and restore the state of a C program which runs concretely, `inspect` does not keep the search history, instead employing stateless search [3]) that can incur high overheads.[1]

A runtime model checker such as `inspect` is potentially "embarrassingly parallel" based on the casual observation that since stateless search does not maintain the search history, different branches of an acyclic state space can be explored concurrently, and with very loose synchronizations. We implemented a parallel version of `inspect` based on this observation, employing a centralized load balancer to distribute work among multiple nodes. Unfortunately, we failed to consistently obtain the linear speedup promised by the apparent parallelism. Deeper investigation revealed the reasons. These reasons, and other features of our algorithm are now summarized:

Avoiding Redundant Computations: Despite our use of *sleep sets* [8] to avoid redundant interleavings among independent transitions, we found that redundant (and, in fact, identical) interleavings were being explored among multiple nodes. The problem was traced to the incremental way of computing backtrack sets in the standard DPOR algorithm (detailed in the rest of this paper), which is well suited for a sequential implementation but not a loosely synchronized distributed implementation. We have developed a heuristic technique to update backtrack sets more aggressively, as detailed in Section 3.4.

Work Distribution Heuristics: Numerous heuristics help achieve efficient work distribution in `inspect`. These include: (i) the straightforward method of employing a single load balancing node (process) and $N-1$ worker nodes (processes); (ii) the concept of a soft limit on the number of backtrack points recorded within a worker node before that node decides to offload work to another worker; and (iii) minimizing communication by offloading work that lies deepest within the stack – points from where the largest number of program-paths are available – so that bigger chunks of work are shipped per communication.

This paper describes these extensions to the DPOR algorithm proposed in [1] and detailed in [2]. Our experiments demonstrate almost linear speedup with increasing number of nodes (CPUs). For example, one of our benchmarks which has eight threads and requires more than 11 hours to finish checking using sequential `inspect` can be checked by the parallel `inspect` within 11 minutes using 65 nodes. The parallel `inspect` gives a speedup of 63.2 out of 65.

[1] Given programs that do not terminate, a stateless search method (such as used in `inspect`) requires depth-bounding or some other technique to ensure termination. This was not an issue in our practical test programs. In this paper, we focus only on checking multithreaded programs that terminate.

Roadmap: Section 2 presents background information on `inspect` and DPOR. Section 3 presents the extended DPOR algorithm used in parallel `inspect`. Section 4 presents implementation detail, and the experiment results, Section 5 the related work, and Section 6 our concluding remarks.

2 Background

2.1 Overview of Inspect

Modeling the library functions employed in, and the runtime environment of multithreaded C programs is non-trivial. To the best of our knowledge, Verisoft [3] is the only model checker capable of checking concurrent C programs without incurring modeling overheads. Unfortunately, Verisoft focuses on concurrent programs that interact through inter-process communication mechanisms. In a multithreaded program, threads can interact not only through explicit synchronization/mutual exclusion primitives, but also through read/write operations on shared data objects. Our runtime model checker `inspect` can handle these details, and can systematically explore all possible interleavings of a multithreaded C program under a specific testing scenario, employing DPOR.

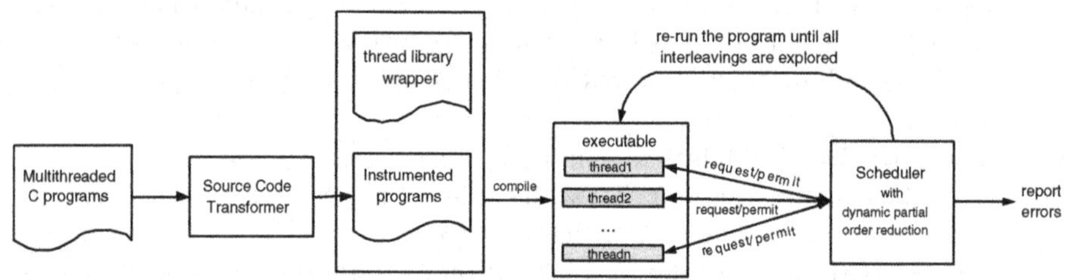

Fig. 1. Inspect's workflow

Figure 1 shows the workflow of `inspect`. The source code transformer instruments the program at the source code level to arrange communications with a scheduler at global interaction points. Here, a thread library wrapper helps intercept thread library calls. Finally, a centralized scheduler embodies the DPOR algorithm, and controls the interleaved executions of the threads according to it. In `inspect`, instrumentation can be done automatically for C programs. The instrumented program is compiled, and the executable is run repeatedly under the control of the scheduler until all relevant interleavings among the threads required by DPOR are explored.

Before performing any operation that might have a side effect on other threads, the instrumented program sends a request to the scheduler. The scheduler can either allow the requesting process to proceed, or block it for any finite duration by postponing a reply.

2.2 Definitions

A multithreaded program can be modeled as a concurrent system, which consists of a finite set of *threads*, and a set of *shared objects*. Threads communicate with each other only through shared objects. Operations on shared objects are called *visible operations*, while the rest are *invisible operations*. We assume threads can only be blocked by visible operations. A *state* of a multithreaded program consists of the global state of all shared objects and the local state of each thread. A *transition* moves the program from one state to the next state by performing one visible operation of a certain thread, followed by a finite sequence of invisible operations, ending just before the next visible operation of that thread.

Given a state s and a transition t, we use the following notations:

- $t.tid$ denotes the identity of the thread that executes t.
- $next(s,t)$ refers to the state which is reached from s by executing t.
- $s.enabled$ denotes the set of transitions that are enabled from s. A thread p is enabled in a state s if there exists some transition t such that $t \in s.enabled$ and $t.tid = p$.
- $s.backtrack$ refers to the backtrack set at state s (Figure 2). $s.backtrack$ is a set of thread identities. Here, $\{t \mid t.tid \in s.backtrack\}$ is the set of transitions which are enabled but have not been executed from s.
- $s.done$ denotes the set of threads examined at s. Similar to $s.backtrack$, $s.done$ is also a set of thread identities. Here, $\{t \mid t.tid \in s.done\}$ is the set of transitions that have been executed from s.

2.3 Dynamic Partial Order Reduction

Partial order reduction (POR) techniques [9] are those that avoid interleaving independent transitions during search.

Given the set of enabled transitions from a state s, partial order reduction algorithms attempt to explore only a (proper) subset of $s.enabled$, and at the same time guarantee that the properties of interest will be preserved. Such a subset is called *persistent set*.

Static POR algorithms compute the persistent set of a state s immediately after reaching it. As for multithreaded programs, persistent sets computed statically will be excessively large because of the limitations of static analysis. For instance, if two transitions leading out of s access an array `a[]` by indexing it at locations captured by expressions `e1` and `e2` (i.e., `a[e1]` and `a[e2]`), a static analyzer may not be able to decide whether `e1=e2` (and hence whether the transitions are dependent or not). Flanagan and Godefroid introduced dynamic partial-order reduction (DPOR) [1] to dynamically compute smaller persistent sets, capitalizing on runtime information.

In DPOR, given a state s, the persistent set of s is not computed immediately after reaching s. Instead, DPOR populates the persistent set of s while searching under s according to depth-first search (DFS). Figure 2 recapitulates the DPOR algorithm. In procedure *update_backtrack_info*, we see how the backtrack state

```
1:  StateStack S;
2:  TransitionSequence T;

3:  DPOR( ) {
4:      State s = S.top;
5:      update_backtrack_info(s);
6:      if (∃ thread p, ∃t ∈ s.enabled, t.tid = p) {
7:          s.backtrack = {p};
8:          s.done = ∅;
9:          while (∃q ∈ s.backtrack \ s.done) {
10:             s.done = s.done ∪ {q};
11:             s.backtrack = s.backtrack \ {q};
12:             let t_n ∈ s.enabled, t_n.tid = q;
13:             T.append(t_n);
14:             S.push(next(s, t_n));
15:             DPOR();
16:             T.pop_back();
17:             S.pop();
18:         }
19:     }
20: }

21: update_backtrack_info(State s) {
22:     for each thread p {
23:         let t_n ∈ s.enabled, t_n.tid = p;
24:         let t_d be the latest transition in T that is dependent and may be co-enabled
              with t_n;
25:         if (t_d ≠ null) {
26:             let s_d be the state in S from which t_d is executed;
27:             let E be {q ∈ s_d.enabled | q.tid = p, or q in T, q happened after t_d
                  and is dependent with some transition in T which was executed by
                  p and happened after q }
28:             if (E ≠ ∅)
29:                 choose any q in E, add q.tid to s_d.backtrack;
30:             else
31:                 s_d.backtrack = s_d.backtrack ∪ {q.tid | q ∈ s_d.enabled};
32:         }
33:     }
34: }
```

Fig. 2. Dynamic partial-order reduction

of a state called s_d*.backtrack* is updated while exploring a state s reached from s_d*.backtrack* under DFS. Observe from line 29 that we add to s_d*.backtrack* a thread id *q.tid*, where s_d is the most recent state, searching back from s, where a transition that depends on transition t_n occurs. When the DFS unwinds to state s_d*.backtrack*, the backtrack set is consulted and the threads recorded in there are scheduled, provided 'done' is not true (line 9). Last but not least, in `inspect`, we employ *sleep sets* [8] to avoid interleaving independent actions.

3 Algorithm

In the DPOR algorithm, the thread ids recorded in the backtrack set of a state s (i.e., *s.backtrack*) help generate different (non-equivalent) executions out of s. These executions can be independently explored. It is this insight that distributed `inspect` capitalizes. In fact, as DPOR is often best implemented through stateless search, it is completely safe to explore the different transitions in the backtrack sets of states concurrently, and with no (or very little) synchronization. With the wide availability of cluster machines, the potential for distributed verification is very high.

To have multiple nodes explore multiple backtrack points concurrently, each cluster node must know: (i) the transition to be executed from a backtrack point; (ii) the portion of the search stack from the initial state to the backtrack point; (iii) the transition sequence from the initial state to reach the backtrack point. All this information is easily obtained from the search stack. A centralized load balancer can help balance the work among multiple nodes, employing very limited synchronizations.

In this section, we first present an overview of the load balancing algorithm (Section 3.1) and the computation of each worker (Section 3.2). Our extended DPOR algorithm is presented over Sections 3.3 and 3.4.

3.1 Load Balancing

In parallel `inspect`, we assign one node of an N-node cluster as the centralized load balancer (Figure 3), and the rest of $N-1$ nodes as workers (a simple initial approach to ease programming). The load balancer monitors the status of all workers for the purpose of partitioning the workload. Two classes of workers are maintained: *busy_workers* – the set of workers busy exploring some parts of the state space, and *idle_workers* – the set of workers which are available for new work (initially all workers).

The load balancer chooses an idle worker, starts checking the program under test on the selected node, and adds this node to the *busy_workers* set (Line 6-9). Then it keeps waiting for messages from busy workers until the *busy_workers* set is empty (Line 10-26). At this stage, all workers have finished exploring their part of state space, which means the whole state space has been explored. In the last step (Line 27-28), the load balancer will send a termination message to every worker to terminate them and exit.

The messages that the load balancer can receive from the workers fall into two categories:

- a request from a busy worker to unload some work to idle workers.
- a report message from a busy worker after it finishes exploring the assigned state space.

While exploring the assigned state space, if a worker ends up having more than a certain number of backtrack points in its stack, it implies that too much work might have been assigned to this worker. In this situation, this worker will send a work unloading request to the load balancer. If there are idle workers available, the load balancer passes along the idle worker's information (line 21-24). Otherwise, it tells the requester that there are no idle worker available (Line 17-20).

```
1: Program P;
2: WorkerSet busy_workers, idle_workers;

3: load_balance( ) {
4:     idle_workers = { all workers in the cluster };
5:     busy_workers = ∅;
6:     let n_a be a worker, n_a ∈ idle_workers;
7:     idle_workers = idle_workers \ {n_a};
8:     start checking P on n_a;
9:     busy_workers = {n_a};
10:    while (busy_workers ≠ ∅) {
11:        receive event e from any worker w;
12:        if(e is work finish notification)
13:            busy_workers = busy_workers \ {w};
14:            idle_workers = idle_workers ∪ {w};
15:        }
16:        else if(e is new work request){
17:            if(idle_workers = ∅){
18:                reply "no idle workers" to w;
19:                continue;
20:            }
21:            let n_b be a worker in idle_workers;
22:            idle_workers = idle_workers \ {n_b};
23:            busy_workers = busy_workers ∪ {n_b};
24:            send n_b's information to w;
25:        }
26:    }
27:    for each worker ∈ idle_workers
28:        send a termination message to worker;
29: }
```

Fig. 3. The load balancing algorithm

3.2 Worker Routine

Each worker (Figure 4) keeps passively waiting for work unloading messages, and has DPOR-enabled depth first search for each assigned state space (Line 7-9). Here a modified DPOR routine (detailed in Section 3.3) is used. The worker exits the while loop and terminates when a termination message is received (Line 4-5). The task description message that a worker receives (Line 6) for starting a new backtrack point includes:

```
worker_node( ) {
    while (true) {
        wait for an incoming message, let it be msg;
        if(msg is terminating)
            return;
        receive task description;
        DPOR();
        send report to the load balancer;
    }
}
```

Fig. 4. The routine that runs on each worker

- the portion of the search stack from the bottom until the backtrack point.
- the transition sequence to reach the backtrack point from the initial state.
- the transition to be executed from the backtrack point

The transition sequence is used to help the worker which is assigned the task to replay the program until the backtrack point. The state stack is necessary to help the node to avoid exploring the backtrack points that other nodes have explored.

Figure 5 illustrates how the workers and the load balancer collaborate. Let a be a busy worker and b an idle one, with a trying to unload some work to b. First a sends a request to the load balancer. If there are idle nodes, the load balancer will return an idle node's id to the worker. In our example, the load balancer tells a that b is idle, whereupon node a will send an unload message to b with all the information needed for b to start searching from an unexplored backtrack point. When b finishes the assigned work, it sends a report to the load balancer.

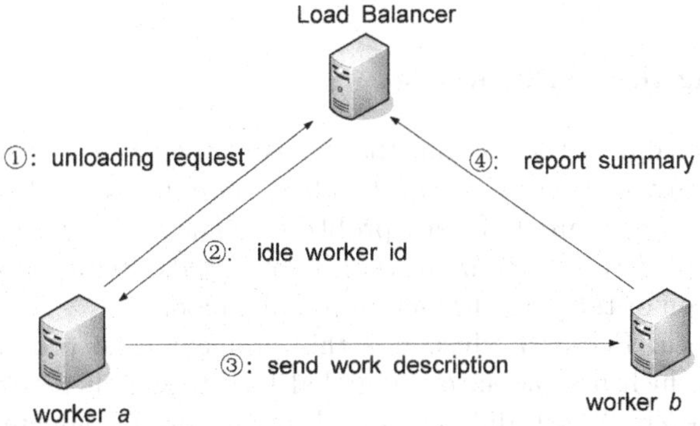

Fig. 5. The message flow between the load balancer and the workers

3.3 Distributed DPOR

Figure 6 shows our distributed DPOR algorithm. Comparing with the original DPOR algorithm in Figure 2, we made the following changes:

- add communication and work unloading primitives (Line 7-8 in Figure 6).
- to avoid the redundant exploration of the state space among multiple nodes, we compute the backtrack points in a different way from the original DPOR algorithm. We will present this in Section 3.4.

In this distributed DPOR, each time after updating the backtrack points, we will check whether the number of backtrack points in the search stack has exceeded a value n (Line 7). Here n is the number of backtrack points in the search stack. If so, the current node decides to unload some of this excess work to the other nodes, as captured in procedure `unload_work`.

To derive the most benefit per exchanged work unloading message, we observe that backtrack points situated deeper in the stack typically have larger numbers of program-paths emanating from them. Based on this heuristic, we choose the deepest state s in the search stack that satisfies $s.backtrack \neq \varnothing$ (Line 29). After unloading a backtrack point from s, on the current node, we will put the thread id of the transition in *s.done* to avoid it being explored by the current node (Line 37-38).

The *unload_work* routine first checks with the load balancer to see if there are any idle nodes. If not, the routine will return immediately (Line 27-28). Otherwise, it finds and sends information pertaining to the deepest backtrack point, along with the transition sequence from the initial state to that backtrack point, to the idle node. The algorithm in Figure 6 does the unload work request each time it enters the DPOR routine. This may lead to repeated failures if there are no idle nodes available for a while (not observed in our experiments). Various heuristic solutions are possible in case it arises in practice (e.g., send aggregated requests more infrequently).

3.4 Updating the Backtrack Set

In dynamic partial order reduction, the persistent set of a given state is computed dynamically. Procedure *update_backtrack_info* in Figure 2 shows how the backtrack points are computed. One problem we encountered with the original DPOR algorithm is that with more than two threads, it may result in redundancy exploration of the same branch in parallel mode.

The example in Figure 7 illustrates this problem. The program has three threads, all of which first acquire the global lock t, and then release the lock. Obviously, there are $3! = 6$ different interleavings for this concurrent program with DPOR.

Assume we use a cluster that has only two worker nodes. We also assume that the bound n in Figure 6 for unloading is 1. Let the two workers be n_0 and n_1, and let the three threads be t_0, t_1 and t_2. Figure 8 shows how the work would be

```
StateStack S;
TransitionSequence T;
Transition t;

DPOR( ) {
   State s = S.top;
   update_backtrack_info(s);                                  ◁ modified, details in Section 3.4
   if (there are more than n backtrack points in the S)                               ◁ added
     unload_work();                                                                   ◁ added
   if (∃ thread p, ∃t ∈ s.enabled, t.tid = p) {
       s.backtrack = {p};
       s.done = ∅;
       while (∃q ∈ s.backtrack \ s.done) {
           s.done = s.done ∪ {q};
           s.backtrack = s.backtrack \ {q};
           let t_n ∈ s.enabled, t_n.tid = q;
           T.append(t_n);
           S.push(next(s, t_n));
           DPOR();
           T.pop_back();
           S.pop();
       }
   }
}

unload_work( ) {
   send a work unload request to the load balancer;
   receive reply rep from the load balancer;
   if(rep says no idle node available)
     return;
   let s be the deepest state in stack S that s.backtrack ≠ ∅;
   let T_s be the transition sequence to reach s from the initial state;
   let S_s be a copy of the sequence of states from the bottom of S to s;
   choose t ∈ s.backtrack;
   let s' be the last state in S_s (i.e. s' is a copy of s);
   s'.backtrack = {t};
   s'.done = s'.done ∪ (s.backtrack \ {t});
   send (S_s, T_s, t) to the idle node;
   s.backtrack = s.backtrack \ {t};
   s.done = s.done ∪ {t};
}
```

Fig. 6. DPOR for parallelization

distributed between the two nodes if we follow the *update_backtrack_info* routine shown in Figure 2.

Let n_0 start concretely executing the program first, and n_1 is idle. When n_0 reaches the end of its trace, we can observe the interleaving of three threads as in

```
global: mutex  t;

thread t0:          thread t1:          thread t2:

lock(t);            lock(t);            lock(t);
unlock(t);          unlock(t);          unlock(t);
```

Fig. 7. A simple example

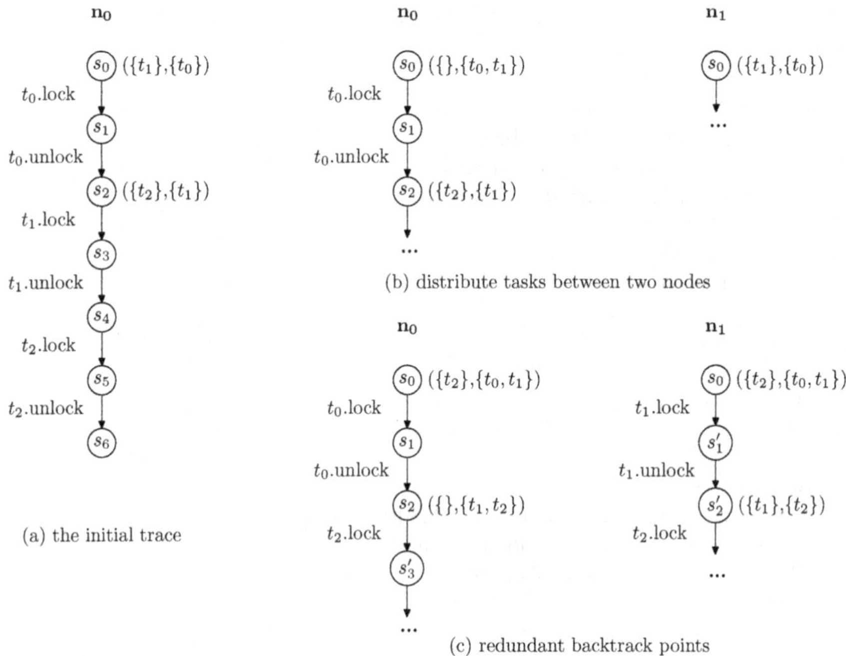

Fig. 8. An example of redundant backtrackings. The sets maintained are (*s.backtrack*, *s.done*).

Figure 8(a). Here, two backtrack points at s_0 and s_2 have been recorded. When the work node n_0 detects this (i.e., more than one backtrack point in the search stack), it will send a request to the load balancer for unloading work. First the load balancer will tell n_0 that n_1 is idle. Second, n_0 will send the backtrack point, transition sequence, copy of the search stack to n_1, following the *unload_work* routine in Figure 6. Then the work node n_1 will receive the message and ready for exploring the state space assigned to it. The left half of Figure 8(b) captures this scenario.

At this point, with respect to the situation in Figure 8(b), n_0 will explore transition t_2*.lock* from the backtrack point s_2, while n_1 will explore transition t_1*.lock* from s_0. Both nodes will update the backtrack information according to their own search stacks. The scenario in Figure 8(c) results, in which both n_0 and

n_1 compute and place t_2 in $s_0.backtrack$ whose transition should be explored from s_0. This will result in redundant explorations being conducted by n_0 and n_1. In the worst case, this kind of redundancy may have all the workers explore the same interleaving, and result in little or no speedup (Our experiments shown in Section 4 confirms this).

```
1:  StateStack S;
2:  TransitionSequence T;

3:  update_backtrack_info(State s) {
4:     for each thread p {
5:        let t_n ∈ s.enabled, t_n.tid = p;
6:        for each t_d ∈ T that is dependent and may be co-enabled with t_n {
7:           let s_d be the state in S from which t_d is executed;
8:           let E be {q ∈ s_d.enabled | q.tid = p, or q in T, q happened after t_d
                 and is dependent with some transition in T which was executed by
                 p and happened after q }
9:           if (E ≠ ∅)
10:             choose any q in E, add q.tid to s_d.backtrack;
11:          else
12:             s_d.backtrack = s_d.backtrack ∪ {q.tid | q ∈ s_d.enabled};
13:       }
14:    }
15: }
```

Fig. 9. Modified update_backtrack_info

This problem is caused by the algorithm shown in Figure 2 computing $s.backtrack$ incrementally with respect to state s. In parallel `inspect`, when a worker unloads work to some idle node, it is possible that the full backtrack set has not yet been associated with states in the copy of the stack being passed along. To solve this problem, given a state s, one must attempt to compute all transitions associated with $s.backtrack$ as aggressively as possible. We observe that the *update_backtrack_info* routine shown in Figure 2 only updates the latest state in the search stack from which the enabled transition in dependent and may be co-enabled with the next transition (Line 25-32 in Figure 2).

The modified *update_backtrack_info* routine is shown in Figure 9. For each to be executed transition t, the new routine will check the stack to find all states from which a dependent and may be co-enabled transition was executed (Line 6 of Figure 9), and update the correspondent backtrack set. With the new routine, we will get the distributed scenario as shown in Figure 10. Note that this is only a heuristic; we do not know of a way to retain loose synchronizations between the threads and still avoid this redundancy.

Correctness: The soundness of the final DPOR algorithm described (employed in parallel `inspect`) follows from the fact that the parallel algorithm is guaranteed

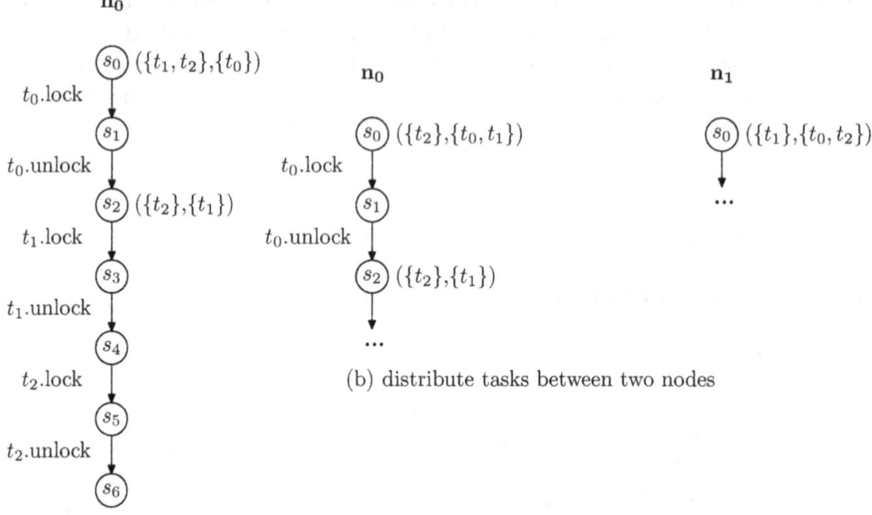

(a) the initial trace

(b) distribute tasks between two nodes

Fig. 10. With the modified *update_backtrack_set*

to compute at least all the backtrack set entries computed by the sequential algorithm for every state. We alter only where this information is computed.

4 Implementation and Experiments

We implemented the parallel `inspect` using MPI [10,11]. MPI (Message Passing Interface) is a message-passing library specification, designed to ease the use of message passing by end users. It is the *de facto* standard of high performance computing. MPI makes writing parallel program much easier, and is supported by virtually all supercomputers and clusters. We used the MPI routines `MPI_Send` and `MPI_Recv` for communication among nodes.

One interesting problem we encountered while we implemented the parallel `inspect` is that the cluster's network file system can be a bottleneck for a parallel runtime checker if there are disk write operations in the program under test. We note that this problem can be easily avoided by using the local disks.

We conducted our experiments on a 72-node cluster with 2GB memory and two 2.4GHz Intel XEON processors on each node. We compiled the program with gcc-4.1.0 and -O3 option. We used LAM-MPI 7.1.1 [12] as the message passing interface. The runtimes that we report are the average runtimes calculated over three runs.

Table 1 shows some benchmarks we have used to test the parallel `inspect`. In Table 1, the second column is the number of threads in each benchmark,

Table 1. Checking time with the sequential `inspect`

benchmark	threads	runs	check using sequential inspect (sec)
fsbench	26	8,192	291.32
indexer	16	32,768	1188.73
aget	6	113,400	5662.96
bbuf	8	1,938,816	39710.43

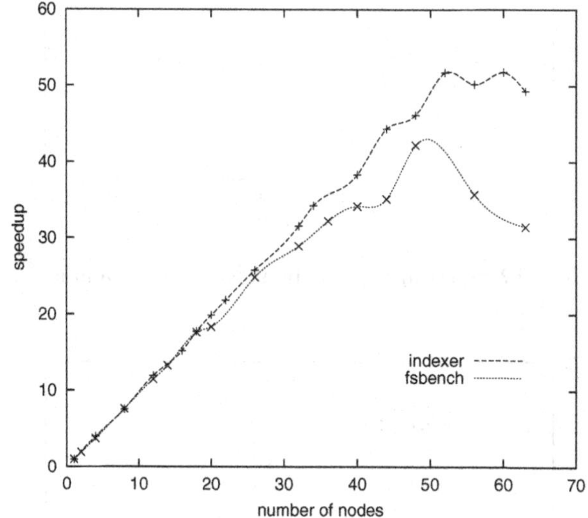

Fig. 11. The speedup of the two benchmarks, *indexer* and *fsbench* from [1]. As the state spaces of these two benchmarks are relatively small, with the number of worker nodes increasing, the communication overhead increases more rapidly than the time reduction we get from distributing the work to more nodes. As a result, we see a degradation of speedup when we use more than 52 nodes to do parallel checking for *indexer*, and more than 48 nodes for *fsbench*.

the third column shows the number of runs needed for runtime checking the program, and the last column shows the time that the sequential `inspect` needs for checking the program.

The first two benchmarks, *indexer* and *fsbench*, are from [1]. *Indexer* captures the scenarios in which multiple threads insert messages into a hash table concurrently. *Fsbench* is an abstraction of the synchronization idiom in Frangipani file system. The third benchmark, *aget* [13] is an ftp client in which multiple threads are used to download different segments of a large file concurrently. The last benchmark, *bbuf* is an implementation of a bounded buffer with four producers and four consumers that have put/get operations on it.

Indexer and *fsbench* are relatively small benchmarks. Using one node in the cluster, the sequential `inspect` takes about 25 minutes to check *indexer*, and

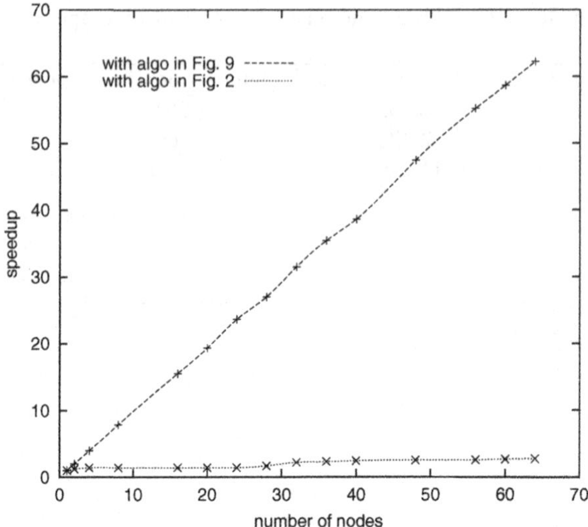

Fig. 12. Speedups on the bounded buffer example

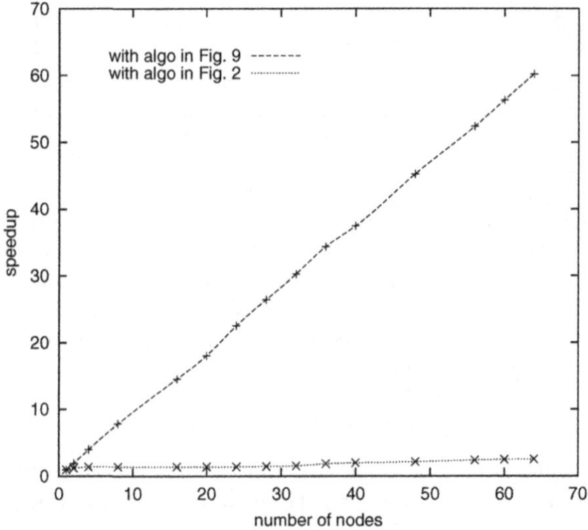

Fig. 13. Speedups on the aget example

5 minutes to check *fsbench*. Using parallel `inspect` and at most 65 nodes (one node as the load balancer and 64 worker nodes), we can check both of them within 40 seconds.

Figure 11 shows the speedup we got using the parallel `inspect` against the sequential `inspect` on *indexer* and *fsbench*. As the performance of using the modified *update_backtrack_info* in Figure 9 does not differ significantly from using the original *update_backtrack_info* in Figure 2, we do not show the comparison in Figure 11.

Figure 12 shows the speedup we got using the parallel `inspect` on *bbuf*. The sequential `inspect` needs more than 11 hours to finish checking the program. During this period of time, `inspect` needs to re-run the program for more than 1.9 million times. As shown in Figure 12, the parallel `inspect` can give us almost linear speedup. It turns out that we can get a speedup of 63.2 out of 64 worker nodes (totally 65 nodes, including the load balancer), and reduce the checking time to 11 minutes. In this figure, we also show the comparison between the speedup we got using the modified *update_backtrack_info* in Figure 9 and the original *update_backtrack_info* in Figure 2. As we can see, without the modification in Figure 9, we get little speedup while the number of nodes increases.

Figure 13 shows the speedup using the parallel `inspect` on *aget*. There are data races in the original *aget*. We fixed those data races and did experiments on the fixed version. We reduced the size of the data package, which *aget* gets from the ftp server, to 512 bytes, to avoid the non-determinism introduced by the network environment. The result again confirms that parallel `inspect` can give out almost linear speedup, and our extension on the original DPOR is efficient.

5 Related Work

Parallel and distributed model checking has been a topic of growing interest, with a special conference series (PDMC) devoted to this topic. An exhaustive literature survey is beyond the scope of this paper. Quite a few distributed and parallel model checkers based on message passing have been developed for Murphi and SPIN [14,15,16,17,18]. Stern and Dill [14] developed a parallel Murphi which distributes states to multiple nodes for further exploration according th the state's signature. They pointed out the idea of coalescing states into larger messages for better network utilization in the context of model checking. Eddy [15] extends the work and studies the parallel and distributed model checking under the multicore architecture. Kumar and Mercer [17] improve the load balancing method in parallel Murphi. Recently Holzmann and Bosnacki [18] design a multicore model checking algorithm to improve SPIN to fully utilize the multicore chips.

Brim et al. [19] propose a distributed partial order reduction algorithm for generating a reduced state space. The algorithm exploits features of the partial order reduction which makes the idea of distributed DFS-based algorithm feasible. Palmer et al. [20,21] propose another distributed partial order reduction algorithm based on the two-phase partial order reduction algorithm.

As far as the authors know, our work is the first effort on using parallelism to speed up runtime model checking for multithreaded programs.

6 Conclusion

Checking time has been the major bottleneck for runtime model checkers such as `inspect`. We design a distributed dynamic partial order reduction algorithm, and develop a parallel version of `inspect`, using parallelism to speed up model checking. Our experiments confirm that parallel `inspect` is quite robust and scales well on a wide variety of nodes. It can give out almost linear speedup compared with the sequential `inspect`.

Acknowledgment

We gratefully acknowledge the computational support provided by the Scientific Computing and Imaging Institute at the University of Utah, thank Eric Swenson and other staff members helping us with the experiments, and thank Sarvani Vakkalanka for reading the draft.

References

1. Flanagan, C., Godefroid, P.: Dynamic Partial-order Reduction for Model Checking Software. In: Palsberg, J., Abadi, M. (eds.) POPL, pp. 110–121. ACM Press, New York (2005)
2. Yang, Y., Chen, X., Gopalakrishnan, G., Kirby, R.M.: UUCS-07-008: Runtime Model Checking of Multithreaded C Programs. Technical report (2007), `http://www.cs.utah.edu/research/techreports/2007/ps/UUCS-07-008.ps`
3. Godefroid, P.: Model Checking for Programming Languages using Verisoft. In: POPL, pp. 174–186 (1997)
4. Holzmann, G.J.: The Spin Model Checker: Primer and Reference Manual. Addison-Wesley, Reading (2004)
5. Robby, D.M.B., Hatcliff, J.: Bogor: an extensible and highly-modular software model checking framework. In: ESEC / SIGSOFT FSE, pp. 267–276 (2003)
6. Henzinger, T.A., Jhala, R., Majumdar, R.: Race checking by context inference. In: PLDI '04. Proceedings of the ACM SIGPLAN 2004 conference on Programming language design and implementation, pp. 1–13. ACM Press, New York (2004)
7. Andrews, T., Qadeer, S., Rajamani, S.K., Rehof, J., Xie, Y.: Zing: A Model Checker for Concurrent Software. In: Cointe, P. (ed.) ECOOP 1996. LNCS, vol. 1098, pp. 484–487. Springer, Heidelberg (1996)
8. Godefroid, P.: Partial-Order Methods for the Verification of Concurrent Systems: An Approach to the State-Explosion Problem. Springer, Heidelberg (1996)
9. Clarke, E.M., Grumberg, O., Peled, D.A.: Model Checking. MIT Press, Cambridge (2000)
10. Snir, M., Otto, S.: MPI-The Complete Reference: The MPI Core. MIT Press, Cambridge (1998)
11. `http://www.mpiforum.org/docs/docs.html`
12. `http://www.lammpi.org/`
13. `http://www.enderunix.org/aget/`
14. Stern, U., Dill, D.L.: Parallelizing the Mur*hi* Verifier. In: Grumberg, O. (ed.) CAV 1997. LNCS, vol. 1254, pp. 256–278. Springer, Heidelberg (1997)
15. Melatti, I., Palmer, R., Sawaya, G., Yang, Y., Kirby, R.M., Gopalakrishnan, G.: Parallel and Distributed Model Checking in Eddy. In: Valmari, A. (ed.) Model Checking Software. LNCS, vol. 3925, pp. 108–125. Springer, Heidelberg (2006)

16. Sivaraj, H., Gopalakrishnan, G.: Random Walk Based Heuristic Algorithms for Distributed Memory Model Checking. Electr. Notes Theor. Comput. Sci. 89(1) (2003)
17. Kumar, R., Mercer, E.G.: Load Balancing Parallel Explicit State Model Checking. Electr. Notes Theor. Comput. Sci. 128(3), 19–34 (2005)
18. Holzmann, G., Bosnacki, D.: Multi-core model checking with Spin (2007)
19. Brim, L., Cerna, I., Moravec, P., Simsa, J.: Distributed Partial Order Reduction of State Spaces. PDMC (1) (2004)
20. Palmer, R., Gopalakrishnan, G.: Partial Order Reduction Assisted Parallel Model Checking. PDMC (2002)
21. Palmer, R., Gopalakrishnan, G.: A distributed partial order reduction algorithm. In: Peled, D.A., Vardi, M.Y. (eds.) FORTE 2002. LNCS, vol. 2529, p. 370. Springer, London, UK (2002)

Some Solutions to the Ignoring Problem

Sami Evangelista and Christophe Pajault

CEDRIC - CNAM Paris
2, rue Cont, 75003 Paris
{evangeli,christophe.pajault}@cnam.fr

Abstract. The ignoring problem refers to the fact that some actions may be infinitely postponed by a state space search algorithm that makes use of partial order reduction (POR). The prevention of this phenomenon is mandatory if one wants to verify more elaborate properties than the deadlock freeness, e.g., safety or liveness properties. We present in this work some solutions to this problem. In order to assess the quality of our propositions, we included them in our model checker Helena. We report the result of some experiments which show that our algorithms yield better reductions than state of the art algorithms like those implemented in the Spin tool.

Keywords: explicit model checking, partial order reduction, ignoring problem, cycle proviso.

Model checking [5], or state space analysis, is a formal method to prove that finite state systems match their specification. Given a model of the system and a property, usually expressed in a temporal logic such as LTL, it explores all the possible configurations, i.e., the state space, of the system to check the validity of the property. Despite its simplicity, its practical application is limited due to the well-known state explosion problem: the state space can be far too large to be explored in a reasonable time.

Partial-order reduction (POR) [18,16,11] is an approach to cope with this problem by tackling one of its main source, the concurrent execution of several components. It is based on the following observation: due to the interleaving semantic of concurrent systems, a set of different executions can have exactly the same effect on the system and be only a permutation of the same sequence. Thus, an efficient way to reduce the state explosion would be to explore only a single or some representative executions and ignore all the others permutations that are equivalent to the chosen ones.

On the basis of this principle, several authors proposed the idea of a selective search algorithm: at each state visited by the algorithm, a set of transitions is computed and only the transitions of this set are used to generate the immediate successors of the state. The execution of the other transitions is postponed and delegated to a future state. Consequently some states may never be explored. In the best case, the state space is reduced in an exponential way.

The ignoring problem, first identified in [18], is a pathological situation that may arise if one does not choose sets carefully: a transition may be infinitely

D. Bošnački and S. Edelkamp (Eds.): SPIN 2007, LNCS 4595, pp. 76–94, 2007.

delayed. This means that the transition selection function can be totally unfair with respect to some process of the system. Though the prevention of this phenomenon is not mandatory if one wants to check if the system deadlocks, it must be resolved for "higher level" properties, e.g., safety or liveness properties. The idea is to enforce an additional condition, called *proviso*, which ensures that the selection function will never forget a transition. By strengthening the acceptance conditions of a set, the proviso may unfortunately cause new states to be generated. It is thus crucial to have an efficient proviso that introduce the least number of states.

We propose in this paper two new versions of this proviso which show good results as our experimentations attested it. The first one, designed for safety properties, can be seen as an optimization of the Spin model checker [12] proviso while the second one targets liveness properties.

The paper is structured as follows. Section 1 contains some basic elements on model checking and partial-order reduction that are needed for the understanding of this paper. The next section introduces different approaches proposed to deal with the ignoring problem. In section 3 we explain our motivations and we show why, in our sense, there is still a need for other algorithms. Our contribution is the two new versions of the proviso presented in sections 4 and 5. We report in section 6 the results of some experiments done with our model checker Helena [8] which implements our propositions as well as state of the art algorithms. At last, section 7 summarizes our contribution.

1 Formal Background

1.1 State Transition Graphs

We will develop our ideas in the frame of state transition graphs (STG). An STG is a directed graph that describes all the possible evolutions of a system.

Definition 1 (State transition graph). *A state transition graph (STG), is a 4-tuple* $(S, s_0, A, \rightarrow)$ *where* S *is a finite set of* **states**; $s_0 \in S$ *is the* **initial state** *of the system;* A *is a set of* **actions**; $\rightarrow \subseteq S \times A \times S$ *is the* **transition relation**, *which is such that* $(s, a, s') \in \rightarrow \wedge (s, a, s'') \in \rightarrow \Rightarrow s' = s''$.

Let $(S, s_0, A, \rightarrow)$ be an STG. If $(s, a, s') \in \rightarrow$ then we note $s \xrightarrow{a} s'$ and we say that s' is a *successor* of s. An action $a \in A$ is *enabled* for $s \in S$, denoted $s \xrightarrow{a}$, iff there exists $s' \in S$ such that $s \xrightarrow{a} s'$. We can also note $s \rightarrow s'$ if there exists $a \in A$ such that $s \xrightarrow{a} s'$. The set of *enabled actions* at a state $s \in S$, denoted $en(s)$, is defined by $en(s) = \{a \in A \mid s \xrightarrow{a}\}$. A state s is a *dead state* iff $en(s) = \emptyset$. For any natural number $n \in \mathbb{N}$, states $s_i \in S$ and actions $a_i \in A$ with $i \in \{1 \dots n\}$, $s_1 \xrightarrow{a_1} \dots s_{n-1} \xrightarrow{a_{n-1}} s_n$ is called an *execution sequence* of length n iff $s_i \xrightarrow{a_i} s_{i+1}$ for all $i \in \{1..n-1\}$. State s_n is said to be *reachable from* s_1. A state is *reachable* iff it is reachable from s_0.

1.2 Partial-Order Reduction

Partial-order reductions [18,16,11] restrict the part of the state space that needs to be explored during verification in such a way that all properties of interest are preserved. The reduction is achieved on-the-fly, i.e., during the state space exploration to avoid the construction of the full state space. The underlying principle is to select for each state some enabled actions that will be executed while the others are postponed and delegated to a future state. This selection mechanism is formalized through the notion of reduction function.

Definition 2 (Reduction function). *Let $(S, s_0, A, \rightarrow)$ be an STG. A reduction function r is a mapping from S to 2^A such that $\forall s \in S, r(s) \subseteq en(s)$.*

When $en(s) = r(s)$ for some state s the function does not provide any reduction. We say that s is *fully expanded.* Otherwise, it is *partially expanded.* An action a is *ignored* in s iff $a \in en(s) \setminus r(s)$.

By applying such a reduction function, one can build a reduced graph.

Definition 3 (Reduced STG). *Let $(S, s_0, A, \rightarrow)$ be an STG and r be a reduction function. The reduced STG $(S_r, s_{0r}, A_r, \rightarrow_r)$ is defined by:*

- $s_{0r} = s_0$, $A_r = A$.
- *$s \in S_r$ iff there is a finite execution sequence $s_0 \xrightarrow{a_0} \ldots \xrightarrow{a_{n-1}} s_n$ such that $s = s_n$ and $a_i \in r(s_i), \forall s_i \in \{s_0 \ldots s_{n-1}\}$.*
- *$(s, a, s') \in \rightarrow_r$ iff $s \in S_r$, $(s, a, s') \in \rightarrow$ and $a \in r(s)$.*

Partial-order reduction for dead states detection. It is clear that a selection function has to respect some rules to preserve properties of interest. This led to several variations of the reduction according to the kind of property specified. However, since the general principle of the partial-order reduction theory is to exploit the commutativity of concurrent actions to limit useless interleavings, all are based on the key notion of independence of actions. Intuitively, two actions a and b are independent if they cannot disable each other and if they commute in any state of the system.

Definition 4 (Independence). *An independence relation is a symmetric and anti-reflexive relation $I \in A \times A$ satisfying the two following conditions for each state $s \in S$ and for each $(a, b) \in I$.*

Enabledness. *if $a, b \in en(s)$ and $s \xrightarrow{b} s'$ then $a \in en(s')$.*
Commutativity. *if $a, b \in en(s)$ then $s \xrightarrow{a} s'' \xrightarrow{b} s'$ and $s \xrightarrow{b} s''' \xrightarrow{a} s'$.*

Two actions a and b are *independent* iff $(a, b) \in I$. Otherwise, they are *dependent* and (a, b) belongs to the relation $(A \times A) \setminus I$.

This independence relation is usually computed at compile time, i.e., before the exploration of the state space, on the basis of a static analysis of the model. An action that only manipulate local variables, e.g., an assignment to a local variable will be typically considered as independent from any other action.

We are now able to enumerate the two following conditions which allow us to compute a *persistent set* (PS) of transitions for a state s.

C0. $r(s) = \emptyset$ iff $en(s) = \emptyset$.

C1. an action that is dependent on an action of $r(s)$ cannot be executed without a transition in $r(s)$ occurring first.

A reduction function that compute persistent sets preserves all the dead states of the system [11] and can thus be used for the detection of such states. The only purpose of C0 is to guarantee that the search algorithm with reduction progresses if the normal one does. The intuition behind condition C1 is that after the execution of any sequence that only includes transitions outside $r(s)$ all the transitions of $r(s)$ will still be executable. Thus we can execute them immediately and delay the execution of the others.

Partial-order reduction for safety properties. A search algorithm that compute persistent sets may infinitely delay the execution of some transitions and miss states of interest. The following additional constraint, called *proviso*, can prevent this phenomenon, called *action ignoring* problem [18].

C2$^{\mathbf{S}}$. For any state $s \in S_r$, $a \in en(s)$ there is s' reachable from s in the reduced graph such that $a \in r(s')$.

This condition ensures that any enabled action will be executed in a state reachable from s. If the reduction function satisfies this condition, it can be showed that the reduced graph is, what Godefroid called, a *trace automaton*. Trace automata have the nice property to preserve the reachability of local states: if a process can reach a given state in the initial graph, then it will also be able to reach this state in the reduced graph. Trace automata can therefore be used to verify a large range of safety properties that include, for example, assertions on local variables.

Partial-order reduction for liveness properties. To preserve liveness properties we must ensure that any cycle of the graph does not contain an enabled transition that is never executed (in the states of the cycle). This leads to a strengthened version of the proviso, denoted C2^{L}.

C2$^{\mathbf{L}}$. A cycle is not allowed if it contains a state in which some action a is enabled, but never included in $r(s)$ for any state s on the cycle.

This condition is usually replaced by the following one, implied by the C1 condition, that can be more easily implemented.

C2$^{\mathbf{L'}}$. Along each cycle of the reduced graph, there is some state s that is fully expanded.

Coupled with another condition (see [5]) that preserves the interleavings of some interesting actions (the *visible* actions), the C2^{L} proviso can be used to compute *ample* sets [16]. A selection function that computes such sets builds a reduced graph that is equivalent to the initial one with respect to LTL-X formulae.

2 Related Works

The safety and liveness provisos are stated as properties of the reduced STG whereas we may want to perform the reduction on-the-fly. Therefore they are usually reformulated as conditions that can be efficiently checked during the construction of the reduced STG and, hence, are tightly linked to the way the search algorithm proceeds and the data structures it handles.

For depth first search (DFS), we can use the fact that every cycle contains a transition that reached the search stack at some point during the search. It is then sufficient to forbid to partially expanded states to reach the stack. This gives a first version of the liveness proviso, denoted $\mathrm{C2}_{\mathrm{s}}^{\mathrm{L}}$ [17]. This proviso is the one implemented by the Spin model checker [12].

$\mathbf{C2_s^L}$. If $r(s) \neq en(s)$ then no action in $r(s)$ may reach a state of the stack.

For safety properties a weaker condition can be defined. We may indeed let a transition reach a state on the stack, provided that another transition leads to a state outside this stack [11].

For breadth first search (BFS), a similar version has been recently introduced in [3].

$\mathbf{C2_q^L}$. If $r(s) \neq en(s)$ then all the actions of $r(s)$ reach a state of the queue.

The intuition behind this condition is that we do not have to worry about ignoring some actions of s since we delegate the problem to the successors of s which all belong to the queue and will be processed later. Once again, the weaker version of this proviso for safety proviso denoted $\mathrm{C2}_{\mathrm{q}}^{\mathrm{S}}$ requires that at least one action leads to a state of the queue.

This idea has been generalized in [4] to general state exploring algorithms, that is, any explicit algorithm that partitions the state space into three mutually disjoint sets: the *open* states that have been met but not expanded yet, the *closed* states that have been met and expanded (and can potentialy be reopened), and the *unmet* states. This new proviso can, for example, be used in directed model checking [7]. An open (or unmet) state is safe in the sense that it can be reached by a partially expanded state without risking to introduce some ignoring phenomenon: the resolution of this problem is delegated to this state that will be explored later. On the other hand, closed states are dangerous destinations since they have already been explored.

In [13], a new technique is proposed which aim is to set up the entire reduction mechanism at compile time. The method is then independent from the search algorithm and can be used, for example, in symbolic model checking. Considering a concurrent system, which is a composition of sequential processes, the authors exploit the fact that a cycle in the state space results from some cycle(s) in the sequential processes of the model. The idea is to statically choose an action in each of these cycles and to mark it as *sticky*. The proviso can then be reduced to the following condition: a persistent set that does not include all the enabled actions may not contain a sticky action.

The *two-phase* algorithm presented in [14] uses an alternative to the in-stack check to verify both safety and liveness properties. It alternates phases in which it fully expand states and phases of expansion of deterministic states, i.e., states in which singleton persistent sets can be computed. For some models the two-phase algorithm can achieve significantly better results than a depth first search that uses the $C2_s^L$ proviso.

3 Motivations

Partial order methods can drastically reduce the verification requirements by eliminating redundant interleavings. In the best case the reduction factor is exponential. However, in many cases they are not as efficient as one would expect. This is mainly due to two factors.

First of all, the computation of persistent sets relies on a static analysis of the model that sometimes produces coarse approximations. *Dynamic partial order reduction*, a proposition to cope with this problem, has been recently introduced by Flanagan and Godefroid [9].

Another source of inefficiencies can come from the resolution of the ignoring problem. Indeed we can identify models for which the use of the "historical" proviso based on an in-stack check yields poor results. We will illustrate this problem with the help of the Petri net depicted on figure 1(a). This net models a solution to the dining philosophers problem in which a philosopher takes two forks atomically. Some places have been duplicated for the sake of clarity. They are drawn as dashed circles. Places i_1, i_2, i_3 and i_4 model the idle state of the 4 philosophers while the eating state is modeled by e_1, e_2, e_3 and e_4. Place f_i models the state of the fork of philosopher i. To seat at the table (transition t_i), the philosopher i must take his fork f_i and the fork of its neighbor, i.e., f_j with $j = i \mod n + 1$. Once is meal finished he goes back to the idle state and puts back his forks (transition r_i).

We have drawn on figure 1(b) the state space of this net built with the $C2_s^L$ proviso. Fully expanded states are double circled[1] and states are numbered according to the order they are visited by the algorithm. It appears that this combination does not reduce the number of states but can only save the execution of two transitions. Indeed, the in-stack check often succeeds and this leads to a full expansion of most states. However, it is clear that an optimal proviso (see figure 1(c)) would not introduce any state since all the cycles of the state space reduced with PS contains the initial state which is fully expanded.

With four philosophers this optimal proviso only saves two states but if we generalize the problem to n philosophers the reduction is much more impressive. Indeed, the full state space and the state space reduced with proviso $C2_s^L$ both have a size in $\mathcal{O}(2^n)$ while the state space reduced with an optimal proviso has $n + 1$ states.

---

[1] We will adopt this graphical convention throughout the paper.

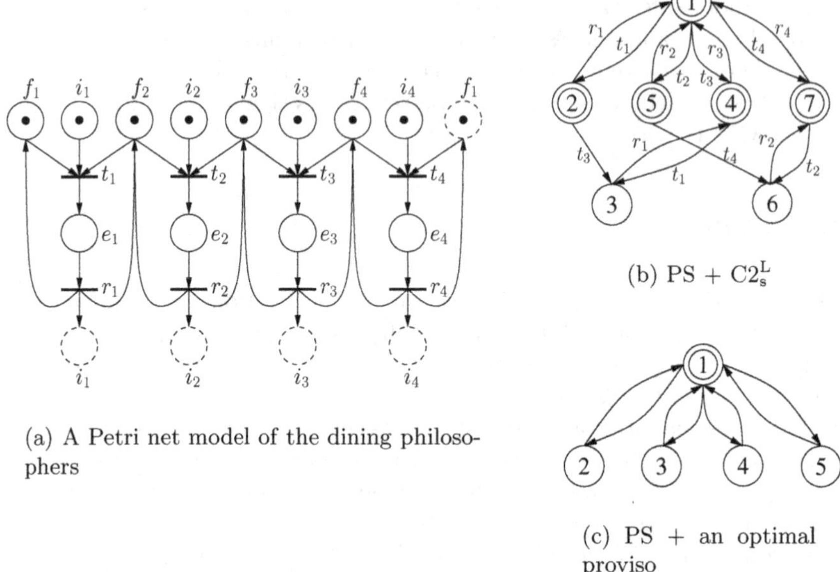

(a) A Petri net model of the dining philosophers

(b) PS + $C2_s^L$

(c) PS + an optimal proviso

Fig. 1. An example that illustrates our motivations

Our intuition is that the ignoring problem is a phenomenon that seldom occurs in practice. By taking a too defensive approach traditional implementations of the cycle proviso such as those based an in-stack check can introduce much more states than necessary. Though our example is not representative as it corresponds to the worst case we can think of, it still illustrates the fact that the $C2_s^L$ proviso is not adapted for some classes of models.

The static proviso [13] may overcome this problem if the sticky transitions are chosen appropriately, e.g., transitions t_1, t_2, t_3 and t_4 in our example, but since it is based on a static analysis of the model its performances may vary according to the input formalism of the model checker. For example, since there is no clear notion of process or loop in high-level Petri nets, the language of our model checker Helena [8], a detection of sticky transitions may produce a coarse approximation containing many useless transitions.

The two phase algorithm [14] also achieves an optimal reduction on this example, but it is based on a principle - always selecting singletons - that can, for some models, be too much strong. For instance, it does not behave very well when processes can act indeterministically. Moreover, it prevents the use of some elaborated techniques that refine the dependency relation, e.g., [2].

Our objective is therefore to devise a proviso that (1) can be an interesting alternative when others fail to efficiently reduce the state space; (2) is not linked to a particular formalism and can be implemented by any model checker.

4 A Proviso for Safety Properties

We propose in this section a new version of the safety proviso that is based on a depth-first search algorithm. This one also performs checks in the stack to avoid an infinite postponement of actions but it considerably relaxes the conditions under which a transition is acceptable.

Figure 2 gives the POR algorithm in a pseudo-code form. The principle of our proviso $C2_e^S$ is to associate to each state s of the stack an integer *expanded* that records the number of fully expanded states on the stack below s, i.e., between s_0 and s. The global variable *expanded* keeps track of this number. Then, when an action a leads from a state s to a state s' on the stack we compare the number of fully expanded states currently on the stack, i.e., the value of $s.expanded$, to the number associated to s', i.e., $s'.expanded$. If the first one is strictly greater then this obviously means that there is a fully expanded state s'' on the stack between s' and s. Hence, s'' is reachable from s and the enabled actions of s will necessarily be executed at a state on the path from s to s''. This can be illustrated with the help of the opposite figure. Enclosed in each state is the value of its *expanded* attribute.

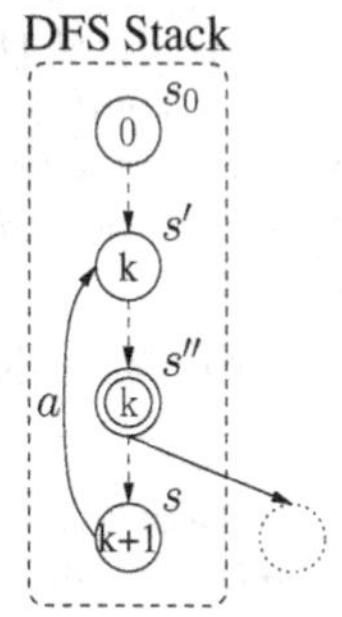

Proviso $C2_e^S$ is clearly better than $C2_s^S$, in the sense that it will always compute smaller persistent sets (but not necessarily smaller graphs). Indeed it can be viewed as an optimization of $C2_s^S$: by removing the *expanded* attribute and by changing the condition of function $C2_E^S$ we obtain the same proviso. The price to pay is a slight increase of the memory requirements. Our proviso requires an additional integer per state (typically 32 bits) for the *expanded* attribute. However, some savings can be done by removing the *expanded* attribute of the states that leave the stack. Indeed, once popped from the DFS stack this attribute is not used anymore by the algorithm. In addition, the space required to store this information is usually small compared to the size of states in a large system. Lastly, we will see in section 6 that this extra memory consumption should, in most cases, be largely compensated by the reduction achieved.

To show the correctness of our proviso we prove that the reduction function has a witness [1]. This notion is defined below.

Definition 5 (Witness function). *Let $\mathcal{T} = (S, s_0, A, \rightarrow)$ be an STG, r a reduction function of $\mathcal{T}$ and $\mathcal{T}_r = (S_r, s_{0r}, A_r, \rightarrow_r)$ be the reduction of $\mathcal{T}$ with respect to r. A mapping $W : S_r \rightarrow \mathbb{N}$ is a witness for r iff:*

$$\forall s \in S_r, r(s) \neq en(s) \Rightarrow \exists (s, a, s') \in \rightarrow_r \text{ such that } W(s') < W(s)$$

The intuition behind this idea of witness function is that for any state s of the reduced graph that is partially expanded we can find a successor s' of s with $W(s') < W(s)$ and to which we delegate the execution of the actions ignored at s. By reitering this operation on s' we obtain a sequence $W(s), W(s'), \ldots$ of decreasing numbers. As the state space is finite, we will necessarily find a state s'' which is such that $W(s'') \geq W(s''')$ for any of its successors s'''. Obviously

```
DFS (s)
H ← H ∪ {s}
s.expanded ← expanded
s.inStack ← true
let P be a persistent set that
   satisfies C2^S_e(s, P) or en(s)
   if there is no such set
if P = en(s) then
   expanded ← expanded + 1
for a ∈ P do
   let s -a-> s'
   if s' ∉ H then DFS(s')
if P = en(s) then
   expanded ← expanded − 1
s.inStack ← false
```

```
C2^S_E (s, P)
for a ∈ P do
   let s -a-> s'
   if
      s' ∉ H or
      ¬s'.inStack or
      s.expanded > s'.expanded
   then
      return true
return false
```

```
SEARCH ()
H ← ∅
expanded ← 0
DFS(s0)
```

Fig. 2. A depth first search algorithm that implements our safety proviso

in such state, $r(s'') = en(s'')$ and all the actions ignored in s that haven't been selected on the path from s to s'' belong to $r(s'')$. It is therefore sufficient to prove that the reduced STG has a witness [1].

Lemma 1. *Proviso $C2^S_e$ implies the safety cycle proviso $C2^S$.*

Proof. Let $W : S_r \to \mathbb{N}$ be a function that enumerates the states of the reduced STG $(S_r, s_{0r}, A_r, \to_r)$ in the order they are removed from the stack : s_0 is mapped to $|S_r| - 1$ while the first state to be popped is mapped to 0. Let F_W be the states of S_r that violate the witness conditions, i.e., defined by

$$F_W = \{s \in S_r \mid r(s) \neq en(s) \land \forall (s, a, s') \in \to_r, W(s') \geq W(s)\}$$

Let us observe the algorithm when it processes a state $s \in F_W$. It holds for all the successors $s' \in S_r$ of s that $s' \in H \land s'.inStack$. Otherwise s' leaves the stack before s and $W(s') < W(s)$ ($\Rightarrow s \notin F_W$). In addition there must be a state s' such that $s \xrightarrow{a}_r s'$ for some $a \in r(s)$ and $s'.expanded < s.expanded$. Otherwise, $r(s) = en(s)$ ($\Rightarrow s \notin F_W$).

Hence, there is a path $s_1 \to_r s_2 \to_r \ldots \to_r s_n$ such that $s' = s_1$, $s_1.inStack \land \cdots \land s_n.inStack$ and $r(s_n) = en(s_n)$. We can define a new function W' such that

1 – $W'(s_1) < W(s)$ and $W'(s_1) < W(s_1)$
2 – $\forall s_i \in \{s_2, \ldots, s_n\}, W'(s_i) < W'(s_{i-1})$ and $W'(s_i) < W(s_i)$
3 – $\forall s \notin \{s_1, \ldots, s_n\}, W'(s) = W(s)$

Let us compare $F_{W'}$ and F_W. Point 1 implies that $s \notin F_{W'}$. In addition, it trivially follows from the three points that $F_{W'} \setminus F_W = \emptyset$, i.e., W' does not introduce a new "violating state". Thus we have $|F_{W'}| < |F_W|$.

By reitering the same operation on W' until $F_W = \emptyset$ we obtain a witness W. □

The different steps of the construction of the witness function are illustrated with the help of the opposite figure. States are numbered according to function W. At each step, the gray state corresponds to the state s of the proof that violates the witness function conditions.

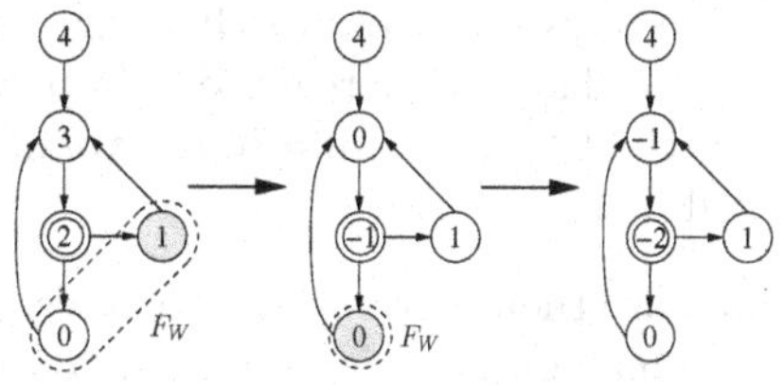

5 A Proviso for Liveness Properties

The conditions that ensure a sound reduction are stronger when one wants to analyze liveness properties, e.g., LTL-X formulae. The reduction must indeed ensure that for any cycle, an action enabled at one of its states will be executed at some state of the cycle. We have seen that a sufficient way to proceed is to fully expand a state on each cycle of the graph.

We would like to adapt the idea of the $C2^S_e$ proviso, presented in the previous section, to the verification of liveness property. Unfortunately, a direct adaptation does not guarantee the desired behavior. We illustrate this problem with the simple graph depicted below.

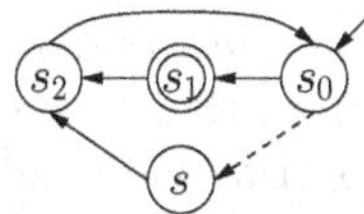

Let us assume that the algorithm first processes state s_0, then pushes s_1 that is fully expanded and finally reaches s_2. Since s_1 is on the stack between s_0 and s_2 the persistent set which consists of the single action that leads from s_2 to s_0 is valid. Now let us suppose that later the algorithm backtracks to s_0 and executes a sequence $s_0 \rightarrow \ldots \rightarrow s$ such that none of the states of this sequence is fully expanded. According to the $C2^S_e$ proviso, the singleton $\{s \rightarrow s_2\}$ is a valid set. Hence, we close a cycle that does not contain any fully expanded state and in which an action may be ignored: $s_0 \rightarrow \ldots \rightarrow s \rightarrow s_2 \rightarrow s_0$.

In order to prevent such situations we will have to perform some additional checks possibly leading to less reductions. We will in particular forbid that state s reaches state s_2 without being fully expanded.

The pseudo-code of our algorithm is given in figure 3. In addition to the *expanded* attribute of proviso $C2^S_e$ the new proviso $C2^L_c$, the *color proviso*, associates some extra information to each state. A state will thus be marked as green, red or orange. This color gives us crucial informations when we want to determine whether an action is allowed or not (see function $C2^L_c$).

green states are safe states. These ones may be reached by any other state without risking of closing an invalid cycle. Intuitively, if a state is green then either it is fully expanded either all its successors are green.

red states are dangerous states. A state may not reach a red state without being fully expanded. This could indeed close a "bad" cycle as in our example. Red states do not belong to the stack anymore.

orange states are potentially dangerous states. An orange state is a state of the stack that can be reached by a partially expanded state under the condition of the $C2_e^S$ proviso: a fully expanded state appears between the two in the DFS stack.

Colors are then attributed as follows.

When a new state is generated and pushed onto the stack we mark it as green if it is fully expanded or orange otherwise. The orange color is attributed in function PUSH_STATE before the computation of the persistent set P to resolve the case where P contains a self-loop transition. Orange states are therefore all the partially expanded states which are in the stack.

An orange state leaving the stack is colored in green if all its successors are green or red otherwise. Hence, while red and green are final states, i.e., the color of a green or red state can not change, orange is a transitory color: once the search terminated, the stack is empty and all states are marked as red or green.

The purpose of lines 13-18 of procedure DFS is to deal with the situation where the state s is partially expanded and reaches a red state s' that was not in H when the persistent set of s was computed. We must then fully expand s, assign it the green color and restart its expansion. In practice we found out that this situation is very unusual.

Let us go back to our previous example and see how our algorithm will proceed on this one. As state s_2 is popped from the stack we color it in red since its only successor, state s_0, is orange, i.e., partially expanded and on the stack. We then backtrack to state s_0 and reach later s. Since s_2 is a red state the action leading from s to s_2 is not allowed if s is not fully expanded. Consequently, we will have to select another set or to fully expand s.

In order to prove the correctness of our proviso we proceed in two steps. We first show that the reduced STG cannot contain a cycle of red states.

Proposition 1. *Let $\mathcal{T} = (S, s_0, A, \rightarrow)$ be an STG and $\mathcal{T}_r = (S_r, s_{0r}, A_r, \rightarrow_r)$ be its reduction obtained using the algorithm of figure 3. Then, there is no cycle of red states in $\mathcal{T}_r$, i.e., $\forall s_1, \ldots, s_n \in S_r$,*

$$s_1 \rightarrow_r s_2 \rightarrow_r \ldots \rightarrow_r s_n \rightarrow_r s_1 \Rightarrow \exists i \in \{1..n\} \mid s_i.\mathit{color} = \mathit{green}$$

Proof. Let us suppose that there is a cycle $s_1 \rightarrow_r s_2 \rightarrow_r \ldots \rightarrow_r s_n \rightarrow_r s_1$ with $s_i.\mathit{color} = \mathit{red}, \forall i \in [1..n]$ and such that s_1 is the first state visited by the algorithm, i.e., pushed onto the stack.

Necessarily during the search we reached a configuration in which

1. States $s_1, \ldots, s_i$ are on top of the stack.
2. $s_1.\mathit{color} = \cdots = s_i.\mathit{color} = \mathit{orange}$.
3. There is $a \in r(s_i)$ such that $s_i \xrightarrow{a} s_j$ and $s_j \in H$.

From now on, we observe this configuration. By assumption, $s_j.\mathit{color} \neq \mathit{green}$, hence, $s_j.\mathit{color} \in \{\mathit{orange}, \mathit{red}\}$. Let us look at these two possibilities.

$s_j.\mathit{color} = \mathit{red}$ ($\Rightarrow s_j$ has left the stack)

We again consider two different cases.

```
DFS (s)
1  H ← H ∪ {s}
2  PUSH_STATE(s)
3  let P be a persistent set that
4     satisfies C2^L_C(s, P) or en(s)
5     if there is no such set
6  if P = en(s) then
7     expanded ← expanded + 1
8     s.color ← green
9 search_loop:
10 for a ∈ P do
11    let s -a-> s'
12    if s' ∉ H then DFS(s')
13    elsif s.color = orange
14        and s'.color = red
15    then
16       s.color ← green
17       P ← en(s)
18       goto search_loop
19 if P = en(s) then
20    expanded ← expanded − 1
21 POP_STATE(s)

SEARCH ()
1  H ← ∅ ; expanded ← 0 ; DFS(s0)
```

```
PUSH_STATE (s)
1  s.inStack ← true
2  s.color ← orange
3  s.expanded ← expanded

POP_STATE (s)
1  s.inStack ← false
2  if s.color = orange then
3     if ∀a ∈ r(s), s -a-> s',
4        s'.color = green
5     then
6        s.color ← green
7     else
8        s.color ← red

C2^L_C (s, P)
1  for a ∈ P do
2     let s -a-> s'
3     if
4        s' ∈ H and
5        (s'.color = red or
6        (s'.color = orange and
7        s'.expanded = s.expanded))
8     then
9        return false
10 return true
```

Fig. 3. A depth first search algorithm that implements our liveness proviso

$s_j \in H$ when $r(s_i)$ is computed
: Necessarily, $s_j.color = red$ when $r(s_i)$ is computed. Otherwise, s_j is on top of s_i in the stack and $s_j.color = orange$ when we reach s_j from s_i. It trivially follows from the condition of the if statement at line 3 of $\mathrm{C2}^{\mathrm{L}}_{\mathrm{C}}$ that $s_j \in H \wedge s_j.color = red \Rightarrow r(s_i) = en(s_i)$, and hence $s_i.color = green$ after the assignment at line 8 of DFS.

$s_j \notin H$ when $r(s_i)$ is computed
: Then, when s_j is reached at line 11 of DFS it holds, by assumption, that $s_j \in H$, $s_j.color = red$ and $s_i.color = orange$. So, s_i is colored in green at line 16.

$s_j.color = orange$ ($\Rightarrow s_j$ is on the stack)
: State s_j was pushed on the stack before s_i. Thus we had $s_j.color = orange$ when $r(s_i)$ was computed. From function $\mathrm{C2}^{\mathrm{L}}_{\mathrm{C}}$, if $s_j \in H \wedge s_j.color = orange$ then $s_j.expanded < s_i.expanded$. Otherwise, we would have $r(s_i) = en(s_i)$ and s_i would be colored in green at line 8 of DFS. Since $s_j.expanded < s_i.expanded$ then there exists s_k with $j < k < i$ such that $r(s_k) = en(s_k)$. Consequently, $s_k.color = green$ from the line 8 of DFS.

So in both cases there is a green state in the cycle. □

Secondly, we prove that if a cycle of the reduced STG contains a green state then it contains a fully expanded state.

Proposition 2. *Let* $\mathcal{T} = (S, s_0, A, \rightarrow)$ *be an STG and* $\mathcal{T}_r = (S_r, s_{0r}, A_r, \rightarrow_r)$ *be its reduction obtained using the algorithm of figure 3. In any cycle* $s_1 \rightarrow_r s_2 \rightarrow_r \ldots \rightarrow_r s_n \rightarrow_r s_1$*, if there is* s_i *such that* $s_i.color = green$ *then there is* s_j *such that* $r(s_j) = en(s_j)$*.*

Proof. We consider in this proof a cycle $s_1 \rightarrow_r s_2 \rightarrow_r \ldots \rightarrow_r s_n \rightarrow_r s_1$ such that $s_i.color = green$ for some $i \in \{1..n\}$.

Let us first suppose that there is a red state in the cycle. If there exists s_i with $s_i.color = red$ then, necessarily, there are s_j and s_k such that $s_j.color = green$, $s_k.color = red$ and $s_j \rightarrow_r s_k$ (otherwise, the cycle would only contain red states). Since it trivially holds that a green state with a red successor is fully expanded our claim is proved for this first case.

Now let us suppose that $\forall i \in \{1..n\}$, $s_i.color = green$. Necessarily, during the search a state s_i reached a state s_j on the stack. Since $s_j.inStack = true$ then $s_j.color \in \{orange, green\}$. Let us look at these two possibilities.

$s_j.color = green$ - It holds for any green state s of the stack that $r(s) = en(s)$.

$s_j.color = orange$ - When s_i leaves the stack (before s_j) it becomes red as it has a non green successor. This goes against our initial assumption that all the states of the cycle are green.

So in both cases there is a fully expanded state in the cycle. □

It is then straightforward to prove the correctness of our liveness proviso.

Lemma 2. *Proviso* $C2_c^L$ *implies the liveness cycle proviso* $C2^L$*.*

Proof. This lemma is a direct consequence of propositions 1 and 2.

Anticipation of the backtrack phase. The red color appears in the graph when some partially expanded state s reaches an orange state. Indeed, once s is popped from the stack it becomes red and this color will be propagated to its predecessors in the stack. This way to proceed is very careful since we assume that the orange states reached by s will be later colored in red. However, there are situations in which we can directly color orange states in green by anticipating the backtrack phase.

We will illustrate the principle of this optimization with the help of figure 4. The letters correspond to the colors of states. Without optimization when state s is processed it reaches the orange state s' and thus becomes red when popped. However, since all the outgoing arcs of s' have been visited and its only successor is green, we know that it will become green when leaving the stack. We can therefore immediately color s' in green. As a direct consequence, state s only reaches green states and can be marked as green.

The implementation of this optimization requires one extra boolean variable per state of the stack which specifies if all the outgoing arcs of the state have

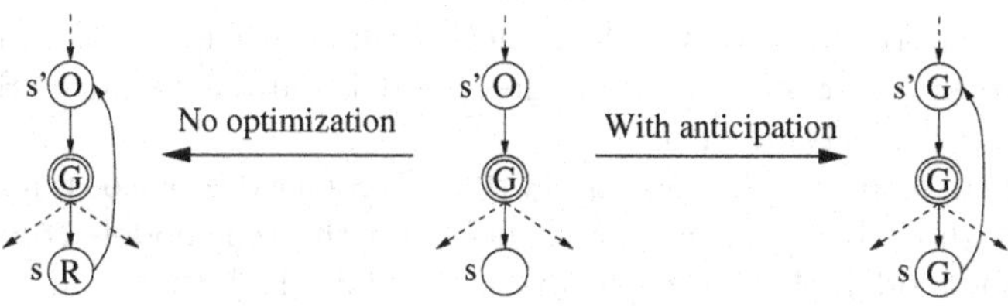

Fig. 4. Illustration of the optimization

been visited. We also introduce an additional color: purple. States colored in purple are states of the stack that will be marked as red when popped. The only purpose of this new color is to ease the implementation of this optimization: purple states are treated as orange states when checking the proviso.

With the optimized proviso, denoted $C2^L_{c\star}$, the algorithm proceeds as follows. When it assigns the green color to the current state or when it executes an action that leads to a green state, the stack is scanned from top to bottom until it meets a green or purple state or an orange state of which some outgoing arcs have not been visited. The green color is assigned to all the states scanned.

Alternatively, when an action leads to a purple or an orange state, the algorithm scans the stack until it meets a green or purple state and colors all the states scanned in purple.

We believe that this optimization has a strong potential insofar as the persistency condition C1 often leads to compute singletons, e.g., with a single transition that only operates on local variables, or to fully expand states. In such situations our optimization is very useful since it allows to assign the green color to most of the states of the stack: as soon as a fully expanded state is met, the green color propagates from top to bottom to all the states of the stack.

If it is clear that our safety proviso outperforms the in-stack check based one, we cannot draw such a conclusion for the color proviso. Proviso $C2^L_s$ and $C2^L_c$ are both based on the notion of dangerous and safe states. With the $C2^L_s$ proviso, dangerous states are all the states of the stack (or more generally, all the closed states [4]) while, on the contrary, with the color proviso, dangerous states do not belong to the stack anymore. It is therefore crucial to experiment these provisos in order to determine which one achieves the best reduction in practice.

6 Experiments

We implemented the algorithms proposed in our model checker Helena [8]. The tool takes as input a high-level Petri net and can verify reachability properties or the presence of dead states. In order to assess the quality of our provisos we also implemented the in-stack and in-queue check based provisos for DFS and BFS which are part of the Spin model checker.

We considered several families of models. Some are simple "toy" examples. Others are communication protocols or mutual exclusion algorithms of which some can be found on the BEEM web portal [15]. We also translated some concurrent Ada software to high-level nets with the help of the Quasar tool (`http://quasar.cnam.fr`). Some of these models can be found in Helena distribution (`http://helena.cnam.fr`).

We observed, as it was the case in [3], that BFS based provisos tend to be less efficient that those based on a DFS. Indeed, on the ten models considered we only found one model (the slotted ring protocol) for which they achieved a better reduction. In addition the difference was pretty insignificant. On other models there were sometimes huge differences. Therefore, we decided not to report the results obtained with BFS based provisos to focus on a comparison between the in-stack check based provisos and our algorithms.

The result of the experimentations are reported in table 1. We performed several searches: without partial order reduction at all (column No POR); without action ignoring resolution (column PS); with a safety cycle proviso (columns $C2_s^S$ and $C2_e^S$); with a liveness proviso (columns $C2_s^L$, $C2_c^L$ and $C2_{c\star}^L$). The numbers reported in columns No POR and PS must therefore be seen as upper and lower bounds when comparing the different provisos.

For each run we report the number of states of the reduced graph and the amount of memory consumed to store the state space. In some cases, we ran out of memory and could not complete the search. This is indicated by a "oom".

For safety properties, a comparison of columns PS and $C2_e^S$ shows that our proviso performs an excellent reduction. On eight models it did not introduce states that were not visited by an algorithm without action ignoring prevention. For Lamport's algorithm, it caused the exploration of a few thousands states which is quite low with respect to the size of the state space of this model. It also doubled the graph size of the resource allocation system. In this model, a process may potentially diverge and perform an infinite sequence that does not include any synchronization. So there actually is some risk of ignoring problem and it is thus obvious that any proviso will necessarily cause the visit of additional states. Nevertheless $C2_e^S$ behaves much better than $C2_s^S$ and on this model.

These results confirm our initial expectations: a DFS seldom closes a cycle that does not contain any fully expanded state. In any concurrent system, there are usually some points of synchronization, e.g., an access to a global variable, the acquisition of a lock. When the processes reach these points it is likely that the algorithm fully expand the state. It seems to us that a weak point of the $C2_s^S$ proviso is that it does not exploit such information on the past of the search that the stack can provide us. Our proviso should therefore be nearly optimal in the sense that it will only disallow the algorithm to close a cycle when this one does not actually contain a fully expanded state.

We also observe that $C2_s^S$ and $C2_s^L$ sometimes brutally increase the graph size. This confirm our initial intuition that these provisos are not adapted to some systems. We can find several models for which these provisos cause the algorithm to visit much more states than really needed. For some examples, e.g., the slotted ring protocol, the resource allocation system, a look at column No POR shows that they even almost cancel the reduction.

Table 1. Comparison of the different provisos implemented in Helena

No POR	PS	PS + Safety proviso $C2^S_s$	$C2^S_e$	PS + Liveness proviso $C2^L_s$	$C2^L_c$	$C2^L_{c\star}$
Simple models						
Load-balancing system (7 clients, 3 servers)						
1 574 530 26.4 MB	72 093 1.2 MB	631 056 10.7 MB	72 093 1.5 MB	630 997 10.7 MB	211 012 4 MB	72 194 1.3 MB
A peer-to-peer communication protocol (8 processes)						
743 580 12.1 MB	163 0.1 MB	72 852 1.2 MB	163 0.1 MB	72 852 1.2 MB	884 830 15.6 MB	252 315 5.2 MB
Resource allocation system (4 processes)						
2 550 759 49.9 MB	72 637 1.5 MB	1 449 206 28.7 MB	151 531 3.6 MB	1 783 881 35.2 MB	754 878 23.2 MB	607 004 15.6 MB
Protocols and mutual exclusion algorithms						
Lamport's mutual exclusion algorithm (4 processes)						
1 914 784 41.02 MB	1 052 518 22.5 MB	1 282 950 27.4 MB	1 055 985 26.7 MB	1 455 606 31.3 MB	1 304 311 31.6 MB	1 304 310 31.6 MB
Peterson's mutual exclusion algorithm (4 processes)						
3 407 946 49.3 MB	259 942 3.7 MB	356 068 5.1 MB	259 942 4.7 MB	356 698 5.1 MB	292 622 4.8 MB	260 608 4.3 MB
Production cell (8 plates)						
oom	396 931 18.2 MB	1 024 422 46.3 MB	396 931 19.1 MB	1 138 954 51.4 MB	495 543 24.2 MB	451 355 21.9 MB
Slotted ring protocol (7 processes)						
439 296 6.1 MB	287 508 4 MB	413 321 5.8 MB	287 508 5.1 MB	437 579 6.1 MB	401 803 6.5 MB	304 417 4.9 MB
Models extracted from programs						
The chameneos (4 tasks)						
oom	415 361 4.7 MB	899 295 10.4 MB	415 361 6.4 MB	899 295 10.4 MB	733 654 10.2 MB	494 123 6.9 MB
The dining philosophers (6 tasks)						
10 888 070 136 MB	109 222 1.3 MB	174 354 2.1 MB	109 222 1.7 MB	174 354 2.1 MB	115 333 1.7 MB	110 190 1.6 MB
A client-server program (4 clients, 2 servers)						
oom	87 129 1.4 MB	99 430 1.6 MB	87 129 1.7 MB	99 430 1.6 MB	159 202 2.8 MB	108 659 1.9 MB

By comparing columns PS and $C2^L_{c\star}$ we can evaluate our proviso in term of number of states it introduces. The results are rather convincing. On seven models out of ten the reductions achieved are very close. For the peer-to-peer protocol and the resource allocation system, the introduction of this additional condition involves an important increase of the graph size. As we mentioned it earlier this fact is not very surprising for the resource allocation system. For the peer-to-peer protocol we will see that our proviso is not adapted to its graph structure.

On the whole, $C2^L_{c\star}$ seems to achieve better reductions than $C2^L_s$. For some models the difference is quite impressive. We can cite the load balancing system or to a lesser extent the production cell. There also are some examples, e.g., Lamport's mutual exclusion algorithm, for which the difference is slighter. We only found two models out of ten for which $C2^L_s$ behaves better: the client-server program and the peer-to-peer communication protocol. For the first one the difference is hardly perceptible. A closer look at the graph structure of the peer-to-peer protocol explains the bad results obtained by $C2^L_{c\star}$ with respect to the $C2^L_s$ proviso. We found out that the situation depicted by the opposite figure often occurred. With the $C2^L_{c\star}$ proviso, when s is processed it may be partially expanded since the fully expanded s'' is between s and s' in the stack. Later, when states $s_1, \ldots, s_n$ are reached, the algorithm expands them fully since s has become red. On the other hand, with the $C2^L_s$ proviso state s may not reach s' without being fully expanded. States $s_1, \ldots, s_n$ can then be partially expanded since they lead to s that has left the stack. This can explain why, on this example, $C2^L_{c\star}$ fully expands much more states than $C2^L_s$.

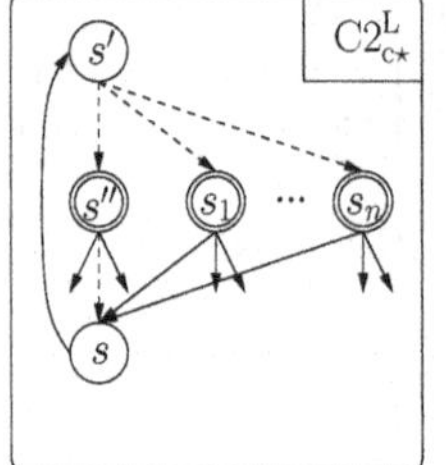

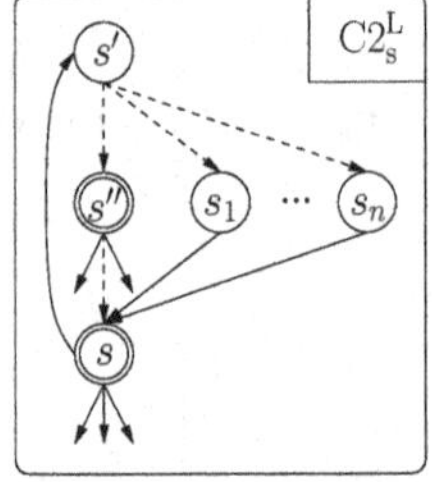

Let us conclude this section with some observations about memory usage. We notice that despite the additional memory it requires per state, $C2^L_{c\star}$ generally outperforms $C2^L_s$. There is only one model - Lamport's algorithm - for which $C2^L_{c\star}$ achieves a better reduction than $C2^L_s$ but consumes more memory. Even in this case, the difference is insignificant. Moreover, as we already pointed it out, memory usage could be optimized by suppressing the expanded attribute of the states that leave the stack.

7 Conclusion

The contribution of this paper is the two new versions of the cycle proviso that resolves the ignoring phenomenon that may arise when applying partial order reduction. The algorithms introduced are simple, easy to implement and can be integrated in any explicit state model checker since they do not rely on any specification language. As a counterpart they assume a DFS exploration of the state space and require the storage of some additional informations. Nevertheless, we have seen that this extra memory consumption is usually compensated by the reduction achieved. A set of experiments revealed that our proviso outperforms state of the art algorithms, like those implemented by the Spin model checker, on many models.

We still plan to perform a more thorough experimentation in order to identify graph structures or classes of models for which our proviso outperforms the others or, on the contrary, is not adapted.

It should also be instructive to compare it with the two-phase algorithm [14] that also seems to outperform the standard proviso on many models - mainly those in which process act in a deterministic way.

At last we have the intuition that the color proviso could be optimized further by weakening the acceptance conditions of a persistent set. When the execution of an action a leads from an orange state o to a red state r the basic question we have to answer is the following one: is there a path leading from r to o or, otherwise stated, is there a path leading from r to a state of the stack? If not, then no cycle of partially expanded states may include the transition $o \xrightarrow{a} r$, and a may be executed without risking of closing an invalid cycle. Such a question can be answered by performing Tarjan's algorithm to detect strongly connected components or one of its variations for LTL model checking [6,10]. However, a comparison of columns PS and $\mathrm{C2}^{\mathrm{L}}_{\mathrm{c}\star}$ of table 1 shows that it is not obvious if this further reduction will compensate the extra memory consumed by Tarjan's algorithm (an additional stack plus at least one integer per state). On several models proviso $\mathrm{C2}^{\mathrm{L}}_{\mathrm{c}\star}$ introduces a very little number of states and it is likely that this will not be the case for these.

Acknowledgements. The authors thank Jean-François Pradat-Peyre for his comments on early drafts of this paper.

References

1. Alur, R., Brayton, R.K., Henzinger, T.A., Qadeer, S., Rajamani, S.K.: Partial-order reduction in symbolic state space exploration. In: Grumberg, O. (ed.) CAV 1997. LNCS, vol. 1254, pp. 340–351. Springer, Heidelberg (1997)
2. Basten, T., Bosnacki, D.: Enhancing partial-order reduction via process clustering. In: Proceedings of the 16th IEEE International Conference on Automated Software Engineering, pp. 245–253. IEEE Computer Society Press, Los Alamitos (2001)
3. Bosnacki, D., Holzmann, G.J.: Improving Spin's partial-order reduction for breadth-first search. In: Godefroid, P. (ed.) Model Checking Software. LNCS, vol. 3639, pp. 91–105. Springer, Heidelberg (2005)
4. Bosnacki, D., Leue, S., Lluch-Lafuente, A.: Partial-order reduction for general state exploring algorithms. In: Valmari, A. (ed.) Model Checking Software. LNCS, vol. 3925, pp. 271–287. Springer, Heidelberg (2006)
5. Clarke, E.M., Grumberg, O., Peled, D.: Model Checking. MIT Press, Cambridge (1999)
6. Couvreur, J.-M.: On-the-fly verification of linear temporal logic. In: Wing, J.M., Woodcock, J.C.P., Davies, J. (eds.) FM 1999. LNCS, vol. 1708, pp. 253–271. Springer, Heidelberg (1999)
7. Edelkamp, S., Leue, S., Lluch-Lafuente, A.: Directed explicit-state model checking in the validation of communication protocols. International Journal on Software Tools for Technology Transfer 5(2-3), 247–267 (2004)

8. Evangelista, S.: High level petri nets analysis with Helena. In: Ciardo, G., Darondeau, P. (eds.) ICATPN 2005. LNCS, vol. 3536, pp. 455–464. Springer, Heidelberg (2005)
9. Flanagan, C., Godefroid, P.: Dynamic partial-order reduction for model checking software. In: Proceedings of the 34th Symposium on Principles of Programming Languages, pp. 110–121. ACM Press, New York (2005)
10. Geldenhuys, J., Valmari, A.: Tarjan's algorithm makes on-the-fly LTL verification more efficient. In: Jensen, K., Podelski, A. (eds.) TACAS 2004. LNCS, vol. 2988, pp. 205–219. Springer, Heidelberg (2004)
11. Godefroid, P. (ed.): Partial-Order Methods for the Verification of Concurrent Systems. LNCS, vol. 1032. Springer, Heidelberg (1996)
12. Holzmann, G.J.: The model checker SPIN. IEEE Transactions on Software Engineering 23(5), 279–295 (1997)
13. Kurshan, R.P., Levin, V., Minea, M., Peled, D., Yenigun, H.: Static partial order reduction. In: Steffen, B. (ed.) ETAPS 1998 and TACAS 1998. LNCS, vol. 1384, pp. 345–357. Springer, Heidelberg (1998)
14. Nalumasu, R., Gopalakrishnan, G.: An efficient partial order reduction algorithm with an alternative proviso implementation. Formal Methods in Systems Design 20(3), 231–247 (2000)
15. Pelánek, R.: BEEM: Benchmarks for explicit model checkers (`http://anna.fi.muni.cz/models/index.html`). In: Proceedings of the 14th International SPIN Workshop. LNCS, Springer, Heidelberg (2007)
16. Peled, D.: All from one, one for all: on model checking using representatives. In: Courcoubetis, C. (ed.) CAV 1993. LNCS, vol. 697, pp. 409–423. Springer, Heidelberg (1993)
17. Peled, D.: Combining partial order reductions with on-the-fly model-checking. In: Dill, D.L. (ed.) CAV 1994. LNCS, vol. 818, pp. 377–390. Springer, Heidelberg (1994)
18. Valmari, A.: A stubborn attack on state explosion. In: Clarke, E., Kurshan, R.P. (eds.) CAV 1990. LNCS, vol. 531, pp. 156–165. Springer, Heidelberg (1991)

Cartesian Partial-Order Reduction

Guy Gueta[1], Cormac Flanagan[2], Eran Yahav[3], and Mooly Sagiv[1]

[1] Tel Aviv University
{guygueta,msagiv}@post.tau.ac.il
[2] University of California at Santa Cruz
cormac@soe.ucsc.edu
[3] IBM T.J. Watson Research Center
eyahav@us.ibm.com

Abstract. Verifying concurrent programs is challenging since the number of thread interleavings that need to be explored can be huge even for moderate programs. We present a *cartesian semantics* that reduces the amount of non-determinism in concurrent programs by delaying unnecessary context switches. Using this semantics, we construct a novel dynamic partial-order reduction algorithm. We have implemented our algorithm and evaluate it on a small set of benchmarks. Our preliminary experimental results show a significant potential saving in the number of explored states and transitions.

1 Introduction

This paper addresses the problem of proving the correctness of a concurrent program, *i.e.*, of showing that all possible program traces satisfy certain correctness properties. We define a *cartesian* partial order reduction technique that allows to safely consider only a subset of these program traces. Our technique can be combined with existing finite state model checkers to yield new algorithms for finite state systems. It can also be combined with abstract interpretation [4] to yield new conservative algorithms for infinite systems. In both cases we expect to obtain significant speedups without sacrificing soundness or completeness. We have implemented a model checker based on cartesian partial order reduction, and provide preliminary experimental results that show a significant reduction in the number of states and transitions explored. Our experiments also compare the performance of our algorithm to the partial order reduction techniques of SPIN [12], and the recent technique of [6]. Compared to these techniques, cartesian partial order reduction saves more states and transitions on most of our example programs.

1.1 Partial Order Reduction

Partial order reduction techniques [8,14,17] combat state explosion by only exploring a representative subset of all possible program traces. In general, however, verifying that a subset of all traces is representative may be as hard as solving the underlying verification problem. Therefore, existing partial order reduction techniques mostly focus on two special cases: "sleep sets" [8, pp. 75] and "persistent sets" [8, pp. 41]. In particular, a

D. Bošnački and S. Edelkamp (Eds.): SPIN 2007, LNCS 4595, pp. 95–112, 2007.

transition is established as persistent by checking for its potential collisions with an infinite future of another thread. Such collisions are traditionally detected via static analysis (e.g., [5]), which may yield coarse results for complicated or pointer-rich code. Alternatively, dynamic partial order reduction [6] infers persistent sets dynamically as part of a stateless search, but is applicable only to cycle-free systems. The algorithm of [5] also infers persistent sets dynamically, but only for thread-local and lock-protected data.

1.2 Main Results

In this paper, we present a new approach for partial order reduction. This approach identifies and exploits a different kind of redundancy than either sleep sets or persistent sets. The strength of our approach stems from the fact that, unlike in persistent sets, where a transition must be checked for conflicts with an *infinite* future of another thread, we only inspect a finite future for collisions, and guarantee safety by exploring both possible extensions at any collision point. In Sec. 4.1, we show that this approach yields significant improvements even over optimal persistent sets. This result is also supported by our preliminary empirical study in Sec. 7.

Our technique is presented as new operational (or execution) semantics that can be applied to both finite and infinite systems. In particular, it can be combined with abstract interpretation in order to conservatively handle infinite traces and infinite state systems.

```
N=12;
boolean A[N,N];
Robot(int x,int y)
 int dirX = 1, dirY = 1;
 while(true)
  A[x,y]=false;
  x += dirX; y += dirY;
  if(x=N-1 or x=0) dirX*=(-1);
  if(y=N-1 or y=0) dirY*=(-1);
  assert(A[x,y]⇒(x=9 or x=2));
  A[x,y]=true;
Main()
 newthread Robot(0,0);
 newthread Robot(4,0);
```

Fig. 1. Two threads implementing robots

A motivating example. The concurrent program of Fig. 1 simulates an arena with two robots which move in different paths. Each robot is represented by a thread that calculates and updates its position in an infinite loop. The program verifies that the robots can meet only at the 9th and the 2nd rows by using an assert instruction (identical to the Java assert). Although this program is quite simple, its state space is relatively large. An attempt to reduce the state space by existing partial order reduction methods is problematic because:

1. Most partial order reduction methods (e.g., persistent sets) are based on a static dependence analysis. Such analyses will fail to establish the independence of the transitions in this program, and therefore yield a poor reduction of the state space.
2. Dynamic partial order reduction [6] requires a stateless search, and so cannot handle examples such as this one, where there are cycles in the state space.
3. The approach of [5] provides limited benefit on this benchmark because it does not contain much thread-local or lock-protected data.

In Sec. 7, we show that our approach saves close to 73% of the transitions that need to be explored for this program.

We present cartesian partial order reduction as an operational (or execution) semantics, which we believe makes it simpler to understand and to establish correctness (see [9]). For example, in contrast to the dynamic analysis of [6], it does not rely on happens-before relations [13]. Also, since it saves intermediate states, it supports cycles and behaves well in transition systems with multiple paths into a single state. Finally, it can be combined with (counter-example driven) abstract interpretation to handle concurrent programs with infinite state spaces (e.g., [19]).

The contributions of this paper can be summarized as follows:

- We present a novel *cartesian semantics* that reduces the nondeterminism in concurrent programs.
- Based on this semantics, we derive a corresponding *cartesian partial order reduction* algorithm that can be used to improve both finite-state model checkers and infinite-state abstract interpreters. Our algorithm identifies dependencies dynamically, avoiding the inherent imprecision of static dependence analyses. It also overcomes the cycle-free restriction of [6], and so is applicable to more programs.
- We present preliminary experimental results showing that our approach can lead to significant savings in the number of explored states and transitions. We also show that our approach is beneficial in cases where traditional partial order reduction methods are unable to reduce the space.

The rest of this paper is organized as follows. Sec. 2 provides an informal overview of our method. Sec. 3 includes basic definitions and notations. Sec. 4 defines our cartesian semantics and shows that it is observationally equivalent to the standard semantics. Sec. 5 and Sec. 6 realize this semantics as a model checking algorithm. Sec. 7 reports initial empirical results on the behavior of this model checking algorithm. Sec. 8 describes related work and Sec. 9 concludes. Appendix A describes the benchmarks from Sec. 7.

2 Overview

This section provides an overview of our approach for the simple concurrent program shown in Fig. 2. The two threads in this program share two variables, x and y, and all variables are initially zero.

Thread 1:	Thread 2:
0: z := 8	0: q := 8
1: x := 1	1: priv := y
2: z := 42	2: q := 42
3: y := 7	3: priv := x
4: w := z	4: nop

Fig. 2. Two threads using shared variables x and y

Whereas traditional model checking would explore all possible interleavings of these two threads, our approach explores only a representative subset of these interleavings, based on the notion of *dependent transitions*. For this program, there are two pairs of dependent transitions: the statement x := 1 (of thread 1) is dependent with `priv` := x (of thread 2); similarly, y := 7 is dependent with `priv` := y. (In this simple example, a static notion of dependence is sufficient. Our approach detects dependencies dynamically, however, thus overcoming the inherent imprecision of statically identified dependencies.)

The key idea of our approach is to find, for each explored state, a sequence of transitions for each thread such that only the *last* transitions in these two sequences are allowed to be dependent (i.e., every pair of transitions other than the last two transitions must be independent). We refer to the two sequences of transitions found for a state as a *cartesian vector* for that state.

For the program's initial state, a suitable cartesian vector is:

T_1: `z:=8; x:=1` T_2: `q:=8; priv:=y; q:=42; priv:=x`

since `z:=8` is independent of all transitions in T_2's sequence, and `x:=1` is independent of all transitions in T_2's sequence except the last. The last transitions `x:=1` and `priv:=x` may be (and indeed are) dependent.

After finding the two sequences, we nondeterministically pick one of them, execute that sequence in its entirety (without a context switch), and then continue exploration from that resulting state. For example, suppose we first execute the sequence T_1: `z:=8; x:=1`. At the resultant state, a suitable cartesian vector is:

T_1: `z:=42; y:=7` T_2: `q:=8; priv:=y`

since only the last pair of transitions are dependent. Again, we nondeterministically pick one of these sequences and execute it entirely, without context switches.

By proceeding in this manner, we eventually explore all possible orderings of the dependent transitions in this program. Fig. 3 shows how our approach explores a representative subset of all possible traces of this program.

As an aside, it is worth noting that the statement `z:=8` in T_1 is a persistent transition, as it has no future collisions with T_2. In principle, this could have allowed exploring only representative traces that begin with `z:=8` as their first step. Establishing that `z:=8` is indeed a persistent transition, however, requires inspection of the future execution of T_2 (which in general, may be infinite). In some cases, the persistence of a transition can be established by a preceding static dependence analysis phase. Like methods based on persistent sets, our approach can also benefit from such static dependence information when it exists. Unlike `z:=8`, the statement `x:=1` is not persistent, as it has a future collision with `priv:=x` in T_2 (as long as `priv:=x` is not executed).

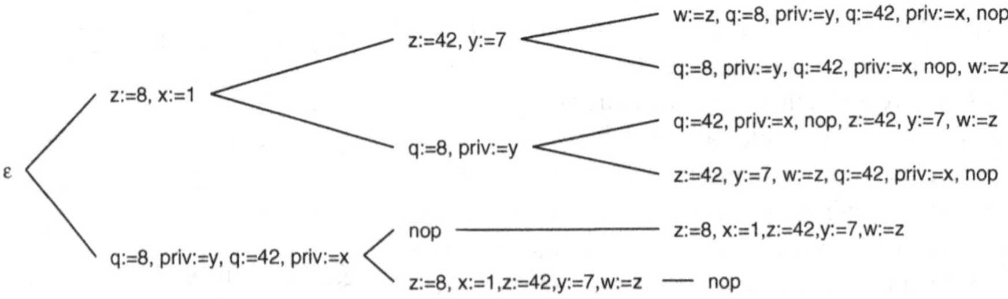

Fig. 3. Exploration of representative traces of the example program of Fig. 2

3 Basic Definitions

We consider a concurrent system composed of a finite set *Threads* of threads. The threads communicate by performing atomic operations on communication objects (e.g. shared variables).

A *state* of the concurrent system consists of the *LocalState* of each thread (the values for all the thread's private variables), and of the *SharedState* (values for all the communication objects). That is, $State = SharedState \times LocalStates$ where $LocalStates = Threads \rightarrow LocalState$. For $ls \in LocalStates$, we write $ls[T \mapsto l]$ to denote the map that is identical to ls except that it maps T to the local state l.

A *transition* moves the system from one state to a subsequent state, by performing an atomic operation of a chosen thread. The transition $t_{T,l}$ of thread T for local state l is defined via a total function: $t_{T,l}$: $SharedState \rightarrow LocalState \times SharedState$. A transition $t_{T,l} \in \tau$ is *enabled* in a state $s = \langle g, ls \rangle$ (where $g \in SharedState$ and $ls \in LocalStates$) if $l = ls(T)$. If $t = t_{T,l}$ is enabled in $s = \langle g, ls \rangle$ and $t(g) = \langle g', l' \rangle$, then we say the execution of t from s produces a unique successor state $s' = \langle g', ls[T \mapsto l'] \rangle$, written $exec(s,t) = s'$ or $s \Rightarrow s'$. We say that *q is reachable from s in the standard semantics* if $s \overset{*}{\Rightarrow} q$.

Notice that in a given state every thread has exactly one enabled transition, therefore no thread can be blocked. This is not restrictive, as blocking or termination of a thread can be modeled by a self loop. Let τ denote the set of all transitions of the system $\tau = \{t_{T,l} | T \in Threads, l \in LocalState\}$.

A *trace* is an infinite sequence $\sigma = s_1, t_1, s_2, t_2, \ldots$ such that for every $i \in \mathbb{N}^+$, $exec(s_i, t_i) = s_{i+1}$. A *trace prefix* is a nonempty (possibly infinite) prefix of a trace, that does not end with a transition. We denote the set of all trace prefixes (of the considered concurrent system) by *Prefix*. A *legal prefix of thread T* is a trace prefix that has at least one transition and all its transitions are executed by thread T.

For $A \in Prefix$, we say that $t \in A$ if t is a transition in A. We denote the last transition of A by $last\_tran(A)$. If there is no transition in A or A is infinite then $last\_tran(A)=\bot$. We denote the first and last states of A by $first(A)$ and $last(A)$ respectively. If A is infinite then $last(A)=\bot$. We denote the set of states in A by $states(A)$.

Our cartesian partial order reduction technique is based on the notion of transitions being *independent*, which essentially means that the order in which these transitions are executed does not matter.

Definition 1 (Independence). *We say that transitions t and t′ of different threads are* independent *if*[1] *for every* $s \in State$: $t, t' \in enabled(s) \implies exec(exec(s,t),t') = exec(exec(s,t'),t)$. *If two transitions of different threads t and t′* are independent, *then we write* $t \parallel t'$, *otherwise we write* $t \nparallel t'$.

4 Cartesian Partial Order Reduction

The standard semantics of multithreaded programs nondeterministically chooses a thread for scheduling right after every transition, but this degree of nondeterminism results in state space explosion. In this section, we present a non-standard *cartesian* semantics that avoids many context switches, while preserving both soundness and completeness.

[1] Sometimes similar definitions require that independent transitions are not disable each other, this is not necessary because two transitions from different threads can never disable each other in the presented concurrent system.

As outlined in Section 2, our cartesian semantics is defined in terms of *cartesian vectors*. Essentially, a cartesian vector (CV) for a state describes a sequence of transitions that each thread can perform without context switches from that state.

Definition 2 (Cartesian Vector). *In a concurrent system with n threads of control, a vector $(p_1, \ldots, p_n) \in$ Prefix^n is a* cartesian vector from a state s *if for every $T_i, T_j \in$ Threads the following holds:*

1. *first*$(p_i) = s$;
2. p_i *is a legal prefix of thread* T_i;
3. $\forall t \in p_i, t' \in p_j : t \not\parallel t' \implies t = last\_tran(p_i) \wedge t' = last\_tran(p_j)$.

Intuitively, this definition implies that if two prefixes are in the same cartesian vector, then only their last transitions may depend on each other. Note that each state may have multiple CVs. In particular, every state has at least the *minimal CV*, which contains exactly one transition for each thread, but many states will also admit larger CVs.

Example 1. For the program of Fig. 2, consider the two trace prefixes from the initial state: p_1 is the sequence `z:=8; x:=1; z:=42` (of thread 1) and p_2 is the sequence `q:=8; priv:=y` (of thread 2). Each prefix accesses different variables, therefore the vector (p_1, p_2) is a cartesian vector for the initial state.

Now consider the longer prefix p'_1: `z:=8; x:=1; z:=42; y:=7`. In this case (p'_1, p_2) is still a cartesian vector because only the last transitions are dependent.

To generate a cartesian vector for any explored state, we assume the existence of an *cartesian function* ϕ: *State* $\rightarrow$ *Prefix*^{n} such that, for every $s \in$ *State*, $\phi(s)$ is a cartesian vector from s. Every state space has at least the *minimal cartesian function*, which simply returns the minimal CV for each state (see Section 5). Section 5 describes an algorithm for computing better CVs.

Given a cartesian function ϕ, we can build a *a cartesian semantics* that uses ϕ as a guide for execution. The intuition behind the cartesian semantics is as follows: when the cartesian semantics starts the execution from a state s it selects a prefix σ from the vector $\phi(s)$ and executes the transitions of σ. When the semantics reaches *last*(σ) (the last state of σ) it starts the procedure again from *last*(σ). If σ is infinite it continues to go over the states of σ forever.

The cartesian semantics generated by ϕ is formalized as two binary relations $\longrightarrow_\phi$ and $\Longrightarrow_\phi$ on states, where $\longrightarrow_\phi$ relates states at the end of prefixes, and is transitively closed, and $\Longrightarrow_\phi$ extends $\longrightarrow_\phi$ to also include intermediate states.

Definition 3. *We define the binary relations $\longrightarrow_\phi$ and $\Longrightarrow_\phi$ on State with respect to a cartesian function ϕ inductively in Fig. 4. Here $\longrightarrow_\phi$ is the relation on final states in which scheduling occurs and $\Longrightarrow_\phi$ is the relation on both final and intermediate states.*

An important property of cartesian semantics is described by the following theorem, which states that the set of local states is identical for the standard semantics and the cartesian semantics. Consequently, if a thread sees a violation of a local safety property (e.g., by using an assert instruction as in Java), then the same thread will see the same violation under the cartesian semantics.

$$s \longrightarrow_\phi s \qquad \text{reflexivity}$$

$$s \longrightarrow_\phi s' \qquad \exists \pi \in \phi(s): s' = \mathit{last}(\pi) \qquad \text{basis}$$

$$\frac{s \longrightarrow_\phi s' \quad s' \longrightarrow_\phi s''}{s \longrightarrow_\phi s''} \qquad \text{transitivity}$$

$$s \Longrightarrow_\phi s \qquad \text{reflexivity}$$

$$s \Longrightarrow_\phi s' \qquad \exists \pi \in \phi(s): s' \in \mathit{states}(\pi) \qquad \text{basis}$$

$$\frac{s \longrightarrow_\phi s' \quad s' \Longrightarrow_\phi s''}{s \Longrightarrow_\phi s''} \qquad \text{pseudo-transitivity}$$

Fig. 4. Inference rules for a cartesian semantics

Theorem 1. *For every cartesian function* ϕ, *if* $s \stackrel{*}{\Rightarrow} \langle g, ls[T \mapsto l]\rangle$ *then there exist* $g' \in \mathit{SharedState}$ *and* $ls' \in \mathit{LocalStates}$ *such that* $s \Longrightarrow_\phi \langle g', ls'[T \mapsto l]\rangle$.

The proof appears in [9].

The situation with global properties is somewhat more complex. To illustrate this situation, consider again the program of Fig. 2, for which we can build a cartesian semantics with the following cartesian vector from the initial state: T_1: `z:=8; x:=1; z:=42`, T_2: `q:=8; priv:=y; q:=42`. This cartesian semantics will never reach a state with $\mathtt{z} = 8$ and $\mathtt{q} = 8$. Therefore, the global property *"there is a state in which* `z`*=8 and* `q`*=8"* cannot be directly proven by using the cartesian semantics. Instead, we can convert this global property into a local property by introducing a dummy thread that merely observes the variables involved in the property (i.e., a thread that reads `z` and `q` in an infinite loop), and then use the cartesian semantics to verify this localized version of the original global property.

4.1 Cartesian Semantics Versus an Optimal Persistent Sets Algorithm

To illustrate the relation between the cartesian semantics and persistent sets, consider the example program shown in Fig. 5 (a). For this example, the program counters of the two threads uniquely define the current value of `x` and `y`, and so we can represent each state simply as a pair of program counters (pc_1, pc_2).

For this program, an optimal persistent sets algorithm will save only one transition, that from the state (3,3), because in any other state, in which the two threads have not terminated, there is a collision between the next step of T1 and a future step of T2 (and, symmetrically, a collision between the next step of T2 and a future step of T1).

In contrast, a suitable cartesian vector for this program's initial state is: $T1$: `x++;x++;x++;` $T2$: `y++;y++;y++`. Hence, the cartesian semantics saves 12 transitions and entirely avoids the states $(1,2)$, $(1,1)$, $(2,1)$, $(2,2)$, as illustrated in

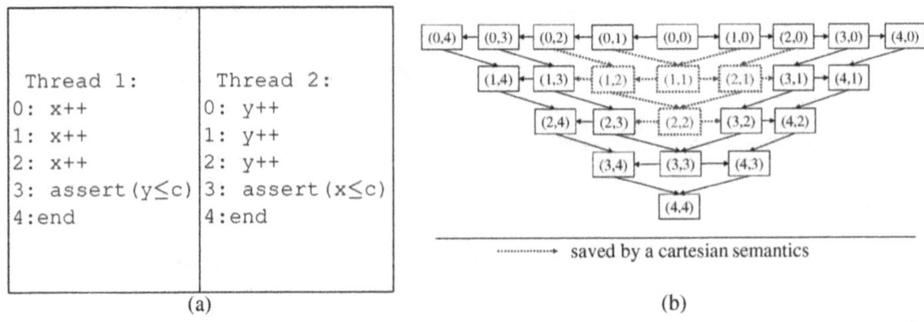

Fig. 5. (a) A simple concurrent program, and (b) reduced state space with a cartesian semantics

Fig. 5 (b). The algorithm we propose in Sec. 6 utilizes this fact and does not explore these states and transitions.

Note that a combination of persistent sets and sleep sets will not reduce these states because sleep sets is not able to reduce states.

5 Computing Cartesian Vectors

In order to build an algorithm based on the cartesian semantics, we need the ability to calculate a cartesian vector for every observed state of the concurrent system. The algorithm `CalcCV` in Fig. 6 computes such CVs. `CalcCV` assumes that the state space is finite or acyclic.

The algorithm starts with a *minimal* CV, where each prefix contains a single transition. Such a vector necessarily satisfies Def. 2. However, for such minimal CVs, the cartesian semantics provides no benefits since it coincides with the standard semantics.

To yield longer prefixes that reduce the explored state space, the algorithm then repeatedly extends this CV with additional transitions, while still satisfying Def. 2. The array `extendable` identifies threads whose prefix can still be extended. Initially, all threads are extendable, and threads are removed from this set as conflicts are detected.

Each iteration of the `while` loop picks some extendable prefix, and tries to extend it with the next transition of that thread. Two complications arise here. First, if the added transition conflicts with the *last* transition of a different prefix, then such conflicts are allowed by Def. 2, but the algorithm records that neither prefix can be further extended.

Second, if a thread is in an infinite loop whose transitions do not conflict with concurrent threads, then that thread has an infinite prefix. To avoid diverging in such situations, the `CalcCV` algorithm avoids extending a prefix once a cycle has been detected. Instead, it marks such prefixes as being *infinite*; these marks are used by the model checking algorithm of the following section.

This cycle check guarantees that, on any finite state system, the `CalcCV` algorithm will eventually terminate, once all threads are exhausted. Indeed, this procedure actually returns a *maximal cycle-free CV*. That is, adding additional transitions to the

```
CalcCV(s) {
  for each i ∈ 1..n do {
    CV[i] = s.NextTrans(s,Tᵢ).nextState(s,Tᵢ);
  }
  extendable = { 1..n }
  for each i,j ∈ 1..n such that i≠j and
      last_tran(CV[i]) is dependent with last_tran(CV[j]) {
    extendable = extendable - {i,j}
  }
  while (extendable≠∅) {        // repeatedly extend CV
    pick any i ∈ extendable
    s = last(CV[i]);
    if( ∃j ≠ i. NextTrans(s,Tᵢ) is dependent
        with some transition in CV[j] (other than the last)) {
      extendable = extendable - {i}
    } else {
      for each j≠i such that NextTrans(s,Tᵢ)
          is dependent with last_tran(CV[j]) {
        extendable = extendable - {i,j}
      }
      if( NextState(s,Tᵢ) in CV[i] and i ∈ extendable ) {
        mark CV[i] as infinite
        extendable = extendable - {i}
      }
      // add this transition to CV
      add NextTrans(s,Tᵢ) and NextState(s,Tᵢ) to CV[i]
    }
  }
  return CV
}
```

Helper functions:
NextTrans(s, T): return $t_{T,l}$ for $s = \langle g, ls[T \mapsto l] \rangle$
NextState(s, T): return exec(s,NextTrans(s,T))

Fig. 6. Algorithm for calculating cartesian vectors.

result of `CalcCV(s)` yields an CV that is either invalid or contains cycles that re-visit previously-explored states.

Note that the order in which our algorithm tries to extend prefixes is arbitrary, and different exploration orders can lead to different resulting CVs. Our implementation of the algorithm uses a round-robin exploration (we did not test the effect of other exploration orders).

The correctness of the algorithm is established in the following lemma, which holds for any finite state system:

Lemma 1. *For every state s,* `CalcCV`*(s) terminates and returns a valid CV.*

The proof appears in [9].

Example 2. The following steps describe an execution of CalcCV from the initial state of the program shown in Fig. 2.

1. At the beginning, both threads are extendable, and each prefix contains only the program's initial state, where both threads are about to execute line 0.
2. T_1 executes `z:=8`, T_2 executes `q:=8`, and no conflicts are detected.
3. T_1 executes `x:=1`, T_2 executes `priv:=y`, and no conflicts are detected.
4. T_1 executes `z:=42`, T_2 executes `q:=42`, and still no conflicts are detected.

5a. The next transition of T_1 is `y:=7`, which conflicts with the previously-executed transition `priv:=y` of T_2, so this thread is no longer extendable.

5b. The next transition of T_2 is `priv:=x`, which conflicts with the previously-executed transition `x:=1` of T_1, so this thread is also no longer extendable.

At this point, the extendable set is empty, so `CalcCV` returns the cartesian vector: T_1: `z:=8; x:=1; z:=42;` T_2: `q:=8; priv:=y; q:=42;`.

Since CalcCV is called for each visited state, a key concern is the running time of this procedure. For our intended application of software model checking, we assume that each transition accesses at most one memory location, and two transitions of different threads are dependent only if they access the same memory location and that at least one of these accesses is a write. Under these assumptions, it is fairly straightforward to implement CalcCV such that its running time is proportional to the size of the resulting CV (that is, to the sum of the lengths of the prefixes in this CV). In particular, each step of the implementation either extends CV or reduces the extendable set.

6 Model Checking Algorithm

Fig. 7 presents a state exploration or model checking algorithm that explores all reachable states of the cartesian semantics, using the subroutine CalcCV to compute cartesian vectors for each reached state. Notice that only the last states of finite prefixes are added to WorkSet (according to the cartesian semantics the exploration does not have to continue from infinite prefixes).

Notice that CalcCV stops only before or after transitions that participate in a memory contention (only such transitions can be detected as dependent), therefore the reduced state space does not contain a state in which two threads (or more) are at the middle of sections without memory contentions. Therefore we can simply identify a class of states that are not present in the reduced state space. It is worth mentioning that in many large programs most of the code does not involve memory contention, therefore many states are saved by our method.

A simple variant of this algorithm executes a few instances of CalcCV in parallel (on different processors). This variant utilizes the fact that CalcCV runs independently on one processor without being affected by what happening on the other processors. Such variant can efficiently utilize a few processors and reduces the running time of the model checking, especially when the calculated CVs are long. We present the pseudo-code of this simple variant in Fig. 8, and evaluate its performance in our experiments.

```
modelCheck(s0) {
  WorkSet = {s0}
  CoveredSet = ∅
  while WorkSet is not empty {
    select and remove s from WorkSet
    if not member(s,CoveredSet) {
      CoveredSet = CoveredSet ∪ { s }
      CV = CalcCV(s)
      for each prefix ∈ CV {
        verify local properties in states(prefix)
        if prefix is not marked as infinite
          WorkSet = WorkSet ∪ { last(prefix) }
    }}}}
```

Fig. 7. A cartesian model checking algorithm based on CalcCV

```
InitThread(s0)
  WorkSet = {s0}
  CoveredSet = ∅
  ActiveThreads = 0
  start a worker thread for each processor
  wait until ( (WorkSet is empty) and (ActiveThreads=0) )
  terminate all worker threads

WorkerThread()
  begin:
  lock {
    if( WorkSet is empty ) goto begin
    ActiveThreads++
    select and remove s from WorkSet
    if member(s,CoveredSet)
      ActiveThreads--
      goto begin
    CoveredSet = CoveredSet ∪ { s }
  }
  CV = CalcCV(s)
  for each prefix ∈ CV
    verify local properties in states(prefix)
    if prefix is not marked as infinite
      lock { WorkSet = WorkSet ∪ { last(prefix) } }
  lock { ActiveThreads-- }
  goto begin
```

Fig. 8. A concurrent variant of the cartesian model checking algorithm

7 Experimental Evaluation

In this section, we describe preliminary experimental results comparing the cartesian algorithm to other exploration algorithms.

Table 1. Number of stored states, transitions, and running time (milliseconds.) of the cartesian and standard exploration algorithms for our benchmarks. In this table, *Conc Time* indicates the running time of the concurrent variant of the cartesian algorithm.

	Standard algorithm			Cartesian algorithm				Percentage of Saving			
Benchmark	**States**	**Transitions**	**Time (ms)**	**States**	**Transitions**	**Time (ms)**	**Conc Time (ms)**	**States**	**Transitions**	**Time**	**Conc Time**
SharedPtr	32131	64262	266	418	12785	47	32	98.7	80.1	82.3	31.9
SharedArray	2276	4552	16	132	1648	0	0	94.2	63.8	99	0
2 Robots	4877	9754	109	56	2635	15	15	98.9	73	86.2	0
3 Robots	326759	980277	1206422	56	6387	62	31	100	99.3	99	50
File System (1 Threads)	9	8	0	N/A	N/A	N/A	N/A	N/A	N/A	N/A	0
File System (2 Threads)	81	144	0	1	16	0	0	98.8	88.9		0
File System (3 Threads)	729	1944	16	1	24	0	0	99.9	98.8	99	0
File System (4 Threads)	6561	23328	437	1	32	0	0	100	99.9	99	0
File System (5 Threads)	59049	262440	24047	1	40	0	0	100	100	99	0
File System (6 Threads)	531441	2834352	2567703	1	48	0	0	100	100	99	0
File System (7 Threads)				1	56	0	0				0
File System (8 Threads)				1	64	0	0				0
File System (9 Threads)				1	72	0	0				0
File System (10 Threads)				1	80	0	0				0
File System (11 Threads)				1	88	0	0				0
File System (12 Threads)				1	96	0	0				0
File System (13 Threads)				1	104	0	0				0
File System (14 Threads)				10	1026	62	32				48.4
File System (15 Threads)				100	10120	563	203				63.9
File System (16 Threads)				1000	99800	5968	2078				65.2
File System (17 Threads)				10000	984000	64204	23000				64.2
Indexer (1 Threads)	5	4	0	N/A	N/A	N/A	N/A	N/A	N/A	N/A	N/A
Indexer (2 Threads)	25	40	0	1	8	0	0	96	80		0
Indexer (3 Threads)	125	300	0	1	12	0	0	99.2	96		0
Indexer (4 Threads)	625	2000	0	1	16	0	0	99.8	99.2		0
Indexer (5 Threads)	3125	12500	47	1	20	0	0	100	99.8	99	0
Indexer (6 Threads)	15625	75000	641	1	24	0	0	100	100	99	0
Indexer (7 Threads)	78125	437500	15297	1	28	0	0	100	100	99	0
Indexer (8 Threads)	390625	2500000	494687	1	32	0	0	100	100	99	0
Indexer (9 Threads)				1	36	0	0				0
Indexer (10 Threads)				1	40	0	0				0
Indexer (11 Threads)				1	44	0	0				0
Indexer (12 Threads)				9	394	16	16				0
Indexer (13 Threads)				81	3528	187	79				57.8
Indexer (14 Threads)				729	31590	1813	625				65.5
Indexer (15 Threads)				6561	282852	17172	6250				63.6
Indexer (16 Threads)				59049	2532546	191421	82859				56.7
2 Philosophers	11	22	0	9	28	0	0	18.2	-27.3		0
3 Philosophers	36	108	0	27	174	0	0	25	-61.1		0
4 Philosophers	119	476	0	94	750	0	0	21	-57.6		0
5 Philosophers	393	1965	16	295	2984	31	31	24.9	-51.9	-93.8	0
6 Philosophers	1298	7788	172	942	11233	187	156	27.4	-44.2	-8.7	16.6
7 Philosophers	4287	30009	1766	2955	41091	1187	969	31.1	-36.9	32.8	18.4
8 Philosophers	14159	113272	29594	9212	145717	11609	11141	34.9	-28.6	60.8	4
9 Philosophers	46764	420876	383219	28675	509218	132078	138703	38.7	-21	65.5	-5
CMIS C=2 N=8	16430	115010	813	51	1627	32	15	99.7	98.6	96.1	53.1
CMIS C=4 N=16	1014131	7098917	10294344	51	3091	47	31	100	100	99	34
CMIS C=8 N=32				51	8035	156	62				60.3
CMIS C=16 N=64				51	25987	735	281				61.8
CMIS C=32 N=128				51	94147	4875	1719				64.7
CMIS C=64 N=256				51	359491	36531	17672				51.6
CMIS C=128 N=256				6	100336	12141	12250				-0.9
CMIS C=127 N=255				11	221954	27860	27328				1.9

We compared the number of states, transitions, and CPU time measured by a standard model checking algorithm (exhaustive exploration without partial order reduction) and by the cartesian algorithm of Fig. 7. The comparison was done for a few benchmark programs, and the results are reported in Table 1. The number of states mentioned in the results is the number of states that the algorithm stores during its execution (i.e. the size of CoveredSet when the algorithm terminates). An empty cell in the table indicates that the algorithm ran out of memory. Additional results and details about the benchmarks can be found in the appendix.

In order to check dependency between transitions, the implementation of the cartesian algorithm conservatively assumes that two transitions are dependent if they have conflicting memory accesses (i.e., one writes and the other reads or writes from the same location). During the execution of CalcCV, the algorithm remembers the memory locations accessed by each thread (in the current CalcCV execution) and uses this information for determining dependency between transitions.

The benchmarks were also tested on SPIN [11], but its partial order reduction algorithm was unable to reduce the state space of any of the benchmarks (i.e. SPIN's partial order reduction did not affect the numbers of states and transitions).

Some of the acyclic benchmarks were tested on the dynamic partial order reduction algorithm from [6] (hereafter, referred to as FG). Because FG is stateless we only compared the number of transitions. For some acyclic benchmarks, the cartesian algorithm executed much fewer transitions than FG, even when FG was combined with sleep sets [8] (e.g. for the SharedArray benchmark, the cartesian algorithm executed only 1648 transitions whereas FG executed more than 10^7 transitions). For some other acyclic benchmarks such as FileSystem, FG executed less transitions than the cartesian algorithm, but in these cases the differences were less significant.

We also implemented the concurrent variant of the cartesian algorithm mentioned in Sec. 6 and run the benchmarks on it using a machine with 4 processors. In some cases (Indexer, FileSystem, CMIS) it saved around 60% of the running time (comparing to the sequential variant).

8 Related Work

A key limitation in model checking concurrent software systems [2] is the notorious state explosion problem. One approach to this problem is to reduce the size of the state space via *abstraction* [4] and abstraction refinement [1,10,3] techniques. A complementary approach is to only explore a (sufficiently large) fraction of the system's state space, via *partial order reduction* techniques.

One standard partial order reduction technique is based on *persistent (or stubborn) sets* [18,8]. This technique computes a subset of the enabled transitions in each visited state, and only explores those transitions. This computed subset is called a *persistent set*, and contains sufficiently many transitions to guarantee certain completeness properties. Our approach can yield improvements even over the most precise persistent sets.

A traditional limitation of persistent sets is that they are typically obtained from a static analysis of the code, via algorithms such as those described in [8]. Hence, the approximations inherent in any static analysis can result in coarse persistent sets, particularly for pointer-rich code. Our algorithm overcomes this limitation by detecting conflicts between transitions dynamically, instead of statically.

The approach of dynamic partial order reduction [6] computes persistent sets on-the-fly by detecting conflicts dynamically, but only performs a stateless search, and extending it to a stateful search has proven quite difficult. In contrast, the algorithm of this paper performs a stateful search, which provides two key improvements over [6]: (1) it can handle systems with cycles; and (2) even on cycle-free systems, storing states avoids repeated explorations of the same parts of the state space.

A number of recent techniques have considered various kinds of *exclusive access predicates* for shared variables that specify synchronization disciplines such as "this variable is only accessed when holding its protecting lock" or "this variable is local to this thread" [15,16,5,7]. These exclusive access predicates can be leveraged to dynamically infer persistent transitions, and so reduce the search space. At the same time, exclusive access predicates can be verified or inferred during reduced state-space exploration. These techniques of [5,16] in particular have demonstrated significant performance improvements for the common cases of thread-local and lock-protected data. However, these techniques are less effective when the synchronization discipline changes during program execution, such as when an object is protected by different variables at different stages during the program's execution.

9 Conclusions

We have presented a new approach *Cartesian* approach to partial order reduction that can be used by model checkers and abstract interpreters. We are encouraged by the empirical results that show improvement over prior approaches for some benchmarks.

References

1. Ball, T., Rajamani, S.: The SLAM Toolkit. In: Berry, G., Comon, H., Finkel, A. (eds.) CAV 2001. LNCS, vol. 2102, pp. 260–264. Springer, Heidelberg (2001)
2. Clarke, E.M., Grumberg, O., Peled, D.A.: Model Checking. MIT Press, Cambridge (1999)
3. Corbett, J.C., Dwyer, M.B., Hatcliff, J., Laubach, S., Robby, C.S.P., Zheng, H.: Bandera: Extracting Finite-State Models from Java Source Code. In: Proceedings of the 22nd International Conference on Software Engineering (2000)
4. Cousot, P., Cousot, R.: Systematic design of program analysis frameworks. In: Symp. on Principles of Prog. Languages, pp. 269–282. ACM Press, New York, NY (1979)
5. Dwyer, M.B., Hatcliff, J., Prasad, V.R., Robby,: Exploiting Object Escape and Locking Information in Partial Order Reduction for Concurrent Object-Oriented Programs. Formal Methods in System Design 25(2–3) (2004)
6. Flanagan, C., Godefroid, P.: Dynamic Partial-Order Reduction for Model Checking Software. In: Proceedings of POPL'2005, 32nd ACM Symposium on Principles of Programming Languages, Long beach (January 2005)
7. Flanagan, C., Qadeer, S.: Transactions for Software Model Checking. In: Proceedings of the Workshop on Software Model Checking, pp. 338–349 (June 2003)
8. Godefroid, P.: Partial-Order Methods for the Verification of Concurrent Systems. LNCS, vol. 1032. Springer, Heidelberg (1996)
9. Gueta, G., Flanagan, C., Yahav, E., Sagiv, M.: Cartesian partial-order reduction. Technical Report TA-CS-2007-052, School of Computer Science, Tel Aviv University (2007) Available at `http://www.cs.tau.ac.il/~guygueta/Cartesian.pdf`

10. Henzinger, T., Jhala, R., Majumdar, R., Sutre, G.: Lazy Abstraction. In: Proc. of the 29th ACM Symposium on Principles of Programming Languages, Portland, pp. 58–70. ACM Press, New York (2002)
11. Holzmann, G.J.: The SPIN Model Checker: Primer and Reference Manual
12. Holzmann, G.J., Peled, D.: An improvement in formal verification. In: Proceedings of the 7th IFIP WG6 International Conference on Formal Description Techniques VII, pp. 197–211. Chapman & Hall Ltd, London, UK (1995)
13. Lamport, L.: Time, clocks, and the ordering of events in a distributed system. Commun. ACM 21(7), 558–565 (1978)
14. Peled, D.: All from one, one for all: on model checking using representatives. In: Courcoubetis, C. (ed.) CAV 1993. LNCS, vol. 697, pp. 409–423. Springer, Heidelberg (1993)
15. Stoller, S.D.: Model-Checking Multi-Threaded Distributed Java Programs. International Journal on Software Tools for Technology Transfer 4(1), 71–91 (2002)
16. Stoller, S.D., Cohen, E.: Optimistic Synchronization-Based State-Space Reduction. In: Garavel, H., Hatcliff, J. (eds.) ETAPS 2003 and TACAS 2003. LNCS, vol. 2619, pp. 489–504. Springer, Heidelberg (2003)
17. Valmari, A.: Stubborn sets for reduced state space generation. In: 10th Conference on Applications and Theory of Petri Nets, pp. 491–515 (1991)
18. Valmari, A.: Stubborn sets for reduced state space generation. In: Rozenberg, G. (ed.) Advances in Petri Nets 1990. LNCS, vol. 483, pp. 491–515. Springer, Heidelberg (1991)
19. Yahav, E.: Verifying safety properties of concurrent Java programs using 3-valued logic. In: Proc. Symp. on Principles of Prog. Languages, pp. 27–40. ACM Press, New York (2001)

A Benchmarks Description

In this appendix we describe the benchmarks.

A.1 Robots

The Robots example shown in Fig. 1. This program simulates an arena with a number of robots that move in different paths, where each robot is represented by a separate thread. Approaches based on static dependence will not be able to determine when a collision is possible, and would yield a poor reduction of the state space. The dynamic partial order reduction of [6] is not applicable for this benchmark, as its statespace contains cycles.

For this benchmark, we consider two configurations: one that uses 2 robots, as shown in Fig. 1, and one with 3 robots in which a new robot is added and set to start from position $(7, 0)$.

Table 1 shows that for both configurations (2 robots, and 3 robots), the cartesian algorithm provides a significant improvement over the standard semantics.

A.2 CMIS

CMIS is a concurrent sorting algorithm which is composed from Merge-Sort and Insert-Sort, its pseudo code appears in Fig. 9. In Table 1, C indicates an array length from which CMIS uses a sequential Insert-Sort (see pseudo code), N indicates the length of the array. In all the cases the input was an array sorted in a descending order (CMIS

```
ConcurrentMergeInsertSort(A, p, r) {
  if( r-p+1 ≤ C )
    InsertSort(A, p, r);
  else {
    q = ⌊(p+r)/2⌋ ;
    run ConcurrentMergeInsertSort(A, p, q) on a child thread ;
    ConcurrentMergeInsertSort(A, q+1, r);
    wait for child thread termination ;
    Merge(A, p, q, r);
  }
  Assert(A is sorted) ;
}

InsertSort(A, p, r) {
  for j = p+1 to r {
    key = A[j];
    i = j - 1 ;
    while ((i > p-1) and (A[i] > key)) {
      A[i+1] = A[i];
      i--;
    }
    A[i+1] = key ;
  }
}

Merge(A, p, q, r) {
  for i = p to r
    draft[i] = A[i] ;
  i = p; j = q+1; k = p;
  while ((i ≤ q) and (j ≤ r)) {
    if( draft[i] ≤ draft[j] )
      A[k++] = draft[i++];
    else
      A[k++] = draft[j++];
  }
  while (i ≤ q)
    A[k++] = draft[i++];
}
```

Fig. 9. The CMIS (Concurrent-Merge-Insert-Sort) benchmark

sorted the array in an ascending order). Our approach does not deal with dynamic thread creation therefore we simulated the dynamic threads creation by using threads that wait on a loop until they receive an appropriate request.

A.3 SharedArray

The code of the SharedArray benchmark is shown in Fig. 10. In this program, there are two threads writing to a shared array in a loop. Each of the threads accesses different

```
N = 64;
int A[N];
int idx0 = 0, idx1 = 1,counter = 1;
Thread i (i = 0,1)
  While( idxi < N) atomic {
      A[idxi]=counter + idxi;
      idxi += 2 ;
  }
  atomic {
    counter = counter + 1 + idx1-i ;
    assert(counter ≤ 2*N + 4) ;
  }
```

Fig. 10. SharedArray Example

portions of the array. In every iteration of the loop each thread reads the value of a shared variable *counter* and updates the array using its value. After finishing the loop each thread updates the value of the shared variable *counter*. The instructions within the atomic blocks (marked by the keyword atomic) are executed together atomically.

Partial order reduction algorithms based on persistent sets will not be able to reduce the state space of this program. This is due to the fact that in every state in which the two threads are still running, every persistent set contains all enabled transitions.

A.4 SharedPtr

The code for the SharedPtr benchmark is shown in Fig. 11. In this benchmark, two threads are performing updates to memory locations identified using a shared pointer p.

The behavior of this example is similar to that of the SharedArray example, in the sense that the threads sometimes access disjoint parts of memory, but in a way that a static partial order reduction approach will not be able to detect.

```
N = 100;
int x=3, y=4, c1=0, c2=0
int* p
Thread 1
  p = &y;
  for(int i=0; i < N; i++) c1 += x;
  *p += 3;
  assert(3 ≤ x,y ≤ 9);
Thread 2
  p = &x;
  for(int i=0; i < N; i++) c2 += y;
  *p += 2;
  assert(3 ≤ x,y ≤ 9);
```

Fig. 11. SharedPtr Example

```
const int size = 128;
const int max = 4;
int[size] table;
int m = 0, w, h;
Thread tid
  while (true) {
    w := getmsg();
    h := hash(w);
    while (cas(table[h],0,w) == false) {
      h := (h+1) % size;
    }
  }
  int getmsg() {
    if (m < max ) {
      return (++m) * 11 + tid;
    } else {
      exit(); // terminate
    }
  }
  int hash(int w) {
    return (w * 7) % size;
  }
```

Fig. 12. Indexer Example (from [6])

A.5 Indexer

This example is taken from [6]. This example has no cycles and behaves well with a persistent sets algorithm. In this benchmark, there are no collisions between the threads when the number of threads is less than 12. As a result, the cartesian algorithm is able to considerably reduce the number of transitions when using up to 11 threads. In contrast, the standard exploration suffers from exponential increase in the number of transitions. Notice that in some cases the number of stored states is 1, this is reasonable because in these cases the threads have no conflicts between them.

A.6 File System

This example is also taken from [6]. It uses up to 17 threads that communicate via a shared memory. The properties of this example are similar to those of the Indexer example.

A.7 Dining Philosophers

This example is the classical dining philosophers program.

On-the-Fly Dynamic Dead Variable Analysis

Joel P. Self and Eric G. Mercer

Department of Computer Science
Brigham Young University
Provo, Utah, USA

Abstract. State explosion in model checking continues to be the primary obstacle to widespread use of software model checking. The large input ranges of variables used in software is the main cause of state explosion. As software grows in size and complexity, the problem only becomes worse. As such, model checking research into data abstraction as a way of mitigating state explosion has become more and more important. Data abstractions aim to reduce the effect of large input ranges. This work focuses on a static program analysis technique called dead variable analysis. The goal of dead variable analysis is to discover variable assignments that are not used. When applied to model checking, this allows us to ignore the entire input range of dead variables and thus reduce the size of the explored state space.

Prior research into dead variable analysis for model checking does not make full use of dynamic run-time information that is present during model checking. We present an algorithm for intraprocedural dead variable analysis that uses dynamic run-time information to find more dead variables on-the-fly and further reduce the size of the explored state space. We introduce a definition for the maximal state space reduction possible through an on-the-fly dead variable analysis and then show that our algorithm produces a maximal reduction in the absence of non-determinism.

1 Introduction

Model checking is a way to automatically verify properties of a system [13, 4, 17, 11, 10]. The model of a system is a directed graph containing a set of vertices and a set of edges. In explicit state model checking, vertices represent states of the system and edges represent transitions between states. When used to verify software, model checking can discover subtle errors in deep execution traces that are easily passed over in traditional software testing techniques. Since model checking is a form of formal verification, the output of a model checker is a proof that the system does or does not satisfy the specified property.

When model checking software, a state is a snapshot of the program at a single program location. The state contains the program location and the values of all of the variables in the program. The program is used to generate successor states given a current state. Every state generated is stored in a *Visited* set, and

D. Bošnački and S. Edelkamp (Eds.): SPIN 2007, LNCS 4595, pp. 113–130, 2007.

every newly generated state is checked against the set to determine if the state is new. A breadth-first or depth-first search is used to explore the entire state space and ultimately verify or disprove the specified property. A single state may have multiple successors due to non-determinism in the program. Non-determinism represents input from an outside source such as user input from a keyboard or input from a sensor. The model checker must generate successor states that represent all possible input values in order to explore all possible scenarios when running the program. Since the size of the reachable state space is exponential in the branching factor of the model, the state space becomes large rather quickly, even for programs with relatively few variables. The rapid growth of the state space is called the state explosion problem.

An important technique for mitigating the state explosion problem in verification is data abstraction [5]. Data abstraction reduces the size of the generated state space by abstracting away data values; in other words, it removes variables from the state to make their values unconstrained. Variables that receive values from a non-deterministic input often have such large domains that removing even a single variable can greatly reduce the effect of state explosion.

Dead variable analysis is a type of data abstraction that determines when the values of variables do not matter in order to simplify a program state. Variables can be either live or dead with respect to a program location. A variable is live at a location when its current value is used. A variable is dead at a location when it is redefined before it is used in some future location, or it is not used in any future location. When a variable is dead at a program location its value does not affect the behavior of the program since it is not used. *Static dead variable analysis* (SDVA) has been implemented in several model checkers including SPIN, XMC, Bandera, IF, and Bebop [12,7,6,3,2,18,16]. When SDVA discovers that a variable is dead at a location, it becomes unnecessary for the model checker to track values for that variable.

Fig. 1(a) is a simple program with labeled locations that we use to illustrate how SDVA helps reduce the cost of state exploration. We must assume that any possible value may be passed into the function; however, for the sake of brevity, we only consider four input patterns. The reachable state space of the program from the four input patterns is shown in Fig. 1(b). There are 13 states in the state space of this program when no dead variable analysis is used. SDVA marks c dead at locations **2**, **3**, and **4**, since c is reassigned at location **4**, and it marks b dead at location **3**, since b is reassigned at location **3**. We can coalesce multiple states into a single state by ignoring dead variables since the values of these variables do not matter. For example, the states s_1 and s_2 in Fig. 1(b) become equivalent when the dead variable c is ignored. We combine these into one state in Fig. 2(a). Similar reductions to Fig. 1(b) are applied to states (s_5, s_6), (s_7, s_8), and (s_{10}, s_{11}). The final reduced state space from SDVA is shown in Fig. 2(a).

SDVA, being a static analysis technique, does not use any of the dynamic run-time information available during model checking. For this reason, SDVA is conservative and only considers a variable dead if its current value is not used on any future paths including infeasible paths that are unreachable in any

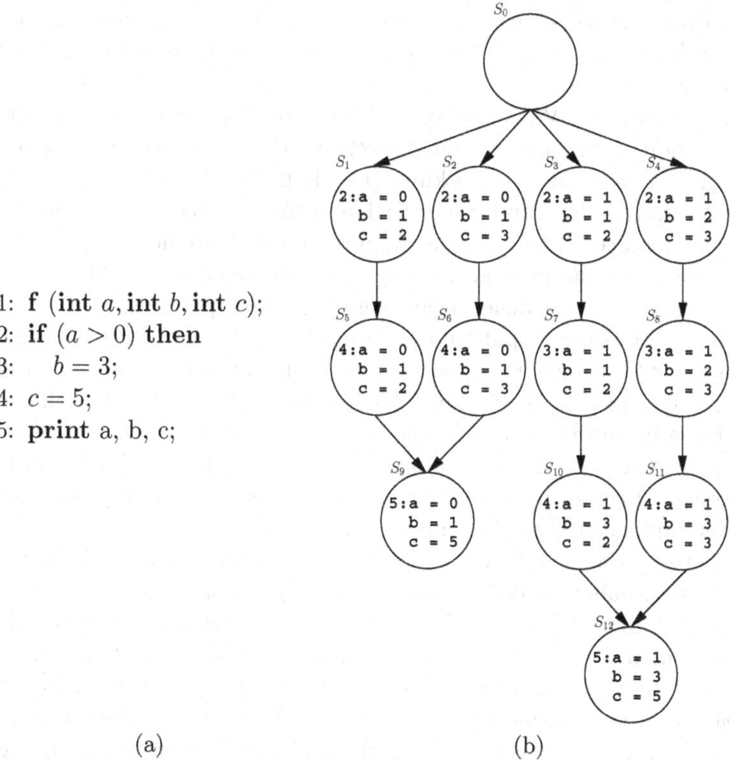

Fig. 1. A simple program and its reachable state space. (a) A simple program with variables dead at several locations. (b) The reachable state space of the program in (a).

program execution. Additionally, when there is a pending pointer dereference in the program, the variable referenced cannot be known until run-time. Variable aliasing in general cannot be computed statically; therefore, in order to be safe, SDVA must assume all variables could be used at the pointer dereference and declare all variables as live. These two issues cause the SDVA to not find the **true** dead variable set for a state; however, run-time information that is readily available during model checking resolves memory aliasing allowing variables to be positively marked as live and other variables to be marked as dead. Run-time information also reveals the exact path taken through the program. A dead variable analysis that uses run time information during model checking is able to discover a more precise dead variable set for each state and possibly generate smaller state spaces. The use of run-time information is the idea behind *dynamic dead variable analysis* (DDVA).

An example of the effects of DDVA can be seen in Fig. 2(b). The state space is generated when variable valuations in addition to program location are used to refine dead variable analysis. When the variable a is greater than zero, it causes the program to go to location **3** which makes b dead at locations **2** and **3**. The refined path allows s_3 and s_4 from Fig. 2(a) to be represented with just a single state, s_3, in Fig. 2(b).

Recent work in DDVA labels variables live or dead dependent on specific future execution paths and is tied directly to the reachable state space of the system [14]. During model checking, [14] simulates single procedure programs forward to discover a partial future path and the variables that are referenced at pointer dereferences. The paths in the program that are not taken in the future are removed from the program. A dead variable analysis on this new program marks more variables as dead because of the missing paths; however, the DDVA algorithm requires user input to determine how far forward to simulate the program in order to achieve the greatest reduction in the state space. Without the correct input value, the algorithm achieves little to no reduction with a substantial increase in verification time and memory used. It is not possible to know what the best explore depth is *a priori* without further analysis. Additionally, the algorithm does not handle programs with loops and non-determinism making DDVA as implemented in [14] impractical to use.

This paper presents a definition of the maximal state space reduction possible from a dead variable analysis and a new algorithm for intraprocedural dynamic dead variable analysis that yields a maximal reduction on single procedure programs with no non-determinism. By triggering analyses only after each trace has been fully determined and by updating states in the reachable state space with new dead variable information, our new algorithm discovers the true set of dead variables for any state. Without non-determinism, the future of an execution path is fixed; however, with non-determinism, the future path is uncertain. A single state can have a future that causes one of its variables be dead and another future where that same variable is live. Variables that become dead after a point of non-determinism cannot be reliably marked as dead before the point of non-determinism without first analyzing the entire reachable state space. In the presence of non-determinism, our algorithm yields the maximum state space reduction that is possible from an on-the-fly dead variable analysis.

2 Related Work

There are currently several relevant works on dead variable analysis in model checking known to us. The work in [3] focuses primarily on showing that live variable analysis defines an equivalence stronger than bisimulation. Static live variable analysis comes at virtually no cost compared to the cost of model checking and is completely orthogonal to other techniques used to attack the state explosion problem [3, 18, 16]. Although SDVA is relatively quick, it only considers program locations in its analysis and can only discover unconditionally dead variables. An analysis that makes use of variable valuations available during model checking, in addition to program locations, can determine more precise paths through the program and find variables that are conditionally dead.

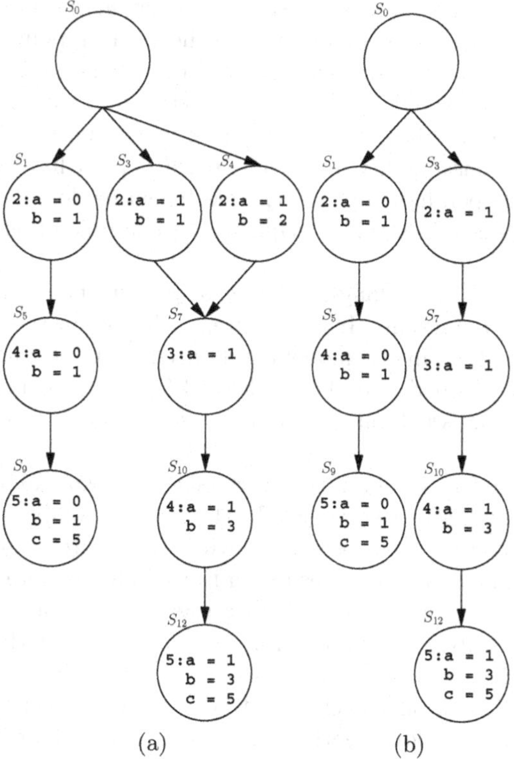

Fig. 2. Two state spaces showing the results of SDVA and DDVA. (a) A reduction of several states from using SDVA. (b) The additional reduction of one state from using DDVA.

The dynamic dead variable analysis in [14] uses run time information to resolve conditional branches and pointer dereferences. In order to do this, the DDVA stops the model checker just before conditional branch points and pointer dereferences are processed and runs a forward analysis. The forward analysis determines a partial path that the program takes in the future and resolves memory aliasing. The forward analysis is terminated either at a user-specified explore depth or at a state with a non-deterministic assignment to a variable. Having a partial path through the program text allows the analysis to use program locations and variable valuations to more precisely determine dead variable sets. The algorithm prunes off portions of the program that are now known to be unreachable given the observed program locations and variable valuations. The normal SDVA is then run on this reduced program to find more precise sets of dead variables.

Although the DDVA in [14] may find more precise sets of dead variables than SDVA, it presents two issues. The first issue is that there is no correlation between explore depths and state space reductions; and the second issue is that no explore depth can give a true dead variable set in the presence of looping structures. The first issue is a consequence of the starting point for each forward analysis and the fact that states cannot have their dead variable sets updated once they have been stored in the *Visited* set. The algorithm does not run a new forward analysis until the model checker runs past the end of the last forward analysis. Consequently, smaller explore depths have shorter analyses but the analyses happen more often. Whereas bigger explore depths have longer analyses, but the analyses are less frequent. An example of such a situation is illustrated in Fig. 3.

Fig. 3 demonstrates how longer explore depths do not always translate to greater state space reductions. In the figure, each box on the left represents a state in the search stack in the model checker. Of particular note are states 10 and 18, where a is defined and then redefined such that a is dead from state 10 to state 17. The forward analysis needs to reach state 18 to discover that a is dead. The way the algorithm is designed, it can only declare a dead in the window of states generated after the start of the forward analysis and before the next non-deterministic assignment. In the forward analysis patterns on the right, each empty rectangle represents the window of states explored by a single forward analysis. The analysis pattern with the smaller explore depth finds that a is dead on the second analysis, and since the analysis starts at state 10, can declare a dead in states 10 through 17. The pattern with the bigger explore depth also finds that a is dead on its second analysis, but since the analysis starts at state 17, it can only declare a dead at state 17; thus, it is impossible to know *a priori* the explore depth to produce the best state space reduction without further analysis of the program structure.

The second issue with the DDVA in [14] is that the true dead variable set for a state is not discovered no matter what explore depth is used. Once states are generated and stored in the *Visited* set they cannot have their dead variable sets updated even if more dead variables are discovered. Additionally, the program text is used for DVA. In the presence of loops, the program text conservatively captures all paths. It has no way to unroll loops and find the exact path taken. These limitations prevent the algorithm from achieving the maximal state space reduction. The goal of this work is to formally define the maximal reduction from DDVA and present an on-the-fly algorithm for computing it.

3 DVA Maximal Reduction

The dead variable abstraction in this work relies on the states and execution paths in the reachable state space and the *control flow graph* (CFG) of the system being verified. A state s is a mapping of variables to a finite domain or $\top$, $s : V \longrightarrow D \cup \{\top\}$, where V is the set of all variables in the system, D is a finite domain, and $\top$ represents an unconstrained or abstracted variable. We use the symbol S to represent the set of all possible mappings of variables to the domain or $\top$. For simplicity, we assume a single initial state, denoted by s_0,

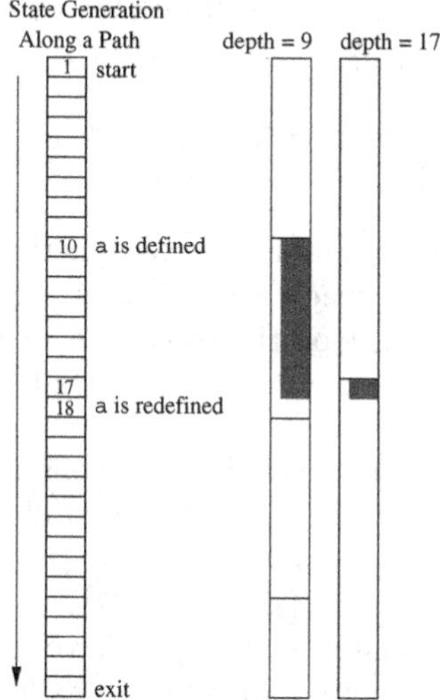

Fig. 3. On the left is the search stack with the variable a defined at state 10 and then redefined at state 18. On the right are two patterns of forward analyses with different explore depths. Highlighted regions show where each analysis marks a as dead.

that contains the initial mapping; although, the results readily extend to systems with multiple initial states.

A control flow graph is a tuple, (N, E), where N is a set of nodes and $E \subseteq N \times N$ is a set of edges connecting nodes. Each node α in the CFG represents a transition that executes atomically in the system. A transition $\alpha \subseteq S \times S$ relates a state with its next state. A transition is enabled in s if and only if there exists an s' such that $\alpha(s, s')$ holds. A transition $\alpha(s, s')$ is valid if α is in the CFG and applying α to s yields s'. A transition is deterministic if and only if for every state s there is at most one s' such that $\alpha(s, s')$ holds. The CFG is used in an iterative dataflow analysis to find dead variables [1]. SDVA and the DDVA in [14] use a CFG to find dead variables in the program. This work uses *execution paths* for the analysis.

An execution path, $\pi = s_0 \stackrel{\alpha_0}{\rightarrow} s_1 \stackrel{\alpha_1}{\rightarrow} \cdots$, is a finite or infinite sequence of states and transitions such that s_0 is the initial state and for every i, $\alpha_i(s_i, s_{i+1})$ is a valid transition and $(\alpha_i, \alpha_{i+1}) \in E$. A path suffix π^i is the suffix of the execution trace π starting at s_i. The set of all states that are in traces that begin with s_0 and contain only the transitions in E constitute the reachable state space of the system $S_R \subseteq S$.

The formal definition we use to mark live and dead variables in a trace makes use of some basic predicates. The predicate $def(v, \alpha)$ is true when the variable v is *defined* by the transition α. Similarly, $used(v, \alpha)$ is true when v is *used* by α. We now give the definition of a variable being live in a transition of an execution path:

Definition 1. *A variable v is live in a transition α_i of an execution path $\pi^i = s_i \xrightarrow{\alpha_i} s_{i+1} \xrightarrow{\alpha_{i+1}} \cdots$ if and only if:*

- *there exists a $j \geq i$ such that $used(v, \alpha_j)$ and*
- *$\neg def(v, \alpha_k)$ for all $i < k < j$*

We use this definition of live variables in the function $live(\pi^i, v)$, which takes π^i, the suffix of the execution trace π starting at s_i, and returns whether the variable v is live in the first state on the trace. If a variable is not live in a state then it is dead. Intuitively, a dead variable is a variable whose current valuation is not used on any future path.

Variables mapped to $\top$ are abstracted and unconstrained. In this way, a state that has abstracted variables can represent many different states. The set of all abstracted variables in a state s is $abstract(s) = \{v \mid s(v) = \top\}$ and the set of concrete variables is $concrete(s) = \{v \mid s(v) \in D\}$.

In order to compare and match states that have differing sets of abstracted variables we define a relation between two states called *contains* denoted $\preceq_c$.

Definition 2. *A state s' is contained in s, denoted $s' \preceq_c s$ if:*

- *$abstract(s') \subseteq abstract(s)$ and*
- *For all variables v in $concrete(s)$, $s'(v) = s(v)$*

A state is contained in another state if the set of abstracted variables of the first state are a subset or equal to the set of abstracted variables of the second state and variables that are concrete in both states are equal.

SDVA only uses the information available in the CFG of the program to do the analysis which admits infeasible paths and produces an imprecise set of dead variables. When a precise execution path through the CFG is used to find dead variables, the true dead variable sets for every state on the trace can be calculated. Finding the true dead variable set for each state in the reachable state space produces an abstract state space that is a *DVA maximal reduction* of the concrete state space.

Definition 3. *An abstract state space S'_R is a **DVA maximal reduction** of the concrete state space S_R if and only if:*

- *For every reachable execution trace starting at the initial state $\pi = s_0 \xrightarrow{\alpha_0} s_1 \xrightarrow{\alpha_1} \cdots$ in the concrete state space, there exists an abstract execution trace $\pi' = s'_0 \xrightarrow{\alpha_0} s'_1 \xrightarrow{\alpha_1} \cdots$ such that for all i, $s_i \preceq_c s'_i$ and $s'_i \in S'_R$*
- *For all states s' in S'_R, and for all variables v in V, if the value of v in s' is not $\top$, then there exists a reachable concrete trace $\pi = s_0 \xrightarrow{\alpha_0} s_1 \xrightarrow{\alpha_1} \cdots$ and an $i \geq 0$ such that $s_i \preceq_c s'$ and $live(\pi^i, v)$*

The original DDVA in [14] uses some runtime information to refine SDVA and find more dead variables; however, it is not able to construct a DVA maximal reduction of a concrete state space and occasionally creates an abstract state space that is no smaller than the state space produced using SDVA. The dynamic dead variable analysis in this work implements Definition 3 on-the-fly to produce a DVA maximally reduced state space in the absence of non-determinism. In the presence of non-determinism, our dynamic dead variable analysis produces the closest approximation to a DVA maximally reduced state space that is possible to produce on-the-fly.

4 Maximal Dynamic Dead Variable Analysis

Our DDVA algorithm achieves a DVA maximal reduction by analyzing fully determined execution paths through the program instead of partial future paths generated from a forward analysis. A fully determined execution path is a single execution path that has been fully explored; it generates no more unique states. An execution path that has reached the exit of the program or a path that has reached an already visited state (representing a path that has entered an infinite loop or merged into an already explored path) are the two kinds of fully determined execution paths. Whenever the search generates a fully determined path, a dead variable analysis is performed. New sets of dead variables for each state in the path are calculated starting with the last state in the path. The exception to this is when a prefix for a trace is unique but all states in its suffix are already in the $Visited$ set. In this case, we can use the dead variable information we already calculated for the suffix to start calculating the dead variables at the last state of the prefix.

When the model checker fully resolves an execution path through the program, the dead variable analysis may find more dead variables for states that have already been explored. A full execution path reveals dynamic run time information of all of the states in the path, allowing the analysis to positively declare variables live or dead. Updating the dead variable sets of visited states requires that they be re-stored in the $Visited$ set. In order to avoid storing states that are later found to be duplicates when their dead variable sets are updated, we use the *contains* relation to ascertain whether a state is unique even before its final dead variable set is generated. In our algorithm, if $s' \preceq_c s$, s' is a newly generated state, and $s \in$ *Visited*, then s' is **not** inserted into *Visited*, because it is contained in s. This pre-emptive duplicate detection saves us from having to generate and store states that are later found to be duplicates.

The new algorithm to dynamically find dead variables, shown in Fig. 4, is remarkably simpler than the work in [14]. The function **dfs** performs a standard depth-first search to enumerate the entire state space of the model. *Stack* is the depth-first search stack. An entry in *Stack* consists of (s, A), with s being a state that includes the location and A being a set of transitions that can be applied to the state to get a next state and location. For our $Visited$ set, we use a hash table that implements the contains relation to compare states. The function $a(s)$ takes a state s and returns the set A, $a : s \longrightarrow A$. A transition $\alpha \in A$ maps a current state onto a next state as defined previously. When a duplicate state is generated (line **11**) or the exit is reached (line **16**), model checking is suspended and a dead variable analysis is run. In the case that the exit of the program is reached, **updateDeadVars** is called with **null** because the entire trace is contained in *Stack*. When a duplicate state is reached, **updateDeadVars** is called with the state in the hash table that matched the newly generated state.

The equation used in **updateDeadVars** to calculate dead variables sets in a state requires as input the previous state's set of dead variables. The variable used for this, $PreviousDeadVars$, is initialized to all variables at line **22** when the exit is reached due to the fact that all variables are dead at the exit. When a partial path is in *Stack* and a path suffix is in $Visited$, we initialize $PreviousDeadVars$ to be the dead variables in the state we matched on, line **24**. Finally, in cases where the exit is not reached because the modeled program enters an infinite loop, the analysis is started with $PreviousDeadVars$ being empty, line **26**, as we cannot determine what the previous state's dead variable set is without entering into an infinite loop ourselves. When a state maps to a non-deterministic assignment in the program, as indicated by the return value of *nonDeterminism*(s_{trace}), line **28**, $PreviousDeadVars$ is set to the empty set, because dead variables discovered after a point of non-determinism cannot be used to calculate the set of dead variables for states before the non-determinism. This point is explained in greater depth at the end of this section.

The equation for the definition of a dead variable is applied at line **31** of **updateDeadVars** to find the set of dead variables for each state in the trace. The function $def(A) = \{v \mid \forall\alpha \in A, def(\alpha, v)\}$ returns the set of variables that are defined in a set of transitions and the function $used(A) = \{v \mid \forall\alpha \in A, used(\alpha, v)\}$ returns the set of variables that are used by a set of transitions. If the analysis finds more dead variables than are currently in the state, the states in *Stack* are updated with their new dead variable sets. Variables that are always live, such as the program location, are never abstracted. The updated states are re-stored in the hash table using the function ***replace***$(Visited, s_{trace}, s')$ (line **34**).

The following is an example run of the algorithm in Fig. 4 that produces the state space shown in Fig. 2(b). The algorithm assumes that SDVA has already been run so that any new dead variables that are found by our DDVA are unioned with the set of dead variables found by the SDVA. Since some states shown in Fig. 2(a) are produced and then later have their dead variable sets updated to become the states in Fig. 2(b), we add a superscript, a or b, to states that differ between the two figures. Our model checking run starts with s_0 as our start state. The state s_0 is pushed onto *Stack* at line **2** and then the depth-first search is called at line **3**. In the main loop of **dfs**, s_0 is peeked at on the top of *Stack*. Line **8** chooses a transition α from s_0's transition set, if there is more than one transition, and removes the transition from the set. Then line **9** uses the transition to produce s_1 from program location **1** of Fig. 1. We check for uniqueness of the newly generated state in lines **10** and **11**. If the state is not contained in any other state in $Visited$, then it is a unique state. The new state in this example is unique so we add it to $Vistited$ and then push it onto *Stack* at lines **14** and **15**. We need to perform a dead variable analysis on each trace after it has been generated, so we check if this trace has finished at line **16** by checking to see if the current state's location is the program exit.

The current trace has not reached the exit so we return to the top of the loop and peek at s_1 on the top of *Stack*. The state s_1 has a single action in its action set. This action is used to produce s_5 which is added to *Visited* and *Stack*. The third time through the main loop of **dfs**, s_5 is peeked at on the top of *Stack* at line **6**. The state s_9, the successor of s_5, is generated and pushed onto *Stack*. Since s_9 is generated at the exit location, we call **updateDeadVars** at line **17**. All variables are dead at the end of the program so the set $PreviousDeadVars$ is set to contain all the variables in the program at line **22**. We iterate backwards through the trace calculating the dead variables for each state starting at the last state. The dead variables of the current state are calculated using the formula on line **31** and then the appropriate variables are marked as dead at line **32**. In this example, no new dead variables are found, so we return from **updateDeadVars**. The fourth time through the main **dfs** loop, s_9 is at the top of *Stack*. It has an empty action set, so it is popped off of *Stack*, and we look at s_5. The state s_5 also has no more children, so it is also popped off *Stack* and then the same process occurs for s_1.

The next action in s_0's action set produces s_3^a. The state s_3^a does not trigger a dead variable analysis and the successor of s_3^a, s_7, also does not trigger an analysis. The next state, s_{10}, leads to s_{12}, which is at the exit, so another dead variable analysis is run. This time the variable b is found to be dead at program locations **2** and **3**. Marking b as dead in s_3^a produces the state s_3^b which replaces the previous state at lines **33** and **34**.

After returning from **updateDeadVars**, s_{12}, s_{10}, s_6, and s_3 are popped off of *Stack*. The next successor of s_0 is s_4 which is contained in s_3^b, so it is not added to the *Stack* or *Visited*. Only s_0 is in *Stack* when **updateDeadVars** is called so no new dead variables are found. Now that s_0's action set is empty, it is popped from *Stack* and state generation has completed.

Our DDVA algorithm is designed on the definitions in the previous section. As such, we claim that using our algorithm to model check single procedure programs without non-determinism produces DVA maximally reduced state spaces on-the-fly by implementing Definitions 2 - 3; however, the presence of non-deterministic assignments to variables can affect the future path from a state so that a state with a non-deterministic assignment can have more than one possible future. These multiple futures of a single state may cause the state to have different sets of dead variables. It is possible that the non-determinism does not actually affect the state's dead variable set, but the only way to know for sure is to examine the entire reachable state space; however, once the entire reachable state space is produced, model checking has finished and there is no longer a need to find more dead variables.

An example of how an execution path can affect states produced before the point of non-determinism is presented in Fig. 5. The function **get_input** represents non-deterministic input from an outside source that ranges over a large finite domain. The variable a is dead at location **2** if c is greater than 2 and the

```
verify ((l_0, s_0))
push(Stack, s_0, a(s_0)))
dfs()

dfs ()
while Stack ≠ ∅ do
  (s, A) := peek(Stack)
  if A ≠ ∅ then
    choose and remove transition α from A
    s' := α(s)
    for all s_i ∈ Visited do
      if s' ⪯_c s_i then
        updateDeadVars(s_i)
        goto: line 5
    Visited := Visited ∪ {s'}
    push(Stack, (s', a(s')))
    if s is at ExitLocation then
      updateDeadVars(null)
  else
    pop(Stack)

updateDeadVars (s_i)
if Stack.LastState is at ExitLocation then
  PreviousDeadVars := V
else if s_i ∉ Stack then
  PreviousDeadVars := abstract(s_i)
else
  PreviousDeadVars := ∅
for s_trace := Stack.LastState to Stack.FirstState do
  if nonDeterminism(s_trace) then
    PreviousDeadVars = ∅
  A := a(s_trace)
  DeadVars := (PreviousDeadVars ∪ def(A)) ∩¬used(A)
  s' = setAbstract(s_trace, DeadVars)
  if s' ≠ s_trace then
    replace(Visited, s_trace, s')
  PreviousDeadVars := DeadVars
```

Fig. 4. Pseudo-code for the maximal DDVA algorithm

path goes through location **4**. A state generated at location **2** could not have a marked as dead because c might be assigned a value less than or equal to 2, making a live. It is possible that every single value returned by **get_input** at location **2** during model checking is greater than 2, which means we can mark a dead at location **2**; however, the only way to check if **get_input** always returns a value greater than 2 is to finish generating the entire reachable state space.

In order to correctly mark variables as dead in the presence of non-determinism, dead variable knowledge gained after a non-deterministic assignment cannot be

```
a = get_input();
c = get_input();
if c > 2 then
    a = 5;
print a, b, c;
```

Fig. 5. A program fragment that has a point of non-determinism that affects what can be declared dead above it

used on states generated before the assignment unless we first generate every possible assignment and future path for the analysis. It is possible that on some models this strategy does find the DVA maximal reduction as it may be the case that the non-determinism in a particular model does not affect dead variable sets in preceding states. We cannot determine on-the-fly whether this is the case, so our algorithm produces state spaces that are not technically DVA maximally reduced when non-determinism is present.

5 Results

We implemented our DDVA algorithm in the Estes model checker developed at the BYU Software Model Checking Lab [15]. Estes uses the GNU debugger as a state generator in order to verify software at the object code level. Since a single line of code from a high level language can easily translate into two or more object code instructions, ways to reduce the size of the explored state space are invaluable. The specific simulator we use as our state generator is based on the Motorola 68hc11 processor and can be found in the Gnu Debugger (GDB) [8]. We use the tools found in the GEL collection of libraries [9] to compile C source code into the binary files that run in the simulator.

In order to implement the contains relation, we need to be able to compare new states with existing states to see if the new state is contained in another state; however, comparing each new state with all the existing states in the $Visited$ set is too unwieldy as the set becomes larger. Since the contains relation stipulates that the values of concrete variables must be equal, we only need to compare each new state with all other states that have the same register values and program location, as these variables are never abstracted. To take advantage of this fact, we implement a chained hash table, where the registers and program location of each state in a chain are equal. When a new state is generated, we hash on the registers and program location to find the correct chain and then compare the state to each of the states in the chain until an exact match or containing state is found, or the end of the chain is reached. If a match or containing state is found, then the new state is discarded. If the new state is unique, it is simply appended to the end of the chain.

We compare the implementation of our DDVA algorithm against normal model checking, model checking with SDVA, and the best and worst runs of the DDVA in [14]. We compare the different techniques running on six different models in the following areas:

- *States generated*: Size of the $Visited$ set at the end of model checking.
- *Wall clock time*: Total time taken to finish model checking.
- *Total memory used*: The total amount of memory used by the model checker to complete a model checking run.
- *Abstraction time*: Total amount of time taken in the dead variable analyses.

We test the algorithms on a number of artificial and real world tests including the main test used to benchmark the DDVA in [14]. The first three models are artificial with no real world objective other than to showcase the kind of state space reductions that are possible with a dynamic dead variable analysis. The last three models are mock-ups of real world functions or programs than can be found in embedded platforms or general purpose computers. The machine used for testing contains an 3GHz Intel Pentium 4 processor and 2GB of RAM. The results are shown in Fig. 6 and Fig. 7.

The data in Fig. 6 and Fig. 7 show how the DDVA in [14] either results in no better reduction than SDVA or has widely varying results depending on the explore depth. Our DDVA on the other hand always has a smaller state space than SDVA, and thus, always has lower memory usage than all of the other methods. For simplicity, the DDVA algorithm in [14] is referred to as *original* in the tables, while our algorithm is referred to as *maximal*.

The `easy3` model is a program with several global integer variables that non-deterministically receive a value at the beginning of the program. The rest of the program contains conditional branches and, depending on values of the variables, all but one variable becomes dead in each branch. The results are shown in the top table of Fig. 6. The example benefits greatly from dead variable analysis. The original DDVA discovers dead variables at the exact same point that SDVA finds dead variables in the example and incurs the time penalty of extra analyses for no state space reduction. Our DDVA reduces the state space and is only slightly slower than SDVA. The original DDVA performs more analyses and thus takes almost twice as long as our DDVA to do its abstraction and yet gains nothing over the static analysis. Our DDVA produces a 35% smaller state space and correspondingly has a lower peak memory usage.

The `littleBranch` model is similar to `easy3`; although, it contains nested conditionals which the original DDVA can take advantage of with the right explore depth. The results are shown in the middle table of Fig. 6. This model, however small, illustrates the difficulty in achieving a good result with the original DDVA. Our DDVA, on the other hand, gives the largest state space reduction, takes the least time to complete, and is able to do this every time without a user specified depth bound.

The `multiBranch` model shown in Fig. 6 is a much larger version of the `littleBranch` model that is used to test the original DDVA. In addition to having deeper nesting than `littleBranch`, `multiBranch` makes use of local variables that are referenced as an offset from the frame pointer. Whenever there is an upcoming pointer dereference, SDVA is forced to declare all variables live. The

Model Name: easy3, **Lines of Code:** 38

Analysis	Explore Depth	States Generated	Total Time	Memory Used (MB)	Abstraction Time
None	N/A	34640	0m12.764s	34.5	0.0s
Static	N/A	15814	0m6.605s	33.80	0.001s
Original best	2	15814	0m10.765s	34.46	3.792s
Original worst	2	15814	0m10.765s	34.46	3.792s
Maximal	N/A	10330	0m8.105s	25.5312	2.017s

Model Name: littleBranch, **Lines of Code:** 57

Analysis	Explore Depth	States Generated	Total Time	Memory Used (MB)	Abstraction Time
None	N/A	864	0m0.442s	30.9	0.0s
Static	N/A	721	0m0.405s	31.4	0.001s
Original best	6	658	0m0.344s	31.43	0.074s
Original worst	2	721	0m0.34s	31.43	0.0492s
Maximal	N/A	530	0m0.223s	23.79	0.0138s

Model Name: multiBranch, **Lines of Code:** 140

Analysis	Explore Depth	States Generated	Total Time	Memory Used (MB)	Abstraction Time
None	N/A	294515	1m49.170s	87.1	N/A
Static	N/A	217454	1m21.780s	74.87	0.002s
Original best	16	176651	1m41.458s	75.79	42.67s
Original worst	5	217478	2m10.965s	83.46	46.35s
Maximal	N/A	145440	2m36.640s	57.99	7.513s

Fig. 6. Results for 3 artificial models. All 3 models are designed to showcase the benefits of using DDVA.

results from this model are shown in the lower table of Fig. 6. This is a good example of a situation where DDVA is engineered to surpass the performance of SDVA; however, again the performance of the original DDVA is unpredictable, and at its worst, generates more states than the static analysis due to the strict state comparison in the hash table. Please note that although our DDVA generates the smallest state space in this example, it incurs a higher run time due to the long chains in the chained table.

Fig. 7 gives the results from the `lexer`, `robot` and `bintree` models. The `lexer` model is patterned after a function in a simple lexical analyzer. The model simulates input as a string of characters which the function reads and then returns a token based on what is in the first one or two characters. The `robot` model simulates a line following robot with three sensors. The robot changes the speed of its left and right motors based on input from the three sensors. In both of these models, our DDVA has the smallest state space and lowest memory usage while taking equal or less time to complete. The `bintree`

Model Name: lexer, **Lines of Code:** 92

Analysis	Explore Depth	States Generated	Total Time	Memory Used (MB)	Abstraction Time
None	N/A	262843	1m28.391s	66.9	0.0s
Static	N/A	226169	1m17.633s	66.32	0.002s
Original best	2	225370	1m51.479s	71.30	31.66s
Original worst	3	226172	1m53.866s	71.13	33.46s
Maximal	N/A	74024	1m45.56s	37.69	4.898s

Model Name: robot, **Lines of Code:** 55

Analysis	Explore Depth	States Generated	Total Time	Memory Used (MB)	Abstraction Time
None	N/A	35865	0m12.838s	35.3	0.0s
Static	N/A	27940	0m10.377s	35.6	0.002s
Original best	2	27940	0m18.675s	36.21	7.947s
Original worst	2	27940	0m18.675s	36.21	7.947s
Maximal	N/A	27784	0m11.494s	29.21	0.552s

Model Name: bintree, **Lines of Code:** 31

Analysis	Explore Depth	States Generated	Total Time	Memory Used (MB)	Abstraction Time
None	N/A	157828	1m0.608s	66.5	0.0s
Static	N/A	154084	1m1.061s	68.4	0.005s
Original best	6	150964	2m14.807s	73.74	72.09s
Original worst	2	154084	2m7.356s	71.47	64.87s
Maximal	N/A	103839	1m7.530s	52.62	16.34s

Fig. 7. Results for 3 real-world models. The `lexer` model is a simple lexical analyzer. The `robot` model simulates a line following robot. The `bintree` model searches a binary tree for a specific node.

model is the only model with a loop in it. This model searches a binary tree for a specific node. Due to algorithmic limitations, the original DDVA typically does not perform well on models with loops because its analysis is tied to the CFG. Our DDVA does much better because it analyzes entire traces through the program which is equivalent to unrolling the loop as many times as needed and then performing dead variable analysis on the unrolled loop as shown in the bottom table of Fig. 7.

6 Conclusions and Future Work

Dead variable analysis is an effective means of reducing the size of the explored state space in model checking while retaining all relevant behaviors of the system. Dynamic dead variable analysis provides a way of finding a larger set of dead variables for each state resulting in even smaller state spaces than those generated using SDVA. Our DDVA greatly improves upon the ideas set forth in the original DDVA of [14] by eliminating the dependence on a user specified explore depth and by producing a DVA maximally reduced state space for models with no non-determinism and the closest possible approximation to a DVA maximally reduced state space in models that contain non-determinism. Our algorithm also correctly addresses looping structures in the analysis.

Our maximal DDVA algorithm is currently limited to single procedure programs. Future work focuses on modifying our DDVA algorithm to work on multi-procedural programs. The easiest way to do this is to declare all global variables as live, and treat every procedure and its local variables as a separate program. As the program returns from a procedure, a dynamic dead variable analysis is run on the trace of states generated through the procedure and dead variables sets for states generated in the procedure are updated.

Other areas of future work include finding ways to speed up run time, adapting the algorithm to different searches, and using a more efficient way of representing dead variables. The current implementation of the algorithm suffers from an increase in run time on large models that can make state space exploration infeasible. This increase in run time comes from the use of a chained hash table and the contains relation. An avenue for future work would be to look into ways to mitigate this problem. Another direction for future work adapts DDVA to work with other search algorithms such as breadth-first search. The benefit of breadth-first search is that paths that reach an error state are guaranteed to be the shortest path to the error. Lastly, the current data structure used to mark dead variables is highly inefficient. Some future work could be dedicated to creating data structures that take less memory to store dead variable information.

References

1. Aho, A.V., Sethi, R., Ullman, J.D.: Compilers: principles, techniques, and tools. Addison-Wesley Longman Publishing Co., Inc, Boston, MA, USA (1986)
2. Ball, T., Rajamani, S.K.: Bebop: A symbolic model checker for Boolean programs. In: Havelund, K., Penix, J., Visser, W. (eds.) SPIN Model Checking and Software Verification. LNCS, vol. 1885, pp. 113–130. Springer, Heidelberg (2000)
3. Bozga, M., Fernandez, J., Ghirvu, L.: State space reduction based on live variables analysis. In: Cortesi, A., Filé, G. (eds.) SAS 1999. LNCS, vol. 1694, pp. 164–178. Springer, Heidelberg (1999)
4. Cimatti, A., Clarke, E.M., Giunchiglia, F., Roveri, M.: NUSMV: A new symbolic model verifier. In: Halbwachs, N., Peled, D.A. (eds.) CAV 1999. LNCS, vol. 1633, pp. 495–499. Springer, Heidelberg (1999)
5. Clarke, E.M., Grumberg, O., Long, D.E.: Model checking and abstraction. ACM Trans. on Programming Languages and Systems 16(5), 1512–1542 (1994)
6. Corbett, J.C., Dwyer, M.B., Hatcliff, J., Laubach, S., Păsăreanu, C.S., Zheng, R., Zheng, H.: Bandera: extracting finite-state models from Java source code. In: International Conference on Software Engineering, pp. 439–448 (2000)

7. Dong, Y., Ramakrishnan, C.R.: An optimizing compiler for efficient model checking. In: FORTE XII / PSTV XIX '99: Proceedings of the IFIP TC6 WG6.1 Joint International Conference on Formal Description Techniques for Distributed Systems and Communication Protocols (FORTE XII) and Protocol Specification, Testing and Verification (PSTV XIX), pp. 241–256. Kluwer, B.V, Norwell (1999)
8. The Gnu project debugger: (2006) Available at `http://sources.redhat.com/gdb/`
9. GNU libraries for 68hc11 and 68hc12: (2005) Available at `http://gel.sourceforge.net/`
10. Havelund, K., Pressburger, T.: Model checking Java programs using Java pathfinder (1998)
11. Henzinger, T.A., Jhala, R., Majumdar, R., Sutre, G.: Software verification with Blast. In: Ball, T., Rajamani, S.K. (eds.) Model Checking Software. LNCS, vol. 2648, pp. 235–239. Springer, Heidelberg (2003)
12. Holzmann, G.J.: The engineering of a model checker: the Gnu i-protocol case study revisited. In: Dams, D.R., Gerth, R., Leue, S., Massink, M. (eds.) Theoretical and Practical Aspects of SPIN Model Checking. LNCS, vol. 1680, Springer, Toulouse, France (1999)
13. Holzmann, G.J.: The Spin Model Checker: Primer and Reference Manual. Addison-Wesley, Reading (2003)
14. Lewis, M.S., Jones, M.D.: A dead variable analysis for explicit model checking. ACM SIGPLAN 2006 Workshop on Partial Evaluation and Program (2006)
15. Mercer, E.G., Jones, M.: Model checking machine code with the GNU debugger. In: Godefroid, P. (ed.) Model Checking Software. LNCS, vol. 3639, pp. 251–265. Springer, San Francisco, USA (2005)
16. Pelánek, R.: On-the-fly state space reductions. Technical Report FIMU-RS-2005-03, Faculty of Informatics Masaryk University Brno (2005)
17. Robby, M., Dwyer, J.: Bogor: an extensible and highly-modular software model checking framework (2003)
18. Yorav, K., Grumberg, O.: Static analysis for state-space reductions preserving temporal logics. Form. Methods Syst. Des. 25(1), 67–96 (2004)

SAT-Based Summarization for Boolean Programs

Gérard Basler*, Daniel Kroening, and Georg Weissenbacher**

Computer Systems Institute, ETH Zurich, 8092 Zurich, Switzerland
`firstname.lastname@inf.ethz.ch`

Abstract. *Boolean programs* are frequently used to model abstractions of software programs. They have the advantage that reachability properties are decidable, despite the fact that their stack is not bounded. The enabling technique is *summarization* of procedure calls. Most model checking tools for Boolean programs use BDDs to represent these summaries, allowing for efficient fix-point detection. However, BDDs are highly sensitive to the number of state variables. We present an approach to over-approximate summaries using Bounded Model Checking. Our technique is based on a SAT solver and requires only few calls to a QBF solver for fix-point detection. Our benchmarks show that our implementation is able handle a larger number of variables than BDD-based algorithms on some examples.

1 Introduction

Boolean programs [1] are frequently used to model software programs. They provide the usual control-flow constructs of an imperative language such as C, but variables are exclusively of Boolean type. The use of Boolean programs as an abstract model has been promoted by the success of the SLAM project [2]. SLAM verifies control-flow dominated properties of Windows device drivers by abstracting an ANSI-C program into a Boolean program. The abstract model of the original program is obtained by means of *Predicate Abstraction* [3]. It contains the same procedures and control flow as the original program, and thus, Boolean programs are a natural formalization. The Boolean variables are used to keep track of predicates over the variables of the original program.

The main advantage of Boolean programs over finite-state transition systems is that their stack allows a precise representation of the behavior of procedure calls, including procedure-local variables and (possibly unbounded) recursive calls. Nevertheless, reachability properties for Boolean programs are decidable [4]: Procedures can access and modify only the topmost element of the stack. Therefore, *summarizing* the procedures prevents a re-evaluation of a call if the same calling context has already been considered before [5].

* Supported by the Swiss National Science Foundation.
** Supported by Microsoft Research through its European PhD Scholarship Programme.

D. Bošnački and S. Edelkamp (Eds.): SPIN 2007, LNCS 4595, pp. 131–148, 2007.

Most existing model checkers compute summaries incrementally at each call site. The reachable states are determined by means of a saturation procedure, which computes and adds summaries until no new states are discovered. Instances of such model checkers are BEBOP [1], which is shipped with SLAM, and MOPED [6]. Both tools use a symbolic representation of states and summaries based on (ordered) Binary Decision Diagrams (BDDs) [7]. Ordered BDDs are a canonical representation of formulas and can be compared efficiently, thus enabling the detection of previously explored portions of the state space.

Unfortunately, in case of a large number of state variables, the BDDs become unmanageably large. Approaches based on SAT-solvers (e.g. [8]) are less sensitive to the number of variables. However, they suffer from the fact that the comparison of sets of states requires a decision procedure for quantified Boolean formulas (QBF), making fix-point detection significantly harder than with BDDs.

We propose a SAT-based summarization technique that reduces the required number of QBF calls significantly. We exploit the following observation about Boolean programs generated by tools such as SLAM: They are *shallow*. Formally, this means that the length of the shortest path from an initial state to any reachable valuation of global and local variables is bounded by a small constant. This bound is called *sequential depth*. Only few programs written in a general purpose programming language such as ANSI-C have this property. A single loop with an integer counter variable may result in a Kripke structure with loop-free paths as long as 2^{32}.

Obviously, a Boolean program may just as well have a sequential depth that is exponential in the number of Boolean variables it contains. However, such a program *must* encode the equivalent of a binary counter using a propositional relation over the Boolean variables. Such models are typically not generated by any of the program analysis tools that we experimented with: Tools based on predicate abstraction generate at least one predicate per loop iteration [9].

In order to avoid the expensive fix-point detection, we generate a *universal* summary, which encodes *all* possible execution traces of the procedure up to its sequential depth, starting from an *uninitialized* calling context. A universal summary is an over-approximation of the fix-point that incremental summarization would yield.

Computing the exact sequential depth is as hard as model checking. To avoid this computation, we use an over-approximation, the *reachability recurrence diameter*, that is commonly used in bounded model checking (BMC) and can be computed by means of a SAT solver.

Related Work. Boolean programs have been introduced as a formalism to represent abstract models generated by SLAM [10]. The success of the SLAM project motivated many researchers to work on even faster model checking algorithms for Boolean programs. The formalism is equally expressive as Pushdown systems, which have been studied long before SLAM was presented: Büchi proved already in 1964 that the set of reachable states of a pushdown system (represented by a string rewriting system) can be expressed in terms of a regular language [4]. This result implies that reachability of states of pushdown systems is decidable.

Sharir and Pnueli introduce summarization as an element of an iterative fix-point detection based dataflow analysis algorithm for a language slightly more expressive than Boolean programs [5]. Ball and Rajamani's model checker BEBOP is based on this work, but uses BDDs to represent states symbolically [1]. Our QBF-based summarization approach (see Section 3) is similar to the algorithm implemented in BEBOP, but uses SAT instead of BDDs. Finkel et al. present an automata-based saturation algorithm that constructs the regular set representing the reachable states of a pushdown system [11]. Esparza presents an optimized version of Finkel's algorithm [6], and Schwoon improves this approach using a BDD-based symbolic representation of pushdown systems [12]. Lal and Reps present a graph-theoretic approach for model checking (weighted) pushdown systems [13]. None of the approaches listed above is based on satisfiability solving techniques.

Recently, several algorithms based on rewriting have been proposed for model checking pushdown systems: Boujjani and Esparza survey approaches that use rewriting to solve the reachability problem for sequential as well as for concurrent pushdown systems [14]. Rewriting-based reachability analysis of concurrent pushdown system is also covered by [15] and [16]. However, the reachability problem for concurrent pushdown is undecidable. Various approaches have been considered to overcome this problem (e.g., [17,18,19] and [15]). We omit a discussion of this work, since our approach does not target concurrent Boolean programs.

Leino's model checker for Boolean programs DIZZY [20] uses SAT-based symbolic simulation. However, the fix-point detection is still done by computing BDDs representing the set of reachable states.

Kroening presents a SAT-based model checker called BOPPO for concurrent pushdown systems *without* recursive procedures [8]. This work comes closest to our approach, since BOPPO uses a SAT-solver for symbolic simulation and a QBF-solver for fix-point detection. Procedure calls can be simulated by dynamic threads. However, in the presence of threads, BOPPO computes an over-approximation of the set of reachable states. Furthermore, BOPPO does not generate summaries for procedures.

Our approach is different from the model checking algorithms listed above, since we compute an over-approximation of the *summaries* of a Boolean program, instead of computing the least fix-point of this set. Still, our algorithm does not yield false positives with respect to reachability properties. To compute this over-approximation, we use Bounded Model Checking (BMC).

BMC was introduced by Biere et al. [21] as a SAT-based alternative to finite-state model checking algorithms that use Binary Decision Diagrams (BDDs) [7]. BMC searches for counterexamples of length at most length k, which is increased iteratively. The approach is complete if k exceeds the *completeness threshold* $\mathcal{CT}$ [22]: If there is no counterexample of length at most $\mathcal{CT}$, then the property in question cannot be violated at all. The *recurrence diameter*, which can be computed using a SAT solver, is an over-approximation of the completeness threshold for reachability properties of finite-state transition systems [22].

Contribution and Outline. We present background on Boolean programs and BMC in Sec. 2. In Section 3, we present a SAT-based model checking algorithm which computes a set of summary edges for each procedure and finds the least fix-point of these sets using a QBF solver. This work is based on the algorithm presented in [1]. To the best of our knowledge, our tool is the first one that implements summarization using SAT and QBF.

In Section 4, we introduce the notion of a *universal summary*, which encodes the unwinding of all possible execution traces of a procedure up to its reachability recurrence diameter. We explain how the use of universal summaries can significantly reduce the number of calls to the QBF solver.

We have implemented these algorithms for model checking Boolean programs and provide experimental results comparing this implementation to a conventional BDD-based algorithm in Section 5.

2 Background

The construction of universal summaries is based on an over-approximation of what we call the *sequential depth* of a procedure. We borrow this idea from *Bounded Model Checking.*

2.1 Bounded Model Checking

BMC is a method for finding logical errors in finite-state transition systems. It is widely regarded as a complementary technique to symbolic BDD-based model checking, and frequently used in the hardware industry; see [23] for a survey of experiments with BMC conducted in industry.

Definition 1 (Finite-State Transition System). *A* Finite-State Transition System $\mathcal{M} = \langle S, T, s_0 \rangle$ *is defined by a finite set of states* S*, a transition relation* $T \subseteq S \times S$*, and an initial state* $s_0 \in S$*.*

Given a finite-state transition system $\mathcal{M}$, an LTL property φ, and a natural number k, a BMC procedure decides whether there exists a sequence of transitions of $\mathcal{M}$ of length k or less that violates φ. SAT-based BMC is performed by generating a propositional formula, which is satisfiable if and only if such a path exists. We write $\mathcal{M} \models_k \varphi$ if all sequences of transitions up to length k satisfy φ.

In practice, the application of BMC is typically restricted to the refutation of safety properties, and is conducted in an iterative manner: Starting with a small initial value of k, k is incremented until either 1) an error is found, or 2) the problem becomes intractable due to the complexity of solving the corresponding SAT instance.

Bounded Model Checking is *complete* iff k reaches a *completeness threshold* $\mathcal{CT}$, which indicates there exists no path in $\mathcal{M}$ that violates ϕ.

Definition 2 (Completeness Threshold [22]). *A* completeness threshold *of a transition system* $\mathcal{M}$ *with respect to a property* φ *is any natural number* $\mathcal{CT}$

such that, given that the property φ is not violated by any sequence of transitions of length up to $\mathcal{CT}$, then it cannot be violated at all, i.e.,

$$\mathcal{M} \models_{\mathcal{CT}} \phi \Longrightarrow \mathcal{M} \models \phi \tag{1}$$

holds.

Clearly, if $\mathcal{M} \models \varphi$, then the smallest $\mathcal{CT}$ is 0, and otherwise it is equal to the length of the shortest counterexample. This implies that finding the smallest $\mathcal{CT}$ is at least as hard as checking $\mathcal{M} \models \varphi$. Consequently, we concentrate on computing an over-approximation of the smallest $\mathcal{CT}$.

The *Reachability Diameter* of a finite-state transition system $\mathcal{M}$ is a completeness threshold for reachability properties of the form $\mathbf{G}p$:

Definition 3 (Reachability Diameter [22]). *Given a finite-state transition system $\mathcal{M}$, the* Reachability Diameter *$rd(\mathcal{M})$ of a $\mathcal{M}$ is the minimal number of steps required for reaching all reachable states.*

The Reachability Diameter corresponds to our notion of the *sequential depth.*

Definition 4 (Reachability Recurrence Diameter [22]). *The* Reachability Recurrence Diameter *with respect to a finite state transition system $\mathcal{M} = \langle S, T, s_0 \rangle$ is the longest loop-free path in $\mathcal{M}$ starting from the initial state s_0:*

$$rrd(\mathcal{M}) \stackrel{def}{=} max\{i | \exists s_1 \dots s_i. \bigwedge_{j=0}^{i-1} T(s_j, s_{j+1}) \wedge \bigwedge_{j=0}^{i-1} \bigwedge_{k=j+1}^{i} s_j \neq s_k\} \tag{2}$$

The Reachability Diameter and the Reachability Recurrence Diameter are only defined for transition systems with a finite state space. However, Boolean programs do not adhere to this restriction, since they contain procedures with call-by-value parameter passing and recursion.

2.2 Semantics of Boolean Programs

We define Boolean programs and their semantics in terms of the control-flow graph of a program. A Boolean program consists of a set of procedures, each of which is represented by its control flow graph (CFG).

As usual, a control flow graph is a directed graph with nodes corresponding to program locations. Without loss of generality, we assume that each procedure has exactly one entry node n_i and one exit node n_e.

In accordance to [1], a state comprises of the program counter n (which is a node in the CFG) and the valuation Ω of the variables *in scope*. Unlike the conventional notion of a program state, a state in a Boolean program does not contain the content of the call stack.

Each edge $\langle n_1, n_2 \rangle$ of the CFG corresponds to a transition $\langle n_1, \Omega_1 \rangle \to \langle n_2, \Omega_2 \rangle$ that relates the values Ω_1 of the variables in scope before the transition to those (Ω_2) after the transition.

We use the following notation to describe transition functions:

- $\Omega(e)$ denotes the evaluation of the expression e according to the valuation Ω of the variables in e. Expressions and their evaluation are defined the usual way.
- We refer to the state before the execution of a transition function as *current* state, and to the state afterwards as *next* state. We use *primed* versions of the variables to distinguish variables that refer to the next state from the variables in the current state. We allow expressions to range over variables in two different states $\langle n_1, \Omega_1 \rangle$ and $\langle n_2, \Omega_2 \rangle$. $(\Omega_1, \Omega_2)(e)$ denotes the evaluation of such an expression e.
- Expressions may also contain non-deterministic choice. While non-deterministic values are traditionally represented by "*", we use a set of non-deterministic choice variables $\iota_1, \ldots \iota_k$ instead. We use ξ to denote a valuation to these variables, and we use $[e]_\xi$ to denote the evaluation of the expression e under the mapping ξ.

In the given setting, only the topmost element of the stack has an immediate impact on the execution of a transition. Therefore, the outcome of a call to a procedure is exclusively determined by the values of the global variables and the actual parameters at the call site. Consequently, each actual call to a procedure **pr** can be *summarized* by a pair of states $\langle n_i, \Omega_i \rangle, \langle n_o, \Omega_o \rangle$, where n_i denotes the entry node of the control flow graph of **pr**, and n_o denotes the corresponding exit node. We use $\Sigma(\mathbf{pr})$ to denote the set of these pairs for a procedure **pr**. Furthermore, we assume in this section that $\Sigma(\mathbf{pr})$ contains the entries for all reachable call contexts. Clearly, $\Sigma(\mathbf{pr})$ is finite for Boolean programs.

For a given entry state, the corresponding exit states[1] are determined by the transition functions of the control flow graph of **pr**. The transition functions are in turn determined by the statements corresponding to the nodes of the control flow graph. We distinguish the following statements:

- The `skip` statement does not modify the variables, but increments the program counter by one.
- The `goto` $\ell_1, \ldots, \ell_m$ statement non-deterministically changes the program counter to one of the program locations $\ell_1, \ldots, \ell_m$ provided as argument. The valuation of the variables does not change.
- The `assume` e statement increases the program counter by one iff the condition e evaluates to `true` in the current state. Otherwise, the `assume` statement has no successor states, i.e., the program terminates.
- The constrained assignment statement $x_1, \ldots, x_k := e_1, \ldots, e_k$ `constrain` e assigns the values of the expressions $e_1, \ldots, e_k$ to the variables $x_1, \ldots, x_k$. The expressions are evaluated in the current state and may contain a non-deterministic choice variables. The constraint e is a predicate that ranges over the variables of the current *and* the next state. It is evaluated in both states, and the statement has no successor state if e does not hold.
- The `return` statement corresponds to the exit node of the control flow graph of **pr**. Whenever it is reached, the current state determines the exit valuation

[1] The use of non-determinism may result in more than one exit valuation.

of the corresponding summary. We assume without loss of generality that all return values are passed to the caller via global variables, i.e., `return` has no parameters. Therefore, the variables are not modified. The program counter of the successor statement is determined by the *caller* of the corresponding procedure **pr**.

- The call $\mathbf{pr}(e_1, \ldots, e_k)$ modifies the global variables according to an *applicable summary* $\langle n_i, \Omega_i \rangle, \langle n_o, \Omega_o \rangle$ in $\Sigma(\mathbf{pr})$. A summary is applicable if a) Ω_i agrees with the current state on the global variables, and b) the evaluation of $e_1, \ldots, e_k$ matches the corresponding actual parameters in Ω_i. (The calling context determines the entry valuation of a summary.)

  Then, the call to $\mathbf{pr}(e_1, \ldots, e_k)$ modifies the global variables according to Ω_o. If more than one summary is applicable, one summary is chosen non-deterministically (analogously to the `goto` statement).

  In the case that an applicable summary exists, the call sets the program counter to the statement that succeeds the call. Otherwise, the statement succeeding the call is never reached.

The statements `skip`, `assume`, the constrained assignment, and procedure calls have a single successor node in the control flow graph (according to the structure of the program). The `return` statement has no successor in the control flow graph, since the program location that succeeds a return statement cannot be determined statically. Goto statements may have more than one successor. Conditional statements like `if-then-else` or `while` loops can be modeled using a combination of the `goto` and `assume` statements.

The recursive nature with respect to $\Sigma(\mathbf{pr})$ of the definition of the semantics indicates that the set of summaries $\Sigma(\mathbf{pr})$ of a Boolean program can be obtained by means of a fix-point computation. Several algorithms that compute the least fix-point of the set $\Sigma(\mathbf{pr})$ in order to determine the set of reachable states have been proposed [1,11,12].

We present a QBF-based algorithm to compute the least fix-point for $\Sigma(\mathbf{pr})$ in the following section, and propose to use a SAT-based over-approximation of this fix-point in Section 4.

3 Summarization Using QBF

In this section we describe how we compute the least fix-point of $\Sigma(\mathbf{pr})$ using forward symbolic execution and QBF-based fix-point detection.

The valuation of a symbolic state is represented in terms of a Boolean formula over non-deterministic choice variables $\iota_1, \ldots, \iota_k$, i.e., we use a parametric representation. Boolean formulas are defined the usual way.

Let N be the set of nodes in a CFG of a Boolean program, let V be the variables of that program.

Definition 5 (Symbolic State). *A* symbolic state *is a triple* $\langle n, \gamma, \omega \rangle$*, where* $n \in N$ *identifies the node in the CFG and is represented explicitly, and* γ *is a Boolean formula over the non-deterministic choice variables and represents the*

Table 1. Conditions on the symbolic transitions $\langle n_1, \gamma_1, \omega_1 \rangle \to \langle n_2, \gamma_2, \omega_2 \rangle$ for the statements `skip`, `goto`, `assume`, and the constrained assignment

Instruction	γ_2	ω_2
`skip`	$\gamma_2 = \gamma_1$	$\omega_2 = \omega_1$
`return`	$\gamma_2 = \gamma_1$	$\omega_2 = \omega_1$
`goto` $\ell_1, \dots \ell_k$	$\gamma_2 = \gamma_1$	$\omega_2 = \omega_1$
`assume` e	$\gamma_2 = (\gamma_1 \wedge \omega_1(e))$	$\omega_2 = \omega_1$
$x_1, \dots, x_k := e_1, \dots, e_k$ `constrain` e	$\gamma_2 = (\gamma_1 \wedge (\omega_1, \omega_2)(e))$	$\omega_2 = (\omega_1[x_1/\omega_1(e_1)] \dots [x_k/\omega_1(e_k)])$

guard *of the state. The component* ω *maps the variables* V *to formulas over* $\iota_1, \dots, \iota_k$*, representing a set of valuations for the variables in the symbolic state.*

Each symbolic state $\langle n, \gamma, \omega \rangle$ represents the set of explicit states

$$\{\langle n, \Omega \rangle | \exists \xi . [\gamma]_\xi \wedge \forall v \in V . \Omega(v) = [\omega(v)]_\xi\}$$

where $\omega(e)$ denotes the evaluation of the expression e according to the mapping ω (analogously to $\Omega(e)$ in Section 2). The symbolic state $\langle \ell_{10}, (\iota_1 \vee \iota_2), \{a \mapsto \iota_1, b \mapsto (\neg\iota_1 \wedge \iota_2)\} \rangle$, for instance, represents the explicit states $\langle \ell_{10}, \{a \mapsto 0, b \mapsto 1\} \rangle$ and $\langle \ell_{10}, \{a \mapsto 1, b \mapsto 0\} \rangle$. The valuation $\langle \iota_1, \iota_2 \rangle = \langle 0, 0 \rangle$ is ruled out by the guard, and the valuations $\langle \iota_1, \iota_2 \rangle = \langle 1, 0 \rangle$ and $\langle \iota_1, \iota_2 \rangle = \langle 1, 1 \rangle$ yield the same explicit state. An unsatisfiable guard indicates that there is no concrete state represented by $\langle n, \gamma, \omega \rangle$ [8].

Before we proceed to introduce our symbolic representation of summaries, we define the transition conditions for the statements `skip`, `goto`, `assume`, and the constrained assignment. In Table 1, we write $\omega[x/e]$ for the mapping that maps x to the formula e, while it agrees with the mapping ω on all other variables. We use γ_1 and ω_1 to refer to the components γ and ω of the current state, and γ_2 and ω_2 to refer to the next state. The program locations are omitted, since they change according to the rules presented in Section 2. The conditions in Table 1 are equivalent to those presented in [8] (except for the `return` statement). According to this table, the components γ and ω are modified as follows:

- In case of a `skip`, `return`, or `goto` statement, γ as well as ω do not change.
- Conditions contributed by `assume` statements are instantiated according to ω_1 and conjoined with the guard γ_1. The symbolic execution terminates if γ_2 is unsatisfiable.
- A constrained assignment updates the mapping ω_2 accordingly. If a constraining condition is present, it is instantiated using ω_1 *and* ω_2, and conjoined with γ_1.

An actual symbolic transition can be characterized by a pair of symbolic states $\langle n_1, \gamma_1, \omega_1 \rangle, \langle n_2, \gamma_2, \omega_2 \rangle$. The first state represents the concrete set of states *before* the transition, and the second the corresponding concrete states *afterwards*. By construction (see Table 1), the components γ_1, γ_2, ω_1, and ω_2 *share* sub-formulas. Therefore, given one of the concrete states $\langle n_1, \Omega_1 \rangle \in \langle n_1, \gamma_1, \omega_1 \rangle$, we can obtain the states that are reachable from $\langle n_1, \Omega_1 \rangle$ via this transition by *constraining* the state $\langle n_2, \gamma_2, \omega_2 \rangle$:

$$\langle n_2, \ \left(\gamma_2 \wedge \bigwedge_{v \in V} \omega_1(v) = \Omega_1(v) \right), \ \ \omega_2 \rangle \tag{3}$$

Continuing our example, we construct the symbolic successor for the state $\langle \ell_{10}, (\iota_1 \vee \iota_2), \{a \mapsto \iota_1, b \mapsto (\neg\iota_1 \wedge \iota_2)\} \rangle$ and the following statement:

$$a := \neg a \ \texttt{constrain} \ (\neg b \vee a')$$

According to Table 1, we obtain $\omega_2 = \{a \mapsto \neg\iota_1, b \mapsto (\neg\iota_1 \wedge \iota_2)\}$ and $\gamma_2 = (\iota_1 \vee \iota_2) \wedge (\iota_1 \vee \neg\iota_2 \vee \neg\iota_1) \equiv (\iota_1 \vee \iota_2)$. We compute the successor states for the concrete state $\langle \ell_{10}, \{a \mapsto 0, b \mapsto 1\} \rangle$ by adding the constraint $\iota_1 = 0 \wedge (\neg\iota_1 \wedge \iota_2) = 1$ to γ_2, ruling out the successor state $\langle \ell_{11}, \{a \mapsto 0, b \mapsto 1\} \rangle$ and leaving us with $\langle \ell_{11}, \{a \mapsto 1, b \mapsto 0\} \rangle$.

If we constrain the transition $\langle n_1, \gamma_1, \omega_1 \rangle, \langle n_2, \gamma_2, \omega_2 \rangle$ with a *symbolic* state $\langle n_1, \gamma_0, \omega_0 \rangle$ (analogously to Equation 3), we obtain a symbolic state that represents the set of states reachable from $\langle n_1, \gamma_0, \omega_0 \rangle$ via this transition:

$$\langle n_2, \left(\gamma_2 \wedge \gamma_0 \wedge \bigwedge_{v \in V} \omega_1(v) = \omega_0(v) \right), \omega_2 \rangle \tag{4}$$

In (4), we assume that the non-deterministic choice variables in $\langle n_1, \gamma_0, \omega_0 \rangle$ differ from those in $\langle n_1, \gamma_1, \omega_1 \rangle$ and $\langle n_2, \gamma_2, \omega_2 \rangle$. This can always be achieved by renaming.

The representation of transitions by means of two symbolic states is not restricted to single transitions, but can be extended to sequences of transitions in the natural way. This representation enables the summarization of compound transitions, and is similar to the concept of *path edges* [1].

Definition 6 (Path edges and summary edges). *A pair of symbolic states* $\langle n_i, \gamma_i, \omega_i \rangle, \langle n_o, \gamma_o, \omega_o \rangle$ *is a* path edge *of procedure* **pr** *iff all of the following hold:*

- n_i *is the entry node of* **pr**.
- $\langle n_i, \gamma_i, \omega_i \rangle$ *is reachable from an initial state of the Boolean program.*
- $\langle n_o, \gamma_o, \omega_o \rangle$ *is reachable from* $\langle n_i, \gamma_i, \omega_i \rangle$ *by a sequence of statements that does* not *contain the* `return` *statement of* **pr** *(unless* n_o *happens to be the corresponding exit node).*

A summary edge *of* **pr** *is a path edge* $\langle n_i, \gamma_i, \omega_i \rangle, \langle n_o, \gamma_o, \omega_o \rangle$*, for which* n_i *corresponds to the entry node, and* n_o *corresponds to the exit node of* **pr**.

Using Definition 6 and Equation 4, we can give a symbolic transition function for the procedure call statement. Assume that we encounter a procedure call

$\mathbf{pr}(e_1,\ldots,e_k)$ and the current state is $\langle n_c,\gamma_c,\omega_c\rangle$. Let $\Sigma_s(\mathbf{pr})$ be the set of symbolic summaries for the procedure **pr**. We use $g_1,\ldots,g_m$ to denote the global variables of the Boolean program, $l_1,\ldots,l_j$ to denote the local variables of the calling context, and $f_1,\ldots,f_k$ to denote the formal parameters of the procedure **pr**.

A summary edge $\langle n_i,\gamma_i,\omega_i\rangle,\langle n_o,\gamma_o,\omega_o\rangle \in \Sigma_s(\mathbf{pr})$ is applicable to the calling context $\langle n_c,\gamma_c,\omega_c\rangle$ iff

1. for all reachable valuations of $g_1,\ldots,g_m,e_1,\ldots,e_k$ in $\langle n_c,\gamma_c,\omega_c\rangle$ there exists a matching valuation to $g_1,\ldots,g_m,f_1,\ldots,f_k$ in $\langle n_i,\gamma_i,\omega_i\rangle$, and
2. γ_o is still satisfiable when the global and formal variables are restricted to the global variables and parameter expressions of γ_c and ω_c according to Equation 4.

The universal quantification in the first condition requires us to use a QBF instance to decide applicability:

$$\forall\xi_c.\ [\gamma_c]_{\xi_c} \Rightarrow \exists\xi_o. \bigwedge_{s\in\{1..m\}} [w_i(g_s)]_{\xi_o} = [w_c(g_s)]_{\xi_c} \wedge \bigwedge_{t\in\{1..k\}} [w_i(f_t)]_{\xi_o} = [w_c(e_t)]_{\xi_c} \wedge [\gamma_o]_{\xi_o} \tag{5}$$

Again, we assume that the non-deterministic choice variables in $\langle n_c,\gamma_c,\omega_c\rangle$ are disjoint from those in the summary edge.

Assuming that (5) holds, we can restrict the symbolic state $\langle n_o,\gamma_o,\omega_o\rangle$ to the states reachable from the calling context $\langle n_c,\gamma_c,\omega_c\rangle$ analogously to (4). By applying the summary, we obtain a new symbolic state $\langle n_r,\gamma_r,\omega_r\rangle$ (the state after the `return` statement) with

$$\gamma_r := \gamma_o \wedge \gamma_c \wedge \bigwedge_{s\in\{1..m\}} w_i(g_s) = w_c(g_s) \wedge \bigwedge_{t\in\{1..k\}} w_i(f_t) = w_c(e_t) \tag{6}$$

and

$$\omega_r(g_1) = \omega_o(g_1),\ldots,\omega_r(g_m) = \omega_o(g_m), \omega_r(l_1) = \omega_c(l_1),\ldots,\omega_r(l_j) = \omega_c(l_j) \tag{7}$$

Now consider the case that (5) does not hold, i.e., $\Sigma_s(\mathbf{pr})$ contains no applicable summary. In that case, a new summary edge must to be computed for the calling context $\langle n_c,\gamma_c,\omega_c\rangle$. For this purpose, we construct a new symbolic state $\langle n_i,\gamma_i,\omega_i\rangle$ which agrees with $\langle n_c,\gamma_c,\omega_c\rangle$ on the global variables, and assign $e_1,\ldots,e_k$ to the formal parameters (using same transition function as the assignment statement). The symbolic state $\langle n_i,\gamma_i,\omega_i\rangle$ serves as entry node for a new path edge, and may eventually yield a new summary edge.

Fix-point Detection. In order to determine the least fix-point of $\Sigma_s(\mathbf{pr})$, our reachability checking performs symbolic simulation of a Boolean program. The algorithm maintains a set $\mathcal{P}$ of path edges and summary edges $\Sigma_s(\mathbf{pr})$ that

```
procedure INSERT(π)
    if π ⊈ P then
        insert π into P
        insert π into W
    end if
end procedure

Initialize P to ∅;
for all pr do Initialize Σ_s(pr) to ∅;
end for
W := {⟨n_0, true, ω_*⟩, ⟨n_0, true, ω_*⟩};          ▷ ⟨n_0, true, ω_*⟩ is initial state
W' := ∅;
while W ≠ ∅ do
    remove π = ⟨n_i, γ_i, ω_i⟩, ⟨n_o, γ_o, ω_o⟩ from W
    if statement of n_o is skip, assume, or assignment then
        π' :=TRANS(π, n_o);
        INSERT(π');
    else if statement of n_o is goto ℓ_1, ..., ℓ_k then
        π_ℓ1, ..., π_ℓk :=TRANS(π, n_o);                 ▷ split path edge
        for all t ∈ {1..k} do
            INSERT(π_ℓt);
        end for
    else if statement of n_o is call pr(e_1, ..., e_k) then
        for all σ_pr ∈ Σ(pr) do
            if APPLICABLE(π, σ_pr) then
                π' :=APPLY(π, σ_pr);
                INSERT(π');
            end if
        end for
        if {σ_pr ∈ Σ(pr) | APPLICABLE(π, σ_pr)} = ∅ then
            construct entry state ⟨n_i, γ_i, ω_i⟩ for pr;
            π' := {⟨n_i, γ_i, ω_i⟩, ⟨n_i, γ_i, ω_i⟩};
            INSERT(π');
            insert π into W'                                ▷ postpone expansion
        end if
    else if statement of n_o is return then
        if π ⊈ Σ_s(pr of n_i) then
            σ := π;                               ▷ encountered new summary edge
            insert σ into Σ_s(pr);
            for all π_c ∈ W' s.t. APPLICABLE(π_c, σ) do
                π' :=APPLY(π_c, σ);               ▷ perform postponed expansion
                INSERT(π');
            end for
        end if
    end if
end while
```

Fig. 1. The SAT based model checking algorithm

have been constructed so far. Our algorithm is similar to the BDD-based model checking algorithm presented in [1]. However, unlike a BDD-based representation of path edges, our representation is not canonical. The price we pay for being able to apply transition functions efficiently is that we need to solve a QBF instance in order to determine whether a path edge is already an element of $\mathcal{P}$.

Let V be the variables of the procedure **pr**. Given two path edges $\langle n_i, \gamma_{i1}, \omega_{i1}\rangle$, $\langle n_o, \gamma_{o1}, \omega_{o1}\rangle$ and $\langle n_i, \gamma_{i2}, \omega_{i2}\rangle, \langle n_o, \gamma_{o2}, \omega_{o2}\rangle$, the latter is *at least as general as* the former iff

$$\forall \xi_1 .\ [\gamma_{o1}]_{\xi_1} \Rightarrow \exists \xi_2 .\ [\gamma_{o2}]_{\xi_2} \wedge \bigwedge_{v \in V} [\omega_{i1}(v)]_{\xi_1} = [\omega_{i2}(v)]_{\xi_2} \wedge [\omega_{o1}(v)]_{\xi_1} = [\omega_{o2}(v)]_{\xi_2} \tag{8}$$

where ξ_1 refers to the non-deterministic choice variables of the first path edge, and ξ_2 to those of the second. Equation 8 holds iff the set of pairs of concrete states represented by the first path edge is a subset of the corresponding set represented by the second. In that case, a further expansion of the path edge $\langle n_i, \gamma_{i1}, \omega_{i1}\rangle, \langle n_o, \gamma_{o1}, \omega_{o1}\rangle$ does not yield any states that are not discovered by expanding the more general path edge.

The pseudo code of our QBF-based algorithm is presented in Figure 1. It resembles the model checking algorithm presented in [1], but uses SAT and QBF instead of BDDs. In line 10, we use ω_* to indicate that the state is initialized non-deterministically.

We use APPLICABLE(π, σ) to denote the condition in Equation 5, where $\pi = \langle n_e, \gamma_e, \omega_e\rangle, \langle n_c, \gamma_c, \omega_c\rangle$ is a path edge that provides the calling context, and σ is a summary edge. Furthermore, APPLY(π, σ) denotes the path edge that we obtain by applying the summary according to equations (6) and (7). The condition in Equation 8 is expressed by $\pi_1 \subseteq \pi_2$ and holds if the path edge π_1 is subsumed by π_2. Finally, we use TRANS(π, n) to denote the application of the transition function of a node n as listed in Table 1.

The algorithm maintains a work-list $\mathcal{W}$ in which all path-edges that are currently explored are stored. Each path edge of this work-list is expanded according to the transition functions described above, until either the guard becomes unsatisfiable or the resulting path edge is already in $\mathcal{P}$. For convenience, we define a procedure `insert`(π), which we use to insert a path edge into the work-list, unless it is already contained in $\mathcal{P}$.

In line 14, the transition functions presented in Table 1 are applied. Whenever the algorithm encounters a `goto` statement, the current path edge is split (see line 17).

Procedure calls are handled in line 22. Matching summary edges are applied immediately. However, if there is no applicable summary edge, we construct an entry state for the called procedure and add a corresponding path edge to the work-list $\mathcal{W}$. Furthermore, we store the current path edge σ in $\mathcal{W}'$, which is examined whenever we add a new summary to $\Sigma(\mathbf{pr})$. Thus, we guarantee that any summary of **pr** that is eventually generated is applied to also σ (see line 39).

Path merging. Splitting the path edge in line 17 of our algorithm in Figure 1 may lead to an explosion of the of the number of path edges. Therefore, we *merge* path edges in our work-list $\mathcal{W}$ whenever possible. Two path edges $\langle n_{i1}, \gamma_{i1}, \omega_{i1}\rangle, \langle n_{o1}, \gamma_{o1}, \omega_{o1}\rangle$ and $\langle n_{i2}, \gamma_{i2}, \omega_{i2}\rangle, \langle n_{o2}, \gamma_{o2}, \omega_{o2}\rangle$ can be merged if $\langle n_{i1}, n_{o1}\rangle$ and $\langle n_{i2}, n_{o2}\rangle$ coincide. In that case, we construct a new path edge $\langle n_{i1}, \gamma_i, \omega_i\rangle, \langle n_o 1, \gamma_o, \omega_o\rangle$ such following conditions hold for γ_i and ω_i:

- $\gamma_i = \left(\gamma_{i1} \wedge \bigwedge_{v \in V} \omega_i(v) = \omega_{i1}(v)\right) \vee \left(\gamma_{i2} \wedge \bigwedge_{v \in V} \omega_i(v) = \omega_{i2}(v)\right)$
- for all $v \in V$, $\omega_i(v) = \omega_{i1}(v) \vee \omega_{i2}(v)$

Analogously, we construct similar conditions for γ_o and ω_o and name the procedure that merges a set of path edges Π MERGE(Π). We deploy a heuristic that postpones the application of certain transitions (e.g. at join nodes in the CFG) in order to increase the number of path edges in $\mathcal{W}$ that can be merged. A similar approach is used by the model checker DIZZY [20], but not in combination with summarization.

4 Universal Summaries

Solving the QBF instances is the primary performance bottleneck of the algorithm presented in the previous section. The majority of the QBF instances is generated by the fix-point detection algorithm (see Equation 8). These QBF instances cannot be avoided if we want to compute the least fix-point of $\Sigma_s(\mathbf{pr})$. However, if we settle for an over-approximation of this fix-point, we can reduce the number of calls to the QBF solver significantly.

The set of path edges consisting of *all* sequences of transitions of a procedure **pr** up to its reachability recurrence diameter (see Def. 3) is such an over-approximation. The definition of the reachability recurrence diameter requires adaption to be applicable to procedures of Boolean programs:

- The reachability recurrence diameter is only defined for finite state system and therefore not applicable to recursive procedure calls.
- The transition function T in Definition 1 is a compound, synchronous transition function that modifies all state variables in each step. A Boolean program is a disjunctive partitioning of *local* transitions, and the advantage of locality is lost if we treat it as a compound transition function.

We address these issues as follows:

- We replace the procedure calls in **pr** by a non-deterministic assignment to all global variables that are potentially changed by the callee. The set of these variables can be obtained by static analysis. The resulting procedure **pr*** is an over-approximation of the behavior of **pr**.
- We still split the path edges, but perform aggressive merging, i.e., we merge at every join node in the CFG. Thus, instead of unwinding the entire compound transition function, each cycle in the CFG is unwound separately. This corresponds to the loop unrolling algorithm used in the CBMC tool [24].

1: **procedure** UNROLL(**pr**)
2: $\mathcal{W} := \{\langle n_i, \mathtt{true}, \omega_* \rangle, \langle n_i, \mathtt{true}, \omega_* \rangle\}$; ▷ $\langle n_i, \mathtt{true}, \omega_* \rangle$ is initial state
3: **for all** nodes $n \in$ CFG(**pr**) **do**
4: $\mathcal{P}(n) := \emptyset$;
5: **end for**
6: assign priorities no nodes: the closer to a `return` statement, the lower;
7: **while** $\mathcal{W} \neq \emptyset$ **do**
8: choose n_o with highest priority s.t. $\exists \langle n_i, \gamma_i, \omega_i \rangle, \langle n_o, \gamma_o, \omega_o \rangle \in \mathcal{W}$;
9: $\mathcal{W}' := \{\langle n_i', \gamma_i', \omega_i' \rangle, \langle n_o', \gamma_o', \omega_o' \rangle \in \mathcal{W} \mid n_o' = n_o\}$;
10: $\mathcal{W} := \mathcal{W} \setminus \mathcal{W}'$;
11: $\pi' :=$ MERGE($\mathcal{W}'$);
12: EXPAND(π', n_o); ▷ expands π' and adds result to $\mathcal{W}$
13: **end while**
14: **assert** (statement of n_o is `return`);
15: **return** π';
16: **end procedure**

Fig. 2. Expanding and merging path edges at every join node

The algorithm in Figure 2 performs aggressive merging by making sure that no path edge can proceed beyond a *join node* unless all other path edges in the work list have "caught up". We achieve this by assigning a priority to each node in the control flow graph. The priority depends on the distance to the exit node: Nodes closer to the `return` statement have a lower priority, and the exit node itself has the lowest priority.

Note that this algorithm fails to proceed beyond a join node of a cycle of the CFG if the procedure EXPAND (see call in line 12) perpetually generates new path edges for this cycle. We prevent this by restricting the path edges generated by EXPAND to the reachability recurrence diameter of **pr**:

Definition 7 (Reachability Recurrence Diameter of procedure). *The* reachability recurrence diameter $rrd(\mathbf{pr})$ *of a Boolean procedure* **pr** *is the* longest *sequence of concrete transitions in* **pr*** *such that no state* $\langle n, \Omega \rangle$ *of the procedure is visited twice.*

Given a set of symbolic path edges $\langle n_i, \gamma_i, \omega_i \rangle, \langle n_o, \gamma_{o,j}, \omega_{o,j} \rangle$, $j \in \{1..n\}$ for a node n_o in procedure **pr***, we can construct a formula (similar to Equation 2) that is satisfiable iff there are n distinct states such that each path edge represents one of them:

$$\exists \xi . \left[\bigwedge_{j=0}^{n-1} \bigwedge_{k=j+1}^{n} \gamma_{o,j} \wedge \gamma_{o,k} \wedge \bigvee_{v \in V} \omega_{o,j}(v) \neq \omega_{o,k}(v) \right]_{\xi} \tag{9}$$

If we keep a record of all path edges that reach a node n (using a set $\mathcal{P}(n)$), we can use Equation 9 to check whether there still exists a sequence of concrete transitions that visits no state at n twice. We use RECURRING($\mathcal{P}(n)$) to denote Equation 9.

```
1: procedure INSERT(π)
2:     if ¬RECURRING(P(n_o) ∪ {π}) then
3:         P(n_o) := P(n_o) ∪ {π};
4:         W := W ∪ {π};
5:     end if
6: end procedure
7: procedure EXPAND(π, n_o)
8:     if statement of n_o is skip, assume, or assignment then
9:         π' :=TRANS(π, n_o);
10:        INSERT(π');
11:    else if statement of n_o is goto ℓ_1, ..., ℓ_k then
12:        π_ℓ1, ..., π_ℓk := TRANS(π, n_o);
13:        for all ℓ ∈ {ℓ_1, ... ℓ_k} do
14:            INSERT(π_ℓ);
15:        end for
16:    else if statement of n_o is a call pr'(e_1, ..., e_k) then
17:        let G ⊆ {g_1, ..., g_m} be globals changed in pr';
18:        π' := π with G assigned non-deterministically;
19:        INSERT(π');
20:    end if
21: end procedure
```

Fig. 3. Unrolling transitions of a Boolean procedure until states repeat

The pseudo-code for the procedure EXPAND is presented in Figure 3. The algorithm checks at each program location whether the reachability recurrence diameter is exceeded. The path edge of the current step is added to $\mathcal{P}(n)$ unless RECURRING$(\mathcal{P} \cup \{\pi\})$ holds (we implicitly assume that path edges with unsatisfiable guards are dropped, too).

Whenever the algorithm encounters a procedure call **pr'**(...), it replaces the transition by a non-deterministic assignment to the globals that are potentially changed by **pr'** (see line 18). Finally, we return the entirely merged path edge π that reaches the exit node of the CFG.

Again, we use $\langle n_i, \texttt{true}, \omega_* \rangle$ to denote the non-deterministically initialized state (see line 2 in Figure 2), i.e., we do not restrict the calling context. Therefore, our algorithm generates a path edge that contains *all* sequences of transitions that do not visit a state twice for an arbitrary calling context.

We use this observation to justify our initial claim: The path edge π obtained by computing UNROLL(**pr**) over-approximates $\Sigma_s(\mathbf{pr})$. We call this π a universal summary.

Definition 8 (Universal summary). *The* universal summary $\Sigma_u(\mathbf{pr})$ *of a procedure* **pr** *is the path edge that we obtain by merging the path edges of all sequences of transitions (the initial state being an unconstrained calling context) of* **pr*** *up to the reachability recurrence diameter of* **pr***, *i.e.,* $\Sigma_u(\mathbf{pr}) :=$ UNROLL(**pr**)*).*

Table 2. Comparison of performance of BEBOP, QBF-based summarization, and universal summaries (timout: $> 2h$)

Benchmark	#vars	BEBOP	QBF-summaries	univ. summ.	violation
SLAM adddevice	434	4m37.4s	0m0.6s	0m1.8s	yes
SLAM nulldevice	434	4m34.0s	0m8.6s	0m1.4s	yes
SLAM pendedcompletedreq	86	0m30.9s	timeout	0m13.5s	yes
SLAM targetrelationneedsref	37	0m0.4s	0m0.5s	0m2.74s	no
SLAM markirppending	11	0m0.4s	0m3.0s	0m18.5s	no
SLAM wmiforward	15	0m0.7s	0m2.0s	0m15.3s	no
TERMINATOR 1	74	timeout	1m55.9s	1m55.9s	yes
TERMINATOR 2	60	88m22.6s	timeout	timeout	yes

The universal summary of **pr** does not only over-approximate $\Sigma_s(\mathbf{pr})$, but also the set of feasible transition sequences. These spurious execution traces are eliminated when $\Sigma_u(\mathbf{pr})$ is applied at all call sites of **pr** according to equations (6) and (7).

However, in case of a cyclic dependency between procedures (i.e., in case of recursion or mutual recursion) the universal summaries cannot be applied. Therefore, we compute the universal summaries of all non-recursive procedures of a Boolean program, and use the algorithm in Figure 1 to handle the remaining recursive procedure calls.

5 Benchmarks

We used SLAM [10] and TERMINATOR [25] to generate eight Boolean programs from Windows device drivers. We compare the performance of our implementation on these examples to the model checker BEBOP, which is part of Microsoft Research's SLAM/SDV toolkit [10] (see Table 2). In addition, we compare the effect of summarization with universal summaries and entirely QBF-based summarization. The column labeled "violation" indicates whether the reachability property we are checking for can be violated or not.

The algorithm that uses universal summaries deploys a heuristic that switches back to QBF-summaries for procedures with universal summaries that are larger than a certain threshold. This typically happens if the procedure contains a lot of non-deterministic assignments.

The benchmarks are incoherent, and we have yet to investigate why this is the case. In some situations (like the `adddevice` benchmark with 434 variables), our implementation is significantly faster than BEBOP. However, this cannot be generalized. Furthermore, in some cases it turns out to be disadvantageous to use universal summaries (see, for instance, the **markirppending** benchmark). The QBF-instances resulting from the combination of universal summaries and QBF-based summarization may become too large for the solver SKIZZO [26]. In the TERMINATOR 2 benchmark, this also happens without universal summaries.

We have a large number of small regression tests that indicate that BDD-based implementations are still faster for Boolean programs with a small number of variables. However, the reason for this may be that we did not profile and optimize our implementation, yet. We intend to make an updated set of benchmarks available as soon as we are able to explain the performance problems on small examples.

6 Conclusion

We present a SAT based model checking algorithm for Boolean programs that uses a QBF solver to compute the least fix-point of the set of summary edges of a procedure. Furthermore, we introduce the concept of *universal summaries*, an over-approximation of the summary edges our initial algorithm computes. By using universal summaries, we reduce the number of calls to the QBF solver significantly.

Our preliminary benchmarks do not allow us to conclude that our approach is in general superior to BDD based model checking. However, some of the results are very promising and indicate that it is worthwhile to further pursue the idea.

Acknowledgements. We would like to thank Vijay D'Silva, Angelo Brillout, and our anonymous reviewers for their valuable comments on this paper.

References

1. Ball, T., Rajamani, S.K.: Bebop: A symbolic model checker for Boolean programs. In: Havelund, K., Penix, J., Visser, W. (eds.) SPIN Model Checking and Software Verification. LNCS, vol. 1885, pp. 113–130. Springer, Heidelberg (2000)
2. Ball, T., Rajamani, S.: Boolean programs: A model and process for software analysis. Technical Report 2000-14, Microsoft Research (2000)
3. Graf, S., Saïdi, H.: Construction of abstract state graphs with PVS. In: Grumberg, O. (ed.) CAV 1997. LNCS, vol. 1254, pp. 72–83. Springer, Heidelberg (1997)
4. Büchi, J.R.: Regular canonical systems. Archive for Mathematical Logic 6, 91 (1964)
5. Sharir, M., Pnueli, A.: Two approaches to interprocedural data dalow analysis. In: Program Flow Analysis: Theory and Applications, pp. 189–233. Prentice-Hall, Englewood Cliffs (1981)
6. Esparza, J., Hansel, D., Rossmanith, P., Schwoon, S.: Efficient algorithms for model checking pushdown systems. In: Emerson, E.A., Sistla, A.P. (eds.) CAV 2000. LNCS, vol. 1855, pp. 232–247. Springer, Heidelberg (2000)
7. Bryant, R.E.: Graph-based algorithms for Boolean function manipulation. IEEE Transactions on Computers 35, 677–691 (1986)
8. Cook, B., Kroening, D., Sharygina, N.: Symbolic model checking for asynchronous Boolean programs. In: Godefroid, P. (ed.) Model Checking Software. LNCS, vol. 3639, pp. 75–90. Springer, Heidelberg (2005)
9. Kroening, D., Weissenbacher, G.: Counterexamples with loops for predicate abstraction. In: Ball, T., Jones, R.B. (eds.) CAV 2006. LNCS, vol. 4144, pp. 152–165. Springer, Heidelberg (2006)

10. Ball, T., Cook, B., Levin, V., Rajamani, S.K.: SLAM and Static Driver Verifier: Technology transfer of formal methods inside Microsoft. In: Boiten, E.A., Derrick, J., Smith, G.P. (eds.) IFM 2004. LNCS, vol. 2999, Springer, Heidelberg (2004)
11. Finkel, A., Willems, B., Wolper, P.: A direct symbolic approach to model checking pushdown systems. ENTCS 9 (1997)
12. Schwoon, S.: Model-Checking Pushdown Systems. PhD thesis, Technische Universität München (2002)
13. Lal, A., Reps, T.: Improving pushdown system model checking. In: Ball, T., Jones, R.B. (eds.) CAV 2006. LNCS, vol. 4144, Springer, Heidelberg (2006)
14. Bouajjani, A., Esparza, J.: Rewriting models of Boolean programs. In: Pfenning, F. (ed.) RTA 2006. LNCS, vol. 4098, Springer, Heidelberg (2006)
15. Bouajjani, A., Esparza, J., Touili, T.: A generic approach to the static analysis of concurrent programs with procedures. In: Principles of Programming Languages (POPL), pp. 62–73. ACM Press, New York (2003)
16. Bouajjani, A., Touili, T.: On computing reachability sets of process rewrite systems. In: Giesl, J. (ed.) RTA 2005. LNCS, vol. 3467, pp. 484–499. Springer, Heidelberg (2005)
17. Qadeer, S., Rehof, J.: Context-bounded model checking of concurrent software. In: Halbwachs, N., Zuck, L.D. (eds.) TACAS 2005. LNCS, vol. 3440, pp. 93–103. Springer, Heidelberg (2005)
18. Touili, T., Sighireanu, M.: Bounded communication reachability analysis of bounded communication reachability analysis of process rewrite systems with ordered parallelism. In: Verification of Infinite State Systems (INFINITY), Elsevier, Amsterdam (2007)
19. Cook, B., Kroening, D., Sharygina, N.: Over-approximating Boolean programs with unbounded thread creation. In: Formal Methods in Computer-Aided Design (FMCAD), pp. 53–59. IEEE Computer Society Press, Los Alamitos (2006)
20. Leino, K.R.M.: A SAT characterization of Boolean-program correctness. In: Ball, T., Rajamani, S.K. (eds.) Model Checking Software. LNCS, vol. 2648, pp. 104–120. Springer, Heidelberg (2003)
21. Biere, A., Cimatti, A., Clarke, E.M., Zhu, Y.: Symbolic model checking without BDDs. In: Cleaveland, W.R. (ed.) ETAPS 1999 and TACAS 1999. LNCS, vol. 1579, pp. 193–207. Springer, Heidelberg (1999)
22. Kroening, D., Strichman, O.: Efficient computation of recurrence diameters. In: Zuck, L.D., Attie, P.C., Cortesi, A., Mukhopadhyay, S. (eds.) VMCAI 2003. LNCS, vol. 2575, pp. 298–309. Springer, Heidelberg (2003)
23. Biere, A., Cimatti, A., Clarke, E.M., Strichman, O., Zhu, Y.: Bounded model checking. Advances in Computers 58, 118–149 (2003)
24. Clarke, E., Kroening, D., Lerda, F.: A tool for checking ANSI-C programs. In: Jensen, K., Podelski, A. (eds.) TACAS 2004. LNCS, vol. 2988, pp. 168–176. Springer, Heidelberg (2004)
25. Cook, B., Podelski, A., Rybalchenko, A.: Terminator: Beyond safety. In: Ball, T., Jones, R.B. (eds.) CAV 2006. LNCS, vol. 4144, Springer, Heidelberg (2006)
26. Benedetti, M.: Evaluating QBFs via symbolic skolemization. In: Baader, F., Voronkov, A. (eds.) LPAR 2004. LNCS (LNAI), vol. 3452, pp. 285–300. Springer, Heidelberg (2005)

LTL Satisfiability Checking

Kristin Y. Rozier[1,*] and Moshe Y. Vardi[2]

[1] NASA Langley Research Center, Hampton, Virginia 23681
Kristin.Y.Rozier@nasa.gov
[2] Rice University, Houston, Texas 77005
vardi@cs.rice.edu

Abstract. We report here on an experimental investigation of LTL satisfiability checking via a reduction to model checking. By using large LTL formulas, we offer challenging model-checking benchmarks to both explicit and symbolic model checkers. For symbolic model checking, we use both CadenceSMV and NuSMV. For explicit model checking, we use SPIN as the search engine, and we test essentially all publicly available LTL translation tools. Our experiments result in two major findings. First, most LTL translation tools are research prototypes and cannot be considered industrial quality tools. Second, when it comes to LTL satisfiability checking, the symbolic approach is clearly superior to the explicit approach.

1 Introduction

Model-checking tools are successfully used for checking whether systems have desired properties [11]. The application of model-checking tools to complex systems involves a nontrivial step of creating a mathematical model of the system and translating the desired properties into a formal specification. When the model does not satisfy the specification, model-checking tools accompany this negative answer with a counterexample, which points to an inconsistency between the system and the desired behaviors. It is often the case, however, that there is an error in the system model or in the formal specification. Such errors may not be detected when the answer of the model-checking tool is positive: while a positive answer does guarantee that the model satisfies the specification, the answer to the real question, namely, whether the system has the intended behavior, may be different.

The realization of this unfortunate situation has led to the development of several *sanity checks* for formal verification [29]. The goal of these checks is to detect errors in the system model or the properties. Sanity checks in industrial tools are typically simple, ad hoc, tests, such as checking for enabling conditions that are never enabled [31]. *Vacuity detection* provides a more systematic approach. Intuitively, a specification is satisfied vacuously in a model if it is satisfied in some non-interesting way. For example,

* Work contributing to this paper was completed at Rice University, Cambridge University, and NASA Langley Research Center, and was supported in part by the Rice Computational Research Cluster (Ada), funded by NSF under Grant CNS-0421109 and a partnership between Rice University, AMD and Cray.

D. Bošnački and S. Edelkamp (Eds.): SPIN 2007, LNCS 4595, pp. 149–167, 2007.

the linear temporal logic (LTL) specification $\Box(req \rightarrow \Diamond grant)$ ("every request is eventually followed by a grant") is satisfied vacuously in a model with no requests. While vacuity checking cannot ensure that whenever a model satisfies a formula, the model is correct, it does identify certain positive results as vacuous, increasing the likelihood of capturing modeling and specification errors. Several papers on vacuity checking have been published over the last few years [2, 3, 8, 27, 26, 30, 34, 37], and various industrial model-checking tools support vacuity checking [2, 3, 8].

All vacuity-checking algorithms check whether a subformula of the specification does not affect the satisfaction of the specification in the model. In the example above, the subformula *req* does not affect satisfaction in a model with no request. There is, however, a possibility of a vacuous result that is not captured by current vacuity-checking approaches. If the specification is *valid*, that is, true in *all* models, then model checking this specification always results in a positive answer. Consider for example the specification $\Box(b_1 \rightarrow \Diamond b_2)$, where b_1 and b_2 are propositional formulas. If b_1 and b_2 are logically equivalent, then this specification is valid and is satisfied by all models. Nevertheless, current vacuity-checking approaches do not catch this problem. We propose a method for an additional sanity check to catch exactly this sort of oversight.

Writing formal specifications is a difficult task, which is prone to error just as implementation development is error prone. However, formal verification tools offer little help in debugging specifications other than standard vacuity checking. Clearly, if a formal property is valid, then this is certainly due to an error. Similarly, if a formal property is *unsatisfiable*, that is, true in *no* model, then this is also certainly due to an error. Even if each individual property written by the specifier is satisfiable, their conjunction may very well be unsatisfiable. Recall that a logical formula φ is valid iff its negation $\neg\varphi$ is not satisfiable. Thus, as a necessary sanity check for debugging a specification, model-checking tools should ensure that both the specification φ and its negation $\neg\varphi$ are satisfiable. (For a different approach to debugging specifications, see [1].)

A basic observation underlying our work is that LTL satisfiability checking can be reduced to model checking. Consider a formula φ over a set *Prop* of atomic propositions. If a model M is *universal*, that is, it contains all possible traces over *Prop*, then φ is satisfiable precisely when the model M does *not* satisfy $\neg\varphi$. Thus, it is easy to add a satisfiability-checking feature to LTL model-checking tools.

LTL model checkers can be classified as *explicit* or *symbolic*. Explicit model checkers, such as SPIN [28] or SPOT [15], construct the state-space of the model explicitly and search for a trace falsifying the specification [12]. In contrast, symbolic model checkers, such as CadenceSMV [32], NuSMV [9], or VIS [5], represent the model and analyze it symbolically using binary decision diagrams (BDDs) [7].

LTL model checkers follow the automata-theoretic approach [45], in which the complemented LTL specification is explicitly or symbolically translated to a Büchi automaton, which is then composed with the model under verification; see also [44]. The model checker then searches for a trace of the model that is accepted by the automaton. All symbolic model checkers use the symbolic translation described in [10] and the analysis algorithm of [17], though CadenceSMV and VIS try to optimize further. There has been extensive research over the past decade into explicit translation of LTL to automata[13, 14, 18, 19, 20, 25, 21, 24, 40, 38, 42], but it is difficult to get a clear sense of the state of the art from a review of the literature. Measuring the performance of LTL satisfiability checking enables us to benchmark the performance of LTL model checking tools, and, more specifically, of LTL translation tools.

We report here on an experimental investigation of LTL satisfiability checking via a reduction to model checking. By using large LTL formulas, we offer challenging model-checking benchmarks to both explicit and symbolic model checkers. For symbolic model checking, we used both CadenceSMV and NuSMV. For explicit model checking, we use SPIN as the search engine, and we tested essentially all publicly available LTL translation tools. We used a wide variety of benchmark formulas, either generated randomly, as in [14], or using a scalable pattern (e.g., $\bigwedge_{i=1}^{n} p_i$). LTL formulas typically used for evaluating LTL translation tools are usually too small to offer challenging benchmarks. Note that real specifications typically consist of many temporal properties, whose conjunction ought to be satisfiable. Thus, studying satisfiability of large LTL formulas is quite appropriate.

Our experiments resulted in two major findings. First, most LTL translation tools are research prototypes and cannot be considered industrial quality tools. Many of them are written in scripting languages such as Perl or Python, which has drastic negative impact on their performance. Furthermore, these tools generally degrade gracelessly, often yielding incorrect results with no warning. Among all the tools we tested, only SPOT can be considered an industrial quality tool. Second, when it comes to LTL satisfiability checking, the symbolic approach is clearly superior to the explicit approach. Even SPOT, the best LTL translator in our experiments, was rarely able to compete effectively against the symbolic tools. This result is consistent with the comparison of explicit and symbolic approach to modal satisfiability [35, 36], but is somewhat surprising in the context of LTL satisfiability in view of [39].

Related software, called `lbtt`,[1] provides an LTL-to-Büchi explicit translator testbench and environment for basic profiling. The `lbtt` tool performs simple consistency checks on an explicit tool's output automata, accompanied by sample data when inconsistencies in these automata are detected [41]. Whereas the primary use of `lbtt` is to assist developers of explicit LTL translators in debugging new tools or comparing a pair of tools, we compare performance with respect to LTL satisfiability problems across a host of different tools, both explicit and symbolic.

The structure of the paper is as follows. Section 2 provides the theoretical background for this work. In Section 3, we describe the tools studied here. We define our experimental method in Section 4, and detail our results in Section 5. We conclude with a discussion in Section 6.

2 Theoretical Background

Linear Temporal Logic (LTL) formulas are composed of a finite set *Prop* of atomic propositions, the Boolean connectives $\neg$, $\wedge$, $\vee$, and $\rightarrow$, and the temporal connectives $\mathcal{X}$ (next time) $\mathcal{U}$ (until), $\mathcal{R}$ (release), $\Box$ (also called $\mathcal{G}$ for "globally") and $\Diamond$ (also called $\mathcal{F}$ for "in the future"). We define LTL formulas inductively:

[1] `www.tcs.hut.fi/Software/lbtt/`

Definition 1. *For every $p \in Prop$, p is a formula. If φ and ψ are formulas, then so are:*

$$\neg\varphi \quad \varphi\wedge\psi \quad \varphi\rightarrow\psi \quad \varphi\,\mathcal{U}\psi \quad \mathcal{G}\varphi$$
$$\varphi\vee\psi \quad \mathcal{X}\varphi \quad \varphi\mathcal{R}\varphi \quad \mathcal{F}\varphi$$

LTL formulas describe the behavior of the variables in $Prop$ over a linear series of time steps starting at time zero and extending infinitely into the future. We satisfy such formulas over *computations*, which are functions that assign truth values to the elements of $Prop$ at each time instant [16].

Definition 2. *We interpret LTL formulas over computations of the form $\pi : \omega \rightarrow 2^{Prop}$. We define $\pi, i \models \varphi$ (computation π at time instant $i \in \omega$ satisfies LTL formula φ) as follows:*

$\pi, i \models p$ for $p \in Prop$ if $p \in \pi(i)$.
$\pi, i \models \varphi\wedge\psi$ if $\pi, i \models \varphi$ and $\pi, i \models \psi$.
$\pi, i \models \neg\varphi$ if $\pi, i \not\models \varphi$.
$\pi, i \models \mathcal{X}\varphi$ if $\pi, i+1 \models \varphi$.
$\pi, i \models \varphi\,\mathcal{U}\psi$ if $\exists j \geq i$, such that $\pi, j \models \psi$ and $\forall k, i \leq k < j$, we have $\pi, k \models \varphi$.
$\pi, i \models \varphi\mathcal{R}\psi$ if $\forall j \geq i$, if $\pi, j \not\models \psi$, then $\exists k$, $i \leq k < j$, such that $\pi, k \models \varphi$.

We define $(\mathcal{F}\varphi)$ as $(true\ \mathcal{U}\varphi)$ and $(\mathcal{G}\varphi)$ as $(\neg\mathcal{F}\neg\varphi)$. We take $models(\varphi)$ to be the set of computations that satisfy φ at time 0, i.e., $\{\pi : \pi, 0 \models \varphi\}$.

In automata-theoretic model checking, we represent LTL formulas using Büchi automata.

Definition 3. *A* **Büchi Automaton** *(BA) is a quintuple $(Q, \Sigma, \delta, q_0, F)$ where:*

Q is a finite set of states.
Σ is a finite alphabet.
$\delta : Q \times \Sigma \rightarrow Q$ is the transition relation.
$q_0 \in Q$ is the initial state.
$F \subseteq Q$ is a set of final states.

A run of a Büchi automaton over an infinite word $w = w_0, w_1, w_2, \ldots \in \Sigma$ is a sequence of states $q_0, q_1, q_2, \ldots \in Q$ such that $\forall i \geq 0$, $\delta(q_i, w_i) = q_{i+1}$. An infinite word w is accepted by the automaton if the run over w visits at least one state in F infinitely often. We denote the set of infinite words accepted by an automaton A by $L_\omega(A)$.

A computation satisfying LTL formula φ is an infinite word over the alphabet $\Sigma = 2^{Prop}$. The next theorem relates the expressive power of LTL to that of Büchi automata.

Theorem 1. [46] *Given an LTL formula φ, we can construct a Büchi automaton $A_\varphi = \langle Q, \Sigma, \delta, q_0, F\rangle$ such that $|Q|$ is in $2^{O(|\varphi|)}$, $\Sigma = 2^{Prop}$, and $L_\omega(A_\varphi)$ is exactly $models(\varphi)$.*

This theorem reduces LTL satisfiability checking to automata-theoretic nonemptiness checking, as φ is satisfiable iff $models(\varphi) \neq \emptyset$ iff $L_\omega(A_\varphi) \neq \emptyset$.

We can now relate LTL satisfiability checking to LTL model checking. Suppose we have a *universal model*, M, that generates all computations over its atomic propositions; that is, we have that $L + \omega(M) = (2^{Prop})^\omega$. We now have that M does *not* satisfy $\neg\varphi$ if and only if φ is satisfiable. Thus, φ is satisfiable precisely when the model checker finds a counterexample.

3 Tools Tested

In total, we tested eleven LTL compilation algorithms from nine research tools. To offer a broad, objective picture of the current state-of-the-art, we tested the algorithms against several different sequences of benchmarks, comparing, where appropriate, the size of generated automata in terms of numbers of states and transitions, translation time, model-analysis time, and correctness of the output.

3.1 Explicit Tools

The explicit LTL model checker SPIN [28] accepts either LTL properties, which are translated internally into Büchi automata, or Büchi automata for complemented properties ("never claims"). We tested SPIN with Promela (PROcess MEta LAnguage) never-claims produced by several LTL translation algorithms. (As SPIN's built-in translator is dominated by TMP, we do not show results for this translator.) The algorithms studied here represent all tools publicly available in 2006, as described in the following table:

Explicit Automata Construction Tools	
LTL2AUT	(Daniele–Guinchiglia–Vardi)
Implementations (Java, Perl)	LTL2Buchi, Wring
LTL2BA (C)	(Oddoux–Gastin)
LTL2Buchi (Java)	(Giannakopoulou–Lerda)
LTL $\rightarrow$ NBA (Python)	(Fritz–Teegen)
Modella (C)	(Sebastiani–Tonetta)
SPOT (C++)	(Duret-Lutz–Poitrenaud–Rebiha–Baarir–Martinez)
TMP (SML of NJ)	(Etessami)
Wring (Perl)	(Somenzi–Bloem)

We provide here short descriptions of the tools and their algorithms, detailing aspects which may account for our results. We also note that aspects of implementation including programming language, memory management, and attention to efficiency, seem to have significant effects on tool performance.

Classical Algorithms. Following [46], the first optimized LTL translation algorithm was described in [24]. The basic optimization ideas were: (1) generate states by demand only, (2) use node labels rather than edge labels to simplify translation to Promela, and (3) use a *generalized Büchi* acceptance condition so eventualities can be handled one at a time. The resulting generalized Büchi automaton (GBA) is then "degeneralized" or translated to a BA. **LTL2AUT** improved further on this approach by using lightweight propositional reasoning to generate fewer states [14]. We tested two implementations of LTL2AUT, one included in the Java-based LTL2Buchi tool and one included in the Perl-based Wring tool.

TMP[2] [18] and **Wring**[3] [40] each extend LTL2AUT with three kinds of additional optimizations. First, in the *pre-translation optimization*, the input formula is simplified

[2] www.bell-labs.com/project/TMP/

[3] www.ist.tugraz.at/staff/bloem/wring.html

using Negation Normal Form (NNF) and extensive sets of rewrite rules. Second, *mid-translation optimizations* tighten the LTL-to-GBA-to-BA translation algorithms. Third, the resulting automata are minimized further during *post-translation optimization*. In the end, TMP produces a BA whereas Wring halts translation with a GBA, which we had to degeneralize.

LTL2Buchi[4] [25] optimizes the LTL2AUT algorithm by initially generating transition-based generalized Büchi automata (TGBA) rather than node-labeled BA to allow for more compaction based on equivalence classes, contradictions, and redundancies in the state space. Special attention to efficiency is given during the ensuing translation to node-labeled BA. The algorithm incorporates the formula rewriting and BA-reduction optimizations of TMP and Wring.

Modella[5] focuses on minimizing the *nondeterminism* of the property automaton in an effort to minimize the size of the product of the property and system model automata during verification [38]. If the property automaton is deterministic, then the number of states in the product automaton will be at most the number of states in the system model. Thus, reducing nondeterminism is a desirable goal. This is accomplished using *semantic branching*, or branching on truth assignments, rather than the *syntactic branching* of LTL2AUT. Modella also postpones branching when possible.

Alternating Automata Tools. Instead of the direct translation approach of [46], an alternative approach, based on *alternating automata*, was proposed in [43]. In this approach, the LTL formula is first translated into an alternating Büchi automaton, which is then translated to a nondeterministic Büchi automaton.

LTL2BA[6] [21] first translates the input formula into a *very weak* alternating automaton (VWAA). It then uses various heuristics to minimize the VWAA, before translating it to GBA. The GBA in turn is minimized before being translated into a BA, and finally the BA is minimized further. Thus, the algorithm's central focus is on optimization of intermediate representations through iterative simplifications and on-the-fly constructions.

LTL→NBA[7] follows a similar approach to that of LTL2BA [19]. Unlike the heuristic minimization of LWAA used in LTL2BA, LTL→NBA uses a game-theoretic minimization based on utilizing a delayed simulation relation for on-the-fly simplifications.

Back to Classics. **SPOT**[8] is the most recently developed LTL-to-Büchi optimized translation tool [15]. It does not use alternating automata, but borrows ideas from all the tools described above. It adds two important optimizations: (1) unlike all other tools, it uses pre-branching states, rather than post-branching states (as introduced in [13]), and (2) it uses BDDs ([6]) for propositional reasoning.

---

[4] `http://ase.arc.nasa.gov/people/dimitra/LTL2Buchi.php`

[5] `http://www.science.unitn.it/~stonetta/modella.html`

[6] `http://www.liafa.jussieu.fr/~oddoux/ltl2ba/`

[7] `http://estragon.ti.informatik.uni-kiel.de/~fritz/ABA-Simulation/ltl.cgi`

[8] `http://spot.lip6.fr/wiki/SpotWiki`

3.2 Symbolic Tools

Symbolic model checkers describe both the system model and property automaton symbolically: states are viewed as truth assignments to Boolean state variables and the transition relation is defined as a conjunction of Boolean constraints on pairs of current and next states [7]. The model checker uses a BDD-based fix-point algorithm to find a *fair path* in the model-automaton product [17]. CadenceSMV[9] [32] and NuSMV[10] [9] both evolved from the original Symbolic Model Verifier developed at CMU [33]. Both tools support LTL model checking via the symbolic translation of LTL to automata described in [10]. CadenceSMV additionally implements heuristics that attempt to reduce LTL model checking to CTL model checking in some cases [4].

4 Experimental Methods

4.1 Performance Evaluation

We ran all tests on Ada, a Rice University Cray XD1 cluster.[11] Ada is comprised of 158 nodes with 4 processors (cores) per node for a total of 632 CPUs in pairs of dual core 2.2 GHz AMD Opteron processors with 1 MB L2 cache. There are 2 GB of memory per core or a total of 8 GB of RAM per node. The operating system is SuSE Linux 9.0 with the 2.6.5 kernel. Each of our tests was run with exclusive access to one node and was considered to time out after 4 hours of run time. We measured all timing data using the Unix `time` command.

Explicit Tools. Each test was performed in two steps. First, we applied the translation tools to the negation of the input LTL formula and ran them with the standard flags recommended by the tools' authors, plus any additional flag needed to specify that the output automaton should be in Promela. Second, each output automaton, in the form of a Promela *never-claim*, was checked by SPIN. In this role, SPIN serves as a search engine for each of the LTL translation tools; it takes a never-claim and checks it for non-emptiness in conjunction with an input model.[12]

In all tests, the model was a *universal* Promela program, enumerating all possible traces over *Prop*. For example, when $Prop = \{A, B\}$, the Promela model is:

```
bool A,B;
/* define an active procedure to generate values for A and B */
active proctype generateValues()
{ do
   :: atomic{ A = 0; B = 0; }
   :: atomic{ A = 0; B = 1; }
   :: atomic{ A = 1; B = 0; }
   :: atomic{ A = 1; B = 1; }
  od }
```

[9] http://www.cadence.com/company/cadence_labs_research.html

[10] http://nusmv.irst.itc.it/

[11] http://rcsg.rice.edu/ada/

[12] It would be interesting to use SPOT's SCC-based search algorithm [23] as the underlying search engine, rather than SPIN's nested depth-first search algorithm [12].

We use the `atomic{}` construct to ensure that the Boolean variables change value in one unbreakable step. Note that the size of this model is exponential in the number of atomic propositions.

Symbolic Tools. We compare the explicit tools with CadenceSMV and NuSMV. To check whether a LTL formula φ is satisfiable, we model check $\neg\varphi$ against a universal SMV model. For example, if $\varphi = (X(a))$, we provide the following input to NuSMV:

```
MODULE main
  VAR
    a : boolean;
    b : boolean;
    c : boolean;
  LTLSPEC !(X(a=1 ))
  FAIRNESS
    1
```

SMV negates the specification, $\neg\varphi$, symbolically compiles φ into A_φ, and conjoins A_φ with the universal model. If the automaton is not empty, then SMV finds a fair path, which satisfies the formula φ. In this way, SMV acts as both a symbolic compiler and a search engine.

4.2 Input Formulas

We benchmarked the tools against three types of scalable formulas: random formulas, counter formulas, and pattern formulas. Scalability played an important role in our experiment, since the goal was to challenge the tools with large formulas and state spaces. All tools were applied to the same formulas and the results (satisfiable or unsatisfiable) were compared. The symbolic tools, which were always in agreement, were considered as reference tools for checking correctness.

Random Formulas. In order to cover as much of the problem space as possible, we tested sets of 250 randomly-generated formulas varying the formula length and number of variables as in [14]. We randomly generated sets of 250 formulas varying the number of variables, N, from 1 to 3, and the length of the formula, L, from 5 up to 65. We set the probability of choosing a temporal operator $P = 0.5$ to create formulas with both a nontrivial temporal structure and a nontrivial Boolean structure. Other choices were decided uniformly. We report median running times as the distribution of run times has a high variance and contains many outliers. All formulas were generated prior to testing, so each tool was run on the *same* formulas. While we made sure that, when generating a set of length L, every formula was exactly of length L and not *up to* L, we did find that the formulas were frequently reducible. Tools with better initial formula reduction algorithms performed well in these tests.

Counter Formulas. Pre-translation rewriting is highly effective for random formulas, but ineffective for structured formulas [18, 40]. To measure performance on scalable, non-random formulas we tested the tools on formulas that describe n-bit binary counters with increasing values of n. These formulas are irreducible by pre-translation rewriting, uniquely satisfiable, and represent a predictably-sized state space. Whereas our measure of correctness for random formulas is a conservative check that the tools find satisfiable formulas to be satisfiable, we check for precisely the unique counterexample for each counter formula. We tested four constructions of binary counter formulas, varying two factors: number of variables and nesting of $\mathcal{X}$'s.

We can represent a binary counter using two variables: a counter variable and a marker variable to designate the beginning of each new counter value. Alternatively, we can use 3 variables, adding a variable to encode carry bits, which eliminates the need for $\mathcal{U}$-connectives in the formula. We can nest $\mathcal{X}$'s to provide more succinct formulas or express the formulas using a conjunction of unnested $\mathcal{X}$-sub-formulas.

Let b be an atomic proposition. Then a computation π over b is a word in $(2^{\{0,1\}})^{\omega}$. By dividing π into blocks of length n, we can view π as a sequence of n-bit values, denoting the sequence of values assumed by an n-bit counter starting at 0, and incrementing successively by 1. To simplify the formulas, we represent each block $b_0, b_1, \ldots, b_{n-1}$ as having the most significant bit on the right and the least significant bit on the left. For example, for $n = 2$ the b blocks cycle through the values 00, 10, 01, and 11. For technical convenience, we use an atomic proposition m to mark the blocks. That is, we intend m to hold at point i precisely when $i = 0 \bmod n$.

For π to represent an n-bit counter, the following properties need to hold:

```
1) The marker consists of a repeated pattern of a 1 followed by n-1 0's.
2) The first n bits are 0's.
3) If the least significant bit is 0, then it is 1 n steps later
   and the other bits do not change.
4) All of the bits before and including the first 0 in an n-bit block flip
   their values in the next block; the other bits do not change.
```

For $n = 4$, these properties are captured by the conjunction of the following formulas:

```
1. (m) && ( [](m -> ((X(!m)) && (X(X(!m))) && (X(X(X(!m))))
                                        && X(X(X(X(m)))))))
2. (!b) && (X(!b)) && (X(X(!b))) && (X(X(X(!b))))
3. []( (m && !b) ->
       ( X(X(X(X(b)))) &&
         X ( ( (!m) &&
            (b -> X(X(X(X(b))))) &&
            (!b -> X(X(X(X(!b))))) ) U m ) ) )
4. [] ( (m && b) ->
        (X(X(X(X(!b)))) &&
          (X ( (b && !m && X(X(X(X(!b))))) U
                (m || (!m && !b && X(X(X(X(b)))) &&
                       X( ( !m && (b -> X(X(X(X(b))))) &&
                            (!b -> X(X(X(X(!b))))) ) U m ) ) ) ) ) ) )
```

Note that this encoding creates formulas of length $O(n^2)$. A more compact encoding results in formulas of length $O(n)$. For example, we can replace formula (2) above with:

```
2. ((!b) && X((!b) && X((!b) && X(!b))))
```

We can eliminate the use of $\mathcal{U}$-connectives in the formula by adding an atomic proposition c representing the carry bit. The required properties of an n-bit counter with carry are as follows:

```
1) The marker consists of a repeated pattern of a 1 followed by n-1 0's.
2) The first n bits are 0's.
3) If m is 1 and b is 0 then c is 0 and n steps later b is 1.
4) If m is 1 and b is 1 then c is 1 and n steps later b is 0.
5) If there is no carry, then the next bit stays the same n steps later.
6) If there is a carry, flip the next bit n steps later and adjust the carry.
```

For $n = 4$, these properties are captured by the conjunction of the following formulas.

```
1. (m) && ( [](m -> ((X(!m)) && (X(X(!m))) && (X(X(X(!m))))
                                     && (X(X(X(X(m))))))))
2. (!b) && (X(!b)) && (X(X(!b))) && (X(X(X(!b))))
3. [] ( (m && !b) -> (!c && X(X(X(X(b))))) )
4. [] ( (m && b) -> (c && X(X(X(X(!b))))) )
5. [] (!c & X(!m)) ->
        ( X(!c) && (X(b) -> X(X(X(X(b))))) &&
                (X(!b) -> X(X(X(X(!b))))) )
6. [] (c -> ( ( X(!b) -> ( X(!c) && X(X(X(X(!b)))) ) ) &&
                          ( X(c) && X(X(X(X(b)))) ) ))
```

Pattern Formulas. We further investigated the problem space by testing the tools on the eight classes of scalable formulas defined by [22] to evaluate the performance of explicit state algorithms on temporally-complex formulas.

$$E(n) = \bigwedge_{i=1}^{n} \Diamond p_i,\ U(n) = (\ldots(p_1\ \mathcal{U}\ p_2)\ \mathcal{U}\ \ldots)\ \mathcal{U}\ p_n,\ R(n) = \bigwedge_{i=1}^{n} (\Box\Diamond p_i \vee \Diamond\Box p_{i+1}).$$

$$U_2(n) = p_1\ \mathcal{U}\ (p_2\ \mathcal{U}\ (\ldots p_{n-1}\ \mathcal{U}\ p_n)\ldots),\ C_1(n) = \bigvee_{i=1}^{n} \Box\Diamond p_i,\ C_2(n) = \bigwedge_{i=1}^{n} \Box\Diamond p_i.$$

$$Q(n) = \bigwedge(\Diamond p_i \vee \Box p_{i+1}),\ S(n) = \bigwedge_{i=1}^{n} \Box p_i.$$

5 Experimental Results

Our experiments resulted in two major findings. First, most LTL translation tools are research prototypes, not industrial quality tools. Second, the symbolic approach is clearly superior to the explicit approach for LTL satisfiability checking.

5.1 The Scalability Challenge

When checking the satisfiability of specifications we need to consider large LTL formulas. Our experiments focus on challenging the tools with scalable formulas. Unfortunately, most explicit tools do not rise to the challenge. In general, the performance of explicit tools degrades substantially as the automata they generate grow beyond 1,000 states. This degradation is manifested in both timeouts (our timeout bound was 4 hours per formula) and errors due to memory management. This should be contrasted with BDD tools, which routinely handle hundreds of thousands and even millions of nodes.

We illustrate this first with run-time results for counter formulas. We display each tool's total run time, which is a combination of the tool's automaton generation time and SPIN's model analysis time. We include only data points for which the tools provide correct answers; we know all counter formulas are uniquely satisfiable. As is shown in Figures 1 and 2,[13] SPOT is the only explicit tool that is somewhat competitive with the symbolic tools. Generally, the explicit tools time out or die before scaling to $n = 10$, when the automata have only a few thousands states; only a few tools passed $n = 8$.

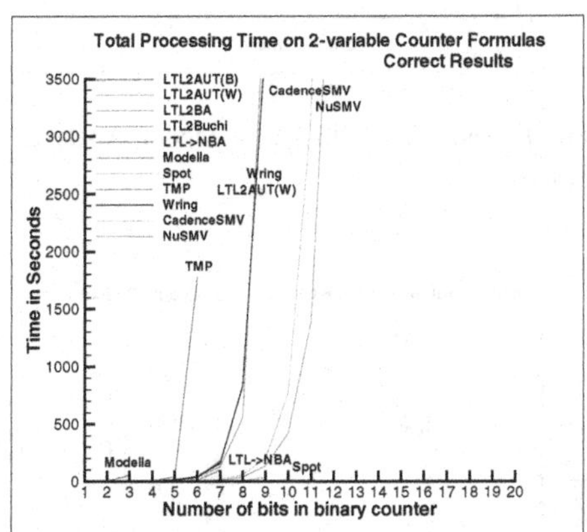

Fig. 1. Performance Results: 2-Variable Counters

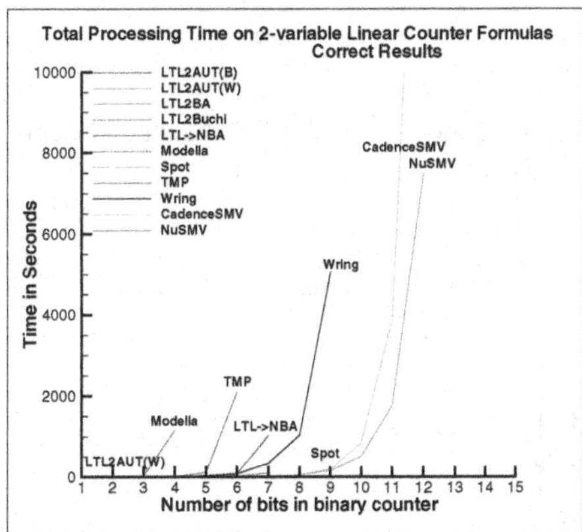

Fig. 2. Performance Results: 2-Variable Linear Counters

Figures 3 and 4 show median automata generation and model analysis times for random formulas. Most tools, with the exception of SPOT and LTL2BA, timeout or die before scaling to formulas of length 60. The difference in performance between SPOT and LTL2BA, on one hand, and the rest of the explicit tools is quite dramatic. Note that up to length 60, model-analysis time is negligible. SPOT and LTL2BA can routinely handle formulas of up to length 150, while the symbolic tools scale past length 200, with run times of a few seconds.

Figure 5 shows performance on the E-class formulas. Recall that $\neg E(n)$ is the formula $\bigvee_{i=1}^{n} \Box \neg p_i$. Since each formula $\Box \neg p_i$ can be translated into an automaton with a fixed number of states, $\neg E(n)$ can be translated into an automaton with $O(n)$ states. Nevertheless, most tools show an unnecessary exponential blow-up. CadenceSMV is the only tool whose performance seems to scale linearly. (The evidence for NuSMV is inconclusive.)

Graceless Degradation. Most explicit tools do not behave robustly and die gracelessly. When LTL2Buchi has difficulty processing a formula, it produces over 1,000 lines of

[13] We recommend viewing all figures online, in color, and magnified.

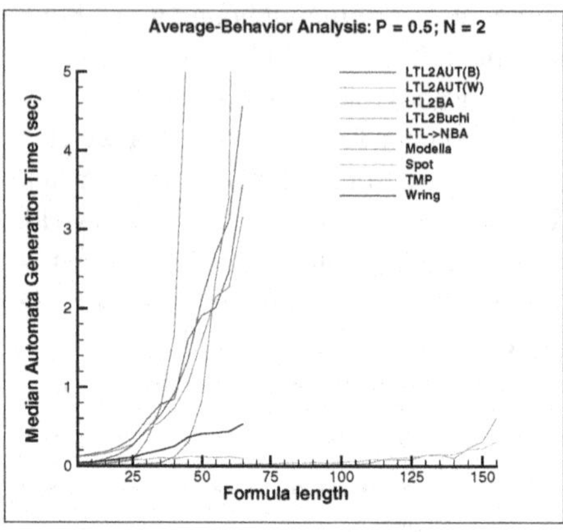

Fig. 3. Random Formulas – Automata Generation Times

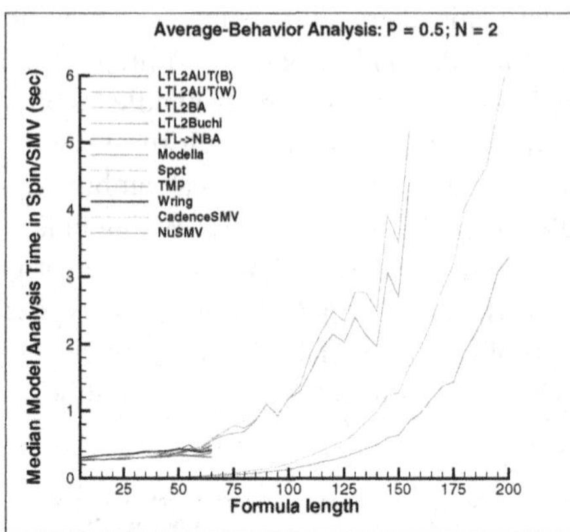

Fig. 4. Random Formulas – Model Analysis Times

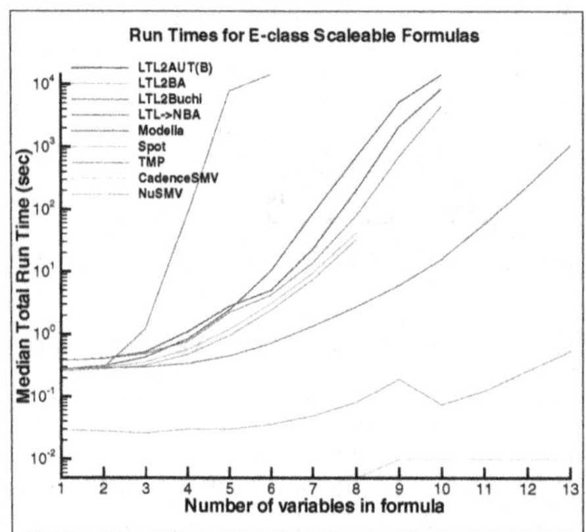

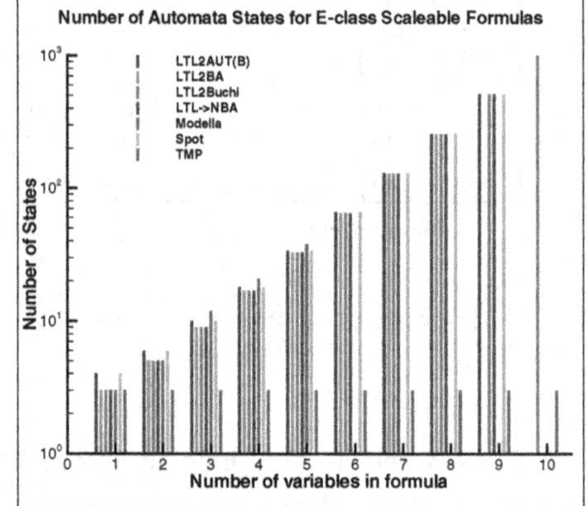

Fig. 5. E-class Formula Data

`java.lang.StackOverflowError` exceptions. LTL2BA periodically exits with "Command exited with non-zero status 1" and prints into the Promela file, "ltl2ba: releasing a free block, saw 'end of formula'." Python traceback errors hinder LTL→NBA. Modella suffers from a variety of memory errors including `*** glibc detected *** double free or corruption (out): 0x55ff4008 ***`. Sometimes Modella causes a segmentation fault and other times Modella dies gracefully, reporting "full memory" before exiting. When used purely as a LTL-to-automata translator, SPIN often runs for thousands of seconds and then exits with non-zero status 1. TMP behaves similarly. Wring often triggers Perl ""Use of freed value in iteration" errors. When the translation results in large Promela models, SPIN frequently yields segmentation faults during its own compilation. For example, SPOT translates the formula $E(8)$ to an automaton with 258 states and 6,817 transitions in 0.88 seconds. SPIN analyzes the resulting Promela model in 41.75 seconds. SPOT translates the $E(9)$ formula to an automaton with 514 states and 20,195 transitions in 2.88 seconds, but SPIN segmentation faults when trying to compile this model. SPOT and the SMV tools are the only tools that consistently degrade gracefully; they either timeout or terminate with a succinct, descriptive message.

A more serious problem is that of incorrect results, i.e., reporting "satisfiable" for an unsatisfiable formula or vice versa. Note, for example, in Figure 5, the size of the automaton generated by TMP is independent of n, which is an obvious error. The problem is particularly acute when the returned automaton A_φ is empty (no state). On one hand, an empty automaton accepts the empty language. On the other hand, SPIN conjoins the Promela model for the never-claim with the model under verification, so an empty automaton, when conjoined with a universal model, actually acts as a universal model. The tools are not consistent in their handling of empty automata. Some, such as LTL2Buchi and SPOT return an explicit indication of an empty automaton, while Modella and TMP just return an empty Promela model. We have taken an empty automaton to mean "unsatisfiable." In Figure 6 we show an analysis of correctness for random formulas. Here we counted "correct" as any verdict, either "satisfiable" or "unsatisfiable," that matched the verdict found by the two SMVs for the same formula as the two SMVs always agree. We excluded data for any formulas that timed out or triggered error messages. Many of the tools show degraded correctness as the formulas scale in size.

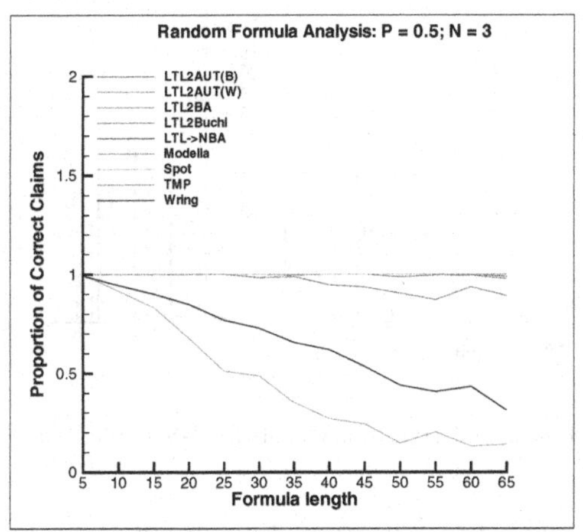

Fig. 6. Correctness Degradation

Does Size Matter? The focus of almost all LTL translation papers, starting with [24], has been on minimizing automata size. It has already been noted that automata minimization may not result in model checking performance improvement [18] and specific attention has been given to minimizing the size of the product with the model [38, 22]. Our results show that size, in terms of both number of automaton states and transitions is not a reliable indicator of satisfiability checking run-time. Intuitively, the smaller the automaton, the easier it is to check for nonemptiness. This simplistic view, however, ignores the effort required to minimize the automaton. It is often the case that tools

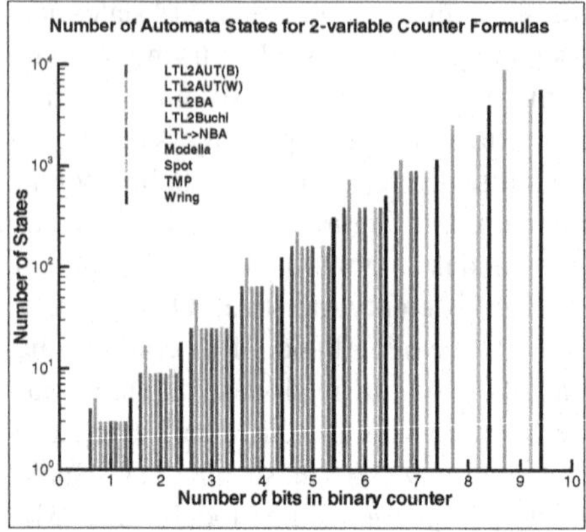

Fig. 7. Automata Size: 2-Variable Counters

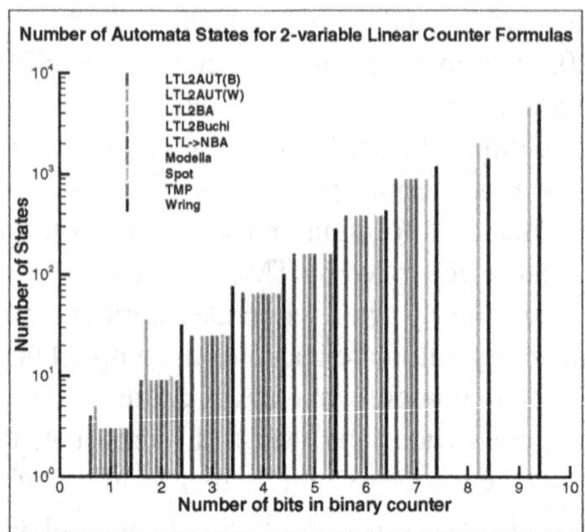

Fig. 8. Automata Size: 2-Variable Linear Counters

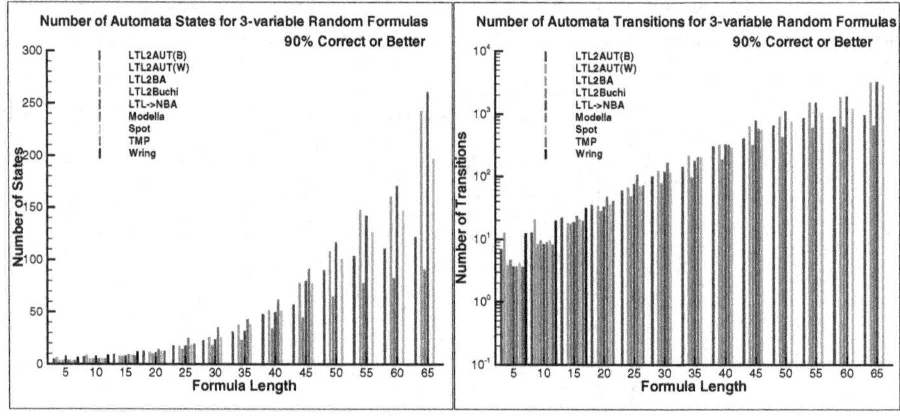

Fig. 9. State and Transition Counts for 3-Variable Random Formulas

spend more time constructing the formula automaton than constructing and analyzing the product automaton. As an example, consider the performance of the tools on counter formulas. We see in Figures 1 and 2 dramatic differences in the performance of the tools on such formulas. In contrast, we see in Figures 7 and 8 that the tools do not differ significantly in terms of the size of generated automata. Similarly, Figure 5, shows little correlation between automata size and run time for E-class formulas.

Consider also the performance of the tools on random formulas. In Figure 9 we see the performance in terms of size of generated automata. Performance in terms of run time is plotted in Figure 11, where each tool was run until it timed out or reported an error for more than 10% of the sampled formulas. SPOT and LTL2BA consistently have the best performance in terms of run time, but they are average performers in terms of automata size. LTL2Buchi consistently produces significantly more compact automata, in terms of both states and transitions. It also incurs lower SPIN model analysis times than SPOT and LTL2BA. Yet LTL2Buchi spends so much time generating the automata that it does not scale nearly as well as SPOT and LTL2BA.

5.2 Symbolic Approaches Outperform Explicit Approaches

Across the various classes of formulas, the symbolic tools outperformed the explicit tools, demonstrating faster performance and increased scalability. (We measured only combined automata-generation and model-analysis time for the symbolic tools. The translation to automata is symbolic and is very fast; it is linear in the size of the formula [10].) We see this dominance with respect to counter formulas in Figures 1 and 2, for random formulas in Figures 3, 4, and 11, and for E-class formulas in Figure 5. For U-class formulas, no explicit tools could handle $n = 10$, while the symbolic tools scale up to $n = 20$; see Figure 10. The only exception to the dominance of the symbolic tools occurs with 3-variable linear counter formulas, where SPOT outperforms both symbolic tools. We ran the tools on many thousands of formulas and did not find a single case in which either symbolic tool yielded an incorrect answer yet every explicit tool gave at least one incorrect answer during our tests.

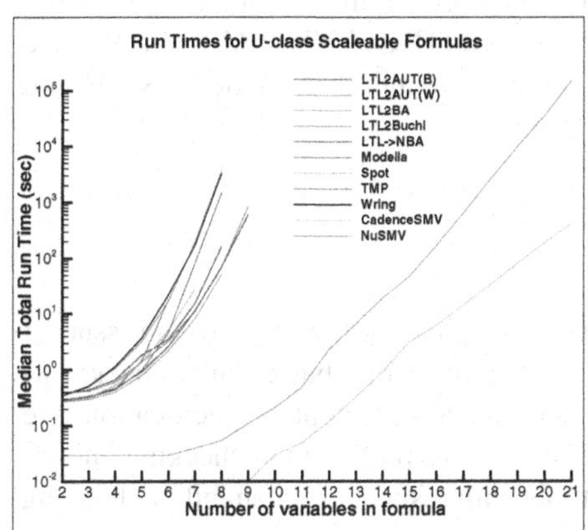

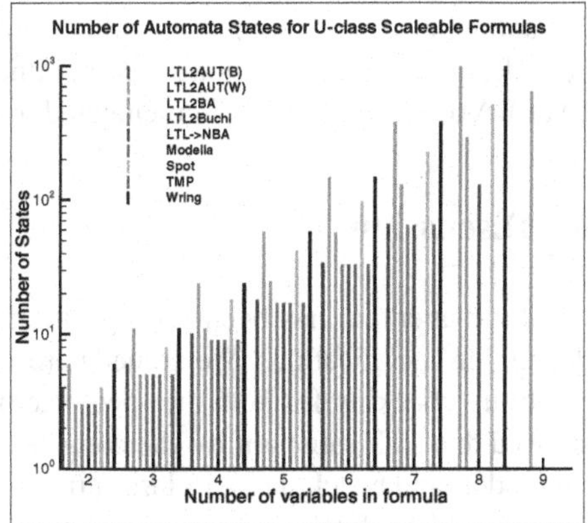

Fig. 10. U-class Formula Data

The dominance of the symbolic approach is consistent with the findings in [35, 36], which reported on the superiority of a symbolic approach with respect to an explicit approach for satisfiability checking for the modal logic K. In contrast, [39] compared explicit and symbolic translations of LTL to automata in the context of symbolic model checking and found that explicit translation performs better in that context. Consequently, they advocate a *hybrid* approach, combining symbolic systems and explicit automata. Note, however, that not only is the context in [39] different than here (model checking rather than satisfiability checking), but also the formulas studied there are generally small and translation time is negligible, in sharp contrast to the study we present here. We return to the topic of model checking in the concluding discussion.

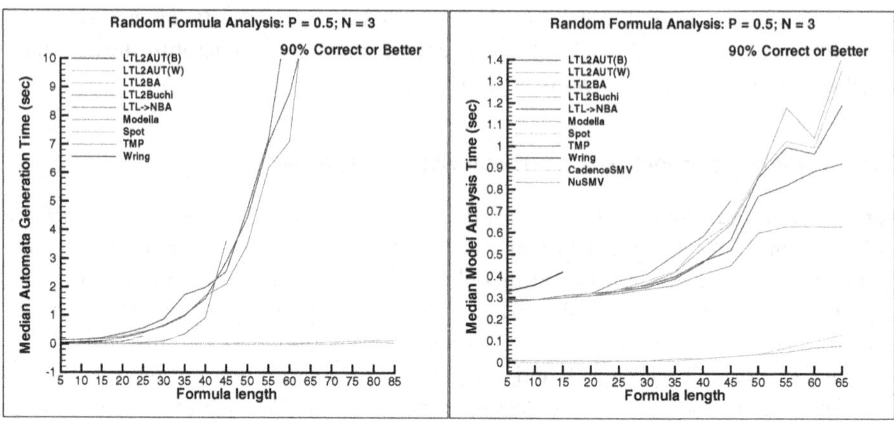

Fig. 11. Automata generation and SPIN Analysis Times for 3-Variable Random Formulas

Figures 3, 4, and 11 reveal why the explicit tools generally perform poorly. We see in the figures that for most explicit tools automata-generation times by far dominate model-analysis times, which calls into question the focus in the literature on minimizing automata size. Among the explicit tools, only SPOT and LTL2BA seem to have been designed with execution speed in mind. Note that, other than Modella, SPOT and LTL2BA are the only tools implemented in C/C++.

6 Discussion

Too little attention has been given in the formal-verification literature to the issue of debugging specifications. We argued here for the adoption of a basic sanity check: satisfiability checking for both the specification and the complemented specification. We showed that LTL satisfiability checking can be done via a reduction to checking universal models and benchmarked a large array of tools with respect to satisfiability checking of scalable LTL formulas.

We found that the existing literature on LTL to automata translation provides little information on actual tool performance. We showed that most LTL translation tools, with the exception of SPOT, are research prototypes, which cannot be considered industrial-quality tools. The focus in the literature has been on minimizing automata size, rather than evaluating overall performance. Focusing on overall performance reveals a large difference between LTL translation tools. In particular, we showed that symbolic tools have a clear edge over explicit tools with respect to LTL satisfiability checking.

While the focus of our study was on LTL satisfiability checking, there are a couple of conclusions that apply to model checking in general. First, LTL translation tools need to be fast and robust. In our judgment, this rules out implementations in languages such as Perl or Python and favors C or C++ implementations. Furthermore, attention needs to be given to graceful degradation. In our experience, tool errors are invariably the result of graceless degradation due to poor memory management. Second, tool developers should focus on overall performance instead of output size. It has already been noted that automata minimization may not result in model checking performance improvement [18] and specific attention has been given to minimizing the size of the product with the model [38]. Still, no previous study of LTL translation has focused on model checking performance, leaving a glaring gap in our understanding of LTL model checking.

References

[1] Ammons, G., Mandelin, D., Bodik, R., Larus, J.R.: Debugging temporal specifications with concept analysis. In: PLDI, Proc. ACM Conf., pp. 182–195 (2003)

[2] Armoni, R., Fix, L., Flaisher, A., Grumberg, O., Piterman, N., Tiemeyer, A., Vardi, M.Y.: Enhanced vacuity detection for linear temporal logic. In: Hunt Jr., W.A., Somenzi, F. (eds.) CAV 2003. LNCS, vol. 2725, Springer, Heidelberg (2003)

[3] Beer, I., Ben-David, S., Eisner, C., Rodeh, Y.: Efficient detection of vacuity in ACTL formulas. Formal Methods in System Design 18(2), 141–162 (2001)

[4] Bloem, R., Ravi, K., Somenzi, F.: Efficient decision procedures for model checking of linear time logic properties. In: Halbwachs, N., Peled, D.A. (eds.) Computer Aided Verification. LNCS, vol. 1633, pp. 222–235. Springer, Heidelberg (1999)

[5] Brayton, R.K., Hachtel, G.D., Sangiovanni-Vincentelli, A., Somenzi, F., Aziz, A., Cheng, S.-T., Edwards, S., Khatri, S., Kukimoto, T., Pardo, A., Qadeer, S., Ranjan, R.K., Sarwary, S., Shiple, T.R., Swamy, G., Villa, T.: VIS: a system for verification and synthesis. In: Alur, R., Henzinger, T.A. (eds.) Computer Aided Verification. LNCS, vol. 1102, pp. 428–432. Springer, Heidelberg (1996)

[6] Bryant, R.E.: Graph-based algorithms for boolean-function manipulation. IEEE Trans. on Computers, vol. C-35(8) (1986)

[7] Burch, J.R., Clarke, E.M., McMillan, K.L., Dill, D.L., Hwang, L.J.: Symbolic model checking: 10^{20} states and beyond. Information and Computation 98(2), 142–170 (1992)

[8] Bustan, D., Flaisher, A., Grumberg, O., Kupferman, O., Vardi, M.Y.: Regular vacuity. In: Borrione, D., Paul, W. (eds.) CHARME 2005. LNCS, vol. 3725, pp. 191–206. Springer, Heidelberg (2005)

[9] Cimatti, A., Clarke, E.M., Giunchiglia, F., Roveri, M.: NuSMV: a new symbolic model checker. It'l J. on Software Tools for Tech. Transfer 2(4), 410–425 (2000)

[10] Clarke, E.M., Grumberg, O., Hamaguchi, K.: Another look at LTL model checking. Formal Methods in System Design 10(1), 47–71 (1997)

[11] Clarke, E.M., Grumberg, O., Peled, D.: Model Checking. MIT Press, Cambridge (1999)

[12] Courcoubetis, C., Vardi, M.Y., Wolper, P., Yannakakis, M.: Memory efficient algorithms for the verification of temporal properties. Formal Methods in System Design 1, 275–288 (1992)

[13] Couvreur, J-M.: On-the-fly verification of linear temporal logic. In: Wing, J.M., Woodcock, J.C.P., Davies, J. (eds.) FM'99 - Formal Methods. LNCS, vol. 1708, pp. 253–271. Springer, Heidelberg (1999)

[14] Daniele, N., Guinchiglia, F., Vardi, M.Y.: Improved automata generation for linear temporal logic. In: Halbwachs, N., Peled, D.A. (eds.) CAV'99. LNCS, vol. 1633, pp. 249–260. Springer, Heidelberg (1999)

[15] Duret-Lutz, A., Poitrenaud, D.: SPOT: An extensible model checking library using transition-based generalized büchi automata. In: MASCOTS, Proc. 12th Int'l Workshop, pp. 76–83. IEEE Computer Society, Los Alamitos (2004)

[16] Emerson, E.A.: Temporal and modal logic (chapter 16). In: Van Leeuwen, J. (ed.) Handbook of Theoretical Computer Science, vol. B, pp. 997–1072. Elsevier, MIT Press, Cambridge (1990)

[17] Emerson, E.A., Lei, C.L.: Efficient model checking in fragments of the propositional μ-calculus. In: LICS, 1st Symp., Cambridge, pp. 267–278 (1986)

[18] Etessami, K., Holzmann, G.J.: Optimizing Büchi automata. In: Palamidessi, C. (ed.) CONCUR 2000. LNCS, vol. 1877, pp. 153–167. Springer, Heidelberg (2000)

[19] Fritz, C.: Constructing Büchi automata from linear temporal logic using simulation relations for alternating büchi automata. In: Ibarra, O.H., Dang, Z. (eds.) CIAA 2003. LNCS, vol. 2759, pp. 35–48. Springer, Heidelberg (2003)

[20] Fritz, C.: Concepts of automata construction from LTL. In: Sutcliffe, G., Voronkov, A. (eds.) LPAR 2005. LNCS (LNAI), vol. 3835, pp. 728–742. Springer, Heidelberg (2005)

[21] Gastin, P., Oddoux, D.: Fast LTL to Büchi automata translation. In: Berry, G., Comon, H., Finkel, A. (eds.) CAV 2001. LNCS, vol. 2102, pp. 53–65. Springer, Heidelberg (2001)

[22] Geldenhuys, J., Hansen, H.: Larger automata and less work for LTL model checking. In: Valmari, A. (ed.) Model Checking Software. LNCS, vol. 3925, pp. 53–70. Springer, Heidelberg (2006)

[23] Geldenhuys, J., Valmari, A.: Tarjan's algorithm makes on-the-fly LTL verification more efficient. In: Jensen, K., Podelski, A. (eds.) TACAS 2004. LNCS, vol. 2988, pp. 205–219. Springer, Heidelberg (2004)

[24] Gerth, R., Peled, D., Vardi, M.Y., Wolper, P.: Simple on-the-fly automatic verification of linear temporal logic. In: Dembiski, P., Sredniawa, M. (eds.) Protocol Specification, Testing, and Verification, August 1995, pp. 3–18. Chapman & Hall, Sydney, Australia (1995)

[25] Giannakopoulou, D., Lerda, F.: From states to transitions: Improving translation of LTL formulae to Büchi automata. In: Peled, D.A., Vardi, M.Y. (eds.) FORTE 2002. LNCS, vol. 2529, Springer, Heidelberg (2002)

[26] Gurfinkel, A., Chechik, M.: Extending extended vacuity. In: Hu, A.J., Martin, A.K. (eds.) FMCAD 2004. LNCS, vol. 3312, pp. 306–321. Springer, Heidelberg (2004)

[27] Gurfinkel, A., Chechik, M.: How vacuous is vacuous. In: Jensen, K., Podelski, A. (eds.) TACAS 2004. LNCS, vol. 2988, pp. 451–466. Springer, Heidelberg (2004)

[28] Holzmann, G.J.: The model checker SPIN (Special issue on Formal Methods in Software Practice). IEEE Trans. on Software Engineering 23(5), 279–295 (1997)

[29] Kupferman, O.: Sanity checks in formal verification. In: Baier, C., Hermanns, H. (eds.) CONCUR 2006. LNCS, vol. 4137, pp. 37–51. Springer, Heidelberg (2006)

[30] Kupferman, O., Vardi, M.Y.: Vacuity detection in temporal model checking. J. on Software Tools For Technology Transfer 4(2), 224–233 (2003)

[31] Kurshan, R.P.: FormalCheck User's Manual. Cadence Design, Inc. (1998)

[32] McMillan, K.: The SMV language. Technical report, Cadence Berkeley Lab (1999)

[33] McMillan, K.L.: Symbolic Model Checking. Kluwer Academic Publishers, Boston (1993)

[34] Namjoshi, K.S.: An efficiently checkable, proof-based formulation of vacuity in model checking. In: Alur, R., Peled, D.A. (eds.) CAV 2004. LNCS, vol. 3114, pp. 57–69. Springer, Heidelberg (2004)

[35] Pan, G., Sattler, U., Vardi, M.Y.: BDD-based decision procedures for K. In: Voronkov, A. (ed.) Automated Deduction - CADE-18. LNCS (LNAI), vol. 2392, pp. 16–30. Springer, Heidelberg (2002)

[36] Piterman, N., Vardi, M.Y.: From bidirectionality to alternation. Theoretical Computer Science 295(1–3), 295–321 (2003)

[37] Purandare, M., Somenzi, F.: Vacuum cleaning CTL formulae. In: Brinksma, E., Larsen, K.G. (eds.) CAV 2002. LNCS, vol. 2404, pp. 485–499. Springer, Heidelberg (2002)

[38] Sebastiani, R., Tonetta, S.: more deterministic vs. smaller büchi automata for efficient LTL model checking. In: Geist, D., Tronci, E. (eds.) CHARME 2003. LNCS, vol. 2860, pp. 126–140. Springer, Heidelberg (2003)
[39] Sebastiani, R., Tonetta, S., Vardi, M.Y.: Symbolic systems, explicit properties: on hybrid approaches for LTL symbolic model checking. In: Etessami, K., Rajamani, S.K. (eds.) CAV 2005. LNCS, vol. 3576, pp. 350–373. Springer, Heidelberg (2005)
[40] Somenzi, F., Bloem, R.: Efficient Büchi automata from LTL formulae. In: Emerson, E.A., Sistla, A.P. (eds.) CAV 2000. LNCS, vol. 1855, pp. 248–263. Springer, Heidelberg (2000)
[41] Tauriainen, H., Heljanko, K.: Testing LTL formula translation into Büchi automata. STTT - Int'l J. on Software Tools for Tech. Transfer 4(1), 57–70 (2002)
[42] Thirioux, X.: Simple and efficient translation from LTL formulas to Büchi automata. Electr. Notes Theor. Comput. Sci, vol. 66(2) (2002)
[43] Vardi, M.Y.: Nontraditional applications of automata theory. In: Hagiya, M., Mitchell, J.C. (eds.) TACS 1994. LNCS, vol. 789, pp. 575–597. Springer, Heidelberg (1994)
[44] Vardi, M.Y.: Automata-theoretic model checking revisited. In: Cook, B., Podelski, A. (eds.) VMCAI 2007. LNCS, vol. 4349, pp. 137–150. Springer, Heidelberg (2007)
[45] Vardi, M.Y., Wolper, P.: An automata-theoretic approach to automatic program verification. In: Proc. 1st LICS, pp. 332–344 (1986)
[46] Vardi, M.Y., Wolper, P.: Reasoning about infinite computations. Information and Computation 115(1), 1–37 (1994)

An Embeddable Virtual Machine for State Space Generation

Michael Weber*

Department of Software Engineering
CWI, Amsterdam, The Netherlands
Michael.Weber@cwi.nl

Abstract. The semantics of modelling languages are not always specified in a precise and formal way, and their rather complex underlying models make it a non-trivial exercise to reuse them in newly developed tools. We report on experiments with a virtual machine-based approach for state space generation. The virtual machine's (VM) byte-code language is straightforwardly implementable, facilitates reuse and makes it an adequate target for translation of higher-level languages like the SPIN model checker's PROMELA, or even C. As added value, it provides efficiently executable operational semantics for modelling languages. Several tools have been built on top of the VM implementation we developed, to evaluate the benefits of the proposed approach.

1 Introduction

Common approaches in state-based model checking employ modeling languages like CSP [11], LOTOS [3], Murϕ [6], DVE [1], or PROMELA [13] to describe actual state spaces. These languages are usually non-trivial: in addition to concepts found in programming languages (scopes, variables, expressions) they provide features like process abstraction, non-determinism, guarded commands, synchronisation and communication primitives, timers, etc.. Implementing an operational model of high-level languages for use in verification tools is consequently not straightforward.

That being said, when developing new verification algorithms and tools it is highly desirable to reuse an already existing modeling language like PROMELA, which has been used in a sizeable number of real-world case studies. In our experience, we identified four main benefits. First, we can reuse existing case studies to test new tools and compare to already published results, instead of having to resort to artificial examples. Secondly, tool developers can concentrate on the implementation of algorithms if the part of how model data enters the developed tool is either reuseable or easily reimplemented, and can be incorporated in whatever infrastructure is dictated by the requirements of a new algorithm. From a user perspective, switching to a model checking tool with compatible

* This research has been partially funded by the Netherlands Organization for Scientific Research (NWO) under FOCUS/BRICKS grant number 642.000.05N09.

D. Bošnački and S. Edelkamp (Eds.): SPIN 2007, LNCS 4595, pp. 168–186, 2007.

input language is made easier, as it avoids the penalty of having to reimplement the model in another formalism, and showing that the semantics have been preserved in the translation. In addition, existing models can be used to benchmark new tools on realistic data sets. Lastly, by taking the virtual machine as an intermediate layer, we can implement (and reuse!) common analyses like dead variable reduction and statement merging independent of the high-level input language.

Contributions. In order to remedy the perceived shortcomings we propose a virtual machine (VM) based approach to state space generation, in which high-level modeling languages are translated to byte-code instructions. Subsequent execution of such byte-code programs with a VM yields state spaces for further use in model checkers, simulators and testing tools. A key point is that the VM is easily embeddable into a host application (for example, a model checker). As such, it should have a formal specification and a straightforwardly implementable execution model, which imposes as few constraints as possible on the tool it is embedded into. In the rest of the paper we present how this can be carried out. We validated the approach with a number of applications based around NIPS, an implementation of the VM described here.

Organisation. In section 2 we describe the virtual machine model and its byte-code semantics. Section 3 summarizes how the virtual machine is used for state space generation in a number of applications: a target for PROMELA compilation, which has been embedded into external-memory and distributed-memory model checkers. As further benefit for tools developers, these tools can be used unchanged to interface with other front-ends, for example, to check C code for embedded systems. We conclude with a summary of related and future work in sections 4 and 5. Appendix A presents benchmark results for our VM implementation to show practical usefulness of our approach.

2 Virtual Machine Specification

The virtual machine (VM) we are using as running example here contains a couple of features not all of which are commonly found at byte-code level in conventional VM architectures like the Java Virtual Machine (JVM) [15]. They are a superset of the features we observed as common in modeling languages. In particular, we have:

Non-determinism. If non-deterministic choice is encountered during executing, the machine offers all possible continuations to the scheduler who then decides which path to take.

Concurrency. Processes can be created, not only statically but also during execution of the model.

Communication. Both, rendezvous and asynchronous channel objects are provided for inter-process communication.

First-class channels. Like in PROMELA and π-calculus [14], channels are first-class values, i.e. they can be sent over channels like any other value, thus allowing for a dynamic communication structure.

Priority scheme. Our byte-code allows to specify which actions have to be given preference. Together with explicit control over externally visible actions, this allows to encode high-level constructs like PROMELA's `atomic` and `d_step`.

Speculative execution. Code sequences like guards are executed speculatively, and changes to the global state are rolled back if the sequence does not run to completion (see Section 2.4). Such non-deterministic effects are naturally not easily replicable in a conventional VM.

External Scheduling. Scheduling decisions are delegated to host applications. This allows for implementation of different scheduling policies which is needed to cater for simulation (interactive scheduling) vs. state space exploration with some search strategy (breadth-first, depth-first, heuristics, interactive, random, or combinations thereof).

The design of our VM was mainly driven by pragmatic decisions: it was our intention to create a model that is simple, efficient and embeddable as component into host applications, with implementation effort split between the VM and compilers targeting it. For example, many instructions make use of the VM's stack because it is trivial for compilers to generate stack-based code for expression evaluation. On the other hand, a stack-based architecture alone is inconvenient for translation of counting loops, thus registers were added. The RISC-like instruction set is motivated by the need for fast decoding inside the instruction dispatcher, the VM's most often executed routine.

Although our machine is a mixture of register-based and stack-based architecture, we are nevertheless dealing with finite state models in this paper by putting bounds on all resources. Concurrency is modeled by interleaving semantics.

A complete specification of a virtual machine suitable as target for PROMELA is available [20]. Our starting point was a simple VM model, which we then extended with features needed to cater for PROMELA's semantics. However, in the interest of reusability we tried to keep these additions as generic as possible (see Section 3.4).

In the following, we will present a formalisation of the VM which is suitable for implementation. We found this an invaluable help in allowing different groups working independently on compilers, byte-code optimizers and the VM itself. It also serves as a reference in case the VM needs to be reimplemented, or for answering questions regarding the semantics of compiled languages.

We start by specifying global and local state, and invariants which translations must preserve. Afterwards we present the byte-code semantics and how scheduling between alternatives is done.

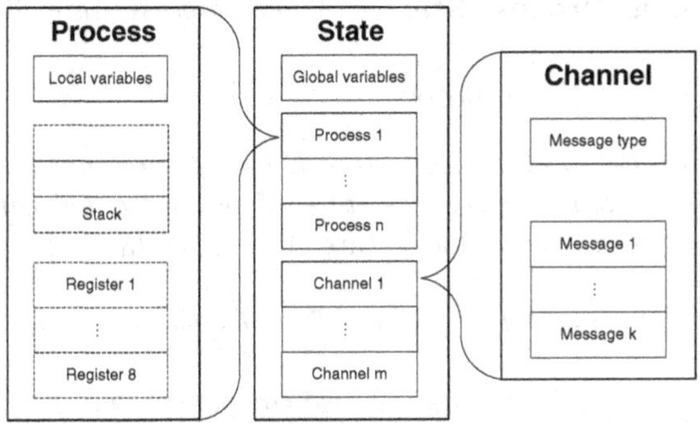

Fig. 1. Overview over the state of the virtual machine. Dotted borders around registers and stack indicate that they are only temporarily part of the machine state, but are not preserved.

2.1 Machine State

The machine's global state as depicted in Figure 1 consists of a few global objects and the local state of its processes.

Definition 1 (Global State). *The global state $\Gamma = \langle \Pi, e, G, \Phi \rangle$ of our virtual machine is a tuple*

$$\Gamma \in \mathit{Processes} \times \mathit{Pid}_{\perp} \times \mathit{Mem} \times \mathit{Channels}$$

with Π denoting a finite set of processes, e the process identifier of a process with exclusive execution privileges ($\perp$ if none), G the global variable store, and Φ the—again finite—set of existing channels (channels are global objects).

We will refer to the set of all global states as Γ as well, if the context makes clear what is meant.

Definition 2 (Process). *A process $\pi = \langle p, M, \Lambda' \rangle$ is a tuple*

$$\pi \in \mathit{Processes} = (\mathit{Pid} \times \mathit{ExecMode} \times \mathit{ProcessState}') \cup \{\mathrm{stop}\}$$

with p denoting a globally unique identifier, $M \in \{\underline{\mathrm{N}}, \underline{\mathrm{A}}, \underline{\mathrm{I}}, \underline{\mathrm{T}}\}$ its execution mode (normal, atomic, invisible, terminated), and Λ' the local state of a process (Definition 3).

Furthermore, we allow the special symbol stop *to denote a deadlocked process which cannot make any further step.*

A process can be either inactive or active.

While a single process can be deadlocked, there might be others which can still continue, so that there is no *global deadlock* yet.

Often, we do not want a global state $\Gamma = \langle \Pi, e, G, \Phi \rangle$ to contain the deadlocked process stop. To simplify notation, we write $\Gamma \neq \mathrm{stop}$ iff no process in Π is deadlocked: $\forall \pi \in \Pi : \pi \neq \mathrm{stop}$.

Definition 3 (Local Process State). *A local process state* $\Lambda' = \langle L, m \rangle$ *is a pair*

$$\Lambda' \in \mathit{ProcessState}' = \mathit{Mem} \times \mathbb{N}$$

and denotes the process-local variable store L and its program counter m.

When a process becomes active, its state Λ' *is augmented with registers* R_0 *and a stack* $D_\epsilon = \epsilon$ *to its* active local state $\Lambda = \langle L, m, R_0, D_\epsilon \rangle$:

$$\Lambda \in \mathit{ProcessState} = \mathit{Mem} \times \mathbb{N} \times \mathit{Registers} \times \mathit{Stack}$$

When it becomes inactive again, its last two components are projected away. As a result, they can only be used for storing temporary *values.*

Definition 4 (Store). *We identify three stores in our virtual machine model: for global (G) and local variables (L), and for registers (R). As usual, we model stores as mappings* $\sigma \in \mathbb{N} \to \mathit{Value}$*, that is for a store* σ*,* $\sigma[i]$ *denotes the store's value at position i. Replacing a value v at position i in the store is written as* $\sigma[i/v]$.

Initial stores are denoted as σ_0 $(\forall i: \ \sigma_0[i] := 0)$. For convenience, we write r_i to reference the ith register $R[i]$.

We added registers to our virtual machine for situations when byte-code effects on the machine's state are not fitting well to a stack model, for instance if values are operated on more than once.

Definition 5 (Data Stack). *Expression evaluation takes place on the data stack component* $D \in \mathit{Stack} = \mathit{Value}^*$ *of a process state. A stack is represented as finite (possibly empty) word* $D = v_n : \cdots : v_1, \quad v_i \in \mathit{Value}, n \in \mathbb{N}$.

We denote the empty stack as $D_\epsilon = \epsilon$.

Communication. Processes can use several ways to communicate values among each other. First, they can use the global store G which can be modified by any process at any time. A more structured way of communication is provided by means of channels. They also offer a model for message-passing synchronization. In our machine, communication channels are typed and bounded, and we distinguish between rendezvous channels and asynchronous channels.

Definition 6. *A* channel $\phi = \langle c, l, t, C \rangle$ *is a tuple*

$$\phi \in \mathit{Channels} = \mathit{ChanId} \times \mathbb{N} \times \mathbb{N} \times \mathit{Message}^*$$

with c denoting a globally unique channel identifier, l the channel capacity, and $C = c_0 : \cdots : c_l$ *its current contents (*c_l *being the last message in the channel). Each message* $c_i \in \mathit{Message} = \mathit{Value}^*$ *consists of a sequence of values of length t.*

Rendezvous channels have zero capacity. A message can temporarily be stored in a channel during rendezvous communication, hence exceeding the capacity of the channel. Such states are internal to the virtual machine and unobservable to its outside. Similarly, asynchronous channels which exceed their capacity automatically fall back to the same behavior as rendezvous channels: send operations on those block until they are within their allowed capacity again.

Definition 7 (Rendezvous Communication). *We define a predicate* sync(Γ) *on a global state* $\Gamma = \langle \Pi, e, G, \Phi \rangle$ *to determine whether rendezvous communication is taking place: at least one channel* $\phi = \langle c, l, t, C \rangle$ *contains more messages than its capacity* l *allows.*

$$\mathrm{sync}(\Gamma) := \begin{cases} \mathrm{true} & \text{if } \exists \phi = \langle c, l, t, C \rangle \in \Phi : \ |C| > l \\ \mathrm{false} & \text{otherwise} \end{cases}$$

2.2 Invariants

Translation to our byte-code language must guarantee the following invariants: as already pointed out in Definition 3, a process becoming active again always resumes execution with register set R_0 and the empty stack D_ϵ. Conversely, at those points in the program when a process may become inactive, the contents of registers and stack are discarded and need not matter for the rest of its execution. This means, that it is unnecessary to consider registers and stack as part of a state vector given to a model checking algorithm.

Because the number of local variables is fixed, a local state Λ' then occupies constant space only.

2.3 Byte-Code Semantics

Having defined the state of our virtual machine, we now proceed by defining the semantics of operations on it. These operations are carried out at process level, with only a single process being active at once.

In the spirit of earlier displays of PROMELA semantics by Holzmann and Natarajan [13], we compose our semantics from several smaller parts by defining four relations to model process activation, internal, intermediate and finally scheduler transitions.

A transition from state Γ_1 to Γ_2 is a relation $\rightarrow_T \in \Gamma \times \Sigma_T \times \Gamma$, with a finite set of labels Σ_T and set of states Γ. If not important, we will elide labels from our presentation. For brevity, we write $\Lambda_1, G_1, \Phi_1 \rightarrow \Lambda_2, G_2, \Phi_2$ instead of

$$\begin{aligned} &\langle \{ \langle p, M, \Lambda_1 \rangle, \pi_1, \ldots, \pi_n \}, e, G_1, \Phi_1 \rangle \\ &\qquad \rightarrow \langle \{ \langle p, M, \Lambda_2 \rangle, \pi_1, \ldots, \pi_n \}, e, G_2, \Phi_2 \rangle \\ &\qquad\qquad \pi_i = \langle p_i, M_i, \langle L_i, m_i \rangle \rangle \text{ for all } 1 \leq i \leq n \end{aligned}$$

State components remaining unchanged in a transition are left out.

Table 1. Load and Store byte-codes

`LDC` c	load constant c onto top of data stack $\langle L, m, R, D\rangle \rightarrow_{int} \langle L, m+1, R, D : c\rangle$
`LDV` g	load variable onto top of data stack $\langle L, m, R, D : a\rangle \rightarrow_{int} \langle L, m+1, R, D : L[a]\rangle$ if $g = \underline{\mathrm{L}}$ $\langle L, m, R, D : a\rangle, G \rightarrow_{int} \langle L, m+1, R, D : G[a]\rangle, G$ if $g = \underline{\mathrm{G}}$
`STV` g	store stack top in variable $\langle L, m, R, D : v : a\rangle \rightarrow_{int} \langle L[a/v], m+1, R, D\rangle$ if $g = \underline{\mathrm{L}}$ $\langle L, m, R, D : v : a\rangle, G \rightarrow_{int} \langle L, m+1, R, D\rangle, G[a/v]$ if $g = \underline{\mathrm{G}}$
`POP` r_i	pop top-most value from stack into register $\langle L, m, R, D : v\rangle \rightarrow_{int} \langle L, m+1, R[i/v], D\rangle$
`PUSH` r_i	push value from register onto stack $\langle L, m, R, D\rangle \rightarrow_{int} \langle L, m+1, R, D : r_i\rangle$

As mentioned before, only one process can be active at any point in time. Thus we define process activation as transition

$$\begin{aligned}&\langle\{\langle p, M, \langle L, m\rangle\rangle, \pi_1, \ldots, \pi_n\}, e, G, \Phi\rangle\\ &\qquad \xrightarrow{p}_{act} \langle\{\langle p, M, \langle L, m, R_0, D_\epsilon\rangle\rangle, \pi_1, \ldots, \pi_n\}, e, G, \Phi\rangle\\ &\qquad\qquad \forall i \in \{1, \ldots, n\} : \ \pi_i = \langle p_i, M_i, \langle L_i, m_i\rangle\rangle\\ &\qquad\qquad\qquad \text{and } e \in \{p, \bot\}, M \neq \underline{\mathrm{T}}\end{aligned}$$

A process needing exclusive execution privileges *must* be activated, otherwise any process can be activated ($e = \bot$). Processes already run to completion ($M = \underline{\mathrm{T}}$) are not activated again.

Next, we define those transitions an active process can possibly take: the *internal-step* relation $\rightarrow_{int} \in \Gamma \times \Gamma$ is the least relation satisfying the rules given below. For reasons of presentation, we divided internal steps into several parts. Note that the byte-code operation to be executed next is determined by indexing program counter m of the currently active process into a global instruction list $\underline{\mathrm{Instr}}$.

Load and Store. Our machine supports usual operations to load constants (`LDC`), and manipulate values of local and global variables (`LDV`, `STV`), as defined in Table 1. The differentiation of local and global store access simplifies byte-code analysis for, e.g., statement merging.

To avoid stack juggling operations like `DUP`, `SWAP`, etc., values can be stored into and retrieved from registers with `PUSH` and `POP`.

Arithmetic and Boolean Operations. Expression byte-codes like `ADD`, `LT`, `AND`, `NEG`, etc., operate on one or more of the stack's top-most entries. Their semantics are obvious and thus only defined exemplarily:

Table 2. Control-flow byte-codes

`JMPNZ` a	jump if non-zero $\langle L, m, R, D : 0\rangle \rightarrow_{int} \langle L, m+1, R, D\rangle$ $\langle L, m, R, D : v\rangle \rightarrow_{int} \langle L, a, R, D\rangle$, if $v \neq 0$
`NDET` a	non-deterministic jump $\langle L, m, R, D\rangle \rightarrow_{int} \langle L, m+1, R, D\rangle$ $\langle L, m, R, D\rangle \rightarrow_{int} \langle L, a, R, D\rangle$
`ELSE` a	else jump $\langle L, m, R, D\rangle \rightarrow_{int} \langle L, m+1, R, D\rangle$ $\langle L, m, R, D\rangle \rightarrow_{int} \langle L, a, R, D\rangle$ if all $\langle L, m+1, R, D\rangle \rightarrow^{*}_{int} \Lambda' \rightarrow_{end}$ stop
`UNLESS` a	unless jump $\langle L, m, R, D\rangle \rightarrow_{int} \langle L, a, R, D\rangle$ $\langle L, m, R, D\rangle \rightarrow_{int} \langle L, m+1, R, D\rangle$ if all $\langle L, a, R, D\rangle \rightarrow^{*}_{int} \Lambda' \rightarrow_{end}$ stop
`CALL` a	call subroutine $\langle L, m, R, D\rangle \rightarrow_{int} \langle L, a, R, D : m+1\rangle$
`RET`	return from subroutine $\langle L, m, R, D : a\rangle \rightarrow_{int} \langle L, a, R, D\rangle$

$$\texttt{OP}_{\otimes} : \quad \langle L, m, R, D : u : v\rangle \rightarrow_{int} \langle L, m+1, R, D : u \otimes v\rangle$$

Control-flow Operations. For control flow changes, we define conditional and unconditional jumps in Table 2. In order to allow explicit modeling of non-determinism, we define `NDET` a as having two possible successor states: one continuing with the next instruction and the other continuing at instruction a. In some situations, it is helpful to allow *conditional non-determinism*, where the existence of one alternative is dependent on the presence or absence of another. For this, we add byte-codes `ELSE` a and its dual `UNLESS` a. They are used in the translation of Promela constructs with similar names, for example.

`CALL` a and `RET` can be used to translate function calls. By default the return address is left on the stack, thus it does not survive if a process becomes inactive. It is in the responsibility of the compiler to store it inside the state vector. This allows for some flexibility when dealing with recursive functions. In general, their treatment requires cooperation between the compiler and an analysis tool working with the generated state space.

Promela itself does not allow function calls, so in the translation these byte-codes are used only for sharing common code blocks. However, they have been also been used to compile method calls of an object-oriented language [21].

Operations on Channels. For inter-process communication, our virtual machine model contains several operations on channels. These include operations to dynamically create channels, query their properties, and manipulate their contents. Both, synchronous and asynchronous channels are supported.

Because of space constraints, we elide their treatment here and refer to the full specification [20]. However, we will return to the topic of synchronous communication in Section 2.4, when discussing process scheduling.

Table 3. Operations for Process Deactivation

`STEP` M'	step complete with mode M' $\langle\{\langle p, M, \langle L, m, R, D\rangle\rangle\} \cup \Pi, e, G, \Phi\rangle$ $\xrightarrow{M'}_{end} \langle\{\langle p, M', \langle L, m+1\rangle\rangle\} \cup \Pi, e', G, \Phi\rangle$ $e' := \begin{cases} p & \text{if } M' \in \{\underline{\text{A}}, \underline{\text{I}}\} \\ \bot & \text{otherwise} \end{cases}$ and $\forall \pi_i \in \Pi : \ \pi_i = \langle p_i, M_i, \langle L_i, m_i\rangle\rangle$
`NEX`	step not executable $\langle L, m, R, D\rangle \rightarrow_{end}$ stop

Spawning New Processes. To start a new process, its current parameters are placed onto the data stack. Specifying the size of these parameters and the start address of its code, a new process is instantiated:

`RUN` k, a run a new process starting at address a

$$\langle\{\pi, \pi_1, \ldots, \pi_n\}, e, G, \Phi\rangle \rightarrow_{int} \langle\{\pi', \pi_1, \ldots, \pi_n, \pi''\}, e, G, \Phi\rangle$$

with $\pi = \langle p, M, \langle L, m, R, D : v_0 : \cdots : v_{k-1}\rangle\rangle$
and $\pi' = \langle p, M, \langle L, m+1, R, D : p''\rangle\rangle$
and $\pi'' = \langle p'', \underline{\text{N}}, \langle L_0[0/v_0, \ldots, k-1/v_{k-1}], a\rangle\rangle$
and $p'' \in \mathit{Pid}$ a unique process identifier

Deactivation of Processes. Following a cooperative multitasking approach, eventually a process allows resumption of other processes by deactivating itself with one of the operations in Table 3.

We introduce `STEP` M as flexible means to control which states become visible to an external scheduler. If further execution of a process is not anticipated (e.g. because of unsatisfied guard conditions or reception attempts on empty channels), process execution may be aborted explicitly by `NEX`. This byte-code instruction can be used to translate guards—boolean conditions which can enable or disable a transition. By attaching an action label to a `STEP`, we can cater for action-based setups as well.

2.4 Scheduling

With all the machinery in place, we now proceed with the relation of *scheduler transitions*, $\rightarrow_{sched}$. We define it in terms of *intermediate transitions* $\rightarrow_{step}$, which is the least relation satisfying

$$\Gamma \xrightarrow{p,M}_{step} \Gamma' \quad \text{if} \quad \Gamma \xrightarrow{p}_{act} \Gamma_0 \rightarrow^*_{int} \Gamma_1 \xrightarrow{M}_{end} \Gamma'$$

This means, that in a machine state Γ some process identified as p is activated, then a number of internal transitions happen, until at some point the process deactivates itself in state Γ', assigning the whole sequence mode M.

In case the machine gets "stuck" without successor states because some process with exclusive execution privileges becomes deadlocked, this process loses them, thus enabling execution possibilities for other processes:

$$\langle \Pi, e, G, \Phi \rangle \xrightarrow{p,M}_{step} \Gamma' \quad \text{if} \quad \langle \Pi, e, G, \Phi \rangle \xrightarrow{e,-}_{step} \text{stop}$$
$$\text{and} \quad \langle \Pi, \bot, G, \Phi \rangle \xrightarrow{p,M}_{step} \Gamma'$$

We can then define the transitions visible to an external scheduler. The approach we took is due to our decision to model rendezvous communication within the interleaving model and thus using an intermediate state which is not revealed to the scheduler. We can distinguish three cases: a process ends a sequence of invisible steps with either a visible transition or a transition leading to deadlock, and no interim rendezvous communication can take place, or, rendezvous communication can take place, with the restriction that the sending and receiving halves of the communication must be consecutive.

Definition 8 (Scheduler Transition). *We define the scheduler transition relation* $\xrightarrow{p}_{sched}$ *as least relation satisfying the following rules.*

- *A scheduler transition consists of a (possibly empty) sequence of invisible steps, followed by a visible step, that is, a step with mode* $\underline{\text{N}}$ *(normal),* $\underline{\text{A}}$ *(atomic) or* $\underline{\text{T}}$ *(terminated). None of the steps is a rendezvous communication.*

$$\Gamma \xrightarrow{p}_{sched} \Gamma' \text{ if } \Gamma = \Gamma_1 \xrightarrow{p,\underline{\text{I}}}_{step} \cdots \xrightarrow{p,\underline{\text{I}}}_{step} \Gamma_{n-1} \xrightarrow{p,M}_{step} \Gamma_n = \Gamma'$$
$$\text{and } \forall i: \neg\text{sync}(\Gamma_i) \text{ and } M \neq \underline{\text{I}} \text{ and } \Gamma' \neq \text{stop}$$

- *Alternatively, if a sequence of invisible steps leads to a deadlocked process, the last step right before the deadlock becomes visible* irrespectively of its mode $\underline{\text{I}}$.

$$\Gamma \xrightarrow{p}_{sched} \Gamma' \text{ if } \Gamma = \Gamma_1 \xrightarrow{p,\underline{\text{I}}}_{step} \cdots \xrightarrow{p,\underline{\text{I}}}_{step} \Gamma_{n-1} \xrightarrow{p,-}_{step} \text{stop}$$
$$\text{and } \forall i: \neg\text{sync}(\Gamma_i) \text{ and } \Gamma' = \Gamma_{n-1}$$

- *Lastly, we allow a rendezvous channel to actually contain one message more than its capacity allows, if the immediately following transition resolves this again by having a rendezvous partner receiving this message, so that said rendezvous channel is within its limits again and the resulting state becomes visible to the scheduler again. In this case the sender loses its execution privilege. It can then be picked up by the receiver. Note that we do not allow a process to have rendezvous communication with itself ($p \neq p'$).*

  With this mechanism, rendezvous communication can be used to pass around execution privileges between processes like in PROMELA.

$$\Gamma \xrightarrow{p}_{sched} \Gamma'' \quad \textit{if} \ \Gamma \xrightarrow{p,M}_{step} \Gamma' = \langle \Pi', e', G', \Phi' \rangle$$
$$\textit{and} \ \langle \Pi', \bot, G', \Phi' \rangle \xrightarrow{p',M'}_{step} \Gamma''$$
$$\textit{and} \ \mathrm{sync}(\Gamma') \ \textit{and} \ \neg\mathrm{sync}(\Gamma'')$$
$$\textit{and} \ p \neq p' \ \textit{and} \ \Gamma'' \neq \mathrm{stop} \ \textit{and} \ M \neq \underline{\mathrm{T}}$$

In all cases, we do not allow a scheduler transition to lead to a global state containing a deadlock process stop.

Our handling of deadlock processes allows us to define a global deadlock state Γ where no process can complete a scheduler transition naturally: there is no Γ' such that $\Gamma \xrightarrow{p}_{sched} \Gamma'$.

Definition 9 (Initial State). *The scheduler starts program execution with the initial state of our machine:* $\Gamma_{init} = \langle \{\langle 1, \underline{\mathrm{N}}, \langle L_0, init \rangle \rangle\}, \bot, G_0, \emptyset \rangle$

The actual interface to run state space generation is not described here, as it is largely based on the same principles as OPEN/CÆSAR [7]. In fact, a preliminary test has shown that we can connect our implementation to CADP [8] with little effort, thus leveraging their large toolset.

3 Applications

The described virtual machine has been utilized successfully in a number of projects[1], which we briefly detail below. On the same time, these projects served as testbed to check whether the virtual machine based approach we advocate is generic enough to accomodate different modelling languages and verification frameworks.

3.1 Promela

We validated our virtual machine-based approach to state space generation by defining a translation from PROMELA to byte-code. As positive side-effect, we obtain an operational semantics for PROMELA which in particular is suitable for classical compiler-based analyses and also for reimplementation. A complete translation procedure is described by Schürmans [20]. Separate from the compiler and thus PROMELA, we developed several common optimizations for static state space reduction on the byte-code level, for example, dead variable reduction and a variant of statement merging.

Although other modeling languages could have been used as well, PROMELA was chosen because it is a truly non-trivial example and it has wide acceptance inside and outside academia.

Benchmarks of our virtual machine show that it performs well enough to be of practical use (Appendix A) on its own. In combination with the projects

[1] `http://www.cwi.nl/~weber/nips/`

described in the following, we could even obtain results which so far have been out of reach.

3.2 An External-Memory Model Checker

The virtual machine is used as state-space generation component in an adaptive external-memory model checking tool [10].

As main memory is still the most restricting factor in state space generation and model checking of industrial-scale models, we developed an algorithm which gradually moves parts of the state space to hard disk when memory fills up. Thus, as long as enough memory is available, it behaves mostly like a regular, memory-bound algorithm.

In unmodified state-space exploration algorithms, checking whether a state has already been visited requires random access to the set of visited states due to commonly used hashtable schemes. In a disk-based setting, such access patterns are prohibitively expensive because they incur large latency when reading from hard disk, in comparison to memory accesses. We get around these limitations by reordering queries such that disk access is avoided if at all possible (through caching strategies) and, failing that, queries are carried out at least in large groups rather than one by one. Besides compression, this allows us also to access the state space stored on disk in a linear fashion, which is orders of magnitude faster than random access.

The amount of main memory available still influences the time needed for full state space generation, however it does not impose a hard limit anymore. With this out of the way, we were able to benchmark our algorithm: the unmodified virtual machine, together with the PROMELA compiler mentioned in Section 3.1 allowed us to use models of real case studies as benchmark material, instead of being constrained to artificial models. In addition, we were able to compare our results with prior experiments.

A short summary is given in Section A. Some of the large models, for example LUNAR scenario 4(d) [23], have previously been reported as exceeding the capabilities of SPIN with 4 GB RAM, with both partial order reduction and `COLLAPSE` enabled. In contrast, we performed state space generation of the mentioned LUNAR scenario with a memory limit of 2.5 GB RAM and without partial order reduction (Appendix A).

3.3 NIPS and DiVinE

An alternative to the external-memory model checker described in Section 3.2, is the use of *distributed algorithms* in verification to get around memory limitations of a single computer. Much research has been devoted to this theme in recent years, for a motivation and recent overview we refer to [4].

The DIVINE library [1] has been conceived as a toolkit and testbed for distributed model checking algorithms, with among other things, an emphasis on LTL model checking. While DIVINE features its own modelling language, DVE, we can apply their algorithms unmodified on PROMELA models, through the use of our virtual machine. In effect, the combination of the two libraries yields a distributed model checker for PROMELA, with, at the time of writing, five different LTL model checking algorithms to choose from.

Moving from a sequential to a distributed setting requires some consideration. In particular, the design of data structures must support relocation to other computers. For our virtual machine, this means that snapshots of its run-time state can be captured and send to another computer. This is particularly easy in our case, as a snapshot is represented opaquely in an architecture-independent, continuous array of binary data which can be written directly to a network connection, without a potentially costly serialization step. Heterogenous distributed environments are supported as well.

In addition, we can redecide on analysis tools without having to modify or rewrite our models, solely depending on the availability of computing resources and hard disk. For example, using DIVINE's distributed algorithms usually gives much faster results. However, if the used computing cluster is busy, a job may spend days in the batch queue before being processed, thus making our external-memory algorithm a viable alternative.

3.4 Model Checking Embedded Systems Software

In the previous sections, we have mainly highlighted the use of our virtual machine as target for PROMELA. Despite it being the initial inspiration, we aimed at designing a generic framework which can cope with different modelling formalisms. As our litmus test we have based the MCESS (short for *Model Checking Embedded Systems Software*) project on our virtual machine. We proceed with a short summary, a more detailed description is given elsewhere [19, Sect. 5.2ff].

Embedded systems based on microcontrollers are often used in safety-critical environments. In MCESS, we address the problem of checking correctness of code written for particular microcontrollers. Regrettably, and despite the sensitivity of the application area, often no formal specifications exist on such projects, so we either have to extract a specification (semi-)manually, or base our analysis *directly* on the implemention under scrutiny. Matters are complicated further by the fact that systems are implemented in a mixture of assembly language and C, most often utilizing specific hardware idiosyncrasies of these severely resource-constrained devices. Previous case studies have shown that existing C model checkers are not directly applicable to such implementations due to the hardware-specific nature [18].

Instead of trying to parse and analyze source code, we chose to compile it with an off-the-shelf C compiler (which is often supplied by the microcontroller vendor), and take the generated binary executable as starting point. We rely on the generated debugging information to present results back to the user. The approach allows us to process assembly and C code in one go. Also, we successfully sidestepped dealing with the complex syntax and even more daunting semantics of C.

Conceptually, assembly language is much easier to formalize, and its semantics are usually precisely described by the vendor. To take a concrete example, we chose the widely used ATMEL ATmega family of microcontrollers, and implemented a translator from ATmeta16 assembly (or rather disassembly, to be precise) to our virtual machine instruction set. For many of the instructions, the translator itself has been *generated* semi-automatically from the semantics given in the ATMEL specification. The critical parts are the hardware dependencies like interrupts (modeled as processes), I/O ports, timers (replaced by non-determinism and abstractions by the compiler), etc.. These require (one-time) manual effort, for example, to obtain a closed system.

A number of factors contribute to the viability of this approach: the type of microcontrollers we are dealing with very space-constrained, typically they have memory in the order of 1024 Bytes. Unsurprisingly, memory allocation is mostly done completely static (no calls to `malloc()`). A limited hardware stack precludes recursive function calls. All these factors make a straight-forward translation much more amenable to yield good results. Deeper analyses can then be layered on top of that.

For state space generation and model checking of such microcontroller programs, we can again utilize the tools described in the previous sections without extra effort. They are well suited to deal with the potentially large state spaces.

4 Related Work

4.1 Promela Semantics

Several formal semantics for PROMELA have been proposed in the past, but it turns out that none of them covers all aspects of the language. The original publication [13] is incomplete in this sense and now partly outdated, as SPIN evolved. It was improved on by a more modular and less implementation-specific approach by Weise [22], but there the handling of nested `do` loops in combination with `goto` statements is unsound. Another incomplete attempt is from Bevier [2]. The specification is a Lisp program and as such peppered with implementation artefacts.

In contrast, we developed a compiler for PROMELA targeting the virtual instruction set defined in Section 2.3. Our translation aims at being faithful to SPIN's PROMELA semantics. It mainly deviates in allowing nested scopes, in order to straighten out the rather confusing static semantics of declarations (variables can be used before being declared). However, we concede that regrettably there are no good means to assure this except continual testing with publicly available models against SPIN as reference implementation.

4.2 Virtual Machines

Virtual machines have been used extensively in Computer Science. A well-known example is the work of Wirth on the Pascal programming language [24].

Independent to our work, two (unpublished, to the best of our knowledge) attempts of virtual machine models for restricted PROMELA-like languages have been brought to our attention [9,17]. Geldenhuys [9] describes a virtual machine as part of the general design of a model checker, while our work is focused on providing a reusable component for state space generation.

ESML [5], the high-level language translated into byte-code is restricted in several ways when compared to PROMELA, and its underlying virtual machine inherits some of these restrictions. For example, it lacks support for asynchronous channels, shared variables and dynamic process creation.

Rosien [17, Section 8] describes some shortcomings of his attempt, for example the lack of arrays, no support for data types beyond integers, unclear semantics for `do` loops or handshake communication inside atomic blocks ("[...] causes undesired results, unexpected atomic deadlocks or otherwise erratic behavior."). Besides that, Rosien's design did not take into account, e.g., distributed settings where successive states may be generated on different computers.

Both papers do not provide a formal model of their VM or of the translation into their byte-code language, making it non-trivial to derive implementations from their work. Neither are implementations readily available.

Bogor. From existing model checking frameworks, we found the Bogor framework [16] closest to the work presented here. It is an extensible framework for software model checking, in particular object-oriented software. Its intermediate representation (BIR) is a high-level guarded command language, not unlike PROMELA. While it can be translated further down to a certain extent, constructs like arrays, locks, exceptions, and high-level control constructs remain, complicating an implementation of its operational semantics.

The Bogor framework consists of a large Java code base, which ruled it out when we were looking into possibilities to interface with other languages. In contrast, our VM implementation itself comprises less than 5000 lines[2] of C and has been interfaced efficiently with C, C++ and Java, and connected to model checking frameworks aimed at high performance like DIVINE.

While Bogor and the work presented here share some common goals, our focus is on embedding into other applications, and thus we aim to show the feasability to provide a reusable *library*, rather than a framework (which might hamper its integration with a host application with incompatible structure.)

From the tool point of view, our aim is not to beat the Bogor framework in terms of features, but rather to provide a small but versatile component which can easily be reused, or written from scratch based on a formal specification.

5 Conclusions

We presented a virtual machine-based approach to state-space generation, in which the virtual machine's instruction set doubles as intermediate language.

[2] According to SLOCCount, `http://www.dwheeler.com/sloccount/`

Assigning operational semantics in such a way makes them straightforwardly implementable, thus encouraging reuse. Among the byte-code instructions are all operations commonly needed for the specification of concurrent systems: non-determinism, process creation, communication primitives, and a way to express scheduler constraints (atomic regions). State-space generators derived in such a way can be small and portable, while benchmarks with a concrete implementation showed that we can obtain practically usable results.

However, some critical thoughts are in order. For example, it is possible to relate analysis results like error traces from the VM back to the original input (PROMELA or C), but there is no stable interface yet available.

Also, a command line simulator is available, yet while working towards integration of our VM implementation in IBM's Eclipse IDE, we found the need for deeper introspection of the VM state. Providing a suitable interface without slowing down state space generation requires some more research. This is worthwhile because we are using the same code for simulation and model checking, thereby foregoing deviations in results. For example, to the best of our knowledge SPIN has been plagued from time to time with the interactive simulation and a model checking run yielding different outcomes.

Nevertheless, with our applications we have shown benefits to be expected through synergy effects of developing an embeddable component for use in third-party tools.

Acknowledgements. We thank Michael Rohrbach and Stefan Schürmans for their implementation efforts and valuable discussions. Theo Ruys brought Rosien's work to our attention. Part of this research has been carried out at RWTH Aachen University.

References

1. Barnat, J., Brim, L., Černá, I., Šimeček, P.: DiVinE the distributed verification environment. In: Leucker, M., van de Pol, J. (eds.) 4th International Workshop on Parallel and Distributed Methods in verifiCation (PDMC'05), Lisbon, Portuga, July 2005 (2005)
2. Bevier, W.: Towards an operational semantics of PROMELA in ACL2. In: Proceedings of the 3rd International SPIN Workshop, April 1997 (1997)
3. Bolognesi, T., Brinksma, E.: Introduction to the ISO specification language LOTOS. In: van Eijk, P.H.J., Vissers, C.A., Diaz, M. (eds.) The Formal Description Technique LOTOS, pp. 23–73. Elsevier Science Publishers, North-Holland (1989)
4. Brim, L.: Distributed verification: Exploring the power of raw computing power. In: Brim, L., Haverkort, B., Leucker, M., van de Pol, J. (eds.) FMICS 2006 and PDMC 2006. LNCS, vol. 4346, pp. 23–34. Springer, Heidelberg (2006)
5. de Villiers, P., Visser, W.: ESML—a validation language for concurrent systems. In: Bishop, J. (ed.): 7-th Southern African Computer Symposium, pages, July 1992, pp. 59–64 (1992)

6. Dill, D., Drexler, A., Hu, A., Yang, C.: Protocol verification as a hardware design aid. In: ICCD '92: Proceedings of the 1991 IEEE International Conference on Computer Design on VLSI in Computer & Processors, Washington, DC, USA, pp. 522–525, IEEE Computer Society (1992)
7. Garavel, H.: OPEN/CAESAR: An open software architecture for verification, simulation, and testing. Lecture Notes in Computer Science 1384, 68–84 (1998)
8. Garavel, H., Lang, F., Mateescu, R.: An overview of CADP 2001. EASST Newsletter 4, 13–24 (2002)
9. Geldenhuys, J.: Efficiency issues in the design of a model checker. Msc. thesis, University of Stellenbosch, South Africa (November 1999)
10. Hammer, M., Weber, M.: To Store or Not To Store reloaded: Reclaiming memory on demand. In: Brim, L., Haverkort, B., Leucker, M., van de Pol, J. (eds.) FMICS 2006 and PDMC 2006. LNCS, vol. 4346, pp. 51–66. Springer, Heidelberg (2007)
11. Hoare, C.A.R.: Communicating Sequential Processes. Prentice-Hall, Englewood Cliffs (1985)
12. Holzmann, G.J.: The engineering of a model checker: the gnu i-protocol case study revisited. In: Dams, D.R., Gerth, R., Leue, S., Massink, M. (eds.) Theoretical and Practical Aspects of SPIN Model Checking. LNCS, vol. 1680, Springer, Heidelberg (1999)
13. Holzmann, G.J., Natarajan, V.: Outline for an operational-semantics definition of PROMELA. Technical report, Bell Laboratories, July 1996 (1996)
14. Milner, R.: The polyadic π-calculus: a tutorial. Technical Report ECS–LFCS–91–180, Laboratory for Foundations of Computer Science, Department of Computer Science, University of Edinburgh, UK, Oct. 1993. In: Bauer, F.L., Brauer, W., Schwichtenberg, H. (ed.): Logic and Algebra of Specification, Springer, Heidelberg (1993)
15. Qian, Z.: A formal specification of java virtual machine instructions for objects, methods and subrountines. Formal Syntax and Semantics of Java, 271–312 (1999)
16. Robby, Dwyer, M.B., Hatcliff, J.: Bogor: an extensible and highly-modular software model checking framework. SIGSOFT Softw. Eng. Notes 28(5), 267–276 (2003)
17. Rosien, M.: Design and implementation of a systematic state explorer. Msc. thesis, University of Twente, The Netherlands (March 2001)
18. Schlich, B., Kowalewski, S.: Model checking C source code for embedded systems. In: Proceedings of the IEEE/NASA Workshop on Leveraging Applications of Formal Methods, Verification, and Validation (ISoLA 2005), September 2005 (2005)
19. Schlich, B., Rohrbach, M., Weber, M., Kowalewski, S.: Model checking software for microcontrollers. Technical Report AIB-2006-11, RWTH Aachen (August 2006)
20. Schürmans, S.: Ein Compiler und eine Virtuelle Maschine zur Zustandsraumgenerierung. Diplomarbeit, RWTH Aachen University (October 2005)
21. Veldema, R.: Personal communication on the Tapir programming language (2006) `http://www2.informatik.uni-erlangen.de/Forschung/Projekte/Tapir/`
22. Weise, C.: An incremental formal semantics for PROMELA. In: Proceedings of the 3rd International SPIN Workshop, April 1997 (1997)
23. Wibling, O., Parrow, J., Pears, A.: Automatized verification of ad hoc routing protocols. In: de Frutos-Escrig, D., Núñez, M. (eds.) FORTE 2004. LNCS, vol. 3235, pp. 343–358. Springer, Heidelberg (2004)
24. Wirth, N.: Pascal-s: A subset and its implementation. In: Barron, D.W. (ed.) Pascal - The Language and its Implementation, pp. 199–259. John Wiley, New York (1981)

A Benchmarks

Our test setup consists of an AMD Athlon 64 3500+ running Linux. We used SPIN 4.2.5 for comparison. SPIN translates PROMELA models into C source code which subsequently is compiled, and then run for the analysis.

By default, SPIN uses data-flow optimizations and statement merging [12] to reduce size of the *explored state space*, thus requiring less time and memory for the task. The optimizations can be disabled optionally (`spin -o1 -o3`). We benchmarked SPIN without said optimizations against our implementation (columns "Unoptimized" in Table 5), and another time with both optimizations enabled, against our *unmodified* VM, but with *path compression* (a variant of statement merging) enabled in our PROMELA compiler.

We compiled the `pan.c` files generated by SPIN from the PROMELA models, and used gcc (version 3.3.5) with option `-O2` (C optimisations), `-DNOREDUCE` (disabling partial-order reduction) and `-DBFS` (enabling breadth-first search). BFS is the main strategy used in NIPS because of the requirements of distributed algorithms, whereas SPIN's default is depth-first search (DFS). We did not implement optimizations used in SPIN's DFS, which is why we compare BFS only.

In our tests, we used models that come with the SPIN distribution. Our experiments show that NIPS (version 1.2.2) is close enough to SPIN both in state vector size (rightmost columns of Table 5) and state space generation speed for our purposes. The actual state count of models is not directly comparable, due to different ways of counting (for example, SPIN counts both halves of a rendezvous communication separately), and due to differing base levels and optimizations. However, crucial behaviour is not optimized away of course.

The size of state vectors, which contain all information needed to restart the virtual machine from (global and local variables, channels, processes), is typically within a few bytes of what is reported by SPIN.

Table 4 shows the results for some large PROMELA models. The experiments were carried out on a 64-bit AMD Opteron™ 248 Dual Processor machine (only one processor used) with 16 GB RAM and a single 200 GB Serial-ATA hard disk, running Linux 2.6.4. For the first two models an arbitrary limit of 2.5 GB RAM was set, whereas the other models were given 16 GB RAM. A full account of the experiments and the models is given in [10].

Table 4. Runs for large PROMELA models. *States visited* are all states, including single-successor states, whereas column *States stored* shows only states with more than one successor. M and G denote factors 10^6 resp. 10^9, GB means Gigabyte.

Model	**States**		**Edges**	**Time**	**Uncompressed**
	visited	**stored**		**[h]**	**storage [GB]**
GIOP1	192.9M	162.5M	664.6M	13:34:21	79.2
LUNAR 4(d)	1.3G	248.3M	1.9G	35:37:29	153.0
HUGO: Hot fail	555.6M	205.3M	864.9M	15:18:16	166.9
LUNAR 4(f)	1.6G	334.6M	2.6G	38:36:02	230.0

Table 5. State Space Generation: A comparison between NIPS and SPIN. PROMELA models are taken from the SPIN distribution. Times are measured as wall-clock time in seconds on an AMD Athlon 64 3500+ running Linux.

Parameter		NIPS Virtual Machine Unoptimized States	Time	NIPS Virtual Machine with Path Compr. States	Time	SPIN 4.2.5 Unoptimized States	Time	SPIN 4.2.5 D. Flow & Stmt. Merge States	Time	NIPS State size in bytes	SPIN State size in bytes
MAX		**eratosthenes**									
	6	170	0.002	34	0.001	195	0.016	128	0.016	130	124
	10	764	0.020	74	0.003	1006	0.018	548	0.018	163	156
	14	2744	0.051	190	0.006	3864	0.026	2263	0.026	229	220
	18	7766	0.166	342	0.012	12035	0.058	6477	0.058	262	252
	22	24092	0.569	626	0.025	41610	0.344	21539	0.344	295	284
	26	69920	1.717	**1162**	0.054	129823	2.430	**69618**	0.430	328	316
	30	146222	3.824	**1710**	0.088	282914	11.855	**130062**	3.855	361	348
	34	**347012**	10.418	**2914**	0.177	713817	171.441	**342028**	26.441	394	380
N	L	**leader**									
3	6	754	0.009	105	0.002	743	0.018	407	0.018	131	116
4	8	5678	0.082	379	0.008	5626	0.037	2410	0.037	186	180
5	10	46091	0.649	1509	0.035	45937	0.268	15791	0.268	249	220
6	12	382465	**6.180**	**6241**	0.176	382151	**3.120**	**106449**	0.120	320	308
N	L	**leader2**									
3	6	4571	0.054	667	0.010	4476	0.027	2430	0.027	138	124
4	8	143373	1.321	**10012**	0.161	142260	0.650	**60052**	0.650	193	188
N		**peterson_N**									
	2	327	0.003	30	0.000	303	0.017	185	0.017	38	40
	3	51118	0.268	**853**	0.012	45927	0.085	**25371**	0.085	50	48
		pftp									
		1378184	**10.033**	301603	4.996	1275180	**3.770**	219167	0.770	189	152
		snoopy									
		124434	2.385	68658	**1.442**	91925	0.436	61624	**0.436**	205	188
N		**sort**									
	5	21245	0.276	572	0.010	14349	0.077	4652	0.077	181	184
	6	152628	1.789	**2019**	0.040	95677	0.576	22350	0.576	215	216

Scalable Multi-core LTL Model-Checking*

J. Barnat, L. Brim, and P. Ročkai

Faculty of Informatics, Masaryk University
Brno, Czech Republic
{barnat,brim,xrockai}@fi.muni.cz

Abstract. Recent development in computer hardware has brought more wide-spread emergence of shared-memory, multi-core systems. These architectures offer opportunities to speed up various tasks – among others LTL model checking. In the paper we show a design for a parallel shared-memory LTL model checker, that is based on a distributed-memory algorithm. To achieve good scalability, we have devised and experimentally evaluated several implementation techniques, which we present in the paper.

1 Introduction

With the arrival of 64-bit technology the traditional space limitations in formal verification may become less severe. Instead, time could quickly become an important bottleneck. This naturally raises interest in using parallelism to fight the "time-explosion" problem.

Much of the extensive research on the parallelization of model checking algorithms followed the distributed-memory programming model and the algorithms were parallelized for networks of workstations, largely due to easy access to networks of workstations. Recent shift in architecture design toward multi-cores has intensified research pertaining to shared-memory paradigm as well.

In [12] G. Holzmann proposed an extension of the SPIN model checker for dual-core machines. The algorithms keep their linear time complexity and the liveness checking algorithm supports full LTL. The algorithm for checking safety properties scales well to N-core systems. The algorithm for liveness checking, which is based on the original SPIN's nested DFS algorithm, is unable to scale to N-core systems. It is still an open problem to do scalable verification of general liveness properties on N-cores with linear time complexity.

A different approach to shared-memory model checking is presented in [15], based on CTL* translation to Hesitant Alternating Automata. The proposed algorithm uses so-called non-emptiness game for deciding validity of the original formula and is therefore largely unrelated to the algorithms based on fair-cycle detection.

In this paper we propose a design for a parallel shared-memory model checking tool, that is based on known distributed-memory algorithms. For the prototype

* This work has been partially supported by the Grant Agency of Czech Republic grant No. 201/06/1338 and the Academy of Sciences grant No. 1ET408050503.

D. Bošnački and S. Edelkamp (Eds.): SPIN 2007, LNCS 4595, pp. 187–203, 2007.

implementation we considered the algorithm by Černá and Pelánek [7]. This algorithm is linear for properties expressible as weak Büchi automata, which comprise majority of LTL properties encountered in practice. Although the worst-case complexity is quadratic, the algorithm exhibits very good performance with real-life verification problems. To achieve good scalability, we have devised several implementation techniques, as presented in this paper, and applied them to the algorithm. We expect, that application of the proposed implementation approaches to other distributed-memory algorithms for LTL model checking may bring similar improvements in scalability on N-core systems.

The main contribution of the paper can thus be seen in giving at least a partial answer to the open research problem. We show that most (see e.g.[10]) of the practically used liveness properties (in fact the complete persistence class [18,8]) can be model-checked using scalable linear time algorithm on multi-core, shared-memory systems.

In Section 2 we summarize the existing parallel algorithms for LTL model checking (*accepting cycle detection*). In Section 3 we present several implementation techniques that were applied to multi-core implementation of the selected algorithm. In Section 4 we report on scalability tests and on comparison with dual-core Nested DFS algorithm.

2 Parallel LTL Model-Checking Algorithms

Efficient parallel solution of many problems often requires approaches radically different from those used to solve the same problems sequentially. Classical examples are list rankings, connected components, depth-first search in planar graphs etc. In the area of LTL model checking the best known enumerative *sequential* algorithms based on fair-cycle detection are the *Nested DFS* algorithm [9,14] (implemented, e.g., in the model checker `SPIN` [13]) and *SCC-based algorithms* originating in Tarjan's algorithm for the decomposition of the graph into strongly connected components (SCCs) [22]. However, both algorithms rely on inherently sequential depth-first search postorder, hence it is difficult to adapt them to parallel architectures. Consequently, different techniques and algorithms are needed. Unlike LTL model checking, the reachability analysis is a verification problem with efficient parallel solution. The reason is that the exploration of the state space can be implemented e.g. using breadth-first search. In the following, we sketch four parallel algorithms for enumerative LTL model checking that are, more or less, based on performing repeated parallel reachability to detect reachable accepting cycles. The reader is kindly asked to consult the original sources for the details.

[MAP] The main idea of the **Maximal Accepting Predecessor Algorithm** [4,6] is based on the fact that every accepting vertex lying on an accepting cycle is its own predecessor. An algorithm that is directly derived from the idea, would require expensive computation as well as space to store all proper accepting predecessors of all (accepting) vertices. To remedy this obstacle, the MAP algorithm stores only a single representative of all proper accepting predecessor for every vertex. The representative is chosen as the *maximal accepting predecessor* accordingly to a presupposed linear ordering $\prec$ of vertices (given e.g. by their memory representation). Clearly, if an accepting vertex is its own maximal accepting predecessor, it lies on an accepting cycle. Unfortunately, it can happen that all the maximal accepting predecessor lie out of accepting cycles. In that case, the algorithm removes all accepting vertices that are maximal accepting predecessors of some vertex, and recomputes the maximal accepting predecessors. This is repeated until an accepting cycle is found or there are no more accepting vertices in the graph.

The time complexity of the algorithm is $\mathcal{O}(a^2 \cdot m)$, where a is the number of accepting vertices and m is the number of edges. One of the key aspects influencing the overall performance of the algorithm is the underlying ordering of vertices used by the algorithm. It is not possible to compute the optimal ordering in parallel, hence heuristics for computing a suitable vertex ordering are used. □

[OWCTY] The next algorithm [7] is an extended enumerative version of the **One Way Catch Them Young Algorithm** [11]. The idea of the algorithm is to repeatedly remove vertices from the graph that cannot lie on an accepting cycle. The two removal rules are as follows. First, a vertex is removed from the graph if it has no successors in the graph (the vertex cannot lie on a cycle), second, a vertex is removed if it cannot reach an accepting vertex (a potential cycle the vertex lies on is non-accepting). The algorithm performs removal steps as far as there are vertices to be removed. In the end, either there are some vertices remaining in the graph meaning that the original graph contained an accepting cycle, or all vertices have been removed meaning that the original graph had no accepting cycles.

The time complexity of the algorithm is $\mathcal{O}(h \cdot m)$ where h is the height of the SCC quotient graph. Here the factor m comes from the computation of elimination rules while the factor h relates to the number of global iterations the removal rules must be applied. Also note, that an alternative algorithm is obtained if the rules are replaced with their backward search counterparts. □

[NEGC] The idea behind the **Negative Cycle Algorithm** [5] is a transformation of the LTL model checking problem to the problem of negative cycle detection. Every edge of the graph outgoing from a non-accepting vertex is labeled with 0 while every edge outgoing from an accepting vertex is labeled with -1. Clearly, the graph contains a negative cycle if and only if it has an accepting cycle.

The algorithm exploits the *walk to root* strategy to detect the presence of a negative cycle. The strategy involves construction of the so called *parent graph* that keeps the shortest path to the initial vertex for every vertex of the graph. The parent graph is repeatedly checked for the existence of the path. If the shortest path does not exist for a given vertex, then the vertex is a part of negative, thus accepting, cycle. The worst case time complexity of the algorithm is $\mathcal{O}(n \cdot m)$, where n is the nubmer of vertices and m is the number of edges. □

[BLEDGE] An edge (u, v) is called a *back-level edge* if it does not increase the distance of the target vertex v form the initial vertex of the graph. The key observation connecting the cycle detection problem with the back-level edge concept, as used in the **Back-Level Edges Algorithm** [1], is that every cycle contains at least one back-level edge. Back-level edges are, therefore, used as triggers to start a procedure that checks whether the edge is a part of an accepting cycle. However, this is too expensive to be done completely for every back-level edge. Therefore, several improvements and heuristics are suggested and integrated within the algorithm to decrease the number of tested edges and speed-up the cycle test.

The BFS procedure which detects back-level edges runs in time $\mathcal{O}(m+n)$. In the worst case, each back-level edge has to be checked to be a part of a cycle, which requires linear time $\mathcal{O}(m+n)$ as well. Since there is at most m back-level edges, the overall time complexity of the algorithm is $\mathcal{O}(m.(m+n))$. □

All the algorithms allow for an efficient implementation on a parallel architecture. The implementation is based on partitioning the graph (its vertices) into disjoint parts. Suitable partitioning is important to benefit from parallelization.

One particular technique, that is specific to automata based LTL model checking, is *cycle locality preserving* problem decomposition [2,16]. The graph (product automaton) originates from synchronous product of the property and system automata. Hence, vertices of product automaton graph are ordered pairs. An interesting observation is that every cycle in a product automaton graph emerges from cycles in system and property automaton graphs. Let A, B be Büchi automata and $A \otimes B$ their synchronous product. If C is a strongly connected component in the automaton graph of $A \otimes B$, then A-projection of C and B-projection of C are (not necessarily maximal) strongly connected components in automaton graphs of A and B, respectively.

As the property automaton origins from the LTL formula to be verified, it is typically quite small and can be pre-analyzed. In particular, it is possible to identify all strongly connected components of the property automaton graph. A partition function may then be devised, that respects strongly connected components of the property automaton and therefore preserves cycle locality. The partitioning strategy is to assign all vertices that project to the same strongly connected component of the property automaton graph to the same sub-problem. Since no cycle is split among different sub-problems it is possible to employ localized Nested DFS algorithm to perform local accepting cycle detection simultaneously.

Yet another interesting information can be drawn from the property automaton graph decomposition. Maximal strongly connected components can be classified into three categories:

Type F: (*Fully Accepting*) Any cycle within the component contains at least one accepting vertex. (There is no non-accepting cycle within the component.)

Type P: (*Partially Accepting*) There is at least one accepting cycle and one non-accepting cycle within the component.

Type N: (*Non-Accepting*) There is no accepting cycle within the component.

Realizing that vertex of a product automaton graph is accepting only if the corresponding vertex in the property automaton graph is accepting it is possible to characterize types of strongly connected components of product automaton graph according to types of components in the property automaton graph. This classification of components into types N, F, and P can be used to gain additional improvements that may be incorporated into the above given algorithms.

3 Implementation Techniques

It is a well known fact, that a distributed-memory, parallel algorithm is straightforwardly transformed into a shared-memory one. However, there are several inefficiencies involved in this direct translation. Several traits of shared-memory architecture may be leveraged to improve real-world performance of such implementations. In this section, we present our approaches at the challenges of shared-memory architecture and its specific characteristics. We will detail the techniques concerning communication, memory allocation and termination detection, and we will show their application on the OWCTY algorithm as described in Section 2. Before doing so, though, let us describe the target platform in more detail.

3.1 Shared-Memory Platform

We work with a model based on threads that share all memory, although they have separate stacks in their shared address space and a special thread-local storage to store thread-private data. Our working environment is POSIX, with its implementation of threads as lightweight processes. Switching contexts among different threads is cheaper than switching contexts among full-featured processes with separate address spaces, so using more threads than there are CPUs in the system incurs only a minor penalty.

Critical Sections, Locking and Lock Contention. In a shared-memory setting, access to memory, that may be used for writing by more than a single thread, has to be controlled through use of mutual exclusion, otherwise, race conditions will occur. This is generally achieved through use of a "mutual exclusion device", so-called mutex. A thread wishing to enter a critical section has to lock the associated mutex, which may block the calling thread if the mutex is locked already by some other thread. An effect called resource or lock contention is associated with this behaviour. This occurs, when two or more threads happen to need to enter the same critical section (and therefore lock the same mutex), at the same time. If critical sections are long or they are entered very often, contention starts to cause observable performance degradation, as more and more time is spent waiting for mutexes.

Role of Processor Cache. There are two fairly orthogonal issues associated with processor cache. First, cache coherence which is implemented by hardware, but its efficiency is affected by programmer, and cache efficiency, which mostly depends on data structures and algorithms employed.

Cache coherence poses an efficiency penalty when there are many processors writing to same area of memory. This is largely avoided by the distributed algorithm, however, locking and access to shared data structures have no other choice. Cache coherence on modern architectures works at a level of cache lines, roughly 64 byte chunks of memory that are fetched from main memory into cache at once.

Modern mutex implementations ensure that the mutex is the only thing present on a given cache line, so it does not affect other data, and, more importantly, it ensures that two mutexes never share a cache line, which would pose a performance penalty.

Recent development in multi-core platforms deals with cache coherence problem in a different, more efficient manner, namely, by sharing the level two cache among two or more cores, therefore reducing the cache coherence overhead significantly. Yet, with the current state of technology, this still does not mitigate the overhead completely.

3.2 Implementing Algorithms in Shared-Memory

The above considerations bring us to the actual algorithm implementation and the associated techniques we came up with. They are all designed to reduce communication overhead, exploiting traits of shared-memory systems that are not available in distributed-memory environments. Consequently, the main goal is to improve scalability of the implementation, which is inversely proportional to communication overhead and its growth with increasing number of threads. That said, keeping in mind the possibility to scale beyond shared-memory systems, we try to keep the implementation in a shape that would make a combined tool to work efficiently on clusters of multi-CPU machines achievable.

When we venture into a strictly shared-memory implementation, one may pose a question, whether a different approach of using a standard serial algorithm modified to allow parallelisation at lower levels of abstraction would give a scalable, efficient program for multi-CPU and/or multi-core systems. Our efforts at extracting such a micro-parallelism in our codebase have been largely fruitless, due high synchronisation cost relative to amount of work we were able to perform in parallel. Although we intend to do more research on this topic, we do not expect significant results.

In the following sections, we explore the possibilities to build on existing distributed-memory approaches, in the vein of statically-partitioned graphs, reducing the overhead using idioms only possible due to locality of memory.

3.3 Communication

Generally, in a distributed computation, all communication is accomplished by passing messages – e.g. using a library like MPI for cluster message passing.

However, in communication-intensive programs, or those sensitive to communication delay, using general-purpose message passing interface is fairly inefficient.

In shared-memory, most of the communication overhead can be eliminated by using more appropriate communication primitives, like high-performance, contention- and lock- free FIFOs (First In, First Out queues). We have adopted a variant of the two-lock algorithm – a decent compromise between performance on one hand and simplicity and portability on the other – presented in [20]. Our modifications involve improved cache-efficiency (by using a linked list of memory-continuous blocks, instead of linked list of single items) and only using a single write-lock, instead of a pair of locks, one for reading and one for writing, since there is ever only one thread reading, while there may be several trying to write.

Every thread involved in the computation owns a single instance of the FIFO and all messages for this thread are pushed onto this single queue. This may introduce a source of resource-contention, where many processes are trying to append messages to a single queue, but considering the message distribution in our system, this turns out to be a negligible problem in practice. With different patterns of communication, a complete lock-free design may be more appropriate (one is given in [20]).

type FIFO of T:
  type Node:
    buffer: array of T
    next: pointer to Node
    read, *write*: integer
  nodeSize: integer (size of *buffer*)
  head, *tail*: pointer to Node
  writeLock: mutex

Fig. 1. FIFO representation

Require: f is a FIFO of T instance, x of type T is an element to enqueue
Ensure: f contains x as its last element
  lock($f.writeMutex$)
  if $f.tail.write = f.nodeSize$ **then**
    $t \leftarrow$ newly allocated Node, all fields 0
  else
    $t \leftarrow f.tail$
  $t.buffer[t.write] \leftarrow x$
  $t.write \leftarrow t.write + 1$
  if $f.tail \neq t$ **then**
    $f.tail.next = t$
    $f.tail = t$
  unlock($f.writeMutex$)

Fig. 2. FIFO enqueue

Require: f is a non-empty FIFO instance
Ensure: front element of f is dequeued and then returned
  if $f.head.read = f.nodeSize$ **then**
    $f.head \leftarrow f.head.next$
  $f.head.read \leftarrow f.head.read + 1$
  return $f.head.buffer[f.head.read - 1]$

Fig. 3. FIFO dequeue

Representation and pseudo-code for enqueue and dequeue algorithms are found in Figures 1, 2 and 3, respectively. The correctness, linearizability and liveness proofs as given in [20] are straightforwardly adapted to our implementation and thus left out.

Alternatives to our implementation, which may be more appropriate in different settings, include a ring-buffer FIFO implementation (if there is a bound on the amount of in-flight data known beforehand, the ring-buffer implementation may be more efficient) and possibly an algorithm based on swapping incoming and outgoing queues (which could be easily implemented as a pointer swap). The latter gives results comparable to the described FIFO method, although the code and locking behaviour is much more complex and error-prone, which made us opt for the simpler FIFO implementation.

3.4 Memory Allocation

In a distributed computation, every process has simply its own memory which it fully manages. In a shared-memory, however, we prefer to manage the memory as a single shared area, since an equal partitioning of available memory and separate management may fall short of efficient resource usage. However, this poses some challenges, especially in allocation-intensive environment like ours.

First, a naïve approach of protecting the allocation routines with a simple mutual exclusion is highly prone to resource contention. Fortunately, modern general-purpose allocator implementations refrain from this idea and have a generally non-contending behaviour on allocation. However, releasing memory back for reuse is more complex to achieve without introducing contention, in a setting where it is often the case that thread other than the one allocating the chunk tries to release it.

There are known general-purpose solutions to this problem, e.g. [19], however they are currently not in widespread use, therefore we have to refrain from the above-mentioned pattern of releasing memory from different than allocating thread, in order to avoid contention and the accompanying slowdown.

The message-passing implementation we employ is pointer-based, in other words, the message sent is only a pointer and the payload (actual interesting message content) is allocated on the shared heap and it may be either reused or released by the receiving thread. Observe however, that releasing the associated memory in the receiving thread will introduce the situation which we are trying to avoid.

We side-step the issue by adding a new communication FIFO to each thread (recall that our communication induces only low overhead and virtually no contention). When a receiving thread decides that the message content needs to be disposed of, instead of doing it itself, sends the message back to the originating thread using the second FIFO. The originating thread then, at convenient intervals, releases the memory in a single batch, having an interesting side-effect of slightly improving cache-efficiency.

3.5 Efficient Termination Detection

Since our algorithms rely on work distribution among several largely independent threads, similarly to a distributed algorithm, we need a specific algorithm for shared-memory termination detection, that would pose minimal overhead and minimal serialisation.

One possible solution is presented in [17], which does not use locking and relies on the system to provide an enqueue-with-wakeup primitive. However, in our system, we have primitives available that support a somewhat different approach: implementation of sleeping/wakeup primitives already relies on locking and we leverage this inherent locking in our termination detection algorithm.

The POSIX threading library offers a mechanism called "condition signalling", which we use to implement thread sleeping and wakeup. A "condition" is a device that allows to be waited-for by its owning thread and "signalling a condition" from another thread will cause the waiting thread to wake up and continue execution. However, this device in itself is race-prone, since the condition may be signalled just before the owner goes to sleep, leading to a deadlock – another signal may never come. Therefore, the condition is always protected by a mutex, which is always locked through the execution of the owner thread and is only atomically unlocked when the thread enters sleep state and atomically reclaimed before waking up.

Since the available mutex implementation allows a lock-or-fail behaviour, as opposed to lock-or-wait which is usually employed for protecting critical sections, we can use the condition device to implement an efficient termination detection algorithm.

Observe, that at any time when a thread is idle, its condition-protecting mutex is unlocked and conversely, whenever the thread is busy, this mutex is locked. So the termination detection algorithm first tries to lock condition mutexes of all worker threads, one by one, using the lock-or-fail behaviour. Then, it proceeds to check the queues. If it succeeded locking all threads and all queues are empty, termination has occurred. Pseudo-code for the algorithm is shown in Figure 4.

We run the termination detection in a dedicated scheduler thread, which also wakes up threads that have pending work. This means that if it has successfully grabbed any locks, queues belonging to those locked threads are checked, and if any is found to be non-empty, the thread is awakened. After every run, all grabbed locks are released again.

Moreover, although this algorithm works correctly as-is, it is rather inefficient if left running in a loop. Therefore, the scheduler thread goes to sleep after every

```
Require: threads: array of Thread, Thread contains idleMutex and idleCondition, fifo
Ensure: termination has occurred iff true is returned
  mutex: Mutex, cond: Condition, held: array of Boolean
  busy ← false
  for t in threads do
    if trylock(t.idleMutex) then
      held[t] ← true
    else
      held[t] ← false
      busy ← true
  for t in threads do
    if not empty( t.fifo ) then
      busy ← true
      if held[t] then
        signal(t.idleCondition)
  for t in threads do
    unlock( t.idleMutex )
  return not busy
```

Fig. 4. Termination Detection in Shared-Memory

iteration, and is woken up by any worker thread that goes idle. This requires a slight modification to the algorithm above, since it adds a race-condition, where the last thread going to sleep wakes up the scheduler, which then runs the algorithm before the calling thread manages to go to sleep, assuming termination did not happen and going to sleep, at which point the system deadlocks, as everyone is idle.

An alternative approach would be to synchronously execute the termination detection algorithm in the thread that has become idle, but due to the nature of the system, the above is more practical code-wise and only incurs very insignificant overhead.

3.6 Implementing OWCTY in Shared-Memory

As can be seen from the pseudo-code (refer to Figure 5), the main OWCTY loop consists of few steps, namely, reachability, elimination and reset. All of them can be parallelised, but only on their own, which requires a barrier after each of them. Only reachability and elimination run in parallel in the current code, reset is to be implemented.

The algorithm uses a BFS state space visitor to implement both reachability and elimination. The underlying BFS is currently implemented using a partition function, i.e., every state is unambiguously assigned to one of the threads. The framework in which the algorithm is implemented offers a multi-threaded BFS implementation based on this kind of state-space partitioning. The algorithm itself is only presented with resulting transition and node-expansion events, unconcerned with the partitioning or communication details.

```
Require: initial is initial state
  S ←Reachability(initial)
  old ← ∅
  while S ≠ old do
    old ← S
    S ←Reset(S)
    S ←Reachability(S)
    S ←Elimination(S)
  return S ≠ ∅
```

Fig. 5. OWCTY Pseudo-code

The barriers are implemented using the termination detection algorithm presented – the computation is initiated by the main thread and the termination detection is then executed in this same thread, which also doubles as a scheduler. When the step terminates, the main thread prepares the next step, spawns the worker threads and initiates the computation again. Since the hash table is always thread-private, i.e. owned exclusively by a single thread, the main thread has to transfer the hash table among different threads in the serial portion of computation. This is nonetheless done cheaply (few pointer operations only) so is probably not worth parallelising.

4 Experiments

4.1 Methodology

The main testing machine we have used is a 16-way AMD Opteron 885 (8 CPU units with 2 cores each). All timed programs were compiled using gcc 4.1.2 20060525 (Red Hat 4.1.1-1) in 32-bit mode, using -O3. This limits addressable memory to 3GB, which was enough for our testing. The machine has 64GB of memory installed, which means that none of the runs were affected by swapping.

For this paper, our main concern is speed and scalability, therefore we focus on these two parameters. Measurement was done using standard UNIX `time` command, which measures real and cpu times used by program. Note that the cpu time given in tables equals to a sum of times spent by individual processors, thus for parallel computations the value of cpu time should exceed the value of real time.

For the experimental evaluation we implemented algorithms upon the state generator from DiVinE [3]. All the models we have used are listed in Table 1 including the verified properties. The models come from the `BEEM` database [21] that contains the models in DiVinE-native modeling language as well as in ProMeLa. We used ProMeLa models for comparison with the `SPIN` model checker. The models are not extremely large, although, their size is sufficient for the time spent on parsing and initialization to be negligible.

Table 1. Models and verified properties

vAcronym	Description	Property (LTL formula)
elevator$_1$	Motivated by elevator ProMeLa model from distribution of SPIN. The cab controller chooses the next floor to be served as the next requested floor in the direction of the last cab movement. If there is no such floor then the controller consider the opposite direction. (3 floors)	If level 0 is requested, the cab passes the level without serving it at most once. $G(r0 \implies (\neg l_0 U(l_0 U(\neg l_0 U(l_0 U (l_0 \wedge open))))))$
elevator$_2$	Same model as elevator, with slightly adjusted parameters to increase state space size. No formula was used with this model.	N/A
leader	Leader election algorithm based on filters. A filter is a piece of code that satisfy the two following conditions: a) if m processes enter the filter, then at most $m/2$ processes exit; b) if some process enter the filter, then at least one of them exits. (5 processes)	Eventually a leader will be elected. $F(leader)$
rether	Software-based, real-time Ethernet protocol whose purpose is to provide guaranteed bandwidth and deterministic, periodic network access to multimedia applications over commodity Ethernet hardware. It is a contention-free token bus protocol for the datalink layer of the ISO protocol stack. (5 Nodes)	Infinitely many NRT actions of Node 0. $G(F(nact0))$
peterson	Peterson's mutual exclusion protocol for N processes. (N=4)	Someone is in critical section infinitely many times. $G(F(SomeoneInCS))$
anderson	Anderson's mutual exclusion protocol for N processes. (N=6)	N/A

4.2 Results

First, we have measured run-times of algorithms presented in Section 2 that were implemented using DiVinE framework and `mpich2` library compiled for

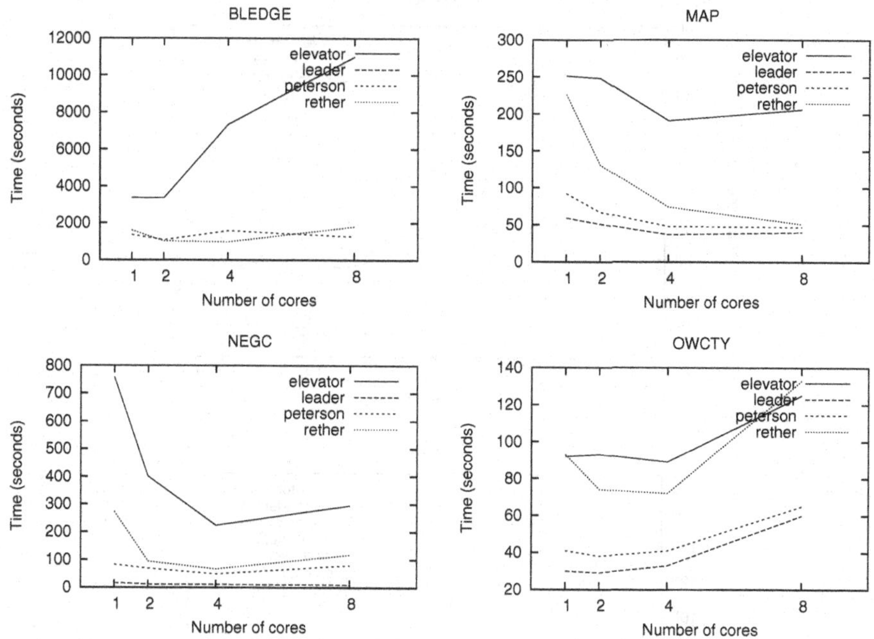

Fig. 6. Scalability of BLEDGE, MAP, NEGC, and OWCTY algorithms implemented using DiVinE and MPI compiled for shared-memory architecture

shared-memory architecture. As shown in Figure 6 these implementations do not exhibit desired scalability on shared-memory architecture, even though they all scale well in a distributed memory environment. Some algorithms have scaled up to 4 cores, but using more cores did not bring any speedup. Under this setting, every MPI node is executed in a separate process.

We have performed more experiments to evaluate the efficiency of techniques introduced in Section 3. We have implemented parallel breadth-first search based reachability and the OWCTY algorithm. Run-times of the thread-optimized BFS reachability and of the thread-optimized implementation of OWCTY algorithm are reported in Figure 7.

The thread-optimized implementations display better scalability behavior, since adding cores reduces computation time at least up to 12 cores, for some models even to 16 cores. Between 12 and 16 cores, the communication overhead reaches a limiting threshold, so adding more does not bring any further speedup and may even impede a slight performance setback.

The actual threshold and curve steepness is generally affected by the partition function used, as well as relative cost of cross transitions. The latter issue partially explains why the MPI versions of algorithms have scalability problems, since the cross transition cost is in this case much higher than in the multi-threaded version.

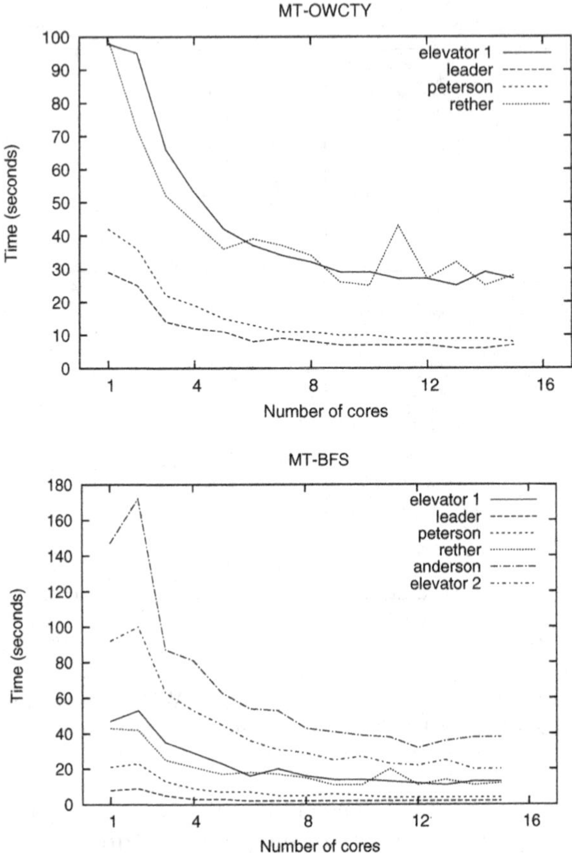

Fig. 7. Scalability of multi-threaded OWCTY and BFS reachability

4.3 Comparison with SPIN

Since the multi-core version of SPIN was not publicly available, in order to make a direct comparison, we run a single reachability on the product automaton graph with SPIN. As SPIN was running only the first procedure of the Nested DFS algorithm we get a good lower bound on runtime of the multi-core SPIN implementation. SPIN was used with parameters -m10000000 -w27 to get the best performance. We have not observed any performance penalty from using bigger stack or hash table than strictly necessary.

We have also measured run-times of a dual-core Nested DFS algorithm as proposed in [12], that was implemented using DiVinE state generator. The run-times are reported in Table 2.

Table 3 gives run-times for SPIN, multi-threaded BFS reachability, and OWCTY cycle detection algorithm, both performed on 16 cores.

Table 2. Parallel Nested DFS in DiVinE

Model	*real*	*cpu*
elevator_1	0:53.4	1:16
leader	0:9.7	0:18.1
peterson	0:24.1	0:33.1
rether	0:45.3	1:5.9

Table 3. Comparison with SPIN

Model	SPIN *reachability*	*BFS reachability*	*OWCTY*
elevator_1	0:14.4	0:12.1	0:26.8
peterson	0:7.4	0:4.2	0:9.2

5 Conclusions

We observe, that the algorithms employed by DiVinE, when augmented with the shared-memory-specific techniques, scale fairly well on multiple cores. Our current OWCTY-based, multi-threaded implementation scales up to 12, and for some models, even to 16 cores, which is a definite improvement over the MPI version.

This fulfills our goal of implementing a scalable multi-core LTL model checker. Thanks to the algorithm used, it has a linear time complexity for majority of LTL properties verified in practice and achieves scalability that makes it practical to use on machines with several CPU cores available.

From the experimental data we see that SPIN outperforms DiVinE in raw speed, but due to SPIN's usage of the Nested DFS algorithm, even if using a parallel nested search, it is bound to execute primary DFS on a single core, which severely limits its scalability potential.

From the profiling work we have done, it is clear that the main bottleneck of DiVinE is its state generator. Improvements in this area should reduce the absolute running times, but will likely negatively affect relative scalability. Therefore, we will continue to work on reducing parallel execution overhead, to maintain or even improve current scalability.

In the pursue of scalability, we also intend to explore alternative approaches to state-space partitioning, non-partitioning approaches and usefulness of load-balancing in this context.

References

1. Barnat, J., Brim, L., Chaloupka, J.: Parallel Breadth-First Search LTL Model-Checking. In: Proc. 18th IEEE International Conference on Automated Software Engineering, pp. 106–115. IEEE Computer Society, Los Alamitos (2003)
2. Barnat, J., Brim, L., Černá, I.: Property Driven Distribution of Nested DFS. In: Proceedinfs of the 3rd International Workshop on Verification and Computational Logic (VCL'02 – held at the PLI 2002 Symposium), University of Southampton, UK, Technical Report DSSE-TR-2002-5 in DSSE, pp. 1–10 (2002)

3. Barnat, J., Brim, L., Černá, I., Moravec, P., Ročkai, P., Šimeček, P.: DiVinE – A Tool for Distributed Verification (Tool Paper). In: Ball, T., Jones, R.B. (eds.) CAV 2006. LNCS, vol. 4144, pp. 278–281. Springer, Heidelberg (2006)
4. Brim, L., Černá, I., Moravec, P., Šimša, J.: Accepting Predecessors are Better than Back Edges in Distributed LTL Model-Checking. In: Hu, A.J., Martin, A.K. (eds.) FMCAD 2004. LNCS, vol. 3312, pp. 352–366. Springer, Heidelberg (2004)
5. Brim, L., Černá, I., Krčál, P., Pelánek, R.: Distributed LTL model checking based on negative cycle detection. In: Hariharan, R., Mukund, M., Vinay, V. (eds.) FST TCS 2001: Foundations of Software Technology and Theoretical Computer Science. LNCS, vol. 2245, pp. 96–107. Springer, Heidelberg (2001)
6. Brim, L., Černá, I., Moravec, P., Šimša, J.: How to Order Vertices for Distributed LTL Model-Checking Based on Accepting Predecessors. In: Proceedings of the 4th International Workshop on Parallel and Distributed Methods in verifiCation (PDMC 2005), pp. 1–12 (2005)
7. Černá, I., Pelánek, R.: Distributed explicit fair cycle detection (set based approach). In: Ball, T., Rajamani, S.K. (eds.) Model Checking Software. LNCS, vol. 2648, pp. 49–73. Springer, Heidelberg (2003)
8. Černá, I., Pelánek, R.: Relating hierarchy of temporal properties to model checking. In: Rovan, B., Vojtáš, P. (eds.) MFCS 2003. LNCS, vol. 2747, pp. 318–327. Springer, Heidelberg (2003)
9. Courcoubetis, C., Vardi, M.Y., Wolper, P., Yannakakis, M.: Memory-Efficient Algorithms for the Verification of Temporal Properties. Formal Methods in System Design 1, 275–288 (1992)
10. Dwyer, M., Avrunin, G., Corbett, J.: Property specification patterns for finite-state verification. In: Ardis, M. (ed.) Proc. 2nd Workshop on Formal Methods in Software Practice (FMSP-98), pp. 7–15. ACM Press, New York (1998)
11. Fisler, K., Fraer, R., Kamhi, G., Vardi, M.Y., Yang, Z.: Is there a best symbolic cycle-detection algorithm? In: Margaria, T., Yi, W. (eds.) ETAPS 2001 and TACAS 2001. LNCS, vol. 2031, pp. 420–434. Springer, Heidelberg (2001)
12. Holzmann, G.: The Design of a Distributed Model Checking Algorithm for SPIN. In: FMCAD, Invited Talk (2006)
13. Holzmann, G.J.: The Spin Model Checker: Primer and Reference Manual. Addison-Wesley, London (2003)
14. Holzmann, G.J., Peled, D., Yannakakis, M.: On Nested Depth First Search. In: The SPIN Verification System, pp. 23–32. American Mathematical Society, 1996. Proc. of the 2nd SPIN Workshop (1996)
15. Inggs, C., Barringer, H.: Ctl* model checking on a shared memory architecture. Formal Methods in System Design 29(2), 135–155 (2006)
16. Lafuente, A.L.: Simplified distributed LTL model checking by localizing cycles. Technical Report 00176, Institut für Informatik, University Freiburg, Germany (July 2002)
17. Leung, H.-F., Ting, H.-F.: An optimal algorithm for global termination detection in shared-memory asynchronous multiprocessor systems. IEEE Transactions on Parallel and Distributed Systems 8(5), 538–543 (1997)
18. Manna, Z., Pnueli, A.: A hierarchy of temporal properties. In: Proc. ACM Symposium on Principles of Distributed Computing, pp. 377–410. ACM Press, New York (1990)
19. Michael, M.M.: Scalable lock-free dynamic memory allocation. SIGPLAN Not. 39(6), 35–46 (2004)

20. Michael, M.M., Scott, M.L.: Simple, fast, and practical non-blocking and blocking concurrent queue algorithms. In: Symposium on Principles of Distributed Computing, pp. 267–275 (1996)
21. Pelánek, R.: BEEM: BEnchmarks for Explicit Model checkers (February 2007) http://anna.fi.muni.cz/models/index.html
22. Tarjan, R.: Depth First Search and Linear Graph Algorithms. SIAM Journal on Computing, 146–160 (1972)

A SystemC/TLM Semantics in PROMELA and Its Possible Applications

Claus Traulsen[1,2], Jérôme Cornet[1], Matthieu Moy[1], and Florence Maraninchi[1]

[1] Verimag, Centre Équation - 2, avenue de Vignate, 38610 GIÈRES — France
[2] Dept. of Computer Science, Christian-Albrechts-Universität zu Kiel, Olshausenstr. 40, 24098 KIEL — Germany

Abstract. SystemC has become a *de facto* standard for the modeling of systems-on-a-chip, at various levels of abstraction, including the so-called *transaction level* (TL). Verifying properties of a TL model requires that SystemC be translated into some formally defined language for which there exist verification back-ends. Since SystemC has no formal semantics, this includes a careful encoding of the SystemC scheduler, which has both synchronous and asynchronous features, and a notion of time. In a previous work, we presented a complete chain from SystemC to a synchronous formalism and its associated verification tools. In this paper, we describe the encoding of the SystemC scheduler into an *asynchronous* formalism, namely PROMELA (the input language for SPIN). We comment on the possible uses for this new encoding.

1 Introduction

SystemC [17] is a C++ library/language used for the description of Systems-on-Chip (SoCs) at different levels of abstraction, from cycle-accurate to purely functional models. It comes with a simulation environment, and is becoming a *de facto* standard in the SoCs industry. SystemC is being increasingly used for writing *Transaction Level Models* (TLM) [7] that allow embedded software development on a virtual prototype of the final chip.

A TL model written in SystemC is based on an *architecture*, *i.e.*, a set of components and connections between them. Components behave *concurrently*. Each component has typed connection *ports*. Its behavior is given by a set of communicating *processes* programmed in full C++ and managed by a non-preemptive *scheduler*. Synchronization mechanisms include *events*, which can be waited for or notified. A process yields control back to the scheduler either by waiting for an event or by waiting for a given period of time to elapse.

Communications between modules proceed by function calls traversing components or communication *channels* (for instance bus models). At the transaction level, such function calls are used to model two types of communication: transactions (atomic exchange of data between modules) and interrupts.

Since the TL models are considered as *reference* models in the SoC design flow, it is necessary to validate properties at this level of abstraction. This is currently done by intensive testing, but formal verification is being investigated

D. Bošnački and S. Edelkamp (Eds.): SPIN 2007, LNCS 4595, pp. 204–222, 2007.

for some years now, in both industry and academia. However, the definition of SystemC, while being an IEEE norm, lacks formal semantics.

Some work on verifying properties of SoC assume that they are described in some parallel formalism inspired by SystemC. Often, this formalism only reflects the subset of the language used for Register Transfer Level (RTL) models and is useless to express the specificities of a TL model (see for instance [9], [5] ; more references in Section 5). Formal verification for RTL designs has been studied a lot, and providing such analysis for designs written in SystemC does not bring new results. Moreover, even if the formalism reflects in some way the transaction level of abstraction, it is often quite far from real SystemC designs.

We are interested in verifying properties of real SystemC designs, at the transaction level. This requires that SystemC and TLM-specific features be translated into some formally defined language for which there exists verification back-ends. This includes a careful encoding of the SystemC scheduler, which has both synchronous and asynchronous features, and a notion of time.

Choosing the formal language in which to translate SystemC is important because it often restricts the set of verification back-ends that can be applied. If we translate SystemC into a symbolic synchronous formalism, we have access to tools like the Lustre [8], SMV [13] or Esterel [2] tool-chains; if we translate it into an asynchronous formalism, we have access to SPIN [10], IF [4], etc. Since the semantics of SystemC processes is neither entirely synchronous, nor entirely asynchronous, any choice implies some encoding. The encoding itself may be responsible for a significant part of the model size.

Another important point is the way time is interpreted. Since SystemC contains explicit constructs to wait for time, the translation into the input language of a timed-model checker like IF [4] or UPPAAL [12] could seem to be an appropriate choice. However, we do not need the full expressive power of timed automata to encode SystemC, and using timed automata would imply to pay the price of the symbolic analysis needed for clocks in the verification back-ends. Consequently, we will choose a discrete interpretation of time in SystemC, and encode timers into some ordinary variables.

In a previous work [16,14], we described a complete chain from SystemC to a synchronous formalism. It is based upon a systematic encoding of SystemC processes into a flavor of synchronous automata. In such a case, SystemC processes are encoded one by one into automata, communicating with an additional automaton that encodes the scheduler specification. The automata corresponding to the user processes are produced specifically to communicate with this scheduler automaton, using additional synchronous signals and the instantaneous dialogue mechanism available in a pure synchronous semantics. The set of automata can then be translated into several synchronous formalisms (SMV [13] input, Lustre), without computing the intrinsic *products* between them, hence delegating the potential state explosion to the verification back-ends that are better equipped to tackle the problem. Another good property of the translation into Lustre is that we get something *executable*. It means that we can, at least, compare the Lustre encoding with the official SystemC semantics, on benchmark programs.

However, the encoding into a synchronous formalism renders manual reading difficult, and the amount of additional synchronizations needed to reflect the semantics of SystemC can be put in question again.

Another approach would be to define a direct semantics by using an *ad hoc* product to represent the effect of the scheduler, that is creating a dedicated parallel composition which would include the main characteristics of the SystemC scheduling specification. While this approach produces more readable results, the fact is that it also requires to create a dedicated model-checker and prevents from using existing verification tools, that deal only with well-known formalisms.

In this paper, we explore the encoding of the SystemC scheduler into an *asynchronous* formalism, namely PROMELA, the input language for the tool SPIN [10]. The translation into PROMELA is another way to give a formal semantics to SystemC/TLM. Thanks to the simulator provided with SPIN, the semantics is executable, and it will be possible to test the faithfulness of our encoding w.r.t. the official scheduler.

So far, we experimented our translations for model-checking and intensive testing of properties like deadlocks and assertions.

The alternative encoding of SystemC into an asynchronous formalism will also allow the comparison of the two verification chains, with respect to the size of the models, the power of the verification tools, etc. In other words, we try to answer the following questions: for a given SystemC model, and a given property of it, is it more efficient to use a synchronous verification chain, or an asynchronous one? This may depend on the type of property, and is still being investigated.

The rest of the paper is structured as follows: Section 2 gives an short introduction to TL modeling with SystemC. Section 3 describes the translation and Section 4 how to use it for verification. We consider related work in Section 5 and conclude in Section 6.

2 Transaction Level Modeling with SystemC

2.1 Subset of SystemC

We briefly describe the main characteristics of SystemC, when used for Transaction Level Models.

Globally, a TLM *component*, or *module*, is an encapsulated piece of code that contains active code (processes to be scheduled by the global scheduler) and passive code (functions offered to the external world, that will be called from a process of another component, by a control flow transfer). Inside such a component, the processes and the functions may share variables and events in order to synchronize with each other. Note that a function code and an active process are conceptually *in parallel*, since the function will be called by another flow of control.

In SystemC, the architecture of the platform is built by a piece of code (the so-called elaboration phase that runs first), but this is conceptually equivalent to a quite traditional architecture-description-language (ADL) (see for instance [6]) that connects the ports exposed by the components.

Communications between modules proceed by function calls traversing components or communications *channels* (for instance bus models). SystemC provides built-in primitive communication channels such as `sc_signal` to model hardware signals at the Register Transfer Level of abstraction. Synchronization associated with the communications is performed by events and shared variables inside modules and/or channels.

In the sequel, we only consider SystemC models at Transaction Level. By such restriction we mean that neither the built-in primitive channels nor the so-called *request update* mechanism (intended for RTL modeling) are used. We will also assume that there is no dynamic creation of processes (see section 3.1 for justification). Otherwise, we fully support other SystemC features.

2.2 A Simple Example

Consider the simple example in Figure 1, consisting of two modules. The first module contains a process that waits for an event $e1$. After receiving the event, it waits an additional 7 ns, before performing some action α. Here α is the abstraction of some real, local computation.When α is finished, the first process will trigger an interrupt in the second module, by calling the function g. The first module also offers an interrupt port by the function f, which will notify the local event $e1$. Similarly, the second module contains a process that waits 5 ns before performing β. Thereafter it will trigger the interrupt in the first module, and wait for the event $e2$, *i.e.* for an interrupt that triggers the function g.

Module 1

```
// Process 1
while(true)
{
  wait(e1);
  wait(7, SC_NS);
  cout << "alpha";
  interrupt_out.g();
}

// Function f
void f()
{
  e1.notify();
}
```

Module 2

```
// Process 2
while (true)
{
  wait(5, SC_NS);
  cout << "beta";
  interrupt_out.f();
  wait(e2);
}

// Function g
void g()
{
  e2.notify();
}
```

Fig. 1. A simple example of a TL model with two modules

While this example is trivial, it contains the relevant parts of a TL model: waiting for event notification, waiting for time and function calls to other modules, which are used to model transactions and interrupts.

There exist three difficulties when defining the semantics of SystemC:

1. The non-preemptive scheduler: we have to ensure that a running process is not interrupted by any other process unless it explicitly relinquishes the control back to the scheduler, by performing a wait either on time or on an event.
2. The SystemC scheduler ensures that time can only elapse when no process is eligible (while SystemC has no control on *real* time, the *simulation* time is merely a counter that the scheduler can decide to increment or not). So all statements are executed instantaneously, except when waiting either for time or for an event that is not notified immediately.
3. Function call communications: they are used for both interrupts and transactions. A process P performing a function call communication lets its control flow go outside its component to finally reach the destination component where a function is executed. The execution of P may continue only after the function call is finished. This means that if the receiver's function performs a `wait()` statement, P will yield the control back to the scheduler, and when elected again will resume its execution in the receiver's function.

3 Expressing SystemC Semantics in Promela

3.1 General Ideas

The Architecture. First, we will abstract from the architecture description part. In a real SystemC design, the function that is actually called when a process P in a module M executes an instruction `p.f()` is determined by the link between the port `p` of M and a port `p'` on another module M' containing a function f' associated with p'.

In the rest of the paper, we will consider that the architecture is hard coded in the function names. In other words, we will consider a process P calling a function f, and another module containing f.

Processes and Functions. The modeling of a SystemC program into Promela transforms each process and each function into a Promela process. SystemC distinguishes several types of processes (`SC_THREAD`, `SC_METHOD`, etc.). We consider here the use of `SC_THREAD`, which is the most general, since the encoding will not benefit from the restrictions enforced on the other types of processes.

We decided to encode the functions as Promela processes in order to keep them well separated from the processes. Thus, the transformation stays modular and is easier to code. Another possibility would have been to do the inlining of the functions inside the processes calling them, and transforming the resulting code into a Promela process. Our choice implies to handle the problem of functions

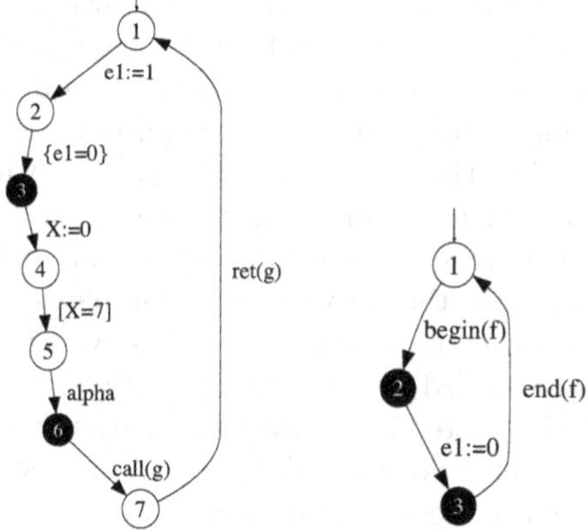

Fig. 2. Automata for Module 1. The left automaton corresponds to Process 1, the right one to function f. The variable X is used to model time. We distinguish between clock guards (square brackets) and guards on variables (curly brackets).

that can be called by multiple different processes. We perform a preprocessing on the SystemC program that consist in duplicating and renaming such functions in order to ensure that each function is called by only one process. This is possible because the function calls we consider are used for *communications* and therefore do not exhibit recursion (this argument also applies when choosing to inline the functions). The number of copies to do for a given function is bounded statically by the number of instantiated processes: while SystemC has recently added a feature to create processes dynamically, this feature is not used (to our knowledge) for Transaction Level models because the number of needed processes is linked to the number of master ports to drive, and ports cannot be created dynamically. In this article's examples, function parameters and return values are not represented but they could be taken into account by using global variables for both.

All time values appearing in the SystemC model must be integer multiples of some basic time granularity. We also assume that all variables can be declared globally, without any naming conflicts. All these restrictions can be ensured by simple preprocessing of the SystemC program without loss of generality.

3.2 Intuitive Idea: Representation with Automata

Our translation to PROMELA can also be seen as a translation into a set of automata. Each process and each function is translated into one interpreted automaton, *i.e.* manipulating some variables. The variables are used 1) to represent shared variables in the SystemC code 2) to encode SystemC events and 3) to count time. In the latter case, we will talk about *clocks*, which will be integers (see later). The transitions hold classically guards on variables as well as assignments. Clocks can either be tested for equality with a constant or a variable, or they can be set to 0. The automata derived from Module 1 of the simple example can be found in Figure 2. They simply reflect the control structure of the SystemC code.

The various automata then have to be asynchronously interleaved, respecting the non-preemptive specification of the scheduler. To obtain this, the automata have two different kinds of states, which we represent as black and white states. Black states represent local control flow: when an automaton is in a black state, it cannot not be preempted by the scheduler. White states basically represent `wait` statements: when an automaton is in a white state, it can be preempted, hence interleaved with any other process. A special case is the one of function calls, which directly transfer the control to the automaton that implements the function. This means we have to synchronize the transitions labeled by `call` (resp. `ret`) with the corresponding transition labeled by `begin` (resp. `end`).

Since we are mainly interested in the synchronization between different modules, we will not describe all the possible data processing inside the modules. This abstracted code could also be represented by encoding its control flow using only black states. The key elements of SystemC are translated in the following way:

`wait(e)`	e:=1 1 {e=0}	`e.notify()`	e:=0
`wait(k ns)`	X:=0 1 [X=k] 2	`wait(e, k ns)`	X:=0 1 e:=1 2 [X=k] {e=0} 3
`f()`	1 begin(f) ... end(f) 3	`port.f()`	call(f) 1 ret(f)

3.3 Detailed Encoding

In the following we will show how our encoding in PROMELA deals with the three problematic parts of SystemC: non-preemptive scheduling, time-elapse and function calls.

Non-Preemptive Scheduling. We distinguish between control points where the scheduler may transfer the control to another process (white states), and internal control points (black states) of one process. The non-preemptive execution of one automaton is realized with an additional shared variable `M` of type `int`. This variable can take the value 0, to mean that any process can perform a step, or N, to mean that the process number N is the only one to be activated. A graphical representation and the actual SPIN encoding are shown in Figure 3.

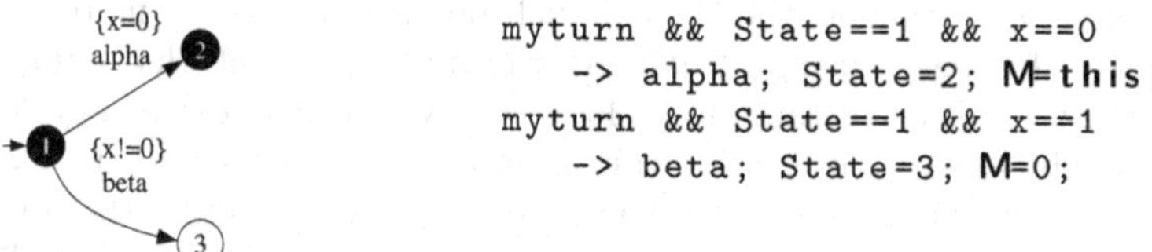

Fig. 3. Representation of non-preemption in PROMELA. The next value of `M` depends on the color of the next state.

This variable is set to 0 by each process that performs a `wait`. Otherwise, a process sets `M` to its own identifier, to indicate that it will take an additional step. For function calls, `M` is used to transfer the control to another process explicitly without the possibility of any other interleaving. We also considered a different encoding that only relied on atomic sections in PROMELA to model non-preemption. We sketch the problems with that approach in Section 3.5.

For simple examples, the use of an extra variable for ensuring atomicity is surely not efficient. We could use the `atomic` or `d_step` statement in PROMELA to ensure that no process can interleave a black state. In the trivial example in Figure 2, where each black state has exactly one incoming and one outgoing transition, we could also merge these and remove the black states all-together. But since the atomic behavior represented by the black states may be any complex control-flow,

X:=0

2

[X=10]

```
active proctype update_clock(){
end:
   do
   :: atomic{timeout && M==0 && X_used
             -> X=X+X_used;}
   od
}
   ...
active proctype A(){
do
:: atomic{myturn && state==1
          -> X=0; X_used=1;M=0;state=2}
:: atomic{myturn && state==2 && X=10
          -> X=0;X_used=0;...}
...
```

Fig. 4. Representation of clocks, which are needed to wait for time, as an automaton and in PROMELA. The process `update_clock` lets time elapse synchronously for all processes. Time is incremented whenever at least one clock is used, and only the time for clocks which are actually used is incremented.

connected to white states by multiple in- and outgoing transitions, this simplification is not possible in the general case.

Clocks. For every process that waits for time, we declare a clock (see Figure 4). We consider *discrete time*, that is every clock is an integer. A dedicated `clock_update` process increments the clocks synchronously as soon as no other process can run, which is tested using PROMELA's `timeout` statement. Hence time will never elapse if there is an instantaneous loop, *i.e.*, when there exists a cycle in the automaton which never performs a wait. Before a wait occurs, the process resets the corresponding clock to zero. We flag for each clock X whether the corresponding process is currently waiting on it, with a Boolean variable X`_used`. A clock is reset to zero when no process waits for it, and it is never increased in this time (it is a dead variable). Hence, the values of the clock are in the range between 0 and the value of the corresponding `wait`. This handling of clocks is similar to the one in discrete time Spin [3].

Function Calls. For each function f, a global Boolean variable `F` is introduced. The effects of f are transformed into:

- calling f: `F` := 1
- returning from the call: {`F` == 0}
- begin of the declaration of f: {`F` == 1}
- end of the declaration: `F` := 0

This is illustrated by Figure 5.

```
...
:: myturn && State==1
   -> f=1; State=2; M=2
:: myturn && State==2 && f==0
   -> State=1;M=this;
...
```

```
...
:: myturn && State==1 && f==1
   -> State=2; M=this;
:: myturn && State==2
   -> alpha; State=3; M=this;
:: myturn && State=3
   -> f=0; State=1; M=1;
...
```

Fig. 5. Representation of function calls in PROMELA. Assume that the caller has the identifier 1 and the function has identifier 2.

Additionally, a `call` sets `M` to the id of the automaton that implements f. Similarly, `end` sets `M` back to the value of the caller. Since each function is called by at most one process, this value is unique. Simply setting M without using F is not sufficient, because we have to make sure that the caller is blocked until the function is completed. Since the function might perform a `wait`, the scheduler could otherwise decide to execute the caller again too early. Similarly, we have to prevent the function from being executed without being called.

If a function is never called, we could simply remove it. On the other hand, it might be the case that our model is only partially defined, that is: one or several modules of the system are not known, and considered as black-boxes (possibly with Byzantine behavior). In this case, we can give an over approximation of the possible behavior of unknown modules, by assuming that a called function can take an arbitrary time, and that each process may call any function at any time. This is reflected by the macro state between `call` and `ret`.

Functions are used both to model interrupts and transactions in TLM. The call representing an interrupt is directly done to another module. On the other hand, transactions are handled by a bus that performs a routing depending on the transaction's address. In the examples, we forget about the bus, and for each transaction directly call the recipient component's function. This simplification assumes we have determined manually to which component each transaction is addressed. In the general case, the code responsible for routing, as well as specific bus behavior can be taken into account by modeling the functions and processes inside the bus, as automata, like any other component. We would then need at least an address parameter for each transaction function calls.

SystemC Events. Each SystemC event (`sc_event`) is encoded using a Boolean variable. The encoding has to reflect the fact that these events are not persistent: if the event is notified before a process waits for it, the notification is lost. This is done by setting the variable to 1 before yielding, which overwrites any previous notifications, the latters done by setting the variable to 0. This encoding assumes that only one process is waiting for the event. When multiple processes wait for the same event, each process taken individually can either miss or get the notifications of the event, depending on its order of execution. This situation can be handled simply by duplicating the event in order to get has many events as waiting processes, with only one waiting process per event. Other notification and wait constructs can be encoded following the same principle, as showed on some additional examples in the array of Section 3.2.

Simple Example. The global definitions and the clock update for the example can be found in Figure 6. First the scheduling variable is declared. The macro `myturn` is an abbreviation to indicate that an automaton is enabled, *i.e.* it is either itself in a black state, or all automata are in white states. Since we do not have variables in the example, we only need to declare the variables for the events. Additionally, we have an integer value and a Boolean flag for each clock, indicating whether we are currently waiting for the clock. Time may elapse, *i.e.* the `update_clock` process is enabled when no other process can perform a step, all processes are in a white state and at least one process waits on time. Using `X=X+X_used` to update time ensures that time will only elapse for a clock that is used.

```
int M=0;
#define myturn (M==0 || M==this)

//Variables
bool e1=0;
bool e2=0;

//Functions
bool f=0;
bool g=0;

//Clocks
#define time_enabled timeout && M==0 && (X_used || Y_used)

int X=0;
bool X_used=0
int Y=0;
bool Y_used=0

active proctype update_clock(){
end:
   do
   :: atomic{time_enabled -> X=X+X_used; Y=Y+Y_used; }
   od
}
```

Fig. 6. Global definitions and the process for synchronous time elapse

The SPIN code for Module 1 can be found in Figure 7. Each process has a variable to store its active state and its id. We could also use the process id that is automatically assigned by SPIN, but using a new value makes it easier to compute the id for function calls, without increasing the number of reachable states. The translation of the automata is straightforward. Each transition becomes an atomic action, that first tests whether the automata can run, *i.e.* is in the right state with the guard evaluating to true. Thereafter the effect of the transition is performed and the new state is set. At last, the scheduling variable is set according to whether the new state is black or white and whether a function call or termination is performed. Since a clock is explicitly set to 0 before each wait, and only at such a point, we also set the clock to "used" when leaving state 3. Similarly, when state 4 is left, we declare the clock as "not used anymore". Labels that abstract real, local computations like `alpha` are printed. The code for Module 2 can be found in Figure 8.

3.4 Validation of the Semantics

Our semantics for SystemC as an encoding in PROMELA is done in order to get the same effect when composing the automata with the asynchronous product of SPIN as when executing the corresponding SystemC code with a valid SystemC scheduler. To check that our semantics was corresponding to SystemC, we instrumented the SystemC models in order to produce test traces. We included in the PROMELA automata the same elements as produced in the SystemC text traces. Each observable action becomes a possible message in a global channel. When an action is performed, the corresponding message is sent to the channel. In order to reduce the size of the channel, the message is read from the channel again directly after. The SystemC trace we want to check is transformed into a `notrace`

```
active proctype module1(){
   byte state=1;
   byte this =1;

   do
   :: atomic{myturn && state==1 -> e1=1;state=2;M=0}
   :: atomic{myturn && state==2 && e1==0 -> state=3;M=this}
   :: atomic{myturn && state==3 -> X=0;X_used=1;state=4;M=0}
   :: atomic{myturn && state==4 && X==7 -> X=0; X_used=0; state=5;M=0}
   :: atomic{myturn && state==5 -> printf("MSC: alpha\n");state=6;M=this}
   :: atomic{myturn && state==6 -> g=1;state=7;M=4}
   :: atomic{myturn && state==7 && g==0 -> state=1;M=this}
   od
}

active proctype fun_f(){
   byte state=1;
   byte this =2;

   do
   :: atomic{myturn && state==1 && f==1 -> state=2;M=this}
   :: atomic{myturn && state==2 -> e1=0;state=3;M=this}
   :: atomic{myturn && state==3 -> f=0;state=1;M=3}
   od
}
```

Fig. 7. PROMELA code for Module 1 with the function f

```
active proctype module2(){
   byte state=1;
   byte this =3;

   do
   :: atomic{myturn && state==1 -> Y=0;Y_used=1;state=2;M=0}
   :: atomic{myturn && state==2 && Y==5 -> Y=0;Y_used=0;state=3;M=0}
   :: atomic{myturn && state==3 -> printf("MSC: beta\n");state=4;M=this}
   :: atomic{myturn && state==4 -> f=1;state=5;M=2}
   :: atomic{myturn && state==5 && f==0 -> state=6;M=this}
   :: atomic{myturn && state==6 -> e2=1;state=7;M=0}
   :: atomic{myturn && state==7 && e2==0 -> state=1;M=this}
   od
}

active proctype fun_g(){
   byte state=1;
   byte this =4;

   do
   :: atomic{myturn && state==1 && g==1 -> state=2;M=this}
   :: atomic{myturn && state==2 -> e2=0;state=3;M=this}
   :: atomic{myturn && state==3 -> g=0;state=1;M=1}
   od
}
```

Fig. 8. PROMELA code for Module 2 with the function g

declaration; now we can use the build-in SPIN test to check whether the behavior of the trace is a valid behavior of the SPIN model. The only problem was to produce all the text traces allowed by the SystemC specification given a SystemC program. While the specification allows any order of execution when multiple processes can be executed, the official SystemC simulator (as well as third party tools) takes only one order, deterministically. A modification of the official simulator existed in the lab, allowing to execute every possible scheduling. We used it to produce every possible traces, and checked that all these traces were included in our semantics.

3.5 Alternative Encoding

We also considered another encoding, which completely relied on PROMELA's atomic sections to model non-preemption. Each state was transformed into a `goto` label, followed by an atomic section that contained all outgoing transitions. Additionally, all black states where combined in one atomic section, including the labels. The semantics of PROMELA ensures that a jump from inside an atomic section to a label which is also contained in an atomic section preserves atomicity. The first problem with this encoding is that we have to inline all functions in order to tell to which point the function returns. But we have the benefit that we do not need the variable `M` for the scheduling, or the variables to hold the current state of each process. Furthermore, the implementation with `goto`s is much more efficient than using a loop with a non-deterministic choice.

But the main problem with this encoding is that the simulator of SPIN interleaves jumps from atomic section to another atomic section (although the documentation and the prover do the opposite). While SPIN proves properties that rely on the fact that such jumps are atomic, it also generates traces that violate the property.

The combination of `goto`s and atomic sections also make it impossible to use partial order reduction. Intuitively, `goto m1` and `atomic{goto m1}` are equivalent when `m1` is *inside* an atomic section, because a single statement is always atomic and every possible interleaving that could occur after the `goto` could as well occur before it. However, for the explicit atomic, SPIN will not allow any interleaving neither after nor before the goto, when partial order reduction is enabled.

```
bool X=0;

active proctype A(){
  assert(X==0);
}
```

```
active proctype B(){
  X=1;
  atomic{goto m0};
  atomic{skip;
    m0: X=0
  }
}
```

Fig. 9. A program whose verification depends on whether partial order reduction is enabled

Consider for example the program in Figure 9. The assertion is violated, when B just executes `X=1` before A is executed. SPIN finds this error, when the program is verified without partial order reduction, while it proves that all assertions hold when partial order reduction is enabled.

Because of these problems, this encoding does not have the benefits of an executable semantics. Therefore, we choose the not so efficient, but more robust encoding as the default.

4 Verification

4.1 Generic Properties

There are a number of properties that should hold for every TL model. First, it should never deadlock. For instance, a deadlock occurs when a process is waiting for an event that is never notified. A deadlock in the SystemC model corresponds directly to the fact that all PROMELA processes are blocked. With SPIN, this can be checked by verifying that no "invalid end states" exist, which is built in the prover. Since we only increase time when at least one process performs a wait on time, it can never be the case that the `clock_update` process runs forever, which would make it impossible for SPIN to detect a deadlock. On the other hand, when all processes terminate, the `update_clock` process will be blocked. Therefore, we explicitly declare the corresponding states as valid end states.

A deadlock might occur in the simple example in Figure 1, if we remove the `wait(5, SC_NS)` statement from the second process. Then the scheduler can choose to execute the second process first, and let it notify the event without a process waiting for it (this is indeed a common error for SystemC programmers). After that, both processes wait for events, but none is ever notified.

Another property we want to check is that no process runs forever without yielding. This can be expressed by the formula $\Box\Diamond M = 0$. For models with clocks, we can also check that time will always elapse, using the formula $\Box\Diamond \mathit{enabled}$ $(\mathit{update\_clock})$.

Of course, these last two properties are liveness formula and can only be checked if all abstractions preserve them (over-approximations of the behaviors preserve safety properties, but do not preserve liveness properties, in general). For the simple example, we do not need to perform any abstractions at all. If, however, the model becomes too large, the first abstraction that comes to mind is to remove all clocks, and to change every clock-guard to *true*. This implies that a process might halt in an arbitrary number of steps before a guard. But the property that a thread is monopolizing the behavior is independent from the clocks, so it can still be verified that way.

These tests work very well on the small example both with the possible deadlock and without. The proof is almost instantaneous, and the number of states remains small. We also checked these properties for the subset of a real-world MPEG decoding platform, which modeled the synchronization between the different components, with good results (see Figure 10).

This example contains many interleavings, a characteristic of real-world platforms. In the bug version, a deadlock may occur. The MPEG example is a modular version, with more parallel automata. All tests were performed on an Intel Celeron with 2.80 GHz and 1 GB RAM.

4.2 Checking Assertions

Checking assertions in the TL model is straightforward. Assertions are simply inserted at the corresponding transition, and directly written into the SPIN code. So

	without bug		with bug		MPEG	
	time (s)	states	time (s)	states	time (s)	states
deadlock	< 0.1	35	< 0.1	9	< 0.1	126
no yielding	< 0.1	49	< 0.1	55	< 0.1	209
time elapse	< 0.1	57	< 0.1	9	< 0.1	226

Fig. 10. Benchmarks for the mpeg example

far, we are mainly using assertions to check that some part of the model is never executed. This could also be modeled using specific error states. Since assertions are always safety properties, they are not effected by possible abstractions.

4.3 Benchmarks

Our test model consists of a chain of modules. The first module triggers an interrupt in the next one. This interrupt notifies an event, allowing the module to trigger an interrupt in the next module, and so on. The last module contains an assertion which is either always false (bug) or always true (no-bug). The latter forces SPIN to compute the whole state space when checking for invalid assertions. While this model may seem artificial, it exhibits the characteristics found in more complex real-world models and leading to state explosion: many processes, synchronized by SystemC events, which can thus be lost depending on the execution order of the various statements. Such study allows to experiment on how the state space that needs to be explored grows depending on parameters. The results presented in Figure 11 focus on the main parameter which is the number of modules. We also tried to experiment with adding an arbitrary number of black states inside the processes, which for clarity is not in the table.

The normal encoding uses the global variable `M`, to assure atomicity, while the `goto` version is our alternative encoding. In order to allow all intended behavior, we disabled partial order reduction when checking the encoding with `goto`.

The entry NT (not tested) indicates that the checking has aborted due to lack of memory. Both encodings find the bug very fast.

When computing the whole state space, we see that the encoding using gotos is more efficient, but the number of states increases exponentially for both encodings. This is due to the increase of white states. We can solve the bug by waiting before the notification, in order to make sure that no event is lost. While this makes the model completely deterministic, the number of states is still growing exponentially. Adding deterministic, local computations, increases the number of reachable states linearly for the normal encoding, and not at all for the encoding with gotos.

4.4 Comments on Performance

There are two possible sources for state explosion, making the model too large for automatic verification: the clocks and the interleaving between the processes.

# modules	3		5		7		9	
	time (s)	states	time (s)	states	time (s)	states	time (s)	states
normal: bug	< 0.1	32	< 0.1	48	< 0.1	64	< 0.1	80
normal: no-bug	< 0.1	3919	0.5	64831	11.8	104576	NT	NT
goto: bug	< 0.1	10	< 0.1	14	< 0.1	18	< 0.1	22
goto: no-bug	< 0.1	287	< 0.1	1535	< 0.1	7679	0.2	36863

# modules	11		13		15		17	
	time (s)	states	time (s)	states	time (s)	states	time (s)	states
normal: bug	< 0.1	104	< 0.1	120	< 0.1	136	< 0.1	152
normal: no-bug	NT	NT	NT	NT	NT	NT	NT	NT
goto: bug	< 0.1	34	< 0.1	38	< 0.1	42	< 0.1	46
goto: no-bug	1.1	172031	7	786431	47	353894	NT	NT

Fig. 11. Benchmarks for the chain call example

Modeling time by integers is usually not a good idea. However, our clocks are always bounded by the time of the corresponding `wait`, which is usually a rather small value, and since the clocks are updated synchronously, the actual increase of the state space is moderate. The size of the state space depends on the maximum time a process waits for, and the number of unrelated `wait` statements in parallel processes.

One way to cope with the state explosion is to use SPIN not for formal verification, but for intensive testing. This is encouraged by the fact that in the benchmark the existing bugs were found very fast. This also allows to use more efficient algorithms in SPIN, like hash-compact search, which only give approximate results.

On the other hand, our benchmark shows that introducing white states lead to state-explosion, while introducing black states has only a minor impact. Typical case-studies contain mostly control-flow, and only a few `waits`; therefore we are confident that we can model check programs of interesting size with our approach.

5 Related Work

The problem of SystemC having no *official* formal semantics is not new. Most of the research work studying SystemC in a formal context starts giving it a semantics in another well-defined formalism.

The majority of the approaches to give a semantics to SystemC are limited to its RTL subset, that is models describing synchronous circuits in detail. For instance, [9] expresses the semantics for the RTL subset in terms of Abstract State Machines. In this work, the processes executes concurrently, while the SystemC specification explicitly says the opposite (*non-preemptive scheduling*). [18] does the same using denotational semantics, but without taking into account the notion of control-flow inside the processes. These previous works have in common the fact that the target formalism that is used does not have concrete tools, and therefore it is impossible to check on examples that the given semantics is faithful. Moreover, the lack of connection to verification tools questions the possible applications for these works.

The approach followed by CheckSyC [5] goes one step further, in the sense that it provides a complete chain from SystemC parsing to formal verification, with relatively good experimental results. The main idea in this work is to recognize and extract well-known synchronous automata from RTL SystemC models and to reuse tools that model-check efficiently synchronous hardware. [19] follows the same idea using the GNU SSA (static single assignment) form of GCC for parsing the code and the synchronous language Signal [1] as the target formalism. Additional benefits, such as compositional reasoning, are presented but still on the RTL subset, whereas we are interested in handling models at higher abstraction levels.

The work in [11] apparently supports any SystemC program, by separating *hardware* (combinatorial functions, FSM, etc., corresponding to the RTL subset) from *software* (other unconstrained SystemC processes) to use different verification approaches. This separation is useless for us, since code for Transaction Level Models, while modeling hardware, falls in the second category. The semantics for SystemC is given by parallel automata with rendez-vous. Variables encoding the status for each process are used in the global state space to model the effect of the scheduler. However, nothing is said on `wait(`*`time`*`)` statements, which is a non-trivial point of the semantics.

We already experimented with the connection of SystemC to a proof engine, with the objective of analyzing Transaction-Level Models. The first output of this work was the tool-chain LusSy [14]. Starting from a SystemC program, we use a SystemC front-end to parse it, generate an intermediate representation called HPIOM made of communicating synchronous automata. We can then generate Lustre or SMV code to connect to a variety of proof engines. The connection to Lustre provides both provability and executability. The work presented here differs on several points: the first one is that LusSy uses a SystemC-independent intermediate formalism, and models the details of the scheduler using an explicit automaton. As opposed to this, we are using here a representation with automata in which the notion of non-preemption is built-in. The details of the scheduler do not need to appear in a separate automaton, but the main scheduling principles are reflected by the automaton encoding, in such a way that the product of SPIN does the intended work. The second difference is that LusSy uses a synchronous formalism, while we are experimenting here with SPIN, which is asynchronous. Finally, the encoding in LusSy over-approximates the possible behavior when time elapses. Whereas the values waited for by the processes determine their order of execution, the encoding considers any possible order. The present work with SPIN computes the actual order in which the processes will be executed. The abstraction in LusSy is conservative for verifying safety properties, but at the expense of larger state spaces.

6 Further Work and Conclusion

We have presented a way of translating TL models written in SystemC into PROMELA. This is one way of giving a formal semantics to SystemC. We use this encoding to perform verification of TL models, like checking for deadlocks and assertions.

The asynchronous encoding seems to be worth further investigation, compared to a synchronous one. When translating SystemC to a synchronous framework, the atomicity between two white states is obtained by a quite complex synchronisation between the automata for the processes, and the automata that represents the scheduler. Conversely, when translating SystemC to PROMELA, the atomicity is built-in. Therefore, if the number of white states is small compared to the number of black states, the formal verification should be easier for the asynchronous encoding

On the other hand, translating SystemC into Lustre or SMV has the advantage of producing a symbolic description of the system that can be exploited by symbolic model-checkers and abstract-interpretation tools.

The use of SPIN is probably better for bug tracking, while the use of a symbolic tool is probably better for performing aggressive abstractions and approximate property verification.

Right now, the transformation from SystemC to PROMELA is manual. While interesting as a first approach to the problem, it would be necessary to implement the principles presented here in a complete tool-chain to apply the approach on a larger case-study and compare it with the synchronous encoding. This would mean to reuse a front-end like Pinapa [15], that we developed for LusSy, a transformation into a structure representing the particular form of automata used here, and a SPIN code generator. We already have a prototype for the data structure and the code generator, but the biggest part of the work is the transformation from the actual SystemC code.

References

1. Benveniste, A., le Guernic, P., Jacquemot, C.: Synchronous programming with events and relations: the Signal language and its semantics. Technical Report 459, IRISA, Rennes, France (1989)
2. Berry, G.: The foundations of Esterel. In: Plotkin, G., Stirling, C., Tofte, M. (eds.): Proof, Language and Interaction: Essays in Honour of Robin Milner (2000)
3. Bosnacki, D., Dams, D.: Discrete-time Promela and Spin. In: Ravn, A.P., Rischel, H. (eds.) FTRTFT 1998. LNCS, vol. 1486, pp. 307–310. Springer, Heidelberg (1998)
4. Bozga, M., Graf, S., Ober, I., Ober, I., Sifakis, J.: The IF toolset. In: 4th International School on Formal Methods for the Design of Computer, Communication and Software Systems: Real Time, SFM-04:RT, Bologna, September 2004. LNCS Tutorials, Springer, Heidelberg (2004)
5. Drechsler, R., Große, D.: CheckSyC: An Efficient Property Checker for RTL SystemC Designs. ISCAS 4, 4167–4170 (2005)
6. Feiler, P.: Architecture Analysis & Design Language (AADL). Technical Report AS5506, SAE International (2004)

7. Ghenassia, F. (ed.): Transaction Level Modeling with SystemC, TLM Concepts and Applications for Embedded Systems. Springer, Heidelberg (2005)
8. Halbwachs, N., Lagnier, F., Ratel, C.: Programming and verifying critical systems by means of the synchronous data-flow programming language LUSTRE. IEEE Transactions on Software Engineering, Special Issue on the Specification and Analysis of Real-Time Systems September 1992 (1992)
9. Hoffmann, D., Gerlach, J., Ruf, J., Kropf, T., Mueller, W., Rosenstiehl, W.: The Simulation Semantics of SystemC. In: DATE, pp. 64–70 (2001)
10. Holzmann, G.J.: The SPIN Model Checker: Primer and Reference Manual. Addison-Wesley Professional, London (2004)
11. Kroening, D., Sharygina, N.: Formal Verification of SystemC by Automatic Hardware/Software Partitioning. In: MEMOCODE 2005, pp. 101–110 (2005)
12. Larsen, K.G., Pettersson, P., Yi, W.: UPPAAL in a Nutshell. Int. Journal on Software Tools for Technology Transfer 1(1–2), 134–152 (1997)
13. McMillan, K.L.: The SMV system (November 06, 1992)
14. Moy, M.: Techniques and Tools for the Verification of Systems-on-a-Chip at the Transaction Level. PhD thesis, INPG, Grenoble, France (December 2005)
15. Moy, M., Maraninchi, F., Maillet-Contoz, L.: Pinapa: An extraction tool for SystemC descriptions of systems-on-a-chip. In: EMSOFT (September 2005)
16. Moy, M., Maraninchi, F., Maillet-Contoz, L.: LusSy: an open Tool for the Analysis of Systems-on-a-Chip at the Transaction Level. Design Automation for Embedded Systems 10(2-3), 73–104 (2006)
17. Open SystemC Initiative. IEEE 1666: SystemC Language Reference Manual (2005) `www.systemc.org`
18. Salem, A.: Formal Semantics of Synchronous SystemC. DATE 1, 10376–10381 (2003)
19. Talpin, J.-P., Le Guernic, P., Shukla, S., Gupta, R.: Compositional behavioral modeling of embedded systems and conformance checking. International Journal on Parallel processing, special issue on testing of embedded systems (2005)

Towards Model Checking Spatial Properties with SPIN*

Alberto Lluch Lafuente

Department of Computer Science, Università di Pisa
lafuente@di.unipi.it

Abstract. We present an approach for the verification of spatial properties with SPIN. We first extend one of SPIN's main property specification mechanisms, i.e., the linear-time temporal logic LTL, with spatial connectives that allow us to restrict the reasoning of the behaviour of a system to some components of the system, only. For instance, one can express whether the system can reach a certain state from which a subset of processes can evolve alone until some property is fulfilled. We give a model checking algorithm for the logic and propose how SPIN can be minimally extended to include the algorithm. We also discuss potential improvements to mitigate the exponential complexity introduced by spatial connectives. Finally, we present some experiments that compare our SPIN extension with a spatial model checker for the π-calculus.

1 Introduction

SPIN [1] is a popular model checker used to verify temporal properties of concurrent systems. Part of its success is due to its efficiency. As a matter of fact, it is used as back-end model checker of various verification tools, like the first version of the Java Pathfinder [2], Bandera [3] or CheckVML [4]. SPIN can also be used [5,6] to check properties of systems described in process algebras like the π-calculus [7].

System specifications in SPIN are given in PROMELA, a high-level language for defining communicating processes, while system properties can be given in a linear-time temporal logic (LTL) [8], in the more expressive formalism of Büchi automata, or by using other ad-hoc mechanisms to express deadlock freedom, satisfaction of local assertions, etc. In that manner SPIN is used to reason about temporal properties of concurrent systems. In some cases, however, one would like to restrict the reasoning to some parts of the system, only. For instance, in a client-server system one would like to express that, under some conditions, two clients can evolve together to reach some undesired state.

Such properties can be expressed by means of spatial logics, that are formalisms for expressing structural properties of models where there is a notion of

* This work has been supported by the EU within the FETPI Global Computing, project IST-2005-016004 SENSORIA (*Software Engineering for Service-Oriented Overlay Computers*).

D. Bošnački and S. Edelkamp (Eds.): SPIN 2007, LNCS 4595, pp. 223–242, 2007.

composition. Besides the usual boolean connectors, spatial logics include ingredients like the connective **0** to represent an empty model or the spatial decomposition | which allows to write formulae $\phi_1|\phi_2$ that are satisfied by models that can be decomposed into two parallel submodels satisfying ϕ_1 and ϕ_2, respectively.

The origins of logics to reason about temporal and spatial properties of systems can be tracked back on early work on logics for reasoning about networks of processes. For instance, the *multiprocess network logic* of [9] considers networks of interconnected processes and proposes a first-order logic with linear temporal modalities and spatial modalities *everywhere*, *anywhere* to respectively refer to the properties of *some* and *any* process connected to the process under consideration. This approach further inspired, amongst others, the logics ICTL* [10] and IPTL [11], *indexed* extensions of CTL* and LTL, respectively. The logic IPTL is actually the propositional fragment of the multiprocess network logic and ICTL* is an extension of CTL* (without the next-time operator) enriched with conjunctions and disjunctions of indexed propositions. In these early works the main focus was on reasoning about properties like mutual exclusion in systems with many identical processes.

More recently, several approaches to the verification of spatial properties have been proposed, on logics either for concurrent software system specifications given in process calculi like the π-calculus [12,13,14] or the ambient calculus [15], or data structures such as heaps [16], trees [17] and graphs [18]. Each such approach proposes a logic that combines spatial connectives with ingredients to reason about model specific aspects (names, childhood, edge adjacency, etc.).

Our goal is to extend the capabilities of SPIN in order to make it able to check spatial properties. We believe that this would be interesting both for system specifications given directly in PROMELA or in other formalisms used by formal methods tools (e.g. the ones cited above) that rely on SPIN for the verification. In most cases, structural aspects are a relevant issue that is worth specifying and verifying.

We achieve this by extending LTL with spatial connectives, much in the line of [14] which proposes a spatial version of a first-order μ-calculus to reason about spatial, temporal and name properties of π-calculus specifications. In contrast with [14] and the rest of the recent spatial logics cited above, we do not introduce the usual void and composition operators. Instead, we introduce second-order process variables that can be instantiated, compared or used to restrict the behavior that a formula refers to. More precisely, $\exists X.\phi$ expresses that ϕ holds for some subset X of the set of system processes, $[\phi]^X$ expresses that ϕ holds for runs restricted to transitions involving processes in set X, and formula $\psi_1 \subseteq \psi_2$ expresses that process expression ψ_1 is contained in process expression ψ_2, where process expressions combine the empty set, singletons formed by process identities, set union and complementation and process set variables. The difference with the multiprocess network logic of [11] and similar works is that our process quantification is not used to reason about connections or local properties of processes but to refer to the behaviour to some processes only.

Our flavour of spatial connectives allows us to compactly express properties that, as far as we can see, are not expressible with the above cited approaches. For instance, the choice of a second-order quantifier has been inspired by the fact that the fixpoint-free fragment of the spatial logic of [18] is captured by Courcelle's monadic second-order logic for graphs [19]. In our case, the usual spatial composition $\phi_1 \mid \phi_2$ can be seen as an abbreviation of $\exists X, Y. X \uplus Y = \mathcal{P} \wedge \lceil \phi_1 \rceil^X \wedge \lceil \phi_2 \rceil^Y$, where $\lceil \phi \rceil^X$ is the *strict* restriction (c.f. Section 2.3) of ϕ under X. It is worth noticing that the use of process quantification and restriction is strictly more expressive than the use of decomposition since the latter does not allow to reason about the whole system inside a decomposition. For instance, recalling the property of a client-server system suggested above we could not extend it to express whether in the undesired situation the server can always evolve to correct the situation. As a more concrete example, consider that one cannot express with the use of the decomposition operator that there is a set of processes X that lead the system to a state where there is another set of processes Y that satisfy a formula ϕ, a property that is expressed in our logic by $\exists X.[\Diamond \exists Y.[\phi]^Y]^X$. We shall see that this is possible because existential quantification is not affected by restriction. In the formula above, for instance, $\exists Y$ quantifies over the whole set of processes of the system and not over X.

After giving the syntax and semantics of the spatial logic, we sketch a basic model checking algorithm and discuss its integration in SPIN. The algorithm is very simple and mainly relies on SPIN's algorithm for LTL model checking. Indeed, we show that verification of the logic can be reduced to checking a certain set of LTL formulae. The extension of SPIN is minimal since it mainly requires us to add the capability of starting the search from a given state and restrict the set of active processes.

Next we face the complexity of the logic, which is strongly influenced by second-order quantification. Indeed, in order to check $\exists X.\phi$ we need to consider all subsets of the set $\mathcal{P}$ of processes of the system, which number is exponential in the size of $\mathcal{P}$. This is a severe drawback on the performance of spatial model checkers. Analyzing all the possible subsets is, however, not always necessary. For instance, a typical property that is used by spatial model checkers is $\neg$**void**$\wedge$ $\neg(\neg$**void** $\mid \neg$**void**$)$, abbreviated with **1**, which expresses that a system has only one component. A property that can be clearly checked in constant time. Take now a formula $1|\phi$, which expresses that a process can be removed such that the remaining system will satisfy ϕ. Clearly, only a linear number of decompositions have to be checked. While these cases can be dealt with by introducing explicit ingredients in the logic, the general problem remains open.

However, we argue that there is space for efficient algorithms. Consider a formula $\exists X.\phi$. Suppose we find that the system restricted to a set Q of processes does not satisfy ϕ. We know that, under some conditions, the system restricted to a superset P of Q simulates the system restricted to Q. For some formulae ϕ we can conclude that ϕ is neither satisfied by the system restricted to P without actually performing the verification. We shall see how to generalize some of these reasonings.

This paper is structured as follows. Section 2 presents the spatial logic for SPIN. Section 3 proposes a model checking algorithm and discusses methods to reduce the verification effort. Section 4 presents comparative empirical results with a spatial logic model checker. A last section concludes the paper and outlines current and future work.

2 Spatial Logic for SPIN

This section defines the syntax and semantics of our logic, which is interpreted over a suitable formalism. We also give some example properties of a well-known problem, namely Dijkstra's dining philosophers problem, and suggestions for spatial property specification patterns.

2.1 Computational Model

We introduce a variant of labeled transition systems as a a suitable representation of the state space of PROMELA models over which our logic will be defined. We first recall the usual notion of (state) labeled transition systems.

Definition 1 (labeled transition system). *A labeled transition system M is a tuple $\langle s_0, S, \rightarrow, L, AP\rangle$, where S is a set of states, $s_0 \in S$ is the initial state, $\rightarrow \subseteq S \times S$ is a transition relation and $L : S \rightarrow 2^{AP}$ is a labeling function mapping states into subsets of AP, a set of atomic predicates representing the observations on states.*

Our notion of labeled transition considers that the system is composed by a set $\mathcal{P}$ of processes.

Definition 2 (composed labeled transition system). *A composed labeled transition system M is a tuple $\langle s_0, S, \rightarrow, L, AP, \mathcal{P}\rangle$, such that $\langle s_0, S, \rightarrow, L, AP\rangle$ is labeled transition system and $\mathcal{P}$ is a finite set of processes that partitions the transition relation, i.e., $\rightarrow = \xrightarrow{\epsilon} \cup \bigcup_{p \in \mathcal{P}} \xrightarrow{p}$, where $\xrightarrow{\epsilon}$ is a set of* empty *transitions used for the usual stutter extension of finite runs*[1].

Composed labeled transition systems roughly approximate PROMELA models without dynamic process creation where processes concurrently execute in an interleaving manner communicating via asynchronous operations[2]. In the rest of the paper we shall use the term *labeled transition systems* or just *systems* to refer to *composed labeled transition systems.*

An *infinite run* of a system M at state s_0, denoted M, s_0 is an infinite sequence $s_0 \rightarrow s_1 \rightarrow \ldots$. A *maximal finite run* is a finite sequence $s_0 \rightarrow s_1 \rightarrow \ldots \rightarrow s_n$

[1] We naively use transition labels above transitions and neglect the definition of labeled transitions as triples or via a labeling function to avoid confusion since only state labels play a role in the semantics.

[2] In PROMELA terminology, this mainly means that the **run** statement and synchronous channels are not allowed.

such that there is no transition $s_n \to s_{n+1}$ in the system. A state s is called *ending state* if there is no transition departing from it. For the sake of simplicity, we assume that systems with finite maximal runs are represented by equivalent systems where the transition relation includes empty transitions that extend finite runs as usual, i.e., given a transition relation $\to$ we define the *stutter extension* of $\to$ by $se(\to) = \to \cup \{s \xrightarrow{\epsilon} s \mid \forall s \in S.(s, s') \notin \to\}$. In words, for each ending state s a self transition $s \xrightarrow{\epsilon} s$ is added. Thus, in the rest of the paper *run* denotes *infinite run.* extend finite runs as usual, i.e., given a transition relation $\to$ we define the *stutter extension* of $\to$ by $se(\to) = \to \cup \{s \xrightarrow{\epsilon} s \mid \forall s \in S.(s, s') \notin \to\}$. In words, for each ending state s a self transition $s \to_s$ is added. Thus, in the rest of the paper *run* denotes *infinite run.* The set of all runs of M starting at s is denoted by $\rho(M, s)$. For a run $r = s_0 \to s_1 \to \ldots s_i \to s_{i+1} \to \ldots$, the *suffix run of* r *starting at* s_i is $r^i = s_i \to s_{i+1} \to \ldots$, while the i-th state of such a run r is denoted by s_i^r. A state $s \in S$ is *reachable* if there is a run r such that $s = s_i^r$ for some $i \in \mathbb{N}$.

Given a system M we define M_P as M *restricted to its subprocesses* $P \subseteq \mathcal{P}$, i.e., $M_P = \langle s_0, S, \to_P, L, AP, \mathcal{P}\rangle$. The restricted transition relation $\to_P$ is defined by $se(\xrightarrow{\epsilon} \cup \bigcup_{p \in P} \xrightarrow{p})$, i.e., the stutter extension of the transitions of processes in P. Thus, the runs of M_P can be seen as the runs of M restricted to P, where a run r restricted to a set of processes P is denoted by r_P and is defined as the maximal prefix of r such that every transition $s \to s'$ belongs to some process in P, i.e., $s \to s' \in \bigcup_{p \in P} \xrightarrow{p}$. If no transition of r belongs to a process outside P then r_P is exactly r. Otherwise, r_P is like r until the first transition $s \to s'$ belonging to a process outside P is encountered. Then the rest of r_P is infinitely extended as explained above.

2.2 Logic Syntax

Once we have a minimal formalism for a PROMELA model, we present the syntax of the spatial logic, where we assume a given system $M = \langle s_0, S, \to, L, AP, \mathcal{P}\rangle$.

Definition 3 (logic syntax). *Let V be a set of process variables. The syntax of our spatial logic is given by the following grammar:*

$$
\begin{array}{lll}
\phi ::= T \mid \neg\phi \mid \phi \vee \phi \mid a & & \textit{(boolean connectives)} \\
\quad\quad \circ\phi \mid \phi\mathbf{U}\phi & & \textit{(temporal connectives)} \\
\quad\quad \psi \subseteq \psi \mid \exists X.\phi \mid [\phi]^X & & \textit{(spatial connectives)} \\
\psi ::= \emptyset \mid \{p\} \mid X \mid \psi \cup \psi \mid \overline{\psi} & & \textit{(set expressions)}
\end{array}
$$

where $a \in AP$, $p \in \mathcal{P}$ and $X \in V$.

In the definition above V is assumed to contain a special variable $\mathcal{X}$ that will be used to record the set of processes under which the system is restricted. We shall describe all ingredients in detail after the definition of the semantics of the logic. Here, we just advance the intuitive meaning of the spatial connectives and the set expressions. The rest of the ingredients constitute the well-known linear temporal logic LTL [8], which we present here in a minimal manner by means of the *next-time* unary operator $\circ$ and the *until* binary operator $\mathbf{U}$. Other typical operators can be derived from these, as we will recall in a next section.

Set connectives are nothing but the empty set, a singleton formed by the identity of a process, a set variable, set union and set complementation (with respect to $\mathcal{P}$). Set inclusion is thus trivially interpreted.

The second-order existential process quantifier binds X with a set of process which we shall see is a subset of the processes of the system. Then, a formula $[\phi]^X$ is valid if ϕ holds for the system restricted to processes in X. However, ϕ might contain further restriction operators which can change the set of process that restrict the system. In this way, we can reason about the behaviour of subcomponents of a system without losing the capacity to refer to the behaviour of the whole system.

Before giving the formal semantics, we define the sets $fn(\phi)$ and $fn(\psi)$ of free variables of a formula ϕ and a set expression ψ. These are defined as expected.

Definition 4 (free variables). *Given a formula ϕ, the set* fn(ϕ) *of* free variables of ϕ *is defined by:*

$$
\begin{aligned}
\mathrm{fn}(T) &= \emptyset \\
\mathrm{fn}(\neg\phi) &= \mathrm{fn}(\phi) \\
\mathrm{fn}(\phi_1 \vee \phi_2) &= \mathrm{fn}(\phi_1) \cup \mathrm{fn}(\phi_2) \\
\mathrm{fn}(a) &= \emptyset \\
\mathrm{fn}(\circ\phi) &= \mathrm{fn}(\phi) \\
\mathrm{fn}(\phi_1 \mathbf{U} \phi_2) &= \mathrm{fn}(\phi_1) \cup \mathrm{fn}(\phi_2) \\
\mathrm{fn}(\psi_1 \subseteq \psi_2) &= \mathrm{fn}(\psi_1) \cup \mathrm{fn}(\psi_2) \\
\mathrm{fn}(\exists X.\phi) &= \mathrm{fn}(\phi) \setminus \{X\} \\
\mathrm{fn}([\phi]^X) &= \mathrm{fn}(\phi) \cup \{X\}
\end{aligned}
$$

Similarly, given a set expression ψ, the set fn(ψ) *of* free variables of ψ *is defined by:*

$$
\begin{aligned}
\mathrm{fn}(\emptyset) &= \emptyset \\
\mathrm{fn}(\{p\}) &= \emptyset \\
\mathrm{fn}(X) &= \{X\} \\
\mathrm{fn}(\psi_1 \cup \psi_2) &= \mathrm{fn}(\psi_1) \cup \mathrm{fn}(\psi_2) \\
\mathrm{fn}(\overline{\psi}) &= \mathrm{fn}(\psi)
\end{aligned}
$$

Obviously, the definition above assumes the usual safe renaming of variables such that variable names are not reused. We will consider closed formulae only, i.e., formulae where every process variable is bound by a quantifier, or in other words, formulae ϕ such that $fn(\phi) = \emptyset$. The notion of free names is crucial to define the equivalence axioms that we shall see in a next section.

2.3 Semantics

The semantics of our logic is interpreted over labeled transition systems.

Definition 5 (logic semantics). *Let $M = \langle s_0, S, \rightarrow, L, AP, \mathcal{P}\rangle$ be a transition system, ϕ, ϕ_1, ϕ_2 be formulae, ψ, ψ_1, ψ_2 be set expressions, $X \in V$ be a second-order process variable, $\sigma : V \rightarrow 2^{\mathcal{P}}$ be a mapping of process variables into sets of processes, $s \in S$ and r be a run of M. The semantics of our logic is given by the following satisfaction relation:*

$$
\begin{array}{lcl}
M, r \models_\sigma T & \Leftrightarrow & \text{true} \\
M, r \models_\sigma \neg\phi & \Leftrightarrow & M, r \not\models_\sigma \phi \\
M, r \models_\sigma \phi_1 \vee \phi_2 & \Leftrightarrow & M, r \models_\sigma \phi_1 \text{ or } M, r \models_\sigma \phi_2 \\
M, r \models_\sigma a & \Leftrightarrow & a \in L(s_0^r) \\
M, r \models_\sigma \circ\phi & \Leftrightarrow & M, r^1 \models_\sigma \phi \\
M, r \models_\sigma \phi_1 \mathbf{U} \phi_2 & \Leftrightarrow & \exists k \in \mathbb{N}. M, r^k \models_\sigma \phi_2 \text{ and } \forall 0 \leq j < k. M, r^j \models_\sigma \phi_1 \\
M, r \models_\sigma \psi_1 \subseteq \psi_2 & \Leftrightarrow & [\![\psi_1]\!]_\sigma \subseteq [\![\psi_2]\!]_\sigma \\
M, r \models_\sigma \exists X.\phi & \Leftrightarrow & \exists P \in 2^{\mathcal{P}}. M, r \models_{\sigma[P/X]} \phi \\
M, r \models_\sigma [\phi]^X & \Leftrightarrow & M, s_0^r \models_{\sigma[\sigma(X)/\mathcal{X}]} \phi \\
M, s \models_\sigma \phi & \Leftrightarrow & \forall r \in \rho(M_{\sigma(\mathcal{X})}, s). M, r \models_\sigma \phi
\end{array}
$$

where $[\![\psi]\!]_\sigma$ is inductively defined by

$$
\begin{array}{lcl}
[\![\emptyset]\!]_\sigma & = & \emptyset \\
[\![\{p\}]\!]_\sigma & = & \{p\} \\
[\![X]\!]_\sigma & = & \sigma(X) \\
[\![\psi_1 \cup \psi_2]\!]_\sigma & = & [\![\psi_1]\!]_\sigma \cup [\![\psi_2]\!]_\sigma \\
[\![\overline{\psi}]\!]_\sigma & = & \mathcal{P} \setminus [\![\psi]\!]_\sigma
\end{array}
$$

Recall that $\mathcal{X}$ is assumed to be a distinguished variable of V which we use to identify the set of processes under which the formula is restricted. Obviously, in the initial environment $\mathcal{X}$ is mapped to the set $\mathcal{P}$ of all processes of the system such that we say that M satisfies ϕ, written $M \models \phi$, whenever $M, s_0 \models_{\sigma[\mathcal{P}/\mathcal{X}]} \phi$ for any σ.

As the last equation of the satisfaction relation defined above suggests, a formula ϕ is satisfied by system M at state s if all runs of M restricted to $\sigma(\mathcal{X})$ starting at ϕ satisfy ϕ. The satisfaction relation for boolean and temporal connectives is the usual one. Recall that $\circ\phi$ holds for a run r iff ϕ holds in the next state after the first state of r, while $\phi_1 \mathbf{U} \phi_2$ requires to ϕ_1 to hold until some point where ϕ_2 holds.

The inclusion of set expressions is defined as expected: $\psi_1 \subseteq \psi_2$ holds in environment σ whenever the set expression ϕ is included in the set expression ϕ_2, both under the environment σ. A formula $\exists X.\phi$ is satisfied by a run r in environment σ whenever there is a set of processes $P \subseteq \mathcal{P}$ for which ϕ holds for r in an environment σ' that is like σ except that variable X is mapped to P. Finally, $[\phi]^X$ holds for a run r of system M whenever all runs of M restricted to $\sigma(X)$ starting from the first state of r satisfy ϕ in a new environment where σ is updated to map $\mathcal{X}$ to $\sigma(X)$.

In addition to the usual boolean and set abbreviations we enumerate the following ones:

$$
\begin{array}{rcll}
\Diamond\phi & \equiv & \neg\Box\phi & \text{eventually} \\
\Box\phi & \equiv & \neg\Diamond\neg\phi & \text{globally} \\
\phi_1\mathbf{R}\phi_2 & \equiv & \neg(\neg\phi_1\mathbf{U}\neg\phi_2) & \text{release} \\
\exists^1 X.\phi & \equiv & \exists X. \bigvee_{p\in\mathcal{P}} X = \{p\} \wedge \phi & \text{first-order quantifier} \\
\forall P.\phi & \equiv & \neg\exists X.\phi & \text{universal quantifier} \\
\lceil\phi\rceil^X & \equiv & [\{\phi\}^X]^X & \text{strict restriction} \\
\phi_1 \mid \phi_2 & \equiv & \exists X, Y. X \uplus Y = \mathcal{P} \wedge \lceil\phi_1\rceil^X \wedge \lceil\phi_2\rceil^Y & \text{composition} \\
\phi_1 || \phi_2 & \equiv & \neg(\neg\phi_1 \mid \neg\phi_2) & \text{dual composition} \\
\mathbf{0} & \equiv & \mathcal{X} = \emptyset & \text{no process} \\
\mathbf{1} & \equiv & \neg\mathbf{0} \wedge (\mathbf{0}||\mathbf{0}) & \text{unique process}
\end{array}
$$

Here $\{\phi\}^X$ is formula ϕ relativized to X, which limits the reasoning in ϕ to processes inside X. This is mainly done by limiting every quantifier inside ϕ to subsets of X and intersecting every set expression with X.

Definition 6 (relativized formula). *A formula ϕ relativized to process variable X is defined by*

$$
\begin{array}{rcl}
\{T\}^X & = & T \\
\{\neg\phi\}^X & = & \neg\{\phi\}^X \\
\{\phi_1 \vee \phi_2\}^X & = & \{\phi_1\}^X \vee \{\phi_2\}^X \\
\{a\}^X & = & a \\
\{\circ\phi\}^X & = & \circ\{\phi\}^X \\
\{\phi_1\mathbf{U}\phi_2\}^X & = & \{\phi_1\}^X\mathbf{U}\{\phi_2\}^X \\
\{\psi_1 \subseteq \psi_2\}^X & = & (\psi_1 \cap X) \subseteq (\psi_2 \cap X) \\
\{\exists Y.\phi\}^X & = & \exists Y.Y \subseteq X \wedge \{\phi\}^X \\
\{[\phi]^Y\}^X & = & \exists Z.Z = Y \cap X \wedge [\{\phi\}^X]^Z
\end{array}
$$

Most of the introduced abbreviations are typical in temporal and spatial logics. Regarding temporal abbreviations, we recall that $\Diamond\phi$ is used to express that ϕ will eventually hold, $\Box\phi$ states that ϕ holds in every reachable state and $\phi_1\mathbf{R}\phi_2$ is the dual of the until operator, satisfied when ϕ_2 holds forever or until some point where both ϕ_1 and ϕ_2 hold. The spatial abbreviations can be used to express the number of processes present in the (sub)system or to reason about decompositions of the system. An interesting abbreviation is the strict restriction, which suggests the way one can force that a quantification that appears under a restriction is limited to the subsets of processes under which the formula is restricted. The strict restriction forbids a formula to refer to processes outside the subsystem under which it is restricted. The best example of use of the strict restriction are the composition operators. For instance, $\phi_1 \mid \phi_2$ holds whenever the processes of a system M can be decomposed into two (possibly empty) disjoint sets P, Q such that M_P, M_Q respectively satisfy ϕ_1, ϕ_2 under strict restriction. This means that ϕ_1 and ϕ_2 cannot refer to processes outside P and Q, respectively. Dually, $\phi_1||\phi_2$ holds whenever for all disjoint decompositions P, Q, M_P satisfies ϕ_1 or M_Q satisfies ϕ_2, both under strict restriction.

2.4 Examples

We illustrate the use of our logic with Dijkstra's dining philosophers problem [20]. Recall that it involves a number of philosophers sitting around a table. There is a plate in front of each philosopher and a fork between each pair of adjacent plates. A philosopher needs two forks to eat the spaghetti on his own plate. The problem is to find a protocol that allows the philosophers to use the forks in such a manner that they can all eat.

A strategy where every philosopher takes his left and right fork as a single atomic action is deadlock free but leads to starvation, i.e., philosophers are not guaranteed to eat infinitely often. On the other hand, consider a strategy where every philosopher decides to pick up his left fork and to not release it before a second fork has been acquired. It is clearly not deadlock free. It suffices to let each philosopher to pick up his left fork such that no philosopher will ever get its right fork.

We might refer to the state space of the problem as the system, where processes correspond to philosophers. In the following examples we will mainly make use of the compositional operator even if equivalent formulae written without such abbreviation are indeed simpler and more efficiently checked. The idea is to use a notation easy to understand to readers that are familiar with spatial logics and to explicit the fact that most of them are expressible in the spatial logic of [14], whose model checker we use in the the comparative experiments of a next section. However, we also give an example of a formula that is not expressible via the composition operator.

Assume that we want to reason about the second version of the problem. We know that it is not deadlock free, but we want to analyze the nature of deadlocks. Suppose that we have have an atomic proposition *deadlock* that holds in deadlock states only. A first spatial property that we might consider is that a deadlock occurs if and only if the system has no processes or all the processes collaborate. In other words, a strict subset of processes cannot lead the system into a deadlock state. This is expressed by the following formula:

$$\textbf{prop1} \equiv (\Diamond \mathit{deadlock}) \wedge (\neg \mathbf{0} \mid ((\Diamond \mathit{deadlock}) \rightarrow \mathbf{0}))$$

Observe that $\mathbf{0}$ necessarily implies *deadlock*. Regarding our comment above, observe that the property could be more compactly and efficiently expressed by the formula $\neg \exists X.X \neq \emptyset \wedge X \neq \mathcal{P} \wedge [\Diamond \mathit{deadlock}]^X$.

Now, we might wonder whether it is true that in every deadlock-free state of the protocol, it is possible to separate the philosophers in two groups such that one of the groups never deadlocks:

$$\textbf{prop2} \equiv \Box(\neg \mathit{deadlock} \rightarrow ((\Box \neg \mathit{deadlock}) \mid T))$$

More generally, we might wonder whether in every deadlock-free state of the protocol, it is possible to separate the philosophers in two groups such that none of the groups ever deadlock:

$$\textbf{prop3} \equiv \Box(\neg deadlock \rightarrow (\Box\neg deadlock \mid \Box\neg deadlock))$$

We also might want to consider properties about starvation. Assume that a proposition $p1eats$ holds in states where philosopher $p1$ is eating. The typical starvation-free property requires each philosopher to be able to eat infinitely often. In our case we can write $\Box\Diamond p1eats$ since by symmetry we know that it suffices to reason about one philosopher.

On the other hand, another interesting property could be whether it is possible, starting from a state in which $p1$ is not eating, to find a group of philosophers that can lead $p1$ into his eating state:

$$\textbf{prop4} \equiv \Box(\neg p1eats \rightarrow (\Diamond p1eats \mid T))$$

Then, we can state a property requiring that, at any state where $p1$ is eating, we can find a group of philosophers that allows $p1$ to eat infinitely often:

$$\textbf{prop5} \equiv \Box(p1eats \rightarrow (\Box\Diamond p1eats \mid T))$$

Finally, we might think of a property stating that a subset of processes can lead $p1$ into its eating state but then a set of processes can make him starve:

$$\textbf{prop6} \equiv \exists X.[\Diamond(p1eats \wedge \exists Y.[\neg\Box\Diamond p1eats]^Y)]^X$$

It is worth noting that this property is not expressible by using the compositional abbreviation.

As an exercise we invite the reader to reason about the validity of the stated properties. The solution is given in Section 4.

2.5 Applications

We give further evidence of the practical interest of our logic by considering the extension of typical property specification patterns for finite-state verification. More precisely, we focus on the patterns identified in [21] (also available on the web[3]). There, patterns are mainly organized according to two categories: occurrence and order. The latter refer to the occurrence of a given event (e.g., absence, universality, existence), while the former regard the relative order in which multiple events occur (e.g., precedence, response, chains). In addition patterns, can be refined by limiting the scope where the property is intended to hold (globally, before or after an event, between two events, etc.). For the sake of simplicity, we will assume here a global scope.

Absence ($\Box\neg\phi$) and universality ($\Box\phi$) are similar patterns to state an invariant property represented by the (not necessarily atemporal) formula ϕ. Indeed, the only actual difference is the point of view of event ϕ: absence is typically used to guarantee that some *undesired* event never happens and universality is used to ensure that a *good* property holds in every reachable state. A typical case where

[3] `http://patterns.projects.cis.ksu.edu/`

one could need spatial connectives is when it is known that the universality or absence of ϕ does not hold, but one is interested in identifying subsystems for which those properties still hold. This is what we did in the previous section regarding the absence of deadlocks.

Existence properties ($\Diamond\phi$) express that some event will eventually happen. In the previous section we used this pattern to ensure the existence of a *bad* event, namely a deadlock and we combined it with spatial connectives to guarantee that only the whole system could make that bad event happen. Typical applications require ϕ to be a *good* event which does not happen if the system has cyclic behaviours where ϕ never happens. Hence, in some cases we could allow such behaviours but require a set of processes to exist that can exit the cyclic behaviour and ensure the existence of ϕ. This can be expressed with the formula $\Box(\neg\phi \rightarrow \exists X.[\Diamond\exists Y = \mathcal{P}.[\Diamond\phi]^Y]^X)$.

Combining the universality and existence patterns also results in the *infinitely often* pattern $\Box\Diamond\phi$ that we used to state absence of starvation in the example of the previous section. By nesting spatial ingredients inside such a pattern we can write a formula $[\Box[\Diamond\phi]^Y]^X$ that can be used to express that in any state reachable by processes of X the processes Y ensure occurrence of ϕ. This might be useful in case we have *bad* processes (X) trying to avoid the *good* event (ϕ) and *good* processes (Y) ensuring the occurrence of the good event.

Precedence of event ϕ_1 over ϕ_2 is expressed by $\neg\phi_1\mathbf{W}\phi_2$, where $\phi_1\mathbf{W}\phi_2$ abbreviates the *weak until* operator $\phi_1\mathbf{U}(\phi_2 \vee \Box\phi_1)$. Response properties ($\Box(\phi_1 \rightarrow \Diamond\phi_2)$) are used to require that every request ϕ_1 will be followed by a response ϕ_2. In both cases we can use spatial connectives to restrict the reasoning to some processes only. For instance, we can strengthen a response property by requiring that a process X alone (e.g., a server) achieves to produce the response. This is stated by $\Box(\phi_1 \rightarrow [\Diamond\phi_2]^X)$.

Chain patterns are used to express relations of complex combinations of events. These include precedence or response relationships consisting of sequences of individual events. We consider the 1-stimulus, 2-response pattern here, expressed by $\Box(\phi_1 \rightarrow \Diamond(\phi_2 \wedge \circ\Diamond\phi_3))$, where ϕ_1 is the request or stimulus and ϕ_2,ϕ_3 are the responses. The formula states that every event ϕ_1 is eventually followed by ϕ_2 and ϕ_3 (in this order). As proposed in the above paragraph, the occurrence of both events can be restricted to different sets of processes, i.e., $\Box(\phi_1 \rightarrow [\Diamond(\phi_2 \wedge [\circ\Diamond\phi_3]^Y)]^X)$.

3 Model Checking

We face here the model checking problem for the spatial logic presented in the previous Section by sketching a basic algorithm and proposing potential improvements.

3.1 Basic Algorithm

The algorithm for checking spatial formulae mainly relies on SPIN's capacity to check LTL formulae. Recall that the mechanism used by SPIN in order to check LTL properties is the so-called *automata-based model checking* approach. Roughly speaking, in order to check that a system M satisfies a formula ϕ a Büchi automaton A is constructed as the intersection of the Büchi automata corresponding to M and $\neg\phi$. Intuitively, A accepts the infinite runs accepted by both the system and the negation of ϕ, i.e., it models the behaviours of the system violating property ϕ.

This is done in SPIN by implementing a Büchi automaton as a special process called *never claim* that is executed concurrently with the system. The executability of the transitions of the never claim depends on boolean expressions on the system variables that represent the atomic propositions of the corresponding formula.

Algorithm check(P,s,σ,ϕ) **switch** ϕ **do**
    case $\psi_1 \subseteq \psi_2$
        return set(ψ_1, σ) $\subseteq$ set(ψ_2, σ) ;
    case $\exists X.\phi_1$
        foreach $P_1 \in 2^{\mathcal{P}}$ **do**
            $\sigma[X] := P_1$;
            if spin(P, s, σ, ϕ_1) **then return** true ;
        return false;
    case $[\phi_1]^X$
        return spin($\sigma[X], s, \sigma, \phi_1$) ;

Fig. 1. Procedure check for checking spatial subformula

Our algorithm exploits the fact that the transitions of the never claim are PROMELA statements which can include, for instance, calls to procedures written in C. The idea is that we convert spatial formulae into maximal LTL subformulae where spatial formulae are substituted by a call to a special verification procedure, which possibly relies on SPIN again. This approach has the benefit to require minimal changes in SPIN.

Thus, the first thing to do is to convert a spatial formula into a set of pure LTL formulae whose atomic propositions are related to spatial subformulae.

Definition 7. *Let ϕ be a formula. The corresponding* flat *formula* flat(ϕ) *is defined by*

$$
\begin{aligned}
\mathrm{flat}(T) &= T\\
\mathrm{flat}(\neg\phi) &= \neg\mathrm{flat}(\phi)\\
\mathrm{flat}(\phi_1 \vee \phi_2) &= \mathrm{flat}(\phi_1) \vee \mathrm{flat}(\phi_2)\\
\mathrm{flat}(a) &= a\\
\mathrm{flat}(\circ\phi) &= \circ\mathrm{flat}(\phi)\\
\mathrm{flat}(\phi_1 \mathbf{U} \phi_2) &= \mathrm{flat}(\phi_1)\mathbf{U}\mathrm{flat}(\phi_2)\\
\mathrm{flat}(\psi_1 \subseteq \psi_2) &= a_{\psi_1 \subseteq \psi_2}\\
\mathrm{flat}(\exists X.\phi) &= a_{\exists X.\mathrm{flat}(\phi)}\\
\mathrm{flat}([\phi]^X) &= a_{[\mathrm{flat}(\phi)]^X}
\end{aligned}
$$

Thus, when converting the negation of a flattened formula into the corresponding never claim, each atomic proposition a_ϕ is actually replaced by a call to `check`(P,s,σ,ϕ). Procedure `check` is depicted in Figure 1. It takes four parameters as input and returns a boolean value. The first parameter is P which represents the set of processes under which the formula is restricted. The second parameter s is the system state from which the formula must be checked. The third parameter is an array σ of processes that ranges over variable names. It implements the environment of process variables. Finally, ϕ is a flat formula.

Observe that the procedure relies on an extension of SPIN which we refer to as `spin`. The extension is minimal and allows to restrict the execution to a subset of processes, start the verification from a given state and record the array σ.

Set expressions are trivially checked via a procedure `set`. Process quantification requires us to consider all possible subsets P_1 of $\mathcal{P}$. For each such set, $\sigma[X]$ is updated with its value and `spin` is called with the new value for σ in order to check ϕ. Finally, process restriction $[\phi_1]^X$ is checked by calling `spin` using the set of processes assigned to X as first parameter.

3.2 Spatial Equivalences

The exponential complexity introduced by the second-order process quantification can be mitigated in some cases by rewriting the formula in an appropriate manner. For instance, a formulae $\exists X.\phi$ is trivially equivalent to ϕ if X is not a free variable of ϕ. As a first step towards such a simplification we introduce a set of structural axioms for spatial formulae which induces an equivalence of formulae.

Definition 8 (spatial equivalence). *The* spatial equivalence *is the least relation $\equiv_s$ on formulae closed under the following axioms:*

$$
\begin{array}{rcll}
\exists X.T & \equiv_s & T & \\
\exists X.\phi_1 \vee \phi_2 & \equiv_s & \phi_1 \vee \exists X.\phi_2 & \text{if } X \notin \text{fn}(\phi_1) \\
\exists X.a & \equiv_s & a & \\
\exists X.\circ\phi & \equiv_s & \circ\exists X.\phi & \\
\exists X.\phi_1 \mathbf{U} \phi_2 & \equiv_s & (\exists X.\phi_1)\mathbf{U}\phi_2 & \text{if } X \notin \text{fn}(\phi_2) \\
\exists X.\phi_1 \mathbf{U} \phi_2 & \equiv_s & \phi_1 \mathbf{U} \exists X.\phi_2 & \text{if } X \notin \text{fn}(\phi_1) \\
\exists X.\psi & \equiv_s & \psi & \text{if } X \notin \text{fn}(\psi) \\
\exists X.\exists Y.\phi & \equiv_s & \exists Y.\exists X.\phi & \\
\exists X.[\phi]^Y & \equiv_s & [\exists X.\phi]^Y & \text{if } X \neq Y \\
[T]^X & \equiv_s & T & \\
[\neg\phi]^X & \equiv_s & \neg[\phi]^X & \\
[\phi_1 \vee \phi_2]^X & \equiv_s & \phi_1 \vee [\phi_2]^X & \text{if } X \notin \text{fn}(\phi_1) \text{ and } \phi_1 \text{ atemporal} \\
[a]^X & \equiv_s & a & \\
[\psi_1 \subseteq \psi_2]^X & \equiv_s & \psi_1 \subseteq \psi_2 & \\
[\exists Y.\phi]^X & \equiv_s & \exists Y.[\phi]^X &
\end{array}
$$

In the definition above a formula ϕ is *atemporal* if it does not contain any temporal operator. Next, we state that the satisfaction relation is closed under spatial equivalence.

Proposition 1. *Let ϕ_1, ϕ_2 be two spatial formulae and M be a transition system. If $\phi_1 \equiv_s \phi_2$ we have $M \models \phi_1$ whenever $M \models \phi_2$.*

Proof (sketch). The proof is trivial: one can basically apply the reasonings usual in propositional logics. The only case that is worth mentioning regards the axiom $\exists X. \circ \phi \equiv_s \circ\exists X.\phi$. But this is not a problem since we assume that the set of processes $\mathcal{P}$ is constant.

In current work we are investigating heuristics for deciding, given a certain formula ϕ_1, how to rewrite it into an equivalent formula ϕ_2 such that checking ϕ_2 requires significantly less effort, possibly by introducing additional axioms for typical abbreviations. For instance, consider formula $\Box\exists X.\Box\phi$. One can easily show that $\Box\Box\phi \equiv \Box\phi$ and $\Box\exists X.\phi \equiv \exists X.\Box\phi$ are equivalence axioms of our logic. This leads to the equivalent formula $\exists X.\Box\phi$ which clearly requires less verification effort with our basic algorithm.

3.3 Exploiting Simulations

Checking $\exists X.\phi$ requires us in general to consider the $2^{\mathcal{P}}$ decompositions of the system. However, in some cases such a formula can be checked more efficiently. Consider for instance formula **1** expressing that there is just one process in the system, which can be checked in constant time, or formulae of the form $(\mathbf{1} \wedge \phi) \mid \psi$ stating that there is a decomposition of the system where one part consists of a single process satisfying ϕ and the rest satisfies ψ, which requires considering a linear number of decompositions, only. Another typical example is the formula $\forall^1 X.\lceil\phi\rceil^X$ or, equivalently, $\mathit{false}||(\mathbf{1} \rightarrow \phi)$ expressing that the system restricted under any single process satisfies ϕ.

A simple way to tackle the problem in specific cases is to explicitly include such abbreviations in the logic and implement ad-hoc procedures for them. However, it is worth studying procedures for the general case. For instance, one can try to exploit the fact that a system approximates the behaviour of its subsystems. We first define a well-known notion of approximation.

Definition 9 (simulation). *Given two transition systems $M_1 = \langle s_1^0, S_1, \rightarrow^1, L_1, AP_1, \mathcal{P}_1\rangle$, $M_2 = \langle s_2^0, S_2, \rightarrow^2, L_2, AP_2, \mathcal{P}_2\rangle$, a relation $R \subseteq S_1 \times S_2$ is a* simulation relation *whenever $s_1 R s_2$ implies:*

- *$L(s_1) = L(s_2)$;*
- *for every transition $s_1 \rightarrow^1 s_1'$ there is a transition $s_2 \rightarrow^2 s_2'$ such that $s_2 R s_2'$.*

If there is a simulation relation R such that $s_1 R s_2$ we say that M_2 at s_1 *simulates* M_1 at s_2, written $M_1, s_1 \preceq M_2, s_2$. If s_1, s_2 are s_1^0,s_2^0 we just say that M_2 *simulates* M_1, written $M_1 \preceq M_2$.

We next observe that under some conditions a subsystem M_P simulates its subsystem M_Q. That this is not true in general can be easily shown. The problem relies in the fact that M_Q might contain empty transitions that are not present in M_Q and that might not be simulated. An example are deadlocks present in M_Q.

A sufficient condition for guaranteeing the that M_P satisfies M_Q is that M_P preserves the ending states of M_Q. This means that in the states where the processes in Q cannot progress, neither can the processes in $P \setminus Q$. A trivial but realistic case where this happens is when the processes in Q do not communicate with processes in $P \setminus Q$. Hence, if we have $Q \subseteq P \subseteq \mathcal{P}$ we say that P is a *fair superset* of Q whenever for any reachable ending state s in M_Q state s is also an ending state in M_P.

Proposition 2 (fair supersets simulate). *Let M be a transition system and P, Q be two sets of processes such that P is a fair superset of Q then, for any $s \in S$:*

$$M_Q, s \preceq M_P, s.$$

Proof (sketch). The identity relation $id = \{(s,s) \mid s \in S\}$ is clearly a simulation relation since both $L(s) = L(s)$ for any $s \in S$ and $\rightarrow_Q \subseteq \rightarrow_P$.

The notion of simulation is sufficient to preserve satisfaction of the temporal logic ACTL* and thus LTL [22] but not our full logic due to the spatial operators. However, we can still identify fragments of our spatial logic that are preserved by fair supersets of processes. The class of preserved formulae is characterized by a type system, which may assign to a formula ϕ the type "$\rightarrow$", meaning that ϕ is preserved by fair supersets or the type "$\leftarrow$", meaning that ϕ is reflected by fairs supersets.

Definition 10 (preserved formulae). *The typing rules are given by*

$$\begin{array}{rl}
T, a :\leftrightarrow & \\
\neg\phi : d^{-1} & \textit{if } \phi : d \\
\phi_1 \vee \phi_2 : d & \textit{if } \phi_1 : d \textit{ and } \phi_2 : d \\
\circ\phi : d & \textit{if } \phi : d \\
\phi_1 \mathbf{U} \phi_2 : d & \textit{if } \phi_1 : d \textit{ and } \phi_2 : d \\
\psi_1 \subseteq \psi_2 :\rightarrow & \textit{if } \psi_1 \subseteq \psi_2 \textit{ antimonotonic} \\
\psi_1 \subseteq \psi_2 :\leftarrow & \textit{if } \psi_1 \subseteq \psi_2 \textit{ monotonic} \\
\exists X.\phi : d & \textit{if } \phi : d \\
[\phi]^X : d & \textit{if } \phi : d
\end{array}$$

where it is intended that $\rightarrow^{-1} = \leftarrow$ and $\leftarrow^{-1} = \rightarrow$. Moreover $\phi :\leftrightarrow$ is a shortcut for $\phi :\rightarrow$ and $\phi :\leftarrow$, while $\phi_1, \phi_2 : d$ stands for $\phi_1 : d$ and $\phi_2 : d$.

In the definition above $\psi_1 \subseteq \psi_2$ *antimonotonic* means that for any pairs of mappings σ_1, σ_2 that ensure that for any variable $X \in V$ it holds $\sigma_1(X) \subseteq \sigma_2(X)$ we have that $[\![\psi_1 \subseteq \psi_2]\!]_{\sigma_2}$ implies $[\![\psi_1 \subseteq \psi_2]\!]_{\sigma_1}$. Monotonicity of process set inclusions is defined similarly.

We now state that preserved (resp. reflected) formulae are indeed preserved (resp. reflected) by fair supersets.

Proposition 3 (preservation). *Let M be a transition system and P, Q be two sets of states such that P is a fair superset of Q, and let ϕ be a formula. Then for any $s \in S, X \in V$ we have*

$$M, s \models_{\sigma[^P/_X]} \phi \;\Rightarrow\; M, s \models_{\sigma[^Q/_X]} \phi \;\; \textit{if } \phi :\rightarrow$$
$$M, s \models_{\sigma[^P/_X]} \phi \;\Leftarrow\; M, s \models_{\sigma[^Q/_X]} \phi \;\; \textit{if } \phi :\leftarrow$$

Proof (sketch). Let us consider the first equation (the other is dual). Note that we have to prove that the satisfaction relation is antimonotonic with respect to any variable X but this clear from the definition of preserved formulae. Regarding the temporal connectives observe that we have M_P simulates M_Q at s.

Proposition 3 gives an intuition on how to improve the check of spatial operators. If, for instance, we have to check whether a system M satisfies formula $\exists X.\phi$ with ϕ being a preserved formula and we find out that $M, s \not\models_{\sigma[^Q/_X]} \phi$ we know that $M, s \not\models_{\sigma[^P/_X]} \phi$ for any fair superset P of Q. Determining the fair supersets of Q can be based on a static analysis. This suggest the improved version of the `check` procedure depicted in Figure 2.

```
Algorithm check(P,s,σ,φ) switch φ do
  case ψ1 ⊆ ψ2
    return set(ψ1, σ) ⊆ set(ψ2, σ) ;
  case ∃X.φ1
    foreach P1 ∈ 2^P do
      valid[P1] := unknown ;
    foreach P1 ∈ 2^P such that valid[P1] ≠ false do
      σ[X] := P1;
      if spin(P, s, σ, φ1) then return true ;
      if preserved(φ) then
        foreach P2 ∈ 2^P such that fair(P2, P1) do
          valid[P2] := false ;
    return false;
  case [φ1]^X
    return spin(σ[X], s, σ, φ1);
```

Fig. 2. Procedure `check` for checking preserved spatial subformulae exploiting supersets

4 Experiments

We compared a first implementation of the basic algorithm as an extension of the SPIN model checker with SLMC [23] a spatial model checker that implements the approach described in [14] for checking spatial properties of π-calculus specifications. The goal of the experiments is to have a first impression of the efficiency of our basic algorithm by comparing it with the only spatial model checker we are aware of.

Before presenting the results we reveal the solution for the validity of the properties described in Section 2.4. Recall that we consider a deadlock solution to Dijkstra's dining philosophers problem consisting in a protocol for the philosophers such that they first try to catch the left fork and then the right one. A philosopher that manages to get both forks is considered to be in its eating state whose only outgoing transition corresponds to releasing both forks at the same time. Properties **prop1**, **prop2**, **prop5** and **prop6** hold while **prop3** and **prop4** do not hold.

Table 1 depicts the results. The second and third columns respectively correspond to the results of the spatial version of SPIN and the SLMC model checker. Each row presents the respective running time (in seconds) achieved when checking the properties described in section 2.4 in PROMELA and π-calculus models of the deadlock solution to Dijkstra's dining philosophers problem. For each property we have tested instances of the problem with increasing number n of philosophers. We restrict the results to two instances per problem with a limit of 10 philosophers and a time limit of 30 minutes.

Table 1. Experimental results

Problem	Spatial SPIN	SLMC
prop1, $n = 9$	0.56	3.60
prop1, $n = 10$	1.19	16.11
prop2, $n = 5$	5.08	0.45
prop2, $n = 6$	21.58	1.71
prop3, $n = 8$	0.13	32.41
prop3, $n = 9$	0.32	240.87
prop4, $n = 3$	0.04	0.14
prop4, $n = 4$	0.10	o.t.
prop5, $n = 5$	26.30	0.26
prop5, $n = 6$	740.37	1.08

We are currently investigating the reasons why the performance of both model checkers drastically differ depending on the property checked. However, the fact that SPIN offers a better performance in some cases is encouraging because our current implementation is limited to the basic algorithm. Additional experiments show that SPIN is much more efficient for exhaustive exploration of the model as well as for deadlock detection.

5 Conclusion

We have proposed a spatial logic for the SPIN model checker. The logic basically extends LTL with spatial connectors to quantify over the set of component processes of a system and restrict a formula under such sets. In such a manner we can express properties of that relate the behaviour of the components of the system.

We have sketched a basic implementation that requires minimal changes in the implementation of SPIN. Next, we have discussed possible ways to reduce the complexity introduced by the second order process quantifier. First, we defined a set of structural axioms under which the satisfaction of spatial formula is closed. Then, we identified a fragment of the logic that is preserved by some *fair* subsystems, such that if we find out that such a formula does not hold for the system restricted to the set of processes Q we can neglect checking ϕ for the fair supersets of Q.

Last, we presented a set of comparative experiments with the spatial model checker SLMC [23] which show that our basic algorithm offers a better performance in some cases. This encourages us to implement the proposed improvements and further study heuristics for an efficient verification of our logic.

In current work we are implementing our whole approach, analyzing its complexity, investigating ways to rewrite formulae into equivalent ones that are more easy to check, and studying trade-offs between the relaxation of the notion of *fair* supersets and the reduction of preserved fragments in order to achieve good performance. A good starting point could be to exploit classical results of compositional reasoning [24] and verification of infinite families of finite-state systems [22]. Potential directions of future research consists of extending the approach to systems with dynamic creation of processes or including first-order predicates in the line of [9] such that also state observations are affected by process restriction.

We also plan to analyze the application of state space reduction techniques in our approach, with a special focus in those techniques implemented in SPIN and in extensions of it. For example, we would like to show whether partial order reduction [25] can be soundly applicable and investigate how to exploit the fact that in the calls to SPIN some of the processes are inactive which means that some interferences of transitions in the whole system can be guaranteed to be absent in some subsystems. As another example, when the focus is on bug finding, the *directed model checking* approach [26] can be used to accelerate the search for errors and possibly provide shorter counterexamples. One can study heuristics to decide the order in which to consider the assignment of subsets to a variable such that errors are found faster.

References

1. Holzmann, G.: The Spin Model Checker, Primer and Reference Manual. Reading, Massachusetts (2004)
2. Havelund, K., Pressburger, T.: Model checking java programs using java pathfinder. International Journal on Software Tools for Technology Transfer 2(4) (2000)

3. Corbett, J.C., Dwyer, M.B., Hatcliff, J., Laubach, S., Pasareanu, C.S., Robby, Z.H.: Bandera: Extracting finite-state models from Java source code. In: 22nd International Conference on Software Engineering (ICSE), IEEE Computer Society Press, Los Alamitos (2000)
4. Varr D., ó.: Automated formal verification of visual modeling languages by model checking. Software and System Modeling 3(2), 85–113 (2004)
5. Song, H., Compton, K.J.: Verifying π-calulus processes by promela translation. Technical Report CSE-TR-472-03, University of Michigan (2003)
6. Wu, P.: Interpreting π-calculus with spin/promela. Technical report, Lab. for Computer Science, Institute of Software, Chinese Academy of Sciences (2001)
7. Milner, R.: Communicating and Mobile Systems: The π-calculus. Cambridge University Press, Cambridge (1992)
8. Manna, Z., Pnueli, A.: The temporal logic of reactive systems. Springer, Heidelberg (1991)
9. Reif, J., Sistla, A.P.: A multiprocess network logic with temporal and spatial modalities. J. Comput. Syst. Sci. 30(1), 41–53 (1985)
10. Browne, M.C., Clarke, E.M., Grumberg, O.: Reasoning about networks with many identical finite state processes. Inf. Comput. 81(1), 13–31 (1989)
11. German, S.M., Sistla, A.P.: Reasoning about systems with many processes. J. ACM 39(3), 675–735 (1992)
12. Caires, L., Cardelli, L.: A spatial logic for concurrency (part II). In: Proceedings of the 13th International Conference on Concurrency Theory, pp. 209–225. Springer, Heidelberg (2002)
13. Caires, L., Cardelli, L.: A spatial logic for concurrency (part I). Inf. Comput. 186(2), 194–235 (2003)
14. Caires, L., Cardelli, L.: Behavioral and spatial observations in a logic for the π-calculus. In: Walukiewicz, I. (ed.) FOSSACS 2004. LNCS, vol. 2987, pp. 72–87. Springer, Heidelberg (2004)
15. Cardelli, L., Gordon, A.D.: Ambient logic. Mathematical Structures in Computer Science (to appear)
16. Reynolds, J.: Separation logic: A logic for shared mutable data structures. In: Logic in Computer Science, pp. 55–74. IEEE Computer Society Press, Los Alamitos (2002)
17. Cardelli, L., Gardner, P., Ghelli, G.: Manipulating trees with hidden labels. In: Gordon, A.D. (ed.) ETAPS 2003 and FOSSACS 2003. LNCS, vol. 2620, pp. 216–232. Springer, Heidelberg (2003)
18. Cardelli, L., Gardner, P., Ghelli, G.: A spatial logic for querying graphs. In: Widmayer, P., Triguero, F., Morales, R., Hennessy, M., Eidenbenz, S., Conejo, R. (eds.) ICALP 2002. LNCS, vol. 2380, pp. 597–610. Springer, Heidelberg (2002)
19. Courcelle, B.: The expression of graph properties and graph transformations in monadic second-order logic. In: Rozenberg, G., (ed.) Handbook of Graph Grammars and Computing by Graph Transformation. World Scientific, pp. 313–400 (1997)
20. Dijkstra, E.W.: Hierarchical ordering of sequential processes. Acta Inf. 1, 115–138 (1971)
21. Dwyer, M.B., Avrunin, G.S., Corbett, J.C.: Patterns in property specifications for finite-state verification. In: ICSE, pp. 411–420 (1999)
22. Clarke, E., Grumberg, O., Peled, D.: Model Checking. MIT Press, Cambridge (1999)

23. Vieira, H.: L.C.: The spatial logic model checker user's manual. Technical Report TR-DI/FCT/UNL-03/2004, Faculty of Science and Technology New University of Lisbon (2004)
24. Berezin, S., Campos, S., Clarke, E.M.: Compositional reasoning in model checking. In: de Roever, W.-P., Langmaack, H., Pnueli, A. (eds.) COMPOS 1997. LNCS, vol. 1536, pp. 81–102. Springer, Heidelberg (1998)
25. Holzmann, G.J., Peled, D.: An improvement in formal verification. In: FORTE. IFIP Conference Proceedings, vol. 6, pp. 197–211. Chapman & Hall, Sydney, Australia (1994)
26. Edelkamp, S., Leue, S., Lluch Lafuente, A.: Directed explicit-state model checking in the validation of communication protocols. STTT 5(2-3), 247–267 (2004)

Model Extraction for ARINC 653 Based Avionics Software*

Pedro de la Cámara, María del Mar Gallardo, and Pedro Merino

University of Málaga
Campus de Teatinos s/n,
29071, Málaga, Spain
{pedro.delacamara}@gmail.com, {gallardo,pedro}@lcc.uma.es

Abstract. One of the most exciting and promising approaches to ensure the correctness of critical systems is *software model checking*, which considers real code, written with standard programming languages like C. One general technique to implement this approach is producing a reduced model of the software in order to employ existing and efficient tools, like SPIN. This paper presents the application of the technique to avionics software constructed on top of an application interface (API) compliant with the ARINC 653 specification (APEX), which is widely employed by the manufacturers in the avionics industry. The paper uses techniques to automatically extract PROMELA models from C source code. These techniques were previously developed by the authors. However, they are now extended to deal with new problems, like real-time aspects and APEX scheduling. In order to close the extracted model during the verification, we built a reusable APEX-specific environment. This APEX environment models the execution engine (i.e. an APEX compliant RTOS) that implements APEX services. Finally, this paper also contains a novel testing method to ensure the correctness of this APEX environment. This testing method uses SPIN to execute official ARINC 653 test cases.

Keywords: Model extraction, software model checking, avionics, APEX, Real Time.

1 Introduction

Application software for avionics, ranging from comfort and measurement software to critical flying control systems, are currently implemented on top of a shared network of processors following standard interfaces like ARINC 653 (Avionics Application Software Standard Interface) [1]. The applications share processors, memory and devices (sensors and input/output devices) and the whole system requires specific scheduling methods with real time features. So the verification of this kind of system is a real trend for model checker practitioners.

It is well known that one major problem of model checking for non-expert engineers is that the technique requires a deep understanding of both the modelling

* This work has been partially supported by the Spanish MEC under grants TIN2004-7943-C04 and TIN 2005-09405-C02-01.

D. Bošnački and S. Edelkamp (Eds.): SPIN 2007, LNCS 4595, pp. 243–262, 2007.

and the property languages supported by the tools. Furthermore, the manual construction process is susceptible to human errors due to misunderstandings or plain programming bugs. This is one reason to start many projects that can generate suitable models with minimal human interaction (see Feaver [9], JPF1 [7] and Bandera [4]). In [6] and [5], the authors develop a model extraction technique to deal with software built on top of well defined APIs. The approach was implemented for SPIN 4 (the same target as that of other related tools like FeaVer or Bandera). In this paper, we extend and apply our method to verify C applications running on top of APEX. The main extensions to our previous work consist in modelling time features and using conformance testing for checking the correctness of our model.

Modelling and verification of avionics software is also described in [10]. The problem of modelling real time in SPIN has been considered in [3]. Although, a detailed comparison with these works is given in Section 8, we may summarize the main contributions of this paper as follows:

1. The method to model *timing events* preserves the size of the state space into the limits suitable for verification with SPIN, like [3]. In addition, our approach can also benefit from abstract matching.
2. The approach in [10] is oriented to the verification of the operating system (OS), and not to the applications running on top of this OS. We apply model extraction techniques to applications (i.e. to its C source code) in order to generate PROMELA+C models. Then we close the extracted models with an environment, which is in fact a model of an APEX-compliant OS. Finally we apply Model Checking to the closed model.
3. Since the verification of the application depends on the correctness of the environment (OS model), we decided to automatically check its correctness. To this end, we employ also SPIN to perform automatic testing, using the ARINC standard test cases [2]. It is important to notice that these test cases are run only one time. Once the correctness of the environment is proven, it can be reused with many application models.

The paper is organized as follows. The preliminary material in Section 2 summarizes our general extraction approach to deal with software constructed on top of well-defined APIs [6]. Section 3 gives an overview of the APEX API and the partitioning scheme for avionics software. The main ideas of the model extraction approach are presented in Section 4 and the details of time modelling in Section 5. Some experimental results that confirm the feasibility of the method is given in Section 6. Section 7 shows the correctness of our approach through testing. Sections 8 and 9 conclude with a more detailed comparison with related works, and the conclusions, respectively.

2 Model Extraction with Well-Defined APIs

Existing approaches to verifying software by model extraction do not specifically address the problem of how to model services provided by the operating system.

They are suitable for source code that only contains library functions that can be executed by the target model checker (see Feaver [7]). When the target model checker cannot directly execute all the operating system calls, it is necessary to add some extra hardness to complete the extracted models.

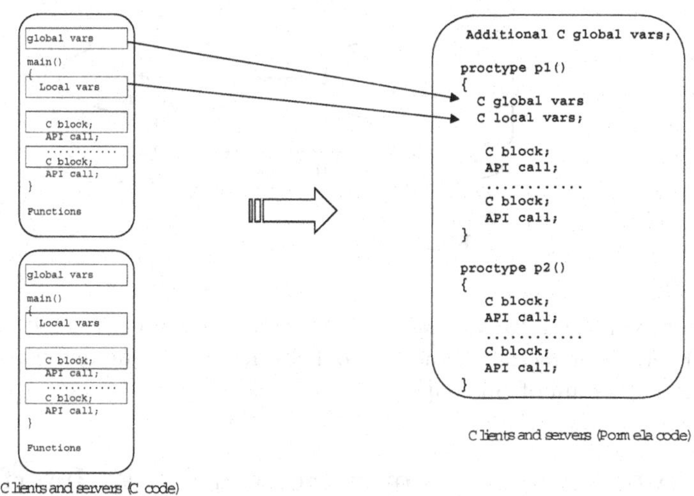

Fig. 1. Mapping scheme in SocketMC

In [6] we considered how to verify concurrent C applications that make extensive use of OS facilities through system calls. In our approach to model extraction, we construct a SPIN oriented model of the behavior of some operating system APIs. This model is used to automatically obtain a correct abstraction of the software that makes use of this API, for instance the Berkley-like Socket API. Following [9], we defined a mapping from the original C code to extended PROMELA. Tool SOCKETMC automatically transforms each API call into PROMELA. The new PROMELA model can be verified with standard SPIN.

As shown in Figure 1, mapping from the original code to PROMELA is done replacing every process (every `main` function) with a `proctype` definition. Then, the body of every proctype is filled using the extensions for C code (`c_decl`, `c_state`, `c_expr` and `c_code`). This is done breaking the C code at the points where a call to API appears. The final PROMELA code preserves the sequential execution of every C block code between two system calls. Thus, when verifying the model, SPIN interleaves blocks and system calls as atomic sentences.

By default, the PROMELA models produced by our model extractor contain all the C variables in the original code. Our method to produce *abstract matching functions*, presented in [5], allows us to automatically reduce the set of variables that should be actually managed to produce the state space. This optimization is also considered for models extracted from APEX based C applications.

This approach can be used for any kind of API, provided that the way of modelling the API calls preserve their semantics. So, in order to verify C applications

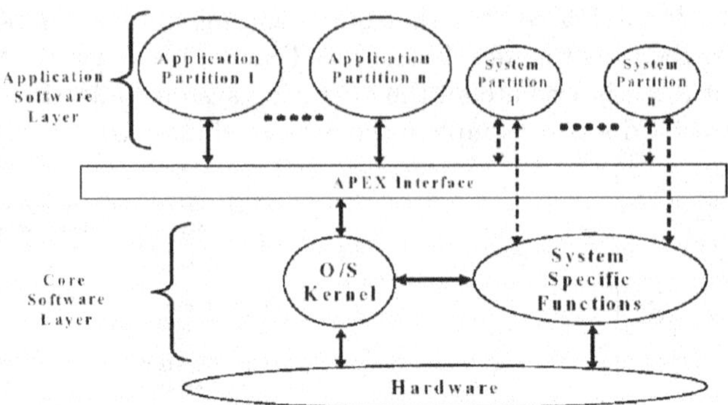

Fig. 2. APEX Interface

written on top of APEX, we only need to correctly model the services provided by APEX and reuse our model extraction tool SOCKETMC. The definition of such API models is the aim of this paper.

3 The ARINC API for Avionics Software: APEX Interface

On-board avionics computing systems have evolved from federated specific computer systems towards generic to modular and integrated computers, like the *Integrated Modular Avionics* (IMA). Most of the federated computers perform basically the same functions (input, processing, and output). A natural way of optimizing resources is to adopt a modular approach: to identify common parts, to standardize interfaces and to encapsulate services. Then, the next step is to share the hardware and software resources by integrating several functions on the same execution platform.

To enable multiple applications to be executed on the same computation resource, while avoiding error propagation, a robust isolation mechanism is used. Isolation is achieved by means of spatial and temporal partitioning, i.e., segregation of memory and time slots allocated to various application parts (or partitions) by means of software and hardware mechanisms.

The *Operating System* (OS) offers the basic and common services for all applications such as load, scheduling, and communication, through a well-defined API conforming to the ARINC 653 specification called APEX. We now briefly describe the main characteristics of APEX (see [1] for a more detailed description).

Partitioning.- One purpose of a core module in an IMA system is to support one or more avionics applications and to allow their independent execution. This can be correctly achieved if the system provides partitioning, i.e., a functional separation of the avionics applications, usually for fault containment (to prevent any partitioned function from causing a failure in another partitioned function) and for ease of verification, validation and certification. A partition is basically the same as a program in a single application environment: it comprises data, its

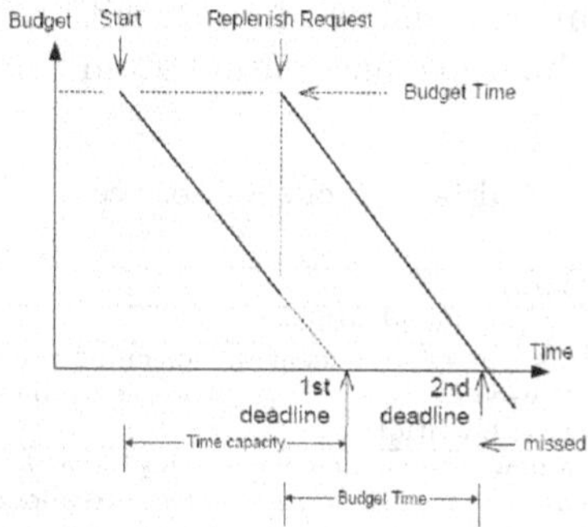

Fig. 3. Process Time Capacity

own context, configuration attributes, etc. For large applications, the concept of multiple partitions relating to a single application is recognized.

APEX *Interface.*- As Figure 2 shows, interface APEX is located between the application software and the OS. It defines a set of facilities provided by the system for application software to control the scheduling, communication, and the status information of its internal processing elements. APEX also provides a common logical environment for the application software that enables independently-produced applications to execute together on the same hardware.

Scheduling.-Specification differences between *partition scheduling* and *process scheduling.* Scheduling of partitions is strictly deterministic over time. The *System Integrator* assigns one or more time windows to each partition. This is done in the fixed configuration within the core module. The scheduling algorithm runs repetitively with a fixed periodicity. Partitions have no priority by themselves. The scheduling unit is an APEX process. Each process has a priority. The scheduling algorithm is priority preemptive. During any process rescheduling event, the OS always selects the highest priority process in the ready state within the partition to receive processor resources. If several processes have the same current priority, the OS selects the oldest one.

Time Management.- As Figure 3 shows, a time capacity is associated with each process, and represents the response time given to the process for satisfying its processing requirements. When a process is started, its deadline is set to the value of the current time plus the time capacity. This deadline time may be postponed by means of service `REPLENISH`. This capacity is an absolute duration of time, not an execution time. This means that a deadline overrun will occur even when the process is not running inside or outside the partition window, but will be acted upon only inside a partition window of its own partition.

Interpartition and Intrapartition communication.- Interpartition communication is defined as the communication among two or more partitions executing either on the same module or on different modules. It may also mean communication between APEX partitions and external equipment. Interpartition communication is conducted via messages. Intrapartition communication mechanisms allow processes to communicate and synchronize with each other. All intrapartition message passing mechanisms must ensure atomic message access.

Table 1. Modelled services

Service	Behaviour
GET_PROCESS_ID	provides a process identifier
GET_PROCESS_STATUS	returns the current status of the specified process. The current status of each process in a partition is available to all processes within that partition.
CREATE_PROCESS	creates a new process and returns its identifier. Partitions can create as many processes as the pre-allocated memory space supports. The consistency among process and partition parameters is checked. Assigning INFINITE_TIME_VALUE to PERIOD and TIME_CAPACITY defines an aperiodic process and a process without DEADLINE, respectively.
SET_PRIORITY	changes the current process' priority. The process is placed as the newest process with that priority in the ready state. Process rescheduling is performed after this service request only when the process whose priority is changed is in the ready or running state.
SUSPEND_SELF	suspends the execution of the current process, if it is aperiodic, until the RESUME service request is issued or the specified time-out value expires.
RESUME	resumes another previously suspended process. The resumed process will become ready if it is not waiting on a resource (delay, semaphore, period, event, message). A periodic process cannot be suspended, so it cannot be resumed.
STOP	makes a process ineligible for processor resources until another process issues START.
START	initializes all attributes of a process to their default values, and resets the runtime stack of the process. If the partition is in NORMAL mode, the process' deadline expiration time and the next release point are calculated.
GET_MY_ID	returns the identifier of the current process.
GET_PARTITION_STATUS	provides the status of the current partition.
SET_PARTITION_MODE	sets the operating mode of the current partition to normal after initialization of the partition is completed. The service is also used to set the partition back to idle (partition shutdown), and to cold start or warm start (partition restart), when a serious fault is detected and processed.
TIMED_WAIT	suspends execution of the requesting process for a minimum amount of elapsed time. Value zero allows the round robin scheduling of processes with the same priority.
PERIODIC_WAIT	suspends the execution of the requesting process until the next release point in the processor time line that corresponds to the period of the process.
GET_TIME	returns the value of the system clock. The system clock is the value of a clock common to all processors in the module.
REPLENISH	updates the deadline of the requesting process with a specified BUDGET_TIME value. It is not allowed to postpone a periodic process deadline past its next release point.

4 Modelling Processes

Following the approach described in [6], our PROMELA model is composed of several application processes, extracted from the application C source code, and an environment that closes the model. During the extraction, the API calls in the original source code are translated into calls to the environment. Consequently, the environment is the process that provides the APEX services to the application processes, and that stores all the state information needed as global data.

We have not modelled every APEX service or functionality. As a first step, we have focussed on what, in our opinion, is the most critical aspect to be modelled in SPIN, that is, the APEX Time Management. Table 1 above shows services modelled with a brief description of their behaviour.

Since the present paper focuses on modelling APEX Time Management, and several APEX features and services are not implemented in this first phase, the following limitations have been imposed: only one partition is allowed, processes cannot be restarted after being stopped, partitions cannot be restarted, error handler, and Health Monitoring and recovering actions are not supported.

4.1 Modelling the Process Scheduling

Applications running on APEX are composed of processes. Processes are scheduled according to the following APEX process scheduling rules: 1) the scheduling unit is an APEX process, 2) each process has a priority, 3) the scheduling algorithm is priority preemptive, 4) during any process rescheduling event, the OS always selects the highest priority process in the ready state, and 5) if several processes have the same current priority, the OS selects the oldest one.

In our model, scheduling is included in the environment and ensures that, in every state, only one PROMELA process is executable by SPIN. Scheduling also ensures that the APEX scheduling rules are followed when selecting a process for processor resources.

Modelling preemption without state explosion. The first issue of modelling APEX scheduling comes from the *process preemption* requirement. APEX specification states that a process may be preempted whenever a re-scheduling event takes place (for instance, when a higher-priority process is resumed after a timeout expiration). Implementing this requirement increases the complexity of the resulting model, which may lead to state explosion during verification.

To solve this problem, we divide the source code into code blocks and APEX API calls, as introduced in [6] (see Figure 1). Code blocks operate only at local scope (i.e. read and write local variables). API calls operate at global scope (i.e. read or write global variables). Notice that application processes can only communicate with other processes or with the environment through API calls.

From the model checking point of view, code blocks perform non-visible local actions, that neither affect other processes nor the environment. Thus, when a process is executing a code block, it does not matter in which code point it is preempted. Therefore we may merge all the sentences of a code block in an *atomic block*, allowing processes to be preemptable only before or after the execution of a code block. The idea of merging local sentences is well known, and it has already used in [6].

API calls behave differently. They use global information and have global effects but, since they are already executed atomically in the real system, it is also correct setting them as atomic in the model.

Controlling process execution. The second important issue when modelling the APEX scheduling is to ensure that the scheduling rules are fulfilled. Scheduling must be able to stop the execution of a process and resume another one. To do this, we use a `provided()` sentence in each PROMELA `proctype` declaration. Sentence `provided()` appends an executability clause to every transition of that process, disabling its execution when it is false. For example, global variable `_curSchProc` in clause "`proctype p1() provided (_curSchProc == _pid)`" stores the pid of the process currently in execution. Thus, sentence `provided()` is only true for the process whose `_pid` matches `_curSchProc`. Thus, the scheduler can control the execution of processes by modifying the `Pid` stored in the variable.

Storing process attributes. Scheduler must keep information about the attributes of each process to correctly realize the context switch. These data are stored as C-structures in the environment, using the embedded-C primitives provided by SPIN 4. Attributes may be static, if their value does not change, or dynamic. Process attributes are shown in Table 2 below.

Due to optimization reasons, only dynamic attributes are included in the SPIN state-vector. Static attributes are marked as `Tracked UnMatched` data (see references [6], [5] and [8]). Hiding these data during the comparison of states (`Matching`) does not discard any significant behaviour, since static attributes are written only once, during the partition initialization phase, when the process is created and the initialization phase is completely deterministic.

Table 2. Process attributes

Static Attributes	
Name	
Base priority	Initial priority
Period	
Time capacity	the amount of time in which the process must finish its work (it is used to calculate the process deadline)
type of deadline	it can be `HARD` or `SOFT`
Dynamic Attributes	
Current priority	
Deadline	Absolute time when time budged will expire.
State	APEX state of the process: `WAITING, RUNNING, DORMANT, READY`.
Waiting cause	Reason why a process is `WAITING` (e.g. for a resource).
Position in queue	If the process is `WAITING` or `READY`, position in the queue of processes waiting for the same cause. This attribute is used when there are several candidates to be awaked/run and the scheduler must choose the oldest one.
Resource	If the process is waiting for a resource, this is its identifier (e.g. a communication port).
Timeout	If the process was suspended with timeout, absolute time when the process will be resumed.
Time wait	If the process called `TIMED WAIT`, absolute time when the process will continue its execution.

Calling the scheduling functionality. Scheduler is called when the so-called re-scheduling events occur. Re-scheduling events are triggered when a change in the environment may modify the executability of one process. Examples of these events are API calls (e.g. `SET_PROCESS_ PRIORITY` and `SUSPEND_SELF`), *time events* (e.g. deadline or timeout expiration), the reception of messages in ports, and intra-partition communication (events up, signaling of semaphores, etc.)

5 Modelling Time

The APEX time management model is based on the notion of *time events*. In respect to model checking with SPIN, a *time event* is a global event, triggered by the environment, and associated to a point in the timeline.

The *time event* concept is related to the classic "tick" signal used in other real-time models. A "tick" signal usually indicates that certain amount of time has elapsed. It is used to interrupt the execution of the model, and to allow the increment or decrement of a time counter. In some cases, increasing/decreasing is not the only action. Other actions, such as awakening a process or notifying a deadline violation, are also carried out as a response to this "tick". In contrast to these signals, *time events* are *only* triggered *when* other actions must be taken. In other words, a *time event* is a special "tick" signal that is only triggered if its effect on the model goes beyond increasing/decreasing a time counter.

Our time management model includes a system clock that keeps track of the time flux, and that is updated by *time events*. That means that the system clock is only updated when a time-related event takes place. If a monitor process observed the system clock during an execution sequence, it would notice that the clock keeps the same value for long time and then, after a *time event* takes place, it jumps to a new value. The most important issue is that the size of the jump is completely dependant on the *time event*, and on the behavior of model itself. It is worth noting that, in terms of model checking, this approach causes a state-space reduction by avoiding "tick" signals that interrupt the model only to update time counters.

5.1 Life-Cycle of *Time Events*

Time events may be armed statically, before starting verification, or dynamically by the environment during execution of the model. The typical life cycle of a *time event* is as follows:

- An application process calls an APEX service (e.g. `TIMED_WAIT(500ms)`).
- The environment (i.e. the APEX OS) takes control and suspends the calling process. Then it arms a `Waiting_Timeout` *time event* that will be triggered `500ms` in the future.
- The environment returns the execution to another ready application process.
- Eventually (i.e. `500ms` in the future), the environment will trigger the *time event*. Then execution of the running process will be interrupted, so that the environment can awake the suspended process.

– Finally, the environment updates the system clock in `500ms`, removes the *time event*, and returns execution to the appropriate application process.

5.2 Implementing and Using *Time Events*

Regarding the implementation details in SPIN, the environment keeps a list with all the armed *time events* as a global state variable. The impact of the list in the state-vector size is not remarkable, since it is optimized for memory saving.

Time events may be used in different ways, depending on how they are armed and triggered. In this project, we have explored two ways of modelling APEX time management in SPIN. They are called *Time Management Types* and each one corresponds to a different modelling requirement. *Time Management Type 1* (TMT1) is used for modelling applications when the execution times of the application code are unknown. *Time Management Type 2* (TMT2) is a refinement of TMT1 taking these execution times into account.

Time Management Type 1: Execution times are not used. In the early stages of software development for industrial processes, execution times are often not available. However, in these first phases, verification by model checking can be very useful as a mean of discarding design errors. Even if execution times are unknown, the piece of software under analysis may already include in the code some time values (inherited from the requirement or design phases). TMT1 provides a model of the environment capable to interpret these time values, but without using specific execution times.

TMT1 makes an over-approximation of the model assuming that the execution of each application code block may take a variable amount of time ranging from 0 to infinite time units, but only at those time points where a *time event* is triggered. Evidently, this over-approximation produces execution traces that will never happen in real execution.

This over-approximation is implemented by the process `TimeEventTrigger`, whose code appears below. This process is in charge of triggering *time events* and runs parallel to the application processes.

```
proctype TimeEventTrigger () {
      do                                   \
      :: (1) ->c_code {ma_Tempus_Fugit();} \
      od;
}
```

Process `TimeEventTrigger` contains an infinite loop with a call to the environment function `ma_Tempus_Fugit` that triggers *time events*, and updates the system clock. Since `TimeEventTrigger` may always be executed, every transition of the model may non-deterministically choose to execute either an atomic application code block (whenever there exists at least one enabled process), or the `TimeEventTrigger` sentence `Tempus_Fugit`.

We now describe the possible execution sequences produced by SPIN when the application code blocks and process `TimeEventTrigger` are interleaved. In the discussion, we denote with $A_0, A_1, \ldots, A_k$ the application code blocks of the model under analysis, $et(A_i)(0 \leq i \leq k)$ being their respective execution times. Similarly, we assume that $T_0, T_1, \cdots$ are the sucessive `TimeEventTrigger` transitions, and that $tp(T_i)$ is the time point associated to the *time event* triggered in T_i. We use $\rightarrow$ to represent the order in which transitions are executed in a given sequence of transitions. It is important to remember that the system clock is only updated during the *time event* triggering which, in this case, means that it is only updated by `Tempus_Fugit`.

Starting with one `TimeEventTrigger` transition T_0, SPIN explores all the following execution sequences:

- $T_0 \rightarrow A_0 \rightarrow A_1 \rightarrow \cdots$, that is, no `TimeEventTrigger` transition takes place. Then, the system clock remains unchanged, and therefore, $et(A_0)+et(A_1)+\cdots = 0$.
- $T_0 \rightarrow A_0 \rightarrow \cdots A_n \rightarrow T_1 \rightarrow \cdots$, that is some application code blocks are executed between T_0 and T_1. After T_1 is triggered, the system clock is updated, and therefore, $et(A_0) + \cdots + et(A_n) = tp(T_1) - tp(T_0)$.
- $T_0 \rightarrow T_1 \rightarrow A_0 \rightarrow \cdots$, that is, the first block A_0 is executed after T_1. This sequence models the behavior where $et(A_0) > tp(T_1) - tp(T_0)$. It can also represent a behavior where execution of A_0 is disabled until the *time event* T_1 is triggered.
- $T_0 \rightarrow T_1 \rightarrow T_2 \rightarrow \cdots$, that is, no application code block is executed. This sequence models the behavior where $et(A_0)$ is infinite. It can also represent a behavior where execution of A_0 is indefinitely disabled.

TMT1 can be used to verify properties related to the ordering of execution of application code blocks (A_i) and `TimeEventTrigger` transitions (T_i). This includes all non-real-time temporal properties usually checked in SPIN. In addition, TMT1 can only deal with *some* of the properties involving real time values. For example, the existential property *"Process P1 is able to do its work before its deadline"* can be checked. SPIN will try to find an execution in which P_1 *is able* to finish successfully. However, property *"Process P1 shall always do its work before its deadline"* cannot be proven because it will always be violated by the execution sequence where one code block has an infinite execution time.

Time Management Type 2: Execution Times are used. The *Time Management Type 2* refines TMT1 by adding information about the *execution times* of the application processes. TMT2 assigns a fixed execution time to each code block. These times may be real data, estimations or even purely hypothetical values.

In a real system, a *time event* may happen at any time as, for instance, during the execution of a code block. However, code blocks are modelled as atomic sentences, and therefore, their execution cannot be interrupted. But this is not a problem, since, by definition, code blocks only perform local computation, with no visible effects on other processes, and it does not matter whether a *time event* is triggered during or just before a code block, as it does not influence the whole behavior of the model.

The strategy of TMT2 is to delay the execution of a code block until it can be executed without being interrupted by *time events*. Whenever a code block is delayed, its remaining execution time is decreased in an amount equal to the delay. This is because the model considers that, in the real system, the code block would be *partially* executed. Eventually, when the remaining execution time is so short that no *time event* can interrupt the code block, the actual code block will be executed.

A special *time control logic*, which is considered part of the environment, is added at the beginning of each code block. Both the whole code block and time control logic are included in an atomic sentence. The following example illustrates the way time control logic works.

```
CP1:
Atomic { /* Init of Time Control Logic of Block 1 */
if RemainingExecTime(_pid) = 0 then
    RemainingExecTime(_pid) = CP1_EXEC_TIME;
end if
if ( (T_NextTimeEvent - CurrentTime) < RemainingExecTime(_pid) then
/* Partial code block execution */
    RemainingExecTime(_pid) = RemainingExecTime(_pid) - (T_NextTimeEvent  - CurrentTime);
    CurrentTime = T_NextTimeEvent;
    Trigger Time Event;
    goto CP1;
else /* Complete code block execution */
    CurrentTime = CurrentTime  + RemainingExecTime(_pid);
    RemainingExecTime(_pid) = 0;
end if
 /* End of Time Control Logic of Block 1 */
  /////////////////////////////////////////////////////////
             APPLICATION CODE BLOCK
  /////////////////////////////////////////////////////////
}
```

Firstly, the time control logic stores the fixed execution time for the code block into the global variable `RemainingExecTime`, which is specifically assigned to the corresponding process. This variable is only updated when its value is zero.

Then, the time to the next armed *time event* is calculated, and if it is possible to completely execute the code block before the next *time event* is triggered, variable `RemainingExecTime` is set back to zero, and the system clock is increased in the same amount. In other words, the elapsed time is equal to `RemainingExecTime`. After setting the system clock, the code block is executed as usual.

Otherwise, if the block code cannot be completely executed, the difference between the next *time event* and the current system clock time is calculated. This value, that represents the time elapsed during which the code block has been partially executed, is subtracted from `RemainingExecTime`. Just after that, the *time event* is triggered, and the process jumps back outside the atomic block. Notice that, as a result of the triggered *time event*, the process may be disabled. Eventually, when the process runs again, it will try to execute the same code block, performing a new iteration of the time control logic. Since this time variable `RemainingExecTime` is not zero, its value is not updated. This iteration goes on until the code block can be completely executed.

This implementation also includes process `TimeEventTrigger`, whose code appears below, and that uses the `timeout` PROMELA sentence to trigger *time events* when the rest of processes are blocked.

```
proctype TimeEventTrigger () {
  do                                          \
  :: (timeout) ->c_code {ma_Tempus_Fugit();}  \
  od;
}
```

In summary, if an *execution event* is a fictitious event that occurs when a code block finalizes its execution, it is possible to state that TMT2 preserves the ordering of *time events* and *execution events.*

However, a question still remains. What happens with the API service calls which are not completely local? The answer is that in a real system, a *time event* cannot interrupt API calls. The concrete effects of a *time event* (for example, a `DEADLINE`) triggered during an API call are mostly implementation dependant. Usually, the effects can be seen after the process returns from the call. In our model, API calls are delayed until all the interrupting *time events* are triggered.

6 Experimental Results

We now present an example to evaluate our APEX environment. The application code has been instrumented in such a way that SPIN generates one execution trace for each possible execution sequence. By analyzing the traces, we may understand the order in which sentences were executed during verification, and the time when it happened (measured with the modelled system clock). We have used *Time Management Type 1.*

The example consists of one process `P1` with the following behaviour. Process `P1` obtains its own identifier (`GET_MY_ID`), modifies its own priority (`SET_PRIORITY`) four times and enters the waiting state (`TIMED_WAIT`) for 500 time units. After awaking, it reads the system clock (`GET_TIME`) and stops itself (`STOP_SELF`). The complete code is shown in Appendix A. Process `init` is shown below.

```
init{ atomic {
    c_code { MODEL_A653_Init(); };
    c_code{
        strcpy (a_att.NAME, "p1");
        a_att.STACK_SIZE = 200;
        a_att.BASE_PRIORITY = 30;
        a_att.PERIOD = INFINITE_TIME_VALUE;
        a_att.TIME_CAPACITY= 5000;
        a_att.DEADLINE = SOFT; };
    A653_CREATE_PROCESS(&a_att, &a_proc, &a_return,p1);
    A653_START(a_proc,&a_return);
    A653_SET_PARTITION_MODE(NORMAL,&a_return);
    run clock();
}; };
```

It creates `P1` (`CREATE_PROCESS`), starts it (`START`) and begins the normal process scheduling by setting the partition in `NORMAL` mode (`SET_PARTITION_MODE`). Since `P1` has a time capacity of 5000 time units, its deadline shall be set 5000 time units. For this example, we modelled a minimal Health Monitoring functionality that stops process `P1` when its deadline is reached.

As described in Section 5.2, Time Management Type 1 makes use of process `TimeEventTrigger` to trigger *time events*. In order to explore every possible sequence of *time events* and application code-blocks, Time Management Type 1 takes advantage of the non-deterministic interleaving between this process and the application processes. In particular, the instrumentation code added to this example generates 10 traces, one for each possible execution sequence. We now discuss them in detail.

Trace 1

Time	Process Executed	Description
0	`TimeEventTrigger`	Next *time event* t = 5000
5000		`DEADLINE`

In this trace, `TimeEventTrigger` runs before `P1` and triggers the `P1-DEADLINE` *time event*. In consequence, the execution is stopped before `P1` can run. In a real system, this behavior takes place if the execution time of the first code-block of `P1` takes more than 5000 time units.

Traces 2-6

The second trace corresponds to the scenario where `P1` is able to execute sentence (`GET_MY_ID`) before its deadline is triggered. Note that after the execution of `GET_MY_ID`, the system time has not advanced.

Time	Process Executed	Description
0	`P1`	CP11: `GET_MY_ID`
0	`TimeEventTrigger`	Next *time event* t = 5000
5000		`DEADLINE`

The next four traces are similar to the previous one. In each of then, `P1` is able to execute one additional sentence `SET_PRIORITY` before the deadline is triggered.

Traces 7-10

Time	Process Executed	Description
0	`P1`	CP11: `GET_MY_ID`
0	`P1`	CP12: `SET_PRIORITY`
0	`P1`	CP13: `SET_PRIORITY`
0	`P1`	CP14: `SET_PRIORITY`
0	`P1`	CP15: `SET_PRIORITY`
0	`P1`	CP15: `TIMED_WAIT`
0	`TimeEventTrigger`	Next *time event* t = 500
500		Awake `P1`
500	`TimeEventTrigger`	Next *time event* t = 5000
5000		`DEADLINE`

In the seventh trace, `P1` enters a waiting state for 500 time units. A *time event* is armed at $t = 500$ and, since no other process is executing, it is triggered.

Finally, the deadline of P1 is triggered. The last three traces show how P1 continues its execution after TIMED_WAIT. The last trace represents the behavior where the execution of P1 is so fast that its deadline is not triggered. SPIN reached depth 30, with state-vector of 228 bytes (107 bytes to store the environment state.) The example confirms that Time Management Type 1 can be used as an over-approximation when there is no information about execution times.

7 Testing the Model of the API

In a real system, application processes use the OS services described in the specification ARINC 653 Part 1 [1]. In the verification model, applications call services provided by the verification environment. To ensure the correctness of the verification, the behavior of the environment services must match the real OS services. As a first step to establish the soundness of the model proposed here, we have carried out an exhaustive testing campaign. The procedure consists in running a battery of *Test Cases*, written in PROMELA+C code, which call every implemented service in every possible condition. Each Test Case provides a fail/pass verdict, depending on the behavior of the services called.

Test Cases are defined considering the ARINC 653 Part 3 "Conformity Test Specification" document [2]. This specification gives a description in natural language of an APEX conformity test-battery. In other words, this battery checks if the APEX services provided by an OS are conformed to the ARINC 653 Part 1 specification. In consequence, it can also be used to check if the services implemented in our environment are also conformant.

Test Cases are classified into functional and robustness tests. Functional tests check that the service works in normal use conditions. Robustness tests check how the service works in abnormal conditions (e.g. it returns the appropriate error codes). The result is a complete conformance test suite. Our work firstly consisted in selecting the test definitions applicable to the current services implemented in the environment. Then we built the PROMELA-C Test Cases and finally we checked that no Test Case returned a fail verdict. The execution of the test cases and the PROMELA model of APEX is done with the validation facilities of SPIN. Due to space restrictions, we cannot describe in detail the codes for Test Cases developed. As an example, Appendix B shows the Test Case checking the SET_PRIORITY service when the PROCESS_ID input parameter is not valid.

It is worth noting that during testing we have used *Time Management Type 2* because we are assuming a deterministic evolution of time.

8 Related Work

Since this paper focuses mainly on modelling the time management aspects of APEX, in this section, we have concentrated on the previous references which have modelled real-time in SPIN.

The proposal presented in [10] shows how to verify a microkernel used in the avionics industry, by constructing a PROMELA model of the Honeywell DEOS operating system. In order to close the OS model, all the possible interactions between the DEOS model and the external world are modelled inside the environment. Basically, this environment includes threads requiring services from the OS and time-related interruption sources. Our work has the opposite goal. We aim at verifying avionics applications which access OS services through the APEX interface. In our case, we semi-automatically extract PROMELA models from applications source code (see [6]). In order to close the application model, we need to use an environment able to provide APEX services to the applications.

In the DEOS environment, one message is periodically generated to indicate that a higher priority thread may become schedulable. After receiving this message, the kernel checks if the current running process must be pre-empted by the higher priority thread. In our case, since the environment is the OS, and the threads are the applications to be verified, whenever a higher priority process becomes schedulable, the environment, that is the OS, disables the execution of the low-priority processes and enables the high-priority one.

The DEOS environment has two time-related interruption sources. The first one periodically interrupts the kernel, in order to check if a higher priority has become schedulable. The second one interrupts the kernel whenever the running process exhausts its time budget. The DEOS environment combines both interruptions in one process, in order to coordinate them and avoid "impossible" behaviours. Similarly, our environment includes a `TimeEventGenerator` process that may be seen as the combination of every time-related interruption source applicable on APEX (waiting timeout expiration, time budget expiration, etc.) However, instead of ticks, our `TimeEventGenerator` triggers *time events*. Each *time events* has an associated *time point*. The environment is able to know the current system time, just by reading the time point value of the last *time event* triggered. This feature allows our environment to provide the system time to the applications. Since both the environment and the applications are aware of system time, it is possible to use timing values in the properties to be verified (i.e. in LTL formulae).

The work presented in [3] is a time extension for PROMELA. The principles explained in that work are generic and may be applicable to different modelling problems. In our case, we aim at modelling the time management as described in the APEX specification. The context of our approach is automatic model extraction of avionics applications and APEX environment modelling. That means that we are in the position of using modelling techniques specially tailored for this context. On the other hand, some of the techniques and assumptions made may not be applicable to other modelling problems.

In the discrete time model of [3], time is divided into slices. The actions take place inside these slices, making it possible to obtain a measure for the time elapsed between events belonging to different slices. However, within a slice, only the relative ordering between events is known. The time elapsed between events is measured in ticks of a global digital clock that is increased by one with every such tick. In our case, a time slice may be considered as the time elapsed between two consecutive *time events*. The main difference is that the time slice size is always variable and depends on model behavior. Furthermore, *time events* may only happen between two atomic blocks of application codes. Another significant difference is that we have identified two different use scenarios, depending on whether the execution time of application code blocks is known or not. If execution time is not known, the environment assumes the worst case over-approximation, that is, the execution time of each code block may be any value from 0 to infinite. In practice, this means that between two *time events*, a process can execute a non-deterministic number of code blocks, unless it makes an API call involving waiting for an event (`TIMED_WAIT`, etc.).

In principle, as in [3], only the relative ordering between events is known within a slice. However, if the execution time of code blocks is known, the environment making it possible to know the absolute time in which a block of code was executed. One important point of the work [3] is that it is compatible with SPIN partial order reduction algorithm (POR). This is not our case, since we use the PROMELA the `provide` sentence which is incompatible with POR. However, this is not a big performance issue for our model, since the main objective of POR is to reduce the state explosion caused by non-deterministic process interleaving. Due to the way in which APEX processes are scheduled, this kind of state explosion rarely appears during verification.

Another related development is the RT-Spin package of [11]. RT-Spin extends PROMELA in order to deal with Real Time. This is the main difference with our work, since we rely on standard PROMELA.

Finally, another main difference with the works referred to above is that most of the environment is implemented in C code. This is done using the embedded C capabilities of SPIN 4. The embedded C code allows us to use data abstraction techniques, as those explained in [5].

9 Conclusions

The first and most important conclusion of this work is that verification of APEX-based avionics applications is feasible with SPIN. We have proven that SPIN is able to model APEX-like Real-Time management in a correct and efficient manner, if the right methods and assumptions are used. Our past experience in modelling APIs ([6], [5]). tells us that other features of APEX (e.g. inter-partition communication, process synchronization, etc) can also be modelled in SPIN. Actually, we are extending SOCKETMC to obtain a more generic model extractor that allows us to automatically verify APEX based applications.

The second conclusion is that verification methods and assumptions must be adapted to each use-scenario. In our case, if application execution times are not known before the verification, then we must use methods and assumptions that cope with this incertitude (i.e. Time Management Type 1). On the other hand, when execution times become available, we must refine the verification using more accurate methods and assumptions (i.e. Time Management Type 2).

In respect to future work, we have several parallel lines of study. First, we plan to expand the set of modelled APEX services. The next step will be to include inter-partition and intra-partition communication services. These new services will be integrated in the ongoing extension of SocketMC[6].

We also want to improve the approach by using memory optimization methods based on data abstraction [5]. We have detected that in some use-scenarios, the execution times are known, but with some degree of incertitude. For these scenarios we want to build a Hybrid Time Management, where execution times are non-deterministically chosen among a limited set of values.

Finally, we realize that APEX static configuration (e.g. ports, partitions, time-schedule, etc.) must also be incorporated into the verification model. For this purpose, we plan to enable our environment to read external static configuration information. In the long term, we want to be able to parse APEX configuration XML files and translate them into a SPIN-friendly configuration.

References

1. ARINC. ARINC Specification 653-2: Avionics Application Software Standard Interface Part 1 - Required Services. Aeronautical Radio INC, Maryland, USA (2005)
2. ARINC. ARINC Specification 653-2: Avionics Application Software Standard Interface Part 3 - Conformity Test Specification. Aeronautical Radio INC, Maryland, USA (2006)
3. Bosnacki, D., Dams, D.: Integrating Real Time into SPIN: A Prototype Implementation. In: Proc. of the FIP TC6 WG6.1 Joint Int. Conf. FORTE XI / PSTV XVIII '98, pp. 423–438. Kluwer, B.V, Boston, MA (1998)
4. Corbett, J.C., Dwyer, M.B., Hatcliff, J., Laubach, S., Pasareanu, C.S.: Bandera: Extracting finite-state models from java source code. In: ICSE '00: Proc.of the 22nd Int. Conf. on Software Engineering, pp. 439–448. ACM Press, New York (2000)
5. de la Cámara, P., Gallardo, M.M., Merino, P.: Abstract matching for software model checking. In: Valmari, A. (ed.) Model Checking Software. LNCS, vol. 3925, pp. 182–200. Springer, Heidelberg (2006)
6. de la Cámara, P., Gallardo, M.M., Merino, P., Sanán, D.: Model checking software with well-defined apis: the socket case. In: FMICS '05: Proc. of the 10th Int. Workshop on Formal methods for Industrial Critical Systems, pp. 17–26. ACM Press, New York (2005)
7. Havelund, K., Pressburger, T.: Model Checking Java Programs using Java Pathfinder. International Journal of Software Tools for Technology Transfer 2(4), 366–381 (2000)
8. Holzmann, G.J., Joshi, R.: Model-driven Software Verification. In: 11th Int. Workshop on Model Checking of Software (SPIN04), pp. 76–91 (2004)
9. Holzmann, G.J., Smith, M.H.: Software model checking: Extracting Verification Models from Source Code. Software Testing, Verification & Reliability 11(2), 65–79 (2001)
10. John Penix, W., Visser, E., Engstrom, A.: Verification of Time Partitioning in the DEOS Scheduler Kernel. In: ICSE '00: Proceedings of the 22nd Int. Conf. on Software Engineering, pp. 488–497. ACM Press, New York (2000)
11. Tripakis, S., Courcoubetis, C.: Extending Promela and Spin for Real Time. In: Margaria, T., Steffen, B. (eds.) TACAS 1996. LNCS, vol. 1055, pp. 329–348. Springer, Heidelberg (1996)

A Code of the Example

```
c_state "PROCESS_ID_TYPE apid" "Local p1"
c_state "RETURN_CODE_TYPE ret" "Local p1"
c_state "SYSTEM_TIME_TYPE time" "Local p1"
proctype  p1 () provided ( _curSchProc == _pid )
{ CP11:
    atomic {
        TRACE(11);
        A653_GET_MY_ID(&(Pp1->apid),&(Pp1->ret),Pp1->_pid);}
  CP12:
    atomic {
        TRACE(12);
        A653_SET_PRIORITY(Pp1->apid,34,&(Pp1->ret)); }
  CP13:
    atomic {
        TRACE(13);
        A653_SET_PRIORITY(Pp1->apid,34,&(Pp1->ret));}
  CP14:
    atomic {
        TRACE(14);
        A653_SET_PRIORITY(Pp1->apid,34,&(Pp1->ret));}
  CP15:
    atomic {
        TRACE(15);
        A653_SET_PRIORITY(Pp1->apid,34,&(Pp1->ret)); }
  CP16:
    atomic {
        TRACE(16);
        A653_TIMED_WAIT(500,&(Pp1->ret),Pp1->_pid);}
  CP17:
    atomic {
        TRACE(17);
        A653_GET_TIME(&(Pp1->time),&(Pp1->ret));
        c_code{
            printf("Time = %u \n",Pp1->time);
            };    }
  CP18:
    atomic {
        TRACE(18);
        A653_STOP_SELF(Pp1->_pid);}
} }
```

B Test Case Checking SET_PRIORITY

```
//P1
proctype P1 () provided ( _curSchProc == _pid ) {
    ...
}

//Master Test

c_state "RETURN_CODE_TYPE ret" "Local Master_Test"

proctype Master_Test () provided ( _curSchProc == _pid ) {

// Invalid Process Id
    atomic {
      A653_SET_PRIORITY(INVALID_PROCESS_ID, HIGH_PROCESS_PRIORITY, &(PMaster_Test->ret));
    }
// Expected RETURN_CODE == INVALID_PARAM
    atomic {
        c_code{
            if ( PMaster_Test->ret == INVALID_PARAM)
```

```
            {
                printf("T-API-PROC-0340:0010 =PASS\n");
            } else
            {
                printf("T-API-PROC-0340:0010 =FAIL\n");
            }
assert(go);
        }
    }
    atomic {
        A653_STOP_SELF(PMaster_Test->_pid);
    }
}

//Init:

c_code {
    PROCESS_ATTRIBUTE_TYPE  a_att;
    PROCESS_ID_TYPE  a_proc;
    RETURN_CODE_TYPE  a_return;
};
c_track "&a_att" "sizeof(PROCESS_ATTRIBUTE_TYPE)" "Matched"
c_track "&a_proc" "sizeof(PROCESS_ID_TYPE)" "Matched"
c_track "&a_return" "sizeof(RETURN_CODE_TYPE)" "Matched"

init{ atomic {

// Init Model
    c_code {
        MODEL_A653_Init();
    };
// Create & Start Master_Test
    c_code{
        strcpy (a_att.NAME, "Master_Test");
        a_att.STACK_SIZE = 200;
        a_att.BASE_PRIORITY = REGULAR_MASTER_PROCESS_PRIORITY;
        a_att.PERIOD = INFINITE_TIME_VALUE;
        a_att.TIME_CAPACITY= INFINITE_TIME_VALUE;
        a_att.DEADLINE = HARD;
    };
    A653_CREATE_PROCESS(&a_att, &a_proc, &a_return,eso2);
    A653_START(a_proc,&a_return);
// Create & Start P1
    c_code{
        strcpy (a_att.NAME, "P1");
        a_att.STACK_SIZE = 200;
        a_att.BASE_PRIORITY = HIGH_PROCESS_PRIORITY;
        a_att.PERIOD = INFINITE_TIME_VALUE;
        a_att.TIME_CAPACITY= INFINITE_TIME_VALUE;
        a_att.DEADLINE = HARD;
    };

    A653_CREATE_PROCESS(&a_att, &a_proc, &a_return,eso2);
    A653_START(a_proc,&a_return);

// Start Scheduling
    A653_SET_PARTITION_MODE(NORMAL,&a_return);
    run clock();
}; };
```

BEEM: Benchmarks for Explicit Model Checkers

Radek Pelánek*

Department of Information Technologies, Faculty of Informatics
Masaryk University Brno, Czech Republic
{xpelanek}@fi.muni.cz

Abstract. We present BEEM — BEnchmarks for Explicit Model checkers. This benchmark set includes more than 50 parametrized models (300 concrete instances) together with their correctness properties (both safety and liveness). The benchmark set is accompanied by an comprehensive web portal, which provides detailed information about all models. The web portal also includes information about state spaces and facilities for selection of models for experiments.

The address of the web portal is `http://anna.fi.muni.cz/models`.

1 Introduction

The model checking field underwent a rapid development during last years. Several new, sophisticated techniques have been developed, e.g., symbolic methods, bounded model checking, or automatic abstraction refinement. However, for several important application domains we cannot do much better than the basic explicit model checking approach — brute force exhaustive state space search. This technique is used by several of the most well-known model checkers (e.g., Spin, Murphi). The application scope of the explicit technique has been extended significantly by progress in computer speed and algorithmic improvements and many realistic case studies showed practical usability of the method. Even some of the software model checkers (e.g., Java PathFinder, Zing) are based on the explicit search.

There is also a significant body of research work devoted to the improvement of explicit model checking. Unfortunately, many papers fail to convincingly demonstrate the usefulness of newly presented techniques. In order to perform high quality experimental evaluation, researchers need to have access to:

- tool in which they can implement model checking techniques,
- benchmark set of models which can be used for comparisons.

At the moment, there is a large number of model checking tools (see [4]), but the availability of benchmark sets is rather poor. The aim of this work is to contribute to the progress in this direction. We present BEEM — a new benchmark set with a web portal.

* Partially supported by GA ČR grant no. 201/07/P035.

D. Bošnački and S. Edelkamp (Eds.): SPIN 2007, LNCS 4595, pp. 263–267, 2007.

This short paper presents the main rationale and design choices behind BEEM. Detailed documentation is given in a technical report [10], which presents description of the modeling language and used models, functionality and realization of the web portal, and an example of an experimental application over the set.

2 Experimental Work in Model Checking

In order to support the need for benchmarks, we present an evaluation of experiments in model checking papers. We have used a sample of model checking publications; experiments in each of these publications were classified into one of the following five categories:

Q1 Random inputs or few toy models.
Q2 Several toy models (possibly parametrized) or few simple models.
Q3 Several simple models (possibly parametrized) or one large case study.
Q4 An exhaustive study of parametrized simple models or several case studies.
Q5 An exhaustive study with the use of several case studies.

Table 1. presents the quality of experiments in papers from our sample (detailed description of the classification and list of all used papers and their classification is given in [10]). Although the classification is slightly subjective, it is clear from Table 1. that there is nearly no progress in time towards higher quality of used models. This is rather disappointing, because more and more case studies are available. Low experimental standards make it hard to assess newly proposed techniques; the practical impact of many techniques can be quite different from claims made in publications. This obstructs the progress of the research in the field. Clearly, a good benchmark set is missing.

The need for benchmarking, better experiments, and thorough evaluation of tools and algorithms is well recognized, e.g., experimentation is a key part of Hoare's proposal for a "Grand Challenge of Verified Software" [6]. There is also significant interest in benchmarks in the model checking community (see e.g., Corbett [3], Avrunin et al. [5], Atiya et al. [1], Jones et al. [8]). Nevertheless, the progress up to date has been rather slow. The main obstacle in developing

Table 1. Quality of experiments reported in model checking papers. We have used a sample of 80 publications which are concerned with explicit model checking and contain an experimental section (for details see [10]). For each quality category, we report number of published papers in years 1994-2006.

	1994	1995	1996	1997	1998	1999	2000	2001	2002	2003	2004	2005	2006
Q1	-	-	1	1	1	1	1	3	2	4	2	1	1
Q2	-	-	3	3	2	3	3	1	2	2	2	1	-
Q3	-	2	1	3	1	2	2	1	3	2	2	4	1
Q4	1	-	-	-	1	-	1	4	1	1	2	-	2
Q5	-	-	-	1	-	-	-	-	1	-	1	-	-

model checking benchmarks is the absence of a common modeling language — each model checking tool is tailored towards its own modeling language and even verification results over the same example are often incomparable.

Although the development of benchmarks is difficult and the model checking community will probably never have a universal benchmark set, we should try to build benchmarks as applicable as possible and steadily improve our experimental analysis. This is the goal of this work.

3 BEEM

Modeling Language. Models are implemented in a *low-level modeling language* based on communicating extended finite state machines (DVE language, see [10] for syntax and semantics). The adoption of a low-level language makes the manual specification of models hard, but it has several advantages. The language has a simple and straightforward semantics; it is not difficult to write own parser and state generator. Models can be automatically translated into other modeling languages — at the moment, the benchmark set includes also *Promela* models which were automatically generated from DVE sources.

Models and Properties. Most of the models are *well-known* examples and case studies. Models span several *different application areas* (e.g., mutual exclusion algorithms, communication protocols, controllers, leader election algorithms, planning and scheduling, puzzles). In order to make the set organized, models are *classified* into different types and categories. The benchmark set is *large* and still growing (at the moment it contains 57 parametrized models with 300 specified instances). *Source codes* of all models are publicly available. Models are briefly described and include *pointers to sources* (e.g., paper describing the case study), i.e., BEEMalso serves as an information portal.

The benchmark set includes also *correctness properties* of models. Safety properties are expressed as reachability of a predicate, liveness properties are expressed in Linear temporal logic. Since an important part of model checking is error detection, the benchmark set includes also *models with errors* (presence of an error is a parameter of a model).

Tool Support. The modeling language is supported by an *extensible model checking environment* — The Distributed Verification Environment (DiVinE) [2]. DiVinE is both a model checking tool and a open and extensible library for a development of model checking algorithms. Researchers can use this extensible environment to implement their own algorithms, easily perform experiments over the benchmark set, and directly compare with other algorithms in DiVinE. Promela models can be used for comparison with the well-known model checker Spin [7].

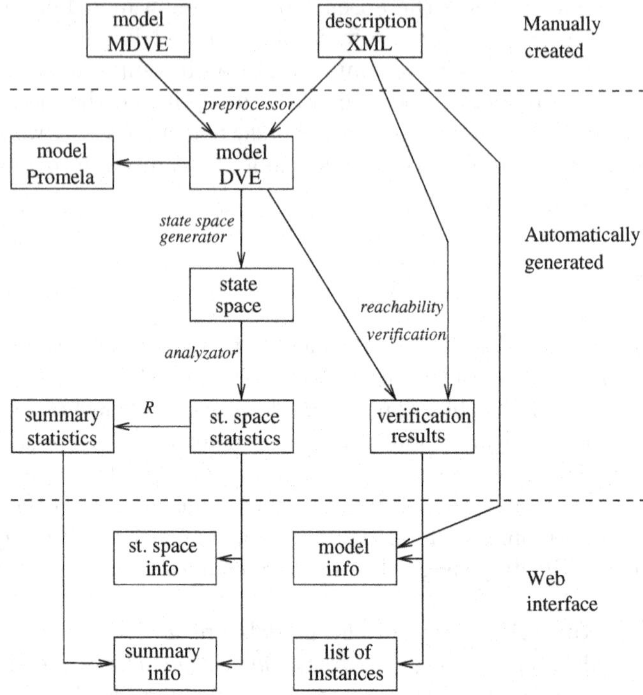

Fig. 1. Overview of the realization of the web portal. The user provides two files: parametrized model and its description. All other information is automatically generated.

Web Portal. The benchmark set is accompanied by an comprehensive web portal, accessible at `http://anna.fi.muni.cz/models`, which *facilitates the experimental work.* The web provides (see Fig 1. for overview of realization):

- presentation of all information about models, their parameters, and correctness properties,
- detailed information about properties of state spaces of models [9] including summary information,
- verification results,
- web form for selection of suitable model instances according to a given criteria,
- instance generator, which can generate both DVE models and Promela models for given parameter values.

All data can be downloaded. Since model descriptions are systematic (XML file), it is easy to write own scripts for manipulation with models and automation of experiments.

4 Summary

The aim of this paper is not to present "the ultimate benchmark set" but rather:

- to provide a ready-made set for those who want to compare different model checking techniques and to facilitate experimental research,
- to encourage higher standards in model checking experiments,
- to stimulate the discussion about benchmarks in the model checking community.

Detailed description of the benchmarks set, example of an experimental application, and direction for the future work can be found in the technical report [10].

Acknowledgement. I thank Pavel Krčál and to members of the DiVinE group, particularly Ivana Černá, Pavel Šimeček and Jiří Barnat, for collaboration, discussions, and feedback.

References

1. Atiya, D.A., Catano, N., Lüettgen, G.: Towards a benchmark for model checkers of asynchronous concurrent systems. In: Fifth International Workshop on Automated Verification of Critical Systems: AVOCs, University of Warwick, United Kingdom (September 12–13, 2005)
2. Barnat, J., Brim, L., Černá, I., Moravec, P., Rockai, P., Šimeček, P.: Divine - a tool for distributed verification. In: Ball, T., Jones, R.B. (eds.) CAV 2006. LNCS, vol. 4144, pp. 278–281. Springer, Heidelberg (2006), `http://anna.fi.muni.cz/divine`
3. Corbett, J.C.: Evaluating deadlock detection methods for concurrent software. IEEE Trans. Softw. Eng. 22(3), 161–180 (1996)
4. Crhová, J., Krčál, P., Strejček, J., Šafránek, D., Šimeček, P.: Yahoda: the database of verification tools. In: Proc. of TOOLSDAY affiliated to CONCUR 2002, FI MU report series (2002) Accessible at `http://anna.fi.muni.cz/yahoda/`
5. Dwyer, M.B., Avrunin, G.S., Corbett, J.C.: Benchmarking finite-state verifiers. International Journal on Software Tools for Technology Transfer (STTT) 2(4), 317–320 (2000)
6. Hoare, T.: The ideal of verified software. In: Ball, T., Jones, R.B. (eds.) CAV 2006. LNCS, vol. 4144, pp. 5–16. Springer, Heidelberg (2006)
7. Holzmann, G.J.: The Spin Model Checker, Primer and Reference Manual. Addison-Wesley, Reading, Massachusetts (2003)
8. Jones, M., Mercer, E., Bao, T., Kumar, R., Lamborn, P.: Benchmarking explicit state parallel model checkers. In: Proc. of Workshop on Parallel and Distributed Model Checking (PDMC'03). ENTCS, vol. 89, Elsevier, Amsterdam (2003)
9. Pelánek, R.: Typical structural properties of state spaces. In: Graf, S., Mounier, L. (eds.) Proc. of SPIN Workshop. LNCS, vol. 2989, pp. 5–22. Springer, Heidelberg (2004)
10. Pelánek, R.: Web portal for benchmarking explicit model checkers. Technical Report FIMU-RS-2006-03, Masaryk University Brno (2006)

C.OPEN and ANNOTATOR: Tools for On-the-Fly Model Checking C Programs*

María del Mar Gallardo[1], Christophe Joubert[2], Pedro Merino[1], and David Sanán[1]

[1] University of Málaga, Campus de Teatinos s/n, 29071, Málaga, Spain
{gallardo,pedro,sanan}@lcc.uma.es
[2] Technical University of Valencia, Camino de Vera s/n, 46022, Valencia, Spain
joubert@dsic.upv.es

Abstract. This paper describes a set of verification components that open the way to perform on-the-fly software model checking with the CADP toolbox, originally designed for verifying the functional correctness of LOTOS specifications. Two new tools (named C.OPEN and ANNOTATOR) have been added to the toolbox. The approach taken fits well within the existing architecture of CADP which doesn't need to be altered to enable C program verification.

1 Introduction

The software model checking problem consists in verifying that a program, *i.e.* an infinite state system described in a high-level language, does not contain errors, such as improper memory access, misuse of system interfaces, or violation of (temporal logic) properties. The verification process is automatic, and the wrong conception of the program is eventually illustrated by means of potential offending behaviors of the system (*e.g.*, counter examples). Traditionally, programs are first analysed to statically remove parts that do not affect the property of interest, using light-weight pre-processing technique such as *program slicing.* The reduced model is then abstracted using *predicate abstraction* and *localization* techniques. Finally, the resulting finite state system is processed by SAT-based, BDD-based or explicit state model checkers.

Existing software model checkers, like SLAM [1] and BLAST [2], are either domain specific (*e.g.*, verification of drivers), language dependent, or based on dedicated algorithms and tools. This paper presents an analysis engine that finds application programming interface (API) usage errors in C programs, similarly to BLAST and SLAM, but rather focusing on a general purpose model checking framework. We describe a set of components, namely C.OPEN and ANNOTATOR, that enable the explicit state verification of C programs by means of the last stable CADP 2006 "Edinburgh" release. The CADP toolbox[1] [3] is a complex

* This work has been supported by the Spanish MEC under grant TIN2004-7943-C04.

[1] CADP web site: "http://www.inrialpes.fr/vasy/cadp".

D. Bošnački and S. Edelkamp (Eds.): SPIN 2007, LNCS 4595, pp. 268–273, 2007.

software suite integrating numerous verification tools. CADP supports the process algebra LOTOS for specification, and offers various tools for simulation and formal verification, including equivalence checkers (bisimulations) and model checkers (temporal logics and modal μ-calculus). The toolbox is designed as an open platform for the integration of other specification, verification and analysis techniques. This is realized by means of APIs which on different levels provide means to extend or exploit the functionalities of the toolbox. These APIs have been used by others to link CADP to other specification languages as well as other verification/testing tools. Here we describe how these APIs have been used by C.OPEN to support C program transformation and abstraction based on XML intermediate representation, and by ANNOTATOR to support on-the-fly data flow analysis and program slicing, namely *influence analysis*, of implicit control flow graphs using *boolean equation systems* (BESs). Our efforts have been driven by the intention to avoid changes to the existing components as much as possible, while providing a sound and efficient framework for C program model checking.

Originality. Our approach differs from previous works, like BLAST and SLAM, in several ways:

1. in the first attempt to connect to the CADP toolbox a model generator (C.OPEN) that automatically extracts implicit *labeled transition systems* (LTSs) from programs written in C programming language, and a static analyzer (ANNOTATOR) that works on implicit abstracted *control flow graphs* (CFGs) described as LTSs,
2. in our emphasis on the verification of distributed protocols (*e.g.*, the Peterson's mutual exclusion (PME) protocol between two processes), using well-specified APIs [4], described as multiple (or multi-instantiated) concurrent independent C programs, rather than on sequential (SLAM) or multi-threaded programs (ongoing work of BLAST),
3. in our use of the OPEN/CÆSAR modular architecture and XML, BES and LTS technologies to represent the state-space and verification problem efficiently and to facilitate the connection to other programming languages, like Promela, and
4. in the way we concentrated this research work on the compiler side, similarly to BANDERA and BOGOR [5] model checking frameworks, but using well-established verification tools of the CADP toolbox as back-end.

2 Software Architecture

The toolset encompasses two sorts of tools (see Figure 1) to verify C programs generated via CADP. (i) The C.OPEN tool provides different means to distill an implicit LTS from a C program. (ii) The static analyser ANNOTATOR enables on-the-fly data flow and influence analysis of implicit LTSs describing abstract CFGs.

Distilling implicit LTSs from a C program. C.OPEN [6] is an addon component for CADP to support C program input to the OPEN/CÆSAR environment [7], though we state that the XML API, called PIXL [8], on which the tool is based, is general enough to attach the C program abstraction process to other verification toolboxes, such as SPIN, via Promela specifications instead of implicit LTSs [4]. The idea that OPEN/CÆSAR environment can be connected to a C compiler and that existing CADP tools can thereby be extended to this new class of specifications is an important step towards re-using well-established verification toolboxes. C.OPEN (400 lines of Shell script) takes as inputs a system

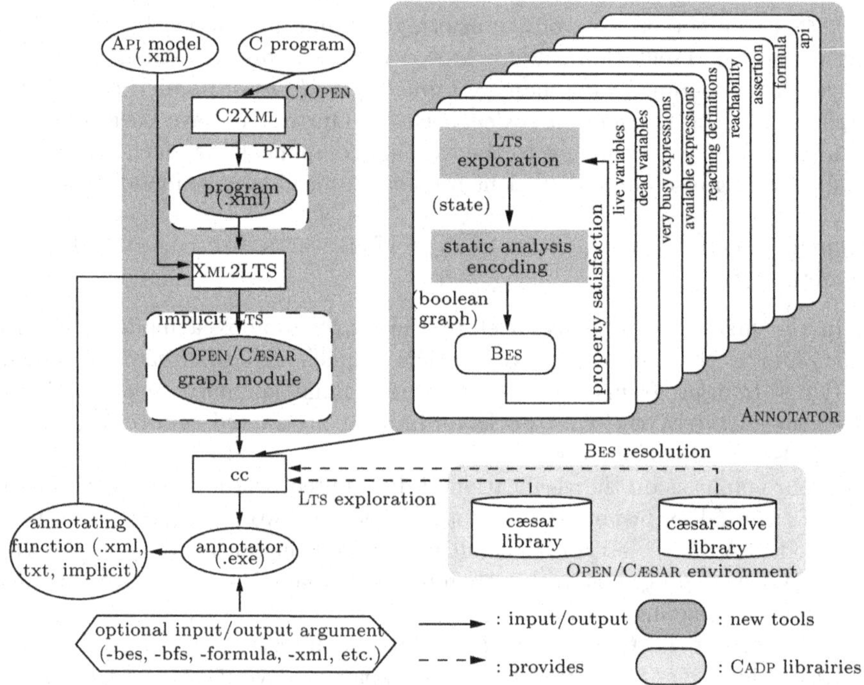

Fig. 1. C.OPEN and ANNOTATOR tools

described by a set of C programs, an operating system API's model represented in XML, and an OPEN/CÆSAR application (*e.g.*, ANNOTATOR). As an output, it generates an executable application (*e.g.*, annotator.exe) by performing the required sequence of tool invocations: 1) a tool, called C2XML (2 000 lines of JAVA), is used with JAVACC and a C grammar (1 000 lines of JAVA), to translate C programs into PIXL compliant XML models; 2) another tool, called XML2LTS (4 500 lines of JAVA), then slices the program models with respect to system APIs to be preserved [9] and it constructs the OPEN/CÆSAR graph module describing the implicit program LTS; 3) finally, the C compiler *cc* is called.

C.OPEN allows to construct abstracted state spaces on-the-fly, and only to the required precision (*w.r.t.* a specific API). It currently offers the possibility to generate either CFG or explicit state space of a program as an implicit LTS.

Analysing implicit CFGs. ANNOTATOR implements standard data flow analysis algorithms on a CFG, by using boolean equation systems (BESs) [10,11]. It also computes various influence analyses [12], generally used for compacting the program state representation, by detecting the relevant program variables in each control point, for a property of interest.

Our static analyser takes as inputs a static analysis to carry out and an LTS describing the CFG of a program, in which instructions are abstracted to the strict necessary information (*i.e.*, modified and defined variables, used expressions, and instruction type). This LTS is represented implicitly by its successor function as an OPEN/CÆSAR program provided by compliant compilers, such as C.OPEN, but existing CADP compilers, such as CÆSAR, could be directly extended to provide such CFGs [13].

ANNOTATOR (6 000 lines of C code) consists of several modules, each one containing the BES translation for a particular static analysis (live variables, very busy expressions, available expressions, reaching definitions, reachability, assertion control, formula and API preservation influence analyses). BESs are represented implicitly by their successor function, in the same way as LTSs in OPEN/CÆSAR. They are handled internally by the CÆSAR_SOLVE [14] library, which offers several on-the-fly resolution algorithms, based on different search strategies (*e.g.*, breadth-first). Dependent on the option selected by the user, the analysis result is written to an XML or textual file. These formats allow post-processing of computed analyses, by directly conveying the result as input to compilers reading these formats, such as C.OPEN, allowing further compilation optimizations.

Availability. The proposed tools are publicly available through the following web pages `http://www.lcc.uma.es/gisum/tools/smc`. C.OPEN and ANNOTATOR, being part of the database of research tools developed using CADP, are also referenced by the CADP web site. Both new tools are rather small, robust and mature (in operation for about a year) and detailed manual pages are provided, as well as more than 25 program examples and step-by-step small case studies. More recently [15], we also defined web services that allow the remote use of C.OPEN and ANNOTATOR, as well as most of CADP verification tools, through the FMICS-jETI platform [16] from a jABC client [17].

Applicability. Concerning applicability, C.OPEN compiles concurrent C programs into the OPEN/CÆSAR intermediate format (*i.e.*, implicit labeled transition system (LTS)), to which efficient CADP model checkers, such as EVALUATOR (evaluation of regular alternation-free μ-calculus formulas) and BISIMULATOR (equivalence checking), are connected. Hence, CTL, ACTL, PDL, PDL-Δ and regular alternation-free μ-calculus properties can be verified on our C input programs. In the PME demonstration, we successfully checked respectively one safety, liveness and fairness property on the C implementation of the protocol and we also reduced the explicit-state space size by 20% using API influence analysis results computed by the ANNOTATOR tool. Furthermore, all analyses that are available in the CADP toolbox can be directly used on our C input programs. Unfortunately, we could not compare our verification framework with well-established software model checkers, like BLAST or SLAM, since they are not dealing with distributed protocols with well-defined APIs yet.

Scalability. ANNOTATOR has been successfully experimented on very large CFGS, extracted from the VLTS benchmark[2], with size up to 10^6 program counters and instructions. Moreover, C.OPEN and ANNOTATOR allow several levels of abstraction of the program instructions present in the LTS model, giving the possibility to verify further properties or to achieve further reductions on the program model.

3 Conclusion and Future Work

The development of an on-the-fly software model checker "from scratch" is a complex and costly task. The open modular architecture adopted for C.OPEN and ANNOTATOR aims at making this process easier, by using the XML intermediate representation, the well-established verification framework of BESS, together with the generic libraries for LTS exploration and BES resolution provided by CADP. For instance, this tool architecture reduces the effort of implementing a new static analysis to its strict minimum: encoding the mathematical definition of the analysis as a BES, and interpreting the result. We plan to continue our work by extending ANNOTATOR with other static analyses (e.g., reset variables analysis [13]) and by interconnecting the two new CADP components with tools extending SPIN, such as SOCKETMC [4] and αSPIN [18].

References

1. Ball, T., Rajamani, S.K.: The slam toolkit. In: Berry, G., Comon, H., Finkel, A. (eds.) CAV 2001. LNCS, vol. 2102, pp. 260–264. Springer, Heidelberg (2001)
2. Beyer, D., Henzinger, T.A., Théoduloz, G.: Lazy shape analysis. In: Ball, T., Jones, R.B. (eds.) CAV 2006. LNCS, vol. 4144, pp. 532–546. Springer, Heidelberg (2006)
3. Garavel, H., Lang, F., Mateescu, R.: An overview of CADP 2001. European Association for Software Science and Technology (EASST) Newsletter 4 (2002) 13–24 Also available as INRIA Technical Report RT-0254 (December 2001)
4. Camara, P., Gallardo, M., Merino, P., Sanán, D.: Model checking software with well-defined apis: the socket case. In: Gnesi, S., Margaria, T., Massink, M. (eds.) Proceedings of the 10th International Workshop on Formal Methods for Industrial Critical Systems FMICS'2005, Lisbon, Portugal, ACM-SIGSOFT, pp. 17–26 (2005)
5. Robby, Rodríguez, E., Dwyer, M.B., Hatcliff, J.: Checking JML specifications using an extensible software model checking framework. Springer International Journal on Software Tools for Technology Transfer (STTT) 8, 280–299 (2006)
6. Gallardo, M., Merino, P., Sanán, D.: Towards model checking c code with open/cæsar. In: Barjis, J., Ultes-Nitsche, U., Augusto, J.C. (eds.) Proceedings of the 4th International Workshop on Modelling, Simulation, Verification and Validation of Enterprise Information Systems MSVVEIS 2006, Paphos, Cyprus, pp. 198–201, Insticc Press (2006)

[2] VLTS web site:
http://www.inrialpes.fr/vasy/cadp/resources/benchmark_bcg.html

7. Garavel, H.: Open/cæsar: An open software architecture for verification, simulation, and testing. In: Steffen, B. (ed.) ETAPS 1998 and TACAS 1998. LNCS, vol. 1384, pp. 68–84. Springer, Heidelberg (1998)
8. Gallardo, M., Martínez, J., Merino, P.: Nuñez, P., Pimentel, E.: Pixl: Applying xml standards to support the integration of analysis tools for protocols. Science of Computer Programming (2006)
9. Gallardo, M., Joubert, C., Merino, P., Sanán, D.: On-the-fly API influence analysis of software. In: Merino, P., Bakkali, M. (eds.) Proceedings of the 2nd International Conference on Science and Technology JICT'07, Málaga, Spain, Spicum (2007)
10. Gallardo, M., Joubert, C., Merino, P.: On-the-fly data flow analysis based on verification technology. In: Drechsler, R., Glesner, S., Knoop, J. (eds.) Proceedings of the 6th International Workshop on Compiler Optimization meets Compiler Verification COCV'2007, Braga, Portugal. Electronic Notes in Theoretical Computer Science, Elsevier, Amsterdam (to appear)
11. Gallardo, M., Joubert, C., Merino, P.: Implementing influence analysis using parameterised boolean equation systems. In: Proceedings of the 2nd International Symposium on Leveraging Applications of Formal Methods, Verification and Validation ISOLA'06, Paphos, Cyprus, 2006, IEEE Computer Society Press, Los Alamitos (To appear)
12. Cámara, P., Gallardo, M., Merino, P.: Abstract matching for software model checking. In: Valmari, A. (ed.) Model Checking Software. LNCS, vol. 3925, pp. 182–200. Springer, Heidelberg (2006)
13. Garavel, H., Serwe, W.: State space reduction for process algebra specifications. Theoretical Computer Science 351(2), 131–145 (2006)
14. Mateescu, R.: Caesar_solve: A generic library for on-the-fly resolution of alternation-free boolean equation systems. Springer International Journal on Software Tools for Technology Transfer (STTT) 8, 37–56 (2006)
15. Gallardo, M., Joubert, C., Merino, P., Sanán, D.: On-the-fly model checking for C programs with extended CADP in FMICS-jETI. In: Proceedings of the 12th IEEE International Conference on Engineering of Complex Computer Systems ICECCS'07, Auckland, New Zealand, IEEE Computer Society Press, Los Alamitos (to appear)
16. Margaria, T., Steffen, B.: Advances in the FMICS-jETI platform for program verification. In: Proceedings of the 12th IEEE International Conference on Engineering of Complex Computer Systems ICECCS'07, Auckland, New Zealand, IEEE Computer Society Press, Los Alamitos (to appear)
17. Margaria, T., Nagel, R., Steffen, B.: Remote integration and coordination of verification tools in jETI. In: Proceedings of the 12th IEEE International Conference on the Engineering of Computer-Based Systems ECBS'05, Greenbelt, MD, USA, pp. 431–436. IEEE Computer Society Press, Los Alamitos (2005)
18. Gallardo, M., Martinez, J., Merino, P., Pimentel, E.: αspin: A tool for abstraction in model checking. Software Tools for Technology Transfer 5(2-3), 165–184 (2004)

ACSAR: Software Model Checking with Transfinite Refinement

Mohamed Nassim Seghir and Andreas Podelski

Universität Freiburg, Georges-Köhler-Allee 52, 79110 Freiburg, Germany

1 Introduction

ACSAR (Automatic Checker of Safety properties based on Abstraction Refinement) is a software model checker for C programs in the spirit of Blast [6], F-Soft [7], Magic [5] and Slam [1]. It is based on the counterexample-guided abstraction refinement (CEGAR) paradigm. Its specificity lies in the way it overcomes a problem common to all tools based on this paradigm. The problem arises from creating more and more spurious counterexamples by unfolding the same (`while`- or `for`-) loop over and over again; this leads to an infinite or at least too large sequence of refinement steps. The idea behind ACSAR is to abstract not just states but also the state changes induced by structured program statements, including for- and while-statements. The use of the new abstraction allows one to shortcut such a "transfinite" sequence of refinement steps.

The divergence of the abstraction refinement loop is not just a theoretical problem but one that hits us in our practical use of software model checker. ACSAR is integrated in a higher order theorem prover, namely Isabelle [3]. It is called, from within Isabelle, for discharging automatically generated verification obligations. Thus, another specificity of ACSAR as a software model checker lies in the way that it is used. We report on our experience of using ACSAR at the end of the paper.

2 A Motivating Example

Let us illustrate the need of abstracting loops through the example in Figure 1(a). This example is taken from the list of benchmarks that were used by McMillan and Jhala [8]. It represents the concatenation of two strings. The key word *assume* does not exist in the C language but it is used for the model checker to express additional assumptions.

A classical refinement generates predicates $i \geq 200, j < 100, i{+}1 \geq 200, j{+}1 < 100, i+2 \geq 200, j+2 < 100 \ldots i+99 \geq 200, j+99 < 100$. The loop is unrolled as many times as the number of loop iterations in a real execution. Moreover, if we want to perform a generic verification for arbitrary string length, by substituting *size* for 100 in line 12 and 21, and $size * 2$ for 200 in line 25, the refinement process completely diverges. The problem is inherent to the CEGAR scheme in its present form (based on state abstraction) where the loop (15, 16, 17, 18, 19, 15) is unfolded over and over again. In this case, neither the interpolation approach nor the split prover method seem to help [8].

D. Bošnački and S. Edelkamp (Eds.): SPIN 2007, LNCS 4595, pp. 274–278, 2007.

```
1  main(){
2
3    char x[101], y[101], z[201];
4    int i,j,k;
5
6    i = 0;
7    while(x[i] != 0){
8      z[i] = x[i];
9      i++;
10   }
11   /* length of x is less than 100 */
12   assume(i < 100);
13
14   j = 0;
15   while(y[j] != 0){
16     z[i] = y[j];
17     i++;
18     j++;
19   }
20   /* length of y is less than 100 */
21   assume(j < 100);
22
23   z[j] = 0;
24   /* prove we don't overflow z */
25   if(i >= 200)
26     {ERROR: goto ERROR;}
27 }
```

(a)

```
main(){

  char x[101], y[101], z[201];
  int i,j,k;

  i = 0;
  while(x[i] != 0){
    z[i] = x[i];
    i++;
  }
  /* length of x is less than 100 */
  assume(i < 100);

  j = 0;
  if(*){
    assume((j_next - j)==(i_next - i));
    i = i_next;
    j = j_next;
  }
  /* length of y is less than 100 */
  assume(j < 100);

  z[j] = 0;
  /* prove we don't overflow z */
  if(i >= 200)
    {ERROR: goto ERROR;}
}
```

(b)

Fig. 1. Example in C code before and after the abstraction

3 Loop Abstraction Approach

As alternative to the iterative unfolding of loops, ACSAR approximates state changes induced by the execution of the loop. The idea of abstracting transitions was previously used to prove the termination of programs [2]. Our use of transition abstraction is in the context of checking safety properties.

3.1 How Does ACSAR Abstract Loops?

ACSAR extracts the list of transition constraints corresponding to the program. Below are the transition constraints corresponding to the loop (15, 16, 17, 18, 19, 15) from the example in Figure 1(a).

$$pc = 15 \wedge y[j] \neq 0 \wedge z'[i] = y[j] \wedge i' = i + 1 \wedge j' = j + 1 \wedge pc' = 15 \quad (1)$$

$$pc = 15 \wedge y[j] = 0 \wedge pc' = 21 \quad (2)$$

A transition constraint is a conjunction of atomic formulas, it expresses a binary relation between a starting state and an arrival state of the program. In atomic formulas, variables marked with primes are evaluated in the arrival state of the transition, otherwise they are evaluated in the starting state. The special variable pc represents the program counter. When an atomic formula does not contain any variable marked with a prime it is called a *guard*. An atomic formula that contains variables with primes is called an *update*. If a variable does not appear marked with a prime in any atomic formula, then it means implicitly that its value does not change when the transition is performed.

The next step is the abstraction phase. In this phase non relevant guards are removed and constraints expressing relations between old and new values of the variables are extracted. For example: the expression $(i' - i) = (j' - j)$ is automatically extracted by ACSAR as both variables i and j increase by the same constant number within the loop. Transition constraints (1) and (2) are replaced by their abstractions (1') resp. (2'). To the difference of transition (1) its abstraction (1') does not loop but it approximates the effect of the loop over the program variables. With this abstraction ACSAR succeeds to prove that the program is safe.

$$pc = 15 \wedge i' - i = j' - j \wedge pc' = 21 \qquad (1')$$
$$pc = 15 \wedge pc' = 21 \qquad (2')$$

Question: How can one express the above abstraction of a loop in terms of a source-to-source transformation on the C program? The problem is that a transition constraint expresses a constraint on the after-value of a transition, but a program statement defines the after-value by the value of an expression. As often, the solution is very simple. We write the transition constraint as a program expression (using an *uninitialized* auxiliary variable `x_next` for the primed version of the variable `x`) and use the program expression in an `assume` statement and then add assignment statements of the form `x = x_next`. See Figure 1(b). The loop (15, 16, 17, 18, 19, 15) is replaced by a nondeterministic 'if' block (the 'nondeterministic' expression is denoted `*`).

What do we gain with loop abstraction? The benefit is two fold:

- We obtain better performance in terms of time and space. Table 1 illustrates a comparison between the loop abstraction approach and a simple approach based on the weakest precondition for refinement. We apply both approaches on different instances of the example of figure 1(a). Column *size* contains different values of the size of input array variables `x` and `y`. Implicitly, the size of `z` is $2 * size$. Using the simple approach, we clearly notice a nonlinear increase of the verification time in function of instance size. With the loop abstraction approach, the execution time is the same and relatively small for all the instances.
- Using the loop abstraction approach, we can verify a generic version (section 2) of the previous example. The abstract transition represents a *parameterization* of all paths corresponding to loop unfolding of different instances of the example program.

Table 1. Performance comparison between the loop abstraction approach and the simple approach

instance	size	time		number of states	
		simple	loop abstraction	simple	loop abstraction
1	10	1.19	0.29	12	5
2	20	2.77	/	22	/
3	50	33.59	/	52	/
4	75	127.72	/	77	/
5	100	336.56	/	102	/

4 ACSAR in Short

ACSAR has the usual ingredients of a software model checker. It receives as input a C file consisting of functions and data structures. Location labels are used to specify a monitor for the property that we want to check. A global control-flow graph is obtained by inlining function bodies into the corresponding call sites. ACSAR translates the program into a set of transition constraints, its canonical representation. The main kernel of ACSAR is composed of two parts: the search engine that explores the state space (building the abstraction on the fly) and the counter example analyzer which increases the precision of the search engine when the abstraction is too coarse. For building the abstraction and, respectively, for checking consistency of transitions, both parts interact with a parameterized constraint solver such as Simplify [4]. ACSAR builds the abstraction of loops on demand, namely when the counter example analyzer has detected that a loop has been unfolded twice. The threshold for the number of unfoldings is a parameter which, for now, is set to two.

5 Experimental Evaluation

ACSAR is used in the Verisoft project[1] as a back-end for the higher order interactive theorem prover Isabelle [3]. Isabelle has a Hoare logic module for the specification and verification of programs [10]. For a Hoare triple $P\ c\ Q$ Isabelle performs the proof of the postcondition Q in three steps: the proof that Q holds, the proof that the program c terminates and the proof that no run time errors occur during the execution of c under the precondition P. For this last step Isabelle generates proof obligations expressing necessary conditions for a safe execution of any command in the program c. For example, given the integer variable x and the command $x := x + 1$, Isabelle generates the proof obligation $MINint \leq x \leq MAXint$. The task of verifying such a proof obligation is automatically delegated to ACSAR. The overall goal is to minimize the 'manual' interaction between the verification engineer and Isabelle. In the (ongoing) interactive verification effort for the Vamos micro-kernel (which is being developed

[1] http://www.verisoft.de

within the Verisoft project), ACSAR automatically discharges about 75% of the (automatically generated) verification obligations (the remaining 25% concern properties that require variable quantification).

Outlook: We are planning to carry over methods for the generation of linear invariants [9] to our approach for abstracting loops. We want also to handle simple array assertions that involve quantifiers; e.g., $\forall i \ (0 \leq i < n) \Rightarrow a[i] = 0$.

References

1. Ball, T., Rajamani, S.K.: The Slam project: debugging system software via static analysis. In: POPL, pp. 1–3 (2002)
2. Cook, B., Podelski, A., Rybalchenko, A.: Abstraction refinement for termination. In: Hankin, C., Siveroni, I. (eds.) SAS 2005. LNCS, vol. 3672, Springer, Heidelberg (2005)
3. Daum, M., Maus, S., Schirmer, N., Nassim Seghir, M.: Integration of a software model checker into Isabelle. In: LPAR, pp. 381–395 (2005)
4. Detlefs, D., Nelson, G., Saxe, J.B.: Simplify: A theorem prover for program checking. Technical Report HPL-2003-148, HP Lab (2003)
5. Chaki, S., et al.: Modular verification of software components in C. In: ICSE, pp. 385–395 (2003)
6. Thomas, A.: Henzinger: Software verification with BLAST. In: Ball, T., Rajamani, S.K. (eds.) Model Checking Software. LNCS, vol. 2648, pp. 235–239. Springer, Heidelberg (2003)
7. Ivancic, F., Shlyakhter, I., Gupta, A., Ganaim, M.K.: Model checking C programs using F-soft. In: ICCD, pp. 297–308 (2005)
8. Jhala, R., McMillan, K.L.: A practical and complete approach to predicate refinement. In: Hermanns, H., Palsberg, J. (eds.) TACAS 2006 and ETAPS 2006. LNCS, vol. 3920, Springer, Heidelberg (2006)
9. Karr, M.: Affine relationships among variables of a program. Acta Inf. 6, 133–151 (1976)
10. Schirmer, N.: A verification environment for sequential imperative programs in Isabelle/HOL. In: Baader, F., Voronkov, A. (eds.) LPAR 2004. LNCS (LNAI), vol. 3452, Springer, Heidelberg (2004)

Instrumenting C Programs with Nested Word Monitors

Swarat Chaudhuri and Rajeev Alur

University of Pennsylvania

1 Introduction

In classical automata-theoretic model checking of safety properties [6], a system model generates a language L of words modeling system executions, and verification involves checking if $L \cap L' = \emptyset$, L' being the language of words deemed "unsafe" by the specification. This view is also used in recent program analyzers like BLAST [5] and SLAM [2], where a specification is a word automaton (or monitor) with finite-state control-flow that accepts all "unsafe" program executions. Typical analysis constructs the "product" of a program and a monitor, in effect *instrumenting* the program with extra commands and assertions, so that the input program fails its specification if and only if the product program fails an assertion. The latter is then checked for possible assertion failures. Monitors also find use in testing and runtime verification, where we try finding assertion violations in the product program at runtime.

One shortcoming of these notations is expressiveness. As finite automata cannot argue about the nested structure of procedure calls and returns in programs, these languages cannot state pre/post-conditions arising in specification languages like JML [4]: "if a file is open right before a call, then it is open when the procedure returns." Nor can they reason about procedural contexts and express properties like: "if a file is opened, it must be closed before control exits the present context." Another issue is that these notations cannot reason modularly about programs. If programs are structured, why not specifications as well?

These problems are overcome if a program execution is modeled by a *nested word* [1] rather than a word. A nested word is obtained by adding, to a word modeling an execution, a set of nested *jump-edges* that connect call sites to their matching returns. A *nested word automaton* processing a nested word reads the symbols in the underlying word just like a word automaton. However, transitions here also take jump-edges into account: while transitioning to a return position (a point in the word with an incoming jump-edge), a nested word automaton can consult its state at the source of the jump-edge, i.e., the call matching the return. Intuitively, the monitor tracks the program's *global control flow* by following the underlying word, and its *local control flow* by following the jump-edges.

This paper presents a specification language—called PAL—based on nested word automata, and a tool to instrument C code using it. This language extends the BLAST specification language [3], and while its richer foundations lets it state context-sensitive properties, it has syntax close to BLAST's and allows easy instrumentation. Monitors in PAL are independent of the programs they are

D. Bošnački and S. Edelkamp (Eds.): SPIN 2007, LNCS 4595, pp. 279–283, 2007.

used to instrument, and work irrespective of whether recursion is present. While they are theoretically only as expressive as monitors in BLAST in the absence of recursion, they are more modular, succinct and comprehensible even in this case. We believe, therefore, that these monitors present an example of *structured specifications*, suitable for structured programs. Finally, while our monitors extend the specification format of a model checker, their use is not limited to static checking. Once a program has been instrumented with a monitor, it can be used for testing or run-time verification as well as static analysis or model checking.

2 Language Description

```
global int infoo = 0;
global int open = 0;
global FILE * stream;

event {  /* event 1 */
 pattern {
   $1=fopen($2,$?);}
 guard { strcmp($2,''dat'')
   ||(open==0 && infoo==1)}
 action {
   if (!strcmp($2,''dat'')){
     open = 1;
     stream = $1;}}
}

event {  /* event 2 */
  pattern { fclose ($1); }
  action { if ($1 == stream)
             open = 0; }}

event {  /* event 3 */
  pattern { $? = foo ($?); }
  local int stored;
  before {
    action { stored = infoo;
             infoo = 1; }}
  after {
    guard { open == 0 }
    action {
      infoo = stored; }}
}
```

Fig. 1. A PAL specification

We present the PAL language via an example. Consider a C program that opens or closes files via calls to `fopen` and `fclose`, and the following requirement, applying to a procedure `foo`: "a secret file `dat` is not opened outside the scope of a file-handling routine `foo`. If `foo`, or a procedure called transitively from it, opens a stream for `dat`, then: (1) no new stream for `dat` is opened without closing the current stream, and (2) any open stream for this file must be closed by the time the top-level call to `foo` returns." Such a discipline follows programmer intuition and prevents security flaws where the main context, unaware that `foo` has left open a sensitive stream, invokes an untrusted program that can now do I/O on the "leaked" stream (for a real instance of this, see Sec. 3).

A PAL monitor for this requirement is shown in Fig. 1. The states of the monitor are encoded by a set of *monitor variables*, and its transitions by a set of `event{...}` blocks. Some monitor variables are *global* and are declared using the keyword `global` — intuitively, global monitor variables may be tested or updated by any event. In addition, each event includes an optional set of *local monitor variables*, declared using the keyword `local`, whose scope is restricted to the current event.

Events are fired by matching *patterns* on statements in the analyzed program. A pattern, specified in a `pattern{...}` block, is an assignment or procedure call with possible "pattern variables" ($?, $1, $2, etc.). During matching, the variables \$1, \$2, etc. match arbitrary C expressions and the variable \$? serves as a wildcard— e.g., the pattern in event 1 matches all calls to `fopen`. For each statement matching the pattern[1] specified in the i-th event, the monitor sets up a precondition and a postcondition using the code in the blocks `before{...}` and `after{...}` in this event. The precondition (similarly, postcondition) checks whether an optional guard—a C expression over monitor and pattern variables, inside a `guard{...}` block—is satisfied by the monitor state right before (after) this statement. If the guard is not satisfied, an assertion violation is reported. Otherwise, the state of the monitor is updated by executing the C code contained within an optional `action{...}` block. This code is allowed to read pattern variables, and read or update monitor variables. For succinctness, we allow guards and actions to be defined outside `before` or `after` blocks (event 1 or 2)—in this case they are assumed to define preconditions.

```
int infoo = 0;
int open = 0;
FILE * stream;

bar() {
  int stored;
  ...
  stored = infoo;
  infoo = 1;
  x = foo(y);
  if (open == 0)
     infoo = stored;
  else ERROR;
  ...
}
```

Fig. 2. Instrumenting using event 3

During instrumentation, code blocks implementing an event's precondition and postcondition are respectively injected before and after statements matching its pattern. Consider a call `x = foo(y)` in a procedure `bar` in a program; on instrumentation using the monitor in Fig. 1, this line in replaced by the chunk of code in Fig. 2. Declarations of the monitor variables are added as well; `stored` is declared locally in `bar`, and `infoo`, `open`, and `stream` are declared globally.

Some may note that this syntax closely resembles that of the BLAST query language. BLAST, too, allows injection of code before or after a program statement using the keywords `before` and `after`. This similarity is a design feature, as our goal was to extend BLAST minimally to obtain a specification language for context-sensitive requirements. The key new features in PAL are local variables and the ability to declare `before` *and* `after` blocks in the same event. This seemingly superficial modification makes a major semantic difference: the control-flow of a monitor is now given by a nested word automaton, rather than a word automaton. Consider our example monitor and an execution of the input program containing a call to `foo`. In the nested word capturing this execution, there is a jump-edge from the call to `foo` to its matching return. Now, as the monitor reads this execution, it can save its state right before control enters `foo` using its local variables, and retrieve this state at the matching return. Thus, it has the power of a nested word automaton that reads the corresponding nested word, consulting its state at the source of an incoming jump-edge while transitioning to a return position. On the other hand, our monitor can use its global variables to pass states *into* invoked procedures such as `foo`, just like a BLAST monitor. More abstractly, this amounts to state updates as it reads the underlying word structure.

[1] Monitors are deterministic—i.e., if more than one pattern is matched at any point, we break the tie by picking the one in the event defined first.

We end this section with some hints to check that the monitor in Fig. 1 specifies our original requirement. The variables `infoo` and `open` track whether `foo` is in the stack and whether `dat` is open, and `stream` stores a possible open stream for `dat`. The variable `stored` is used to infer whether control is back to the top-level context calling `foo`. The rest is easily verified.

3 Implementation and Case Studies

We have implemented PAL on top of the current implementation of BLAST. The specification and analysis modules in BLAST are orthogonal: the former generates C code instrumented with a monitor, while the latter checks the generated code for assertion failures. We extend BLAST's specification module to permit PAL monitors, and analyze the generated code statically as well as dynamically. The source code of our implementation, along with the examples that we now discuss, is available at `http://www.cis.upenn.edu/~swarat/tools/pal.tar.gz`.

File descriptor leak in `fcron`. A monitor as in Sec. 2 could be used to prevent a reported bug (`http://nvd.nist.gov/nvd.cfm?cvename=CVE-2004-1033`) in Version 2.9.4 of `fcron`, a periodic command scheduler for Linux. Here, the main function of a binary (`fcrontab`) calls a routine `parseopt`, which calls a routine `is_allowed` to check if a user is "allowed", which calls a procedure that opens, but forgets to close, a stream for a secret file `fcron.allow`. After control returns to the main context, the program starts a process with a name derived from an environment variable. However, an attacker can change the value of this variable to start a malicious program that reads `fcron.allow` via the open file stream.

This error may be prevented by a policy that allows `parseopt` to open `fcron.allow`, but not to leak its descriptor. In addition, we could require that this secret file is not opened outside the scope of `parseopt`. This policy makes intuitive sense: as `parseopt` is a routine verifying a username, it is reasonable that it, or procedures it calls transitively, opens the file of allowed users. However, by the principle of least privilege, this file should only be opened when necessary, i.e., when `parseopt` is on the stack. A monitor expressing these requirements looks very similar to the one in Fig. 1. On instrumenting `fcron` with this monitor, we find a policy violation within a few random tests (model-checking using BLAST is not a good strategy due to the call to `strcmp` in the monitor).

Stack-sensitive security properties. Consider the security property: "A program must not execute a sensitive operation `write` at any point when an untrusted routine `foo` is on the stack." In the Java and C# languages, such policies are automatically enforced by the run-time environment, using the mechanism of *stack inspection*. In C, they may be enforced dynamically using a monitor—however, traditional monitors cannot express such properties of the stack, so that a nested word monitor is needed. Of course, such monitors could also be used in static analysis or software model checking.

Fig. 3 shows a monitor for the above requirement. The global variable `infoo` tracks if `foo` is in the stack, and a guard ensures that writes only happen outside the scope of `foo`.

We note that PAL may also be used to state some requirements of this nature that *cannot* be enforced via stack inspection. Consider the property: "If an untrusted procedure has ever been on the stack, a certain sensitive operation must not be executed." The rationale is that an untrusted routine may cause a side-effect that proves to be dangerous at a future point, so that if we call one, we must strengthen the security policy. However, since the culpable routine may no longer be on the stack when violation occurs, stack inspection does not help in this case. On the other hand, it is easy to state such properties in PAL; code for a sample monitor is available on our webpage.

```
global int infoo = 0;

event {
  pattern { write(); }
  guard { infoo == 0 }
}

event {
  pattern {$? = foo($?);}
  local int stored;
  before {
    action { stored = infoo;
             infoo = 1; }}
  after {
    action { infoo = stored; }}
}
```

Fig. 3. Stack-sensitive security

Logging policies. PAL also finds use in stating *logging policies* enforced in large development efforts such as Windows. Consider the property: "whenever a procedure returns an error value, the error must be logged via a routine `log` before control leaves the current procedural context." Now, different development groups may call `log` via different wrapper functions; however, the logging policy is fixed across groups and thus independent of the wrappers. In order to track if control has returned from a wrapper to the original context, we need a PAL monitor.

While we do not have access to industrial code bases where such policies are most natural, we have, as a proof of concept, applied this monitor on hand-coded examples and found policy violations using BLAST and random tests.

Acknowledgement. We thank Zhe Yang for valuable suggestions.

References

1. Alur, R., Madhusudan, P.: Adding nested structure to words. Developments in Language Theory, 1–13 (2006)
2. Ball, T., Rajamani, S.: The slam toolkit. In: Computer Aided Verification, 13th International Conference (2001)
3. Beyer, D., Chlipala, A.J., Henzinger, T.A., Jhala, R., Majumdar, R.: The BLAST query language for software verification. In: Giacobazzi, R. (ed.) SAS 2004. LNCS, vol. 3148, pp. 2–18. Springer, Heidelberg (2004)
4. Burdy, L., Cheon, Y., Cok, D., Ernst, M., Kiniry, J., Leavens, G.T., Leino, R., Poll, E.: An overview of JML tools and applications. In: Workshop on Formal Methods for Industrial Critical Systems, pp. 75–89 (2003)
5. Henzinger, T.A., Jhala, R., Majumdar, R., Necula, G.C., Sutre, G., Weimer, W.: Temporal-safety proofs for systems code. In: Brinksma, E., Larsen, K.G. (eds.) CAV 2002. LNCS, vol. 2404, pp. 526–538. Springer, Heidelberg (2002)
6. Holzmann, G.J.: The model checker SPIN. IEEE Transactions on Software Engineering 23(5), 279–295 (1997)

Author Index

Lecture Notes in Computer Science

For information about Vols. 1–4477

please contact your bookseller or Springer

Vol. 4600: H. Comon-Lundh, C. Kirchner, H. Kirchner (Eds.), Rewriting, Computation and Proof. XVI, 273 pages. 2007.

Vol. 4595: D. Bošnački, S. Edelkamp (Eds.), Model Checking Software. X, 285 pages. 2007.

Vol. 4592: Z. Kedad, N. Lammari, E. Métais, F. Meziane, Y. Rezgui (Eds.), Natural Language Processing and Information Systems. XIV, 442 pages. 2007.

Vol. 4591: J. Davies, J. Gibbons (Eds.), Integrated Formal Methods. IX, 660 pages. 2007.

Vol. 4590: W. Damm, H. Hermanns (Eds.), Computer Aided Verification. XV, 562 pages. 2007.

Vol. 4588: T. Harju, J. Karhumäki, A. Lepistö (Eds.), Developments in Language Theory. XI, 423 pages. 2007.

Vol. 4584: N. Karssemeijer, B. Lelieveldt (Eds.), Information Processing in Medical Imaging. XIII, 775 pages. 2007.

Vol. 4583: S.R. Della Rocca (Ed.), Typed Lambda Calculi and Applications. XI, 395 pages. 2007.

Vol. 4581: A. Petrenko, M. Veanes, J. Tretmans, W. Grieskamp (Eds.), Testing of Software and Communicating Systems. XII, 379 pages. 2007.

Vol. 4574: J. Derrick, J. Vain (Eds.), Formal Techniques for Networked and Distributed Systems – FORTE 2007. XI, 375 pages. 2007.

Vol. 4573: M. Kauers, M. Kerber, R. Miner, W. Windsteiger (Eds.), Towards Mechanized Mathematical Assistants. XIII, 407 pages. 2007. (Sublibrary LNAI).

Vol. 4572: F. Stajano, C. Meadows, S. Capkun, T. Moore (Eds.), Security and Privacy in Ad-hoc and Sensor Networks. X, 247 pages. 2007.

Vol. 4569: A. Butz, B. Fisher, A. Krüger, P. Olivier, S. Owada (Eds.), Smart Graphics. IX, 237 pages. 2007.

Vol. 4559: N. Aykin (Ed.), Usability and Internationalization, Part I. XVIII, 661 pages. 2007.

Vol. 4549: J. Aspnes, C. Scheideler, A. Arora, S. Madden (Eds.), Distributed Computing in Sensor Systems. XIII, 417 pages. 2007.

Vol. 4548: N. Olivetti (Ed.), Automated Reasoning with Analytic Tableaux and Related Methods. X, 245 pages. 2007. (Sublibrary LNAI).

Vol. 4547: C. Carlet, B. Sunar (Eds.), Arithmetic of Finite Fields. XI, 355 pages. 2007.

Vol. 4546: J. Kleijn, A. Yakovlev (Eds.), Petri Nets and Other Models of Concurrency – ICATPN 2007. XI, 515 pages. 2007.

Vol. 4543: A.K. Bandara, M. Burgess (Eds.), Inter-Domain Management. XII, 237 pages. 2007.

Vol. 4542: P. Sawyer, B. Paech, P. Heymans (Eds.), Requirements Engineering: Foundation for Software Quality. IX, 384 pages. 2007.

Vol. 4541: T. Okadome, T. Yamazaki, M. Makhtari (Eds.), Pervasive Computing for Quality of Life Enhancement. IX, 248 pages. 2007.

Vol. 4539: N.H. Bshouty, C. Gentile (Eds.), Learning Theory. XII, 634 pages. 2007. (Sublibrary LNAI).

Vol. 4538: F. Escolano, M. Vento (Eds.), Graph-Based Representations in Pattern Recognition. XII, 416 pages. 2007.

Vol. 4537: K.C.-C. Chang, W. Wang, L. Chen, C.A. Ellis, C.-H. Hsu, A.C. Tsoi, H. Wang (Eds.), Advances in Web and Network Technologies, and Information Management. XXIII, 707 pages. 2007.

Vol. 4536: G. Concas, E. Damiani, M. Scotto, G. Succi (Eds.), Agile Processes in Software Engineering and Extreme Programming. XV, 276 pages. 2007.

Vol. 4534: I. Tomkos, F. Neri, J. Solé Pareta, X. Masip Bruin, S. Sánchez Lopez (Eds.), Optical Network Design and Modeling. XI, 460 pages. 2007.

Vol. 4531: J. Indulska, K. Raymond (Eds.), Distributed Applications and Interoperable Systems. XI, 337 pages. 2007.

Vol. 4530: D.H. Akehurst, R. Vogel, R.F. Paige (Eds.), Model Driven Architecture- Foundations and Applications. X, 219 pages. 2007.

Vol. 4529: P. Melin, O. Castillo, L.T. Aguilar, J. Kacprzyk, W. Pedrycz (Eds.), Foundations of Fuzzy Logic and Soft Computing. XIX, 830 pages. 2007. (Sublibrary LNAI).

Vol. 4528: J. Mira, J.R. Álvarez (Eds.), Nature Inspired Problem-Solving Methods in Knowledge Engineering, Part II. XXII, 650 pages. 2007.

Vol. 4527: J. Mira, J.R. Álvarez (Eds.), Bio-inspired Modeling of Cognitive Tasks, Part I. XXII, 630 pages. 2007.

Vol. 4526: M. Malek, M. Reitenspieß, A. van Moorsel (Eds.), Service Availability. X, 155 pages. 2007.

Vol. 4525: C. Demetrescu (Ed.), Experimental Algorithms. XIII, 448 pages. 2007.

Vol. 4524: M. Marchiori, J.Z. Pan, C.d.S. Marie (Eds.), Web Reasoning and Rule Systems. XI, 382 pages. 2007.

Vol. 4523: Y.-H. Lee, H.-N. Kim, J. Kim, Y. Park, L.T. Yang, S.W. Kim (Eds.), Embedded Software and Systems. XIX, 829 pages. 2007.

Vol. 4522: B.K. Ersbøll, K.S. Pedersen (Eds.), Image Analysis. XVIII, 989 pages. 2007.

Vol. 4521: J. Katz, M. Yung (Eds.), Applied Cryptography and Network Security. XIII, 498 pages. 2007.

Vol. 4519: E. Franconi, M. Kifer, W. May (Eds.), The Semantic Web: Research and Applications. XVIII, 830 pages. 2007.

Vol. 4517: F. Boavida, E. Monteiro, S. Mascolo, Y. Koucheryavy (Eds.), Wired/Wireless Internet Communications. XIV, 382 pages. 2007.

Vol. 4516: L. Mason, T. Drwiega, J. Yan (Eds.), Managing Traffic Performance in Converged Networks. XXIII, 1191 pages. 2007.

Vol. 4515: M. Naor (Ed.), Advances in Cryptology - EUROCRYPT 2007. XIII, 591 pages. 2007.

Vol. 4514: S.N. Artemov, A. Nerode (Eds.), Logical Foundations of Computer Science. XI, 513 pages. 2007.

Vol. 4513: M. Fischetti, D.P. Williamson (Eds.), Integer Programming and Combinatorial Optimization. IX, 500 pages. 2007.

Vol. 4511: C. Conati, K. McCoy, G. Paliouras (Eds.), User Modeling 2007. XVI, 487 pages. 2007. (Sublibrary LNAI).

Vol. 4510: P. Van Hentenryck, L. Wolsey (Eds.), Integration of AI and OR Techniques in Constraint Programming for Combinatorial Optimization Problems. X, 391 pages. 2007.

Vol. 4509: Z. Kobti, D. Wu (Eds.), Advances in Artificial Intelligence. XII, 552 pages. 2007. (Sublibrary LNAI).

Vol. 4508: M.-Y. Kao, X.-Y. Li (Eds.), Algorithmic Aspects in Information and Management. VIII, 428 pages. 2007.

Vol. 4507: F. Sandoval, A. Prieto, J. Cabestany, M. Graña (Eds.), Computational and Ambient Intelligence. XXVI, 1167 pages. 2007.

Vol. 4506: D. Zeng, I. Gotham, K. Komatsu, C. Lynch, M. Thurmond, D. Madigan, B. Lober, J. Kvach, H. Chen (Eds.), Intelligence and Security Informatics: Biosurveillance. XI, 234 pages. 2007.

Vol. 4505: G. Dong, X. Lin, W. Wang, Y. Yang, J.X. Yu (Eds.), Advances in Data and Web Management. XXII, 896 pages. 2007.

Vol. 4504: J. Huang, R. Kowalczyk, Z. Maamar, D. Martin, I. Müller, S. Stoutenburg, K.P. Sycara (Eds.), Service-Oriented Computing: Agents, Semantics, and Engineering. X, 175 pages. 2007.

Vol. 4501: J. Marques-Silva, K.A. Sakallah (Eds.), Theory and Applications of Satisfiability Testing – SAT 2007. XI, 384 pages. 2007.

Vol. 4500: N. Streitz, A. Kameas, I. Mavrommati (Eds.), The Disappearing Computer. XVIII, 304 pages. 2007.

Vol. 4499: Y.Q. Shi (Ed.), Transactions on Data Hiding and Multimedia Security II. IX, 117 pages. 2007.

Vol. 4498: N. Abdennahder, F. Kordon (Eds.), Reliable Software Technologies – Ada Europe 2007. XII, 247 pages. 2007.

Vol. 4497: S.B. Cooper, B. Löwe, A. Sorbi (Eds.), Computation and Logic in the Real World. XVIII, 826 pages. 2007.

Vol. 4496: N.T. Nguyen, A. Grzech, R.J. Howlett, L.C. Jain (Eds.), Agent and Multi-Agent Systems: Technologies and Applications. XXI, 1046 pages. 2007. (Sublibrary LNAI).

Vol. 4495: J. Krogstie, A. Opdahl, G. Sindre (Eds.), Advanced Information Systems Engineering. XVI, 606 pages. 2007.

Vol. 4494: H. Jin, O.F. Rana, Y. Pan, V.K. Prasanna (Eds.), Algorithms and Architectures for Parallel Processing. XIV, 508 pages. 2007.

Vol. 4493: D. Liu, S. Fei, Z. Hou, H. Zhang, C. Sun (Eds.), Advances in Neural Networks – ISNN 2007, Part III. XXVI, 1215 pages. 2007.

Vol. 4492: D. Liu, S. Fei, Z. Hou, H. Zhang, C. Sun (Eds.), Advances in Neural Networks – ISNN 2007, Part II. XXVII, 1321 pages. 2007.

Vol. 4491: D. Liu, S. Fei, Z.-G. Hou, H. Zhang, C. Sun (Eds.), Advances in Neural Networks – ISNN 2007, Part I. LIV, 1365 pages. 2007.

Vol. 4490: Y. Shi, G.D. van Albada, J. Dongarra, P.M.A. Sloot (Eds.), Computational Science – ICCS 2007, Part IV. XXXVII, 1211 pages. 2007.

Vol. 4489: Y. Shi, G.D. van Albada, J. Dongarra, P.M.A. Sloot (Eds.), Computational Science – ICCS 2007, Part III. XXXVII, 1257 pages. 2007.

Vol. 4488: Y. Shi, G.D. van Albada, J. Dongarra, P.M.A. Sloot (Eds.), Computational Science – ICCS 2007, Part II. XXXV, 1251 pages. 2007.

Vol. 4487: Y. Shi, G.D. van Albada, J. Dongarra, P.M.A. Sloot (Eds.), Computational Science – ICCS 2007, Part I. LXXXI, 1275 pages. 2007.

Vol. 4486: M. Bernardo, J. Hillston (Eds.), Formal Methods for Performance Evaluation. VII, 469 pages. 2007.

Vol. 4485: F. Sgallari, A. Murli, N. Paragios (Eds.), Scale Space and Variational Methods in Computer Vision. XV, 931 pages. 2007.

Vol. 4484: J.-Y. Cai, S.B. Cooper, H. Zhu (Eds.), Theory and Applications of Models of Computation. XIII, 772 pages. 2007.

Vol. 4483: C. Baral, G. Brewka, J. Schlipf (Eds.), Logic Programming and Nonmonotonic Reasoning. IX, 327 pages. 2007. (Sublibrary LNAI).

Vol. 4482: A. An, J. Stefanowski, S. Ramanna, C.J. Butz, W. Pedrycz, G. Wang (Eds.), Rough Sets, Fuzzy Sets, Data Mining and Granular Computing. XIV, 585 pages. 2007. (Sublibrary LNAI).

Vol. 4481: J. Yao, P. Lingras, W.-Z. Wu, M. Szczuka, N.J. Cercone, D. Ślęzak (Eds.), Rough Sets and Knowledge Technology. XIV, 576 pages. 2007. (Sublibrary LNAI).

Vol. 4480: A. LaMarca, M. Langheinrich, K.N. Truong (Eds.), Pervasive Computing. XIII, 369 pages. 2007.

Vol. 4479: I.F. Akyildiz, R. Sivakumar, E. Ekici, J.C.d. Oliveira, J. McNair (Eds.), NETWORKING 2007. Ad Hoc and Sensor Networks, Wireless Networks, Next Generation Internet. XXVII, 1252 pages. 2007.

Vol. 4478: J. Martí, J.M. Benedí, A.M. Mendonça, J. Serrat (Eds.), Pattern Recognition and Image Analysis, Part II. XXVII, 657 pages. 2007.